Oracles of God

Oracles of God

Perceptions of Ancient Prophecy
in Israel after the Exile

JOHN BARTON

Darton, Longman and Todd
London

First published in 1986 by
Darton, Longman and Todd Ltd
89 Lillie Road, London SW6 1UD

© 1986 John Barton

ISBN 0 232 51666 9

British Library Cataloguing in Publication Data

Barton, John
    Oracles of God: perceptions of ancient
    prophecy in Israel after the Exile.
    1. Bible. O.T.—Criticism, interpretation,
    etc.   2. Prophets
    I. Title
    221.8′29163   BS1198

    ISBN 0–232–51666–9

Phototypeset by Input Typesetting Ltd, London SW19 8DR
Printed and bound in Great Britain by
Anchor Brendon Ltd, Tiptree, Essex

for Katie

Contents

Preface

It is six years since John Todd asked me to write a book on Old Testament prophecy, and it is perhaps fitting to begin by thanking him for his patience. I decided from the first to work in the topsy-turvy fashion of starting with the 'final form of the text', that is, with the prophets as we now encounter them in the Bible, and working back towards the prophets as they really were. Six years later I have still not progressed beyond the fifth or sixth century BC, but there seems already enough material for one book. The approach I have adopted, and most of the conclusions I have reached, were presented in a sketchy form to the Old Testament seminar here in Oxford in 1980, and in a little more detail to the joint meeting of the British and Dutch Old Testament Societies at Zeist in 1982, in my paper ' "The Law and the Prophets." Who are the Prophets?'. I am most grateful for the helpful comments of colleagues on both occasions, and most particularly for detailed advice from James Barr – whose continuing interest in this project has been a source of both encouragement and stimulation. How greatly I am indebted to his own work should be obvious to any reader. It is a great pleasure to record my gratitude to Ernest Nicholson, who has read the entire typescript, and has helped and supported me in so many ways over the years in which I have been working on it.

This has been a good time to work in Oxford in Old Testament studies, and I am conscious of a debt to all my colleagues here, who have provided a specially stimulating atmosphere in which to study and teach the Old Testament: Ian Brayley, John Day, Eric Heaton (to whose recommendation I owe the original invitation to write this book), Paul Joyce, Rex Mason, Anthony Phillips, and Peter Southwell – in addition, of course, to the two professors already mentioned. I am grateful, too, to my former tutor and supervisor, John Austin Baker, who first awoke my interest in the prophets and, indeed, in the Old Testament in general; and to my own pupils, who have had to listen to many of the ideas here in a much vaguer form.

Writing a book is in one sense the loneliest of tasks, but in another it is always a team effort. An academic book would have no content without a library behind it, and I could not have wished for more help than I have had in the Theology Faculty Library here from Wilma Minty and her assistants. It needs to be written somewhere, and I must thank Rachel Hawes and W. Herbert Chivers for lending me (respectively) a flat and a rectory in which to work uninterruptedly at two crucial stages in producing this one. Above all, it needs a publisher: Lesley Riddle, of Darton, Longman and Todd, has been both patient in bearing with my delays and extremely helpful at all stages of production.

Most of the final draft of the book was written in the rectory just mentioned during August this year, thanks in part to the wettest summer for many years but most of all to the forbearance of my wife – without whom I would probably write nothing at all – and my daughter, to whom it is dedicated, with much love, as a poor substitute for a much more interesting holiday.

John Barton
St Cross College, Oxford
December 1985

Abbreviations

ASTI	Annual of the Swedish Institute
BWANT	Beiträge zur Wissenschaft vom Alten und Neuen Testament
BZAW	Beihefte zur *Zeitschrift für die alttestamentliche Wissenschaft*
CBQ	*Catholic Biblical Quarterly*
EvThBeih	Beihefte zu *Evangelische Theologie*
HTR	*Harvard Theological Review*
HUCA	Hebrew Union College Annual
IDB	*The Interpreter's Dictionary of the Bible.* Nashville, I–IV 1962, Supplement 1976.
JAAR	*Journal of the American Academy of Religion*
JBL	*Journal of Biblical Literature*
JCS	*Journal of Cuneiform Studies*
JE	*The Jewish Encyclopedia*, ed I. Singer. 12 vols. New York and London 1901–6.
JSOT	*Journal for the Study of the Old Testament*
JSOTS	*Journal for the Study of the Old Testament*, Supplement Series
JTS	*Journal of Theological Studies*
OS	*Oudtestamentische Studiën*
RB	*Revue Biblique*
RHR	*Revue de l'histoire des religions*
SBL	Society of Biblical Literature
SBTh	Studies in Biblical Theology
SR	*Studies in Religion/Sciences Religieuses*
ThPQ	*Theologisch-Praktische Quartalschrift* of the *Theologische Zeitschrift*
TLZ	*Theologische Literaturzeitung*
TU	Texte und Untersuchungen

TWNT	*Theologisches Wörterbuch zum Neuen Testament,* ed G. Kittel. 10 vols. Stuttgart 1933–74 = *Theological Dictionary of the New Testament.* Grand Rapids, Mich., and London 1964–76.
VT	*Vetus Testamentum*
VTS	*Vetus Testamentum,* Supplement Series
WMANT	Wissenschaftliche Monographien zum Alten und Neuen Testament
WUNT	Wissenschaftliche Untersuchungen zum Neuen Testament
ZAW	*Zeitschrift für die alttestamentliche Wissenschaft*
ZNW	*Zeitschrift für die neutestamentliche Wissenschaft*

Introduction

I

The great figures of any nation's history may be important for either of two reasons: for what they do, or for what they are afterwards thought to have done. Historians of ancient Israel have commonly been interested in figures of the first kind. Studies of the origins of Israel used to be concerned with the identity and character of Moses or of the patriarchs; nowadays they are more likely to concentrate on the nameless groups that constituted the 'tribes of Yahweh' from which the nation may have taken its origins: but in either case the concern is with those who, not simply in name but in historical reality, made Israel what it was. In the same way the primary interest in studying the prophets of Israel has usually been to determine what difference these people actually made, either to the course of the nation's history, or to the development of its religious thought. This is why scholarship has always concentrated on the great pre-exilic prophets from Amos to Jeremiah, and until recently has not devoted much attention to their successors after the Exile. The pre-exilic classical prophets, so it has been thought, were crucially important in shaping the direction of religious thought in Israel, whereas those who came after them in general did little more than mirror the religious culture within which they worked: such creative ideas as there were in the post-exilic age owed their inspiration to other groups in society (such as priests or scribes), and the prophets had lost the initiative.

Where this tendency has been challenged in recent years, it has usually been because scholars have come to believe that post-exilic prophets had more influence than they have been credited with – in other words, it has been part of a desire to 'rehabilitate' figures too hastily depreciated by older scholarship. Post-exilic prophecy,

1

it is implied, was more important than used to be thought: that is, it achieved more and was less derivative than conventionally supposed, contributing as much to the thought of its day as the pre-exilic prophets had contributed to theirs.

The heirs of those who change the life and thought of a nation as much as both pre- and post-exilic prophets did may not, however, remember them for what they really achieved, but for reasons with little or no basis in historical reality. Equally, they may remember other people as great leaders or teachers who to the modern historian seem likely to have been scarcely important at all, or even not to have existed. The importance of Moses for Judaism of the Second Temple period has very little to do with 'the historical Moses'; for the historian of Judaism nothing would be changed if it could be shown that Moses was a pure invention. His importance in the post-exilic age lay in what he was thought to have done, and questions about the reliability of the post-exilic picture of him are questions about the history of the second millennium BC, not about Second Temple Judaism. It so happens that there are historical figures for whom both sorts of question are equally interesting: the real Socrates and the Socrates of Plato are both important for the history of philosophy – so, for that matter, are the real Plato and the Plato of Platonism. The same is unlikely to be true of Abraham, Isaac, or Jacob, who are surely more important for the traditions about them than ever they were in life, at least if the criterion of a person's importance is his influence on subsequent history. Of them we might say what H. G. Gadamer said of Achilles: 'The reality of the representation is greater than that of the original it represents: the Achilles of Homer is more real than the original Achilles.'[1]

The prophets of Israel present examples of both types. Some matter both because they crucially affected the development of Israel's religious thought or even the events of its political and social history, and because they claimed a place in tradition; others seem to the historian little more than names, yet these names have lived on and attracted to themselves a great wealth of lore and a great weight of loyalty and affection. Examples of the first kind might be Isaiah and Jeremiah; of the second, Elijah and Habakkuk. No doubt there is also a third type: prophets whose work had a far-reaching effect on their people, but who have vanished from the tradition. In the nature of the case there will not be much the historian can say about them, though sometimes we may infer their existence from the shape of the gaps in our available evidence, arguing (for example) that the ground must have been in some measure prepared for Amos's startling proclamation of the end of Israel's election by Yahweh, or attributing changes in the theology of the post-exilic community to the activity of otherwise unknown prophetic groups. But there is already plenty of work to do in studying those whose names we do possess. Given the importance that the classical prophets in particular undoubtedly did have in the development of Israelite 'Yahwism' into monotheistic Jewish faith, it is scarcely surprising that so much attention has been paid to them as real historical figures. Nevertheless, the question how the prophets were regarded in subsequent tradition is also worth asking, and this is the question I shall try to answer in this book. Hence the subtitle 'Perceptions of Ancient Prophecy in Israel after the Exile'.

I believe that this question has not previously been treated in any systematic way, though there are a number of works that contribute to parts of it. I hope that the reception of biblical prophecy in Judaism of the Second Temple period will commend itself as an inherently interesting topic; but naturally it could also be seen as part of a larger subject, the history of Israelite prophecy as a whole. Just as the pre-exilic classical prophets have attracted the greatest number of specific studies, so they have also dominated histories of prophecy, even those that in principle are concerned with every period in its development. Books on prophecy thus usually regard as primarily a matter of prolegomena the shadowy predecessors of the great prophets of the eighth century, who flicker in and out of the pages of the historical books of the Old Testament, always just out of the focus of our eyes; and in the same way they treat as little more than a tailpiece the question of what became of prophecy in the post-exilic age, as prophetic inspiration died away and the authority of the Law took its place. At the moment I am not concerned either to attack or defend this *evaluation* of the history of prophecy, but only to suggest that an alternative strategy might also be defended. We might begin at the end of the process, with the period in which prophecy was widely agreed to have ceased and collections of prophetic oracles existed in what were coming to be seen as 'holy scriptures'. The present work is self-contained, but in its closing pages it points forward to some possible implications for the study of pre-exilic prophecy which I hope one day to follow up in a second volume.

Perhaps it should be made clear at the outset that in beginning at the end, and thus concentrating attention on that favourite of so much recent biblical interpretation, the text in its final form, I am not trying to make a case for 'canonical' or structuralist criticism. Nor have I any desire to urge that my procedure is methodologically superior to the traditional approach which begins at the beginning, or that it is 'better', according to some literary or religious principle. Of course any student of the Bible is a child of his own time, and I do not suppose that it would have occurred to me to begin with the reception of the prophets in post-prophetic Judaism if canonical criticism, text-immanent exegesis, and *Wirkungsgeschichte* had not been in the air. Nevertheless my disclaimer of any hidden hermeneutical agenda is seriously meant. This book is a historical study, a contribution to the intellectual history of Israel 'after the Exile' (a period that will need closer definition); it is not an attempt to prescribe new methodological rules for biblical study.

If the technique of beginning at the end has any peculiar merits (and of course I should not attempt it if I did not think it had), they are twofold. First, there is some value in novelty. By approaching a familiar subject from a new angle we sometimes see things that we had overlooked before, though they were there all the time. Secondly, I share Rudolf Smend's belief that in studying a text as complex as the Old Testament there is an advantage in beginning from what is known and proceeding by stages to reconstruct what is unknown, rather than starting with hypothetical 'earliest stages' and coming late in the day to the text in its present form;[2] for this more familiar route tends to mean that we have already made up our minds on many issues before ever we confront the text itself, and can no longer see it with any freshness of perception. It is worth remembering that it was Julius Wellhausen's decision to study the prophets *before* studying the Pentateuchal texts on which he 'knew' (because he had been told) they depended, that he came to embrace Graf's hypothesis that the prophets were in reality earlier than 'the Law'. Not everyone will regard this example as a commendation of the approach I am adopting, but for my part I cannot think of any higher aim for an Old Testament specialist than to try, however falteringly, to imitate the example of Wellhausen. No doubt there is a certain irony in describing the present form of the Old Testament text as 'what is known', as I have just done; for in practice this 'known' text turns out on examination to be little more

4

than a morass of shifting questions. To discover how it was read, and how the 'prophets' who figure in it were understood in post-exilic Judaism, is not noticeably easier than to reconstruct the $n^e bi'im$ who preceded Amos, as most traditional books on prophecy begin by doing. But if the attempt has thrown up innumerable problems, they are at least different problems, and I hope that others will think them worth pursuing further.

II

'Israel after the Exile' suggests rather than defines a period. Most of the material I shall be examining belongs to the later part of the post-exilic age, in effect to the period which is handled in books on New Testament 'background' – from the middle or late third century BC to about the beginning or middle of the second century AD. The range is roughly that covered by the new series 'Cambridge Commentaries on Writings of the Jewish and Christian World, 200 BC to AD 200',[3] but with some bias to the earlier part of that period and a considerable interest in later Old Testament books which somewhat antedate its upper limit. Around this central period, however, there is a penumbra which I should want to leave rather vague. At the lower end, I shall sometimes draw on patristic writings which may help in clarifying early Christian and Jewish ideas about prophecy even though they derive from a much later time, and I shall frequently have to refer to rabbinic texts whose date is notoriously uncertain.

My reason for using the vague phrase 'in Israel after the Exile', however, rather than 'in Israel in the Hellenistic age', 'in early Christianity and its environment', or something of that sort, has to do with the upper limit of the period concerned. This is essentially defined not by date but by the appearance of a particular idea: the idea that 'prophecy' belongs to the past. As we shall see, the belief that prophetic inspiration is a characteristic feature of an age that has now passed away is in practice compatible with a recognition of the inspiration of some of one's contemporaries. The crucial feature is not an absolute dogma that prophecy has decisively ceased, but simply a sense that the prophets of old form a distinctive group which differs in significant ways from contemporary persons who may resemble them, with the result that these earlier figures

5

can be described collectively as 'the prophets', 'the former prophets', 'God's servants the prophets' and so forth. Such a sense is certainly already present in the 'Deuteronomistic History' of Joshua–Kings, and in redactional additions to the books of the pre-exilic and exilic prophets, particularly Jeremiah, many of which have a deuteronomistic flavour. This, according to most scholarly opinion about the 'deuteronomists', means that the idea of the 'old prophets' as forming a coherent group or line of succession during the period brought to a close by the Babylonian sack of Jerusalem goes back to the years of the Exile itself. Similarly, the book of Zechariah can speak of 'the former prophets' in a summarizing way (1:3–6), and even if these words are not those of Zechariah himself, they probably do not long postdate the Restoration of the late sixth century in which he was involved. Although, therefore, material from the sixth and fifth centuries will not be at the centre of our interest in this study, reference will have to be made to some of these texts, as our earliest evidence for Jewish conceptions of what the great prophets had said and done.

It will readily be seen that this introduces a certain complication into the task in hand. I have been speaking as if a period in which prophets were active in Israel, but there were no harmonizing 'traditions' about them, was followed by one in which prophets were important simply as a memory, and fresh prophecy no longer occurred. But though there certainly was a time after which it was no longer acceptable to claim to be a prophet in exactly the same sense as the 'biblical' prophets, there is a considerable period of overlap in which an awareness of 'the prophets' as a past phenomenon co-existed with a claim by individuals to stand in their succession and not to differ qualitatively from them. Haggai and Zechariah clearly attest this transitional conception, and it may be that other post-exilic prophecies that appear under the name of a real post-exilic prophet, rather than being pseudonymously attributed to an earlier figure or appended anonymously to an existing collection, bear witness to the same idea: Joel and Obadiah may be examples of this.

The scope of this book is defined, then, by a corpus of texts, rather than strictly by a set of dates. In principle any material is relevant which tells us how prophecy was understood within Judaism (understood to include the early Christian community as originally a Jewish sect) once the idea had arisen that a primary 'prophetic age' had come to an end. Within the Old Testament itself we shall thus need to take account of the conception of prophecy implied by the redaction of the Deuteronomistic History and of Chronicles, and by additions to the words of the pre-exilic prophets so far as these can be established. Redaction criticism, however, is an uncertain art, and not too much weight will be allowed to fall on what are inevitably very hypothetical reconstructions. More attention will be paid to the later books of the Old Testament and Apocrypha, and to the large body of texts generally called (for short) the Pseudepigrapha. The New Testament, the Qumran texts, and the works of Philo and Josephus will naturally play a major role, and some early patristic texts (principally the 'Apostolic Fathers') will also be used.

The list of texts so far given will scarcely be surprising. If we want to find out what Jewish writers in the post-exilic age thought about prophecy, it makes obvious sense to look at their writings and to examine passages in them that deal explicitly with the subject. But the matter is complicated by the fact that 'prophecy' in our period was not seen only as the defining characteristic of a particular sort of *person*; it was also the name of a type of *literature*. The Hebrew Bible does not only contain books which purport to tell of the deeds and to record the words of prophets. It also contains books called 'Prophets', and when Jewish and Christian writers talk of 'the Prophets' they mean the books as often as the people. This produces, as we shall see, an effect of mutual influence, or (we might say) of mutual contamination. Once a book is classified as a 'Prophet', then anything it contains can easily come to be thought characteristic of 'prophecy': if the book of the Prophet Isaiah includes narratives about the history of Israel, then this will tend to imply that writing historical narratives is a 'prophetic' task; for the modern distinction between the prophet Isaiah as the hero of the book and the prophet Isaiah as its author is not drawn. Conversely, once 'Prophet' comes to be used as a generic classification for a particular group of books, it will be assumed that their authors were all 'prophets', that is, figures who stand in the succession that runs back through Jeremiah, Amos, Elijah, and Nathan, all the way to Moses himself. And this will lead to a whole string of assumptions about the character and inspiration of these authors quite remote from anything a modern student of the Bible might be likely to say about them.

In examining post-exilic notions of prophecy, then, we shall have to include also some investigation of what in our period was thought to constitute a prophetic *book*. (For the sake of brevity, 'prophets' will be used to mean prophetic people, 'Prophets' prophetic books.) This means that our study will include a treatment of two matters that may be more surprising than those outlined so far. First, it should be evident from what has just been said that one cannot hope to grasp what was thought about 'prophecy' in Judaism of the Second Temple period without some consideration of the canon; for as it stands the Hebrew canon contains a section called *Prophets* ($n^e bi'im$). Two questions need to be asked here: which books were reckoned as 'Prophets' in our period, and what did this designation imply about their character and the character of their authors? We shall see that answers to these questions are often assumed by scholars who write about the reception of Scripture in Judaism and Christianity, but that the issue is really much more complicated than it seems.

Clearly the question of which books are 'Prophets' needs to be resolved before we can ask how they were understood in the various writings of our period, and accordingly I shall begin with a discussion of the Prophetic canon. But a second matter which is potentially fruitful for discovering how prophecy was understood, but which introduces a further level of complexity, arises from this very discussion. To anticipate a point that can be established only by a rather painstaking examination of sources bearing on the history of the canon: it seems to me that many of the pseudonymous works written in the last couple of pre-Christian centuries were intended to be read as 'Prophetic' books, and were designed to be accepted as equal in authority and inspiration to those that now appear as *Prophets* in the traditional Hebrew Scriptures. If this is so, then such books can be used as evidence for the conceptions of prophecy prevalent in their day, not just because in them we often find references to the books now in the Prophetic canon, but also because they are themselves *imitations* of those books. From an imitation one does not necessarily learn much of the true character of the original, for some imitations are bad imitations; but one can learn a great deal about how the imitator *saw* the original. From the later books of the Old Testament and Apocrypha, then, and from some of the Pseudepigrapha, it may be possible to learn a good deal, indirectly, about the way the books we call prophetic were being read in this period.

To take an example which will be handled in more detail later: to the modern, critical reader it is immediately apparent that there is all the difference in the world between the book of Amos and the book of Jonah, not just in terms of the historical background and the religious conceptions or world-views of the two books, but also and chiefly at the level of genre. Amos is a collection of prophetic oracles, though it does include a very small amount of narrative (in chapter 7); Jonah is a tale or legend about a prophet. It is probable, however, that to the first readers of Jonah, and indeed to its writer, no important difference – certainly no *generic* difference – was perceived. What must the author and first readers of Jonah have supposed was the essence of a 'Prophetic' book, if they produced something like the book of Jonah when they had a chance to write one for themselves? Clearly their idea of a 'Prophet' was radically different from ours. In the course of this study I shall suggest that similar questions can usefully be asked in relation to such books as Tobit and Daniel, and to some of the Enoch literature.

At this stage the reader may well react by protesting that this literature does not claim to be 'prophetic' at all, and that to introduce it can only cloud the issue. This objection can be met only by first investigating the status of the canon in our period: a further reason for beginning with this question. But the hypothesis that much Jewish pseudepigraphical literature is designed to be read as 'Prophecy' (in the senses to be defined as we proceed) underlies only some parts of my reconstruction of post-exilic ideas about prophecy. There is enough overt reference to books whose 'Prophetic' status is in any case not in doubt for quite a clear picture to emerge, even without the help of these additional sources of information.

When we have established *how* 'prophecy' was understood in post-exilic Judaism – and there are a number of different conceptions attested in the literature – we have still not answered the question *why*. This is, indeed, a much more difficult question, since at least in part it requires more knowledge of the social context of Jewish literature than we possess. I shall suggest reasons where I think they can reasonably be advanced, but remain agnostic where the evidence seems simply insufficient. Since sociological study of the setting of post-exilic literature is now widely practised, however, this will sometimes mean taking sides in debates which cannot yet be said to have reached any conclusion. The vexed question of the origins of 'apocalyptic' is the most obvious case where this is so. It will be seen that my own 'solution' of the problem is, in effect, to try to redefine our terms so that it no longer arises – an old trick, but one which I think may still have a future, at least in relation to this peculiarly contentious issue. It is clear that my proposals, if accepted, would have implications for New Testament study, but I have tried to avoid venturing too far down that perilous road. In general my aim is to be simply descriptive: to register and classify conceptions of prophecy that occur in the period. The literature of the New Testament is a rich source for this inquiry, but most of the questions debated among New Testament scholars do not arise in the present context. Any view that is attested within the New Testament is a view that occurs in our period: whether it was held by the person to whom it is attributed is an important question, but not a question I shall be asking.

III

Although it could hardly be said that this book is short of notes, it will be obvious to the specialist reader that I have not read all the secondary literature that might be relevant to the topics I discuss; and that even where I have read it I do not always cite it. On such a large subject, even quite a long book is bound to be fairly impressionistic if it is to aim at presenting a picture on a reasonable scale. What I have written is not a comprehensive text-book in which every relevant text and article is fully discussed, but a long essay, setting out the case for seeing the place held by 'ancient prophecy' in post-exilic thought in what I believe is a rather new way. Quotations from primary sources, though they are quite extensive, are still no more than samples taken from a vast corpus which I am conscious of being far from mastering. This does not, of course, excuse errors, but it may explain omissions. Especially in chapters 5–8 the reader needs to be clear that I have not even attempted to provide a comprehensive list of all relevant texts, and have seldom cited secondary literature when the texts seemed to speak for themselves. Full bibliographies are available in many indispensable books: the new Schürer, D. E. Aune's *Prophecy in Early Christianity*, J. Blenkinsopp's *A History of Prophecy in Israel*, and the various anthologies of apocryphal and pseudepigraphical works now so freely available. My own work depends heavily on many of these learned works. To use an image which will recur in the body of the book: I am trying to draw some new maps, but I did not discover any of the terrain I am mapping. The present work represents an attempt at fresh interpretation of widely-known data; it cannot be called 'research'.

Hebrew and Greek have been transliterated on the simplest system I can devise, on the principle that readers who know these languages will not need anything more complicated, and that those who do not will hardly welcome it. In Greek, omega is represented by $\hat{o}$ and eta by $\hat{e}$; the smooth breathing is not marked at all; and iota subscript appears as (i); otherwise everything should be self-explanatory. In Hebrew, I have rarely marked the difference between the 'hard' and 'soft' forms of the letters *bgdkpt*, except that *th* is regularly used in the feminine endings *-ôth* and *-ath*. Apart from the dot under *ḥ* when it stands for ḥeth, diacritical marks unfamiliar in European languages have been avoided: hence I have freely used forms such as 'midrash', especially as so many such words can be treated more or less as loan-words in English, at least for a book on the Bible. So far as possible I have preferred not to abbreviate the titles of rabbinic works, and in the body of the text have avoided even abbreviations for biblical books, in an attempt to produce reasonably continuous prose. Quotations are taken from commonly-used translations, though sometimes I have made small changes without calling attention to them. For Josephus and Philo I have generally followed the Loeb editions; for the Bible, the Revised Standard Version; and for the Pseudepigrapha, either Charles or Charlesworth. I have often quoted at length where a reference alone might have been thought enough, again in order to make my argument continuous and self-contained; and perhaps also to whet the appetite of any reader not familiar with the texts quoted, for the ultimate aim of any study such as this must be to send the reader back to the original texts to draw his or her own conclusions from them.

1

The Prophets in the Canon

I

Biblical scholars sometimes lament that for all their labours over the last hundred years and more, people still read the Bible in just the same way as they did before critical study began. Sometimes, indeed, this dejection lowers their confidence to such an extent that they begin to ask whether biblical criticism was a mistake in the first place. The study of the prophets, however, can be claimed as one of the success stories in the history of the critical study of the Bible. Within the mainstream of Christian thought in the West, 'prophecy' has come to mean something very close to what it means in critical Old Testament scholarship. When Christian writers and church leaders speak of the *prophetic* role of the Church or its members, they are nearly always referring consciously to the distinguishing marks of 'classical' prophecy as reconstructed by a century of biblical criticism. In modern Christian usage, to call someone a prophet is generally to imply that he has something to say that poses a challenge to a complacent world. The challenge may include forebodings of disaster to come, if it is not heeded; but these will not be mere prognostications of a clairvoyant sort. They will be understood as the inevitable consequences of present sin which a change of course could, at least in principle, avert.

Now this use of the word 'prophecy' is soundly based in Old Testament scholarship, and in adopting it the modern Church shows that in this respect at least it has heard what biblical specialists have been saying to it. Most of those who influence opinion in the mainline Churches would reject the use of the word 'prophecy' to describe the kind of speculations about the date of the end of the world, often based on numerological investigations of the text of Daniel or Revelation, which have characterized many fundamen-

13

talist sects. And in declaring that such crystal-gazing is not what 'prophecy' means in biblical religion, they follow in the footsteps of Wellhausen and Duhm.[1]

It is, however, perfectly true that English usage outside the ecclesiastical world has still not adopted this as the natural meaning of 'prophecy'. By far the commonest use of the word in everyday English continues to be in reference to prediction of the future. On hearing that the Bible contains *prophetic* books the ordinary person will assume that it contains *predictions*, and in this he will be following an assumption that almost everyone held until the late nineteenth century. When writers on periods later than biblical times want to refer to texts that claim supernatural insight into the future, nothing is more natural for them than to speak of 'prophecies'. Thus Keith Thomas, in his study *Religion and the Decline of Magic*, heads his chapter on the pseudonymous texts, allegedly predicting future events, which enjoyed such a vogue in the sixteenth century, 'Ancient Prophecies',[2] and he shows no awareness whatever that the term could mean anything else. This is an entirely sensible use of the word 'prophecy' in modern English, where it most often refers to the kind of text that biblical scholars generally call 'apocalyptic' – a fact from which, as we shall see, many confusions result. 'Prophecy = prediction' could be said to have been a more or less self-evident equation for most of Christian history.

But if mainstream Christianity, and hence Western culture in general, has taken 'prophecy' to be virtually synonymous with 'prediction', in Jewish tradition it has long been customary to think of a 'prophet' primarily as an accredited teacher of the moral law, one who hands on to succeeding generations inspired commentary on the Torah. Moses himself, after all, was a prophet, and the prophetic books are used in the liturgy of the synagogue to reinforce and draw out the meaning of the Torah, the authoritative teaching that Moses delivered. How far such a perception of prophecy goes back is a question that will concern us later, but there is no doubt that it is a dominant one within Judaism. This idea of the prophet as a divinely-inspired teacher is almost as far from the classical prophet reconstructed by Duhm and his successors as is the apocalyptic visionary of Christian tradition. To describe Amos, proclaiming the imminent end of an Israel blind to all moral demands, as 'a teacher of the moral law', may well seem to anyone

14

who has fully felt the impact of his original message to be damning him with faint praise. Within Judaism, Martin Buber saw it as one of his tasks to resist this domestication of the great prophets.[3] Nevertheless, it is just as important a use of the term 'prophet' as the more typically Christian concern with 'foretelling'.

Now a good index to which of these three ways of understanding prophecy predominates in someone's mind is to ask him to name the prophetic books of the Old Testament. A student of the Bible who is familiar with the modern critical estimate of the prophets will almost always begin: Amos, Hosea, Isaiah, Micah, Jeremiah . . . He will include neither Daniel (since that is 'apocalyptic', not prophecy) nor any of the historical books. A traditional Catholic Christian, untouched by biblical criticism, would reel off the list of books which printed Latin Bibles frequently head *libri prophetici*, which run as follows: The Twelve (in various orders), Isaiah, Jeremiah, Lamentations, Baruch, Ezekiel, and Daniel (with or without the 'apocryphal' additions). But a Jew could be expected to list the *Prophets* of the Hebrew Scriptures: Joshua, Judges, Samuel, Kings, Isaiah, Jeremiah, Ezekiel, and the Twelve.

It does not take much effort to see that there is a considerable degree of correlation between these three lists and the three different conceptions of prophecy held by those who adhere to them. In particular, the typical Christian list, including Baruch and Daniel, has a clear orientation towards the predictive side of prophecy, while the Jewish list, by lumping history and more obviously 'prophetic' activity together and excluding the more crassly predictive books, signals a preference for seeing 'prophets' as *tradents*, those who stand in a line of historical succession and hand on tradition from one generation to the next. Since the lists in question do in fact correspond to the prophetic portion of the canonical form of Scripture accepted by Christians and Jews respectively, it is no great step to conclude that there is a causal connection: either the shape of the canon has influenced how the prophets are understood, or the conception of prophecy in the two communities has influenced their arrangement of the canon. In either case the reasons for the difference between Christian and Jewish Bibles in their arrangement and selection of 'prophetic' books is worth investigating, and it seems a sensible place to begin a study of the different ways in which prophecy was perceived in ancient times.

15

II

Eschatology or ethics? If Christians and Jews have differed in which of these they take to be the typical concern of 'prophetic' books, neither community can be accused of reading into the prophets interests that are simply not there at all. Indeed, in our English Bibles the Old Testament ends with a passage in which the two stand side by side in perfect harmony:

> Remember the law of my servant Moses, the statutes and ordinances that I commanded him at Horeb for all Israel. Behold, I will send you Elijah the prophet before the great and terrible day of the LORD comes. And he will turn the hearts of the fathers to their children, and the hearts of children to their fathers, lest I come and smite the land with a curse (Malachi 4:4–6 [Heb. 3:22–4]).

Nevertheless, the way the canon is ordered for Jews and Christians respectively has often been seen as predisposing the reader to let one concern or the other prevail as the key to the whole prophetic corpus. A presentation of this fairly uncontroversial point will help to show why, in recent years, it has come to be suggested that we have in it a clue to the history of the process of canonization itself.

There is a long tradition in Judaism, classically formulated by Maimonides,[4] that the Hebrew Scriptures are to be seen as consisting of three concentric circles. In the centre stands the Pentateuch or Torah. Its central position does not only indicate that its authority is superior to that of all other Scripture; it also means that all other Scripture is to be understood as generically similar to Torah. The Prophets come next, commenting on the Torah and helping the reader to apply its teaching by providing (especially in the historical books) examples of righteous and unrighteous conduct and (especially in the 'latter Prophets') precepts and warnings. The Writings or Hagiographa, the third division of the Hebrew Bible, encircle both Torah and Prophets and provide a further level of exposition, a little lower in authority than the Prophets, but still divinely inspired.

It is perhaps in the liturgy that this understanding comes most clearly to light, when the solemn reading of the Torah is followed by a lesson from the prophets (the *haftarah*) chosen for its appropriateness in explicating the word of God spoken in the Law. As

16

C. Perrot attractively puts it, 'La Torah est la lumière, une lumière intense et trop forte pour nos pauvres yeux. Des verres fumés sont nécessaires pour en soutenir l'éclat et mieux apprécier la portée du rayonnement. Tel est le rôle de la lecture complémentaire tirée des Prophètes.'[5] The Prophets act as filters, to make the unapproachable light of the Torah bearable for human eyes; and they are therefore indispensable aids to understanding and observing the Torah, and so share in its authority and prestige.[6]

This being so, it is not surprising to find rabbinic sayings in which not only the Pentateuch but the other two divisions of Scripture as well are called 'Torah'. In the Midrash on Psalm 78 we find:

> Let not a man say, The Psalms are not Torah; they are Torah, and the Prophets too are Torah, and the riddles [Proverbs?] and the parables [?] are also Torah.[7]

But there is plenty of evidence already in the New Testament that 'law' could be used to mean 'Scripture', with no distinction between the three divisions. Thus John 10:34 introduces the quotation from Psalm 82:6 ('I said, you are gods') with the words 'Is it not written in your law?'; in Romans 3:19 the catena of psalm-verses assembled to show the universality of human wickedness is said to be designed to silence all mankind because such is the purpose of all that 'the law' says;[8] and in 1 Corinthians 14:21 a quotation from Isaiah 28:11–12 is referred to as written 'in the law'. It is clear from such specific uses of *torah* or *nomos* that the rest of Scripture was perceived as essentially the same sort of thing as the Torah proper, and that its importance lay here, not in any features related to the genres of which the different divisions were composed.[9]

Even without the evidence of this usage, however, it is abundantly plain that in Jewish tradition the rest of Scripture is generally assimilated to the model of Torah. As the new Schürer puts it, 'for the Jew, the books of the Bible are not primarily works of law, or of exhortation and comfort, or of edification and history. They are Torah, a divine instruction, commandment and revelation addressed to Israel.'[10]

Of course the extension of the term *torah* beyond the limits of the Pentateuch does not even stop at the Writings, for Mishnah and Talmud may be seen as further concentric circles beyond the Prophets and the Writings. They are, after all, only the codification of the oral Torah, which according to the famous saying at the

17

beginning of Pirqe Aboth had been handed down from Moses just as the written Torah had been.[11] Alongside the recognition that the individual books in the Prophets and the Writings derived from separate authors living later than Moses, there is also a strong tradition treating them in the same way as the oral Torah – that is, regarding them as having been already known (at least implicitly) to Moses himself. Thus:

> R. Joshua b. Levi said, Every prophet concerned himself [only] with his own prophecy, except for Moses, who spoke all the words of the prophets as well as his own.[12]

On this view, when the prophets came to write their own books they were drawing on words already prepared for them by Moses. As we shall see on many occasions, 'authorship' is an exceedingly fluid concept for the rabbis, and not too much about the mechanism of prophetic inspiration should be read out of a saying such as this.

The desire to attribute every valid tradition of whatever kind to Moses frequently produces suggestions which considered in all their logical implications are somewhat bizarre, but which are hardly intended to be treated as watertight theories. For example, according to a legend in Menahot 29b, God once allowed Moses to see R. Akiba expounding the Torah. Moses failed altogether to understand what he heard, but was reassured when a disciple asked R. Akiba, 'Master, how do you know this?' and the rabbi replied, 'It is a *halakah* of Moses given at Sinai.'[13] Moses here is the 'source' of all teaching given in his name, much as a Cabinet minister is the 'author' of all documents issued in the name of his Department; he need not necessarily understand them all. To try to extract a 'doctrine' of Scripture from sayings such as these is to lose one's sense of proportion. But however little we really learn about the character of prophetic inspiration from such texts, they do very strongly confirm that all Scripture, and indeed all authentic 'tradition' outside Scripture, was and is seen in Judaism as in some sense derived from or dependent on the Torah in the narrower sense of the term, the teaching given by Moses himself. It is entirely consonant with this that the Prophets and the Writings are together referred to as *qabbalah*, 'tradition', in rabbinic usage, when they need to be specifically distinguished from the Torah proper, the Pentateuch.

One of the most striking effects of this subordination of all other

18

Scripture to the Torah is the blurring of what to us are significant distinctions within the other divisions of the canon. For example, rabbinic literature fails to see any significant distinction between what we would call the 'historical' books (Joshua–Kings) and the 'prophetic' books (Isaiah–Malachi). It is customary now to speak of these as the 'Former Prophets' and the 'Latter Prophets' respectively, but so far as we know these terms do not antedate the eighth century AD – in other words, we owe them to the Masoretes. In literature older than this period the phrase 'former prophets' simply means 'prophets of long ago': thus in Sotah 48b 'the former prophets' are said to be either Samuel, David and Solomon, or alternatively the pre-exilic prophets as opposed to Haggai, Zechariah and Malachi (the second possibility corresponding to the use of the expression in Zechariah 1:4).[14] Hints of the later division may perhaps be found in 2 Maccabees 2:13 ('the books about the kings and the prophets'); and in the fact that so far no *pesher* commentaries on the Former Prophets have been found at Qumran, though there *is* such a commentary on the Psalms, which in the Hebrew canon does not figure among the Prophets at all. But on the whole no difficulty seems to have been found in grouping histories and prophecies together as 'Prophets'.

A tempting explanation for this is that writing history was felt to be an essentially 'prophetic' activity in any case. Josephus, as we shall see, thinks that it takes a prophet to write reliable history, and as early as Chronicles prophets figure as historians: see, for example, 2 Chronicles 9:29, 11:15, 20:34, and 32:32. But my own impression is that the perception that the Prophets form a unity rests on a difference of outlook from our own which goes deeper than this. The rabbinic view of the matter can be seen most clearly in a passage from the Talmud which is always cited in discussions of the Hebrew ordering of Scripture, and which will concern us later as evidence for the antiquity of the tripartite canon:

Our Rabbis taught: The order of the Prophets is, Joshua, Judges, Samuel, Kings, Jeremiah, Ezekiel, Isaiah, and the Twelve Minor Prophets. Let us examine this. Hosea came first, as it is written [Hosea 1:2]: God spoke first to Hosea. But did God speak first to Hosea? Were there not many prophets between Moses and Hosea? R. Johanan, however, has explained that he was the first of the four prophets who prophesied at that period, namely,

19

Hosea, Isaiah, Amos, and Micah. Should not then Hosea come first? – Since his prophecy is written along with those of Haggai, Zechariah and Malachi, and Haggai, Zechariah and Malachi came at the end of the prophets, he is reckoned with them. But why should he not be written separately and placed first? – Since his book is so small, it might be lost [if copied separately]. Let us see again. Isaiah was prior to Jeremiah and Ezekiel. Then why should not Isaiah be placed first? – Because the book of Kings ends with a record of destruction and Jeremiah speaks throughout of destruction and Ezekiel commences with destruction and ends with consolation and Isaiah is full of consolation; therefore we put destruction next to destruction and consolation next to consolation.[15]

This passage has innumerable interesting features; but for the moment the important one is the explanation ascribed to Johanan b. Zakkai to account for the order of the Prophets which 'our Rabbis taught'. The modern reader is likely to be struck most forcibly by the inadequacy of claiming that Jeremiah 'speaks throughout of destruction' or that Isaiah is 'full of consolation'.[16] But this conceals a feature which is in reality far more startling: the entire failure to grasp that Kings and Jeremiah – history and prophecy – simply belong to different genres. For us the most obvious difference between the 'destruction' at the end of Kings and the 'destruction' spoken of by Jeremiah is that the first is past, the second future. Kings is a record of what has happened, whereas the prophecies, whether of weal or woe, in the Latter Prophets are for what still lies in the future. For it to seem natural to ignore that distinction and to treat historical narrative and predictive prophecy as the same kind of thing, the Prophetic scriptures have to be read with concerns quite different from ours.[17] Once we see that the importance of the Prophets lies, for the rabbis, *neither* in their accuracy as a record of the past *nor* in the information they provide about the future, but chiefly in the effectiveness with which they bear witness to God's consistency in remaining true to the character revealed in the Torah – punishing transgression, yet never forsaking his covenant with his people[18] – then we can begin to understand why our distinction between record and prediction, and hence between Former and Latter Prophets, was not functional in the world of the Talmud.

In the traditional Jewish understanding of the canon, then, Torah is the essential category in the light of which all else is to be understood. Prophetic books are to be seen primarily as an aid to a better understanding of the teaching given through Moses, in much the same way as mishnah and gemarah; and the prophets who were their authors should be seen as teachers – proto-rabbis, we might almost say – handing on the authentic teaching of Moses to succeeding generations. In respect of their function, prophets are no different from the 'elders' or the 'men of the Great Synagogue' of Pirqe Aboth 1:1 – tradents of authentic tradition. The organization of the canon, with Prophets forming an outer circle around the Pentateuch, perfectly mirrors this conception, it would seem.

III

By contrast, the canon of the Greek Bible, which has come down to us (suspiciously enough) only in Christian tradition, apparently implies a quite different understanding of Scripture, and with it an equally different perception of prophecy. At least in a large majority of manuscripts, the Septuagint seems to preserve an ordering of the books which gives the Old Testament a primarily historical or perhaps eschatological orientation. It would probably be widely agreed that the Greek canon is also, though in a looser sense than the Hebrew, tripartite, but instead of concentric circles its three parts may be seen as three sections of a tightly-stretched cord. At one end the cord is firmly attached to the past: the Bible begins with a section of historical books, among which there is no distinction of rank such as exists in the Hebrew Scriptures between Pentateuch and Former Prophets.[19] The order is the same as in English Bibles up to the end of Esther (though Esther itself includes the additional passages which appear in the English Apocrypha), but there are then added Judith, Tobit, and (usually) 1 and 2 Maccabees. At the other end, attached to the future, stand the books of the prophets, in varying order, but always including Daniel and the 'Lamentations of Jeremiah', as the book is explicitly called in Greek manuscripts (there is no attribution in the Hebrew Scriptures). In the centre is a section of material which has little internal cohesion (scarcely more than the very heterogeneous documents that form the Writings in the Hebrew arrangement), but which Greek and

Latin Bibles sometimes call 'didactic' books. This section comprises, in fact, what modern scholarship generally dubs 'wisdom literature' – Proverbs, Job, Ecclesiastes, Ecclesiasticus, the Wisdom of Solomon – together with the Psalms and the Song of Songs. It may be plausible to say that, if the other sections are concerned respectively with past and future, the 'didactic' books look to the conduct of life in the present; in a sense, they have the same *function* as the Torah has in the Hebrew canon, though they do not of course have the same position of superior *authority* in respect of the other books. There are in fact no grades of authority within the Greek canon: all the books stand on an equal footing. The thrust of the whole arrangement is strongly eschatological. Scripture is a linear account of the divine purpose, from the creation to the consummation promised through the prophets, and it ends on an expectant note, with God's promises awaiting their fulfilment.[20]

We have seen that the Torah is central for the Hebrew Scriptures not only in the sense that it is the most important part of the canon, but also because it provides the model for the rest of Scripture: in so far as a book is canonical Scripture, it is Torah-like in character. Now in the same way it may be argued that prophecy is not only the climax and completion of the Greek Old Testament Scriptures, promising a glorious culmination to the story of God's creative work begun in Genesis, but also the essential key to understanding the Bible as a whole. In so far as a book is canonical Scripture, it is prophetic in character. Just as all scriptural books can by extension be called 'Torah' in Judaism, so in Christian tradition all scriptural books can be called 'prophecy', since what matters in Scripture is above all its ability to point to the fulfilment of God's plans.

The clearest example of this usage is in 2 Peter, where we read that 'no *prophecy* of Scripture is a matter of private interpretation, because no prophecy ever came by the impulse of man, but men moved by the Holy Spirit spoke from God' (2 Peter 1:20–1). This surely implies both that the whole of Scripture can be called 'prophecy' – it is unlikely that the author meant to refer only to the second division – and also that it is to be understood as 'prophecy' in the characteristically Christian sense: predictions about the fulfilment of God's promises. For a Christian of this persuasion all Scripture is prophecy, just as for a Jew all Scripture is Torah. But of course the section called 'prophetic books' is the part of the Bible where this eschatological note can be heard *par excellence*. By placing

22

the prophets at the end of the canon, the Greek tradition and its Latin descendants ensure that the Old Testament will be heard as pointing beyond itself to some future fulfilment, and that the reader will take eschatology, rather than ethics, as the guiding thread through the multifarious books of which Scripture is composed.

The appropriateness of the LXX arrangement for a Christian reading of the Old Testament, and its ready compatibility with the traditional Christian understanding of prophecy as eschatological prediction, is very apparent.[21] Thanks in large measure to the work of A. C. Sundberg, it has become possible to argue that the convenience of the LXX ordering for a Christian reading of Scripture is, indeed, no accident, but that the Greek Bible in its present form was a Christian collection from the beginning, just as the Hebrew Bible was a Jewish one. To show how this conclusion is reached, however, we need to look first at standard theories about the development of both Greek and Hebrew canons.

IV

Since the work of Elias Levita in the fifteenth century, the traditional view among both Jews and Christians has been that the contents and arrangement of the Hebrew Bible were fixed by Ezra.[22] The recognition that a number of biblical books are later than Ezra even in origin, however, has long since led scholars to abandon this picture, and it has been replaced by an alternative theory which is so widely held that it can by now be called 'traditional' itself. The essential element on which nearly all modern scholars agree is that the tripartite arrangement of the Hebrew Scriptures is the best clue to the history of their canonization. The Torah was the first of the three divisions to be accorded canonical status, and in this, many would think, Ezra may well have been at least partly instrumental, though naturally the authority of most of the Pentateuch was agreed even before his work. The Prophets were the next group of scriptures to be 'closed'. Whatever date is assigned to this, it needs to be early enough to explain why Daniel is excluded from the Prophets and relegated to the Writings: so the middle of the second century BC commends itself to many. Finally, the Writings remained in a fluid state until about the end of the first century of the Christian era. It is usually held that a mishnah recorded in M. Yadaim 3:5 shows

23

that there was still uncertainty at this time about the status of one or two books, notably the Song of Songs and Ecclesiastes. At one time the debates about canonicity reported there were glorified with the title 'the council of Jamnia (or Yavneh)'.[23] But it is now generally acknowledged that this expression distorts the character of the discussions recorded in the Mishnah, which does not so much report a definitive set of rulings on the canon as point to continuing uncertainty about the limits of the third scriptural division, the Writings – an uncertainty which may have persisted even into the second century AD. However, from the fact that the two 'Solomonic' books were the subject of uncertainty we can reasonably conclude that most of the Writings were not, and so can see the present canon as effectively fixed by the end of the New Testament period.[24]

This theory has a double advantage. Not only does it explain the fact that the Hebrew Bible is tripartite; it also allows us to think that the order in which the books were canonized bears some relation to the order in which they were written. Thus, though it is true that the Pentateuch in its final form is a product of the post-exilic age, most scholars would still see it as the expansion of a core which is extremely old. If we accept the consensus brought about through the work of Gerhard von Rad and Martin Noth, then the underlying framework or the *Grundschrift* of the JE strands really is the ancient foundation-document of Israel, so that it seems intuitively probable that the finished work which enshrines it should have been the first part of the Bible to achieve canonicity.[25] The 'Deuteronomistic History' – the Hebrew Bible's 'Former Prophets' – is usually dated in the exilic period, while the books of the Latter Prophets were mostly complete by about the middle of the third century BC, even on the least conservative theories. The latest works in the Old Testament (Chronicles, Ruth, Esther) are all in the Writings, and for the most part the books which are supposed to have been discussed 'at Jamnia' (the Song of Songs and Ecclesiastes) are among the latest to have been written, according to majority opinion. Thus the theory that the three divisions of Scripture were canonized in the order in which they now stand does justice to our feeling that the older is likely to have seemed the more authoritative, even if in some cases books were not actually as old as they were believed to be.

The consensus view is sufficiently uncontroversial for there to be no need to set out all the evidence on which it is based, but four

24

points may be singled out for mention here, since they will play an important role in subsequent discussion.

(1) The prologue to Ecclesiasticus, which can be dated fairly accurately in the late second century BC, seems already to be familiar with a tripartite division of Scripture:

> A legacy of great value has come to us through *the law, the prophets, and the writers who followed in their steps* . . .
>
> My grandfather Jesus, having devoted himself more and more to reading *the law and the prophets and the other books of the fathers,* and having gained sufficient ability in these matters, was brought to the point of himself writing down some of the things that have a bearing on education in wisdom . . .
>
> Works do not have the same force when spoken in their own Hebrew and when translated into another language. Not only so, but even *the law itself and the prophets and the rest of the books* have no small difference when read in the original.

This shows, it is argued, (a) that Scripture already had three divisions, but (b) that the third did not yet have an 'official' name; which is what we should expect, given that (a) the canon developed as outlined above but (b) the Writings, as they were later to be known, were not yet hard and fast.

(2) In Luke 22:44 the risen Jesus instructs his disciples in the scriptural testimonies which show that the Messiah had to suffer before entering into his glory, and the Scriptures are described as 'the law, the prophets and the psalms'. Again we find here the first two divisions under their usual titles, but the third is referred to, *pars pro toto*, by the name of one of its component books – the book from which Christians drew most of their *testimonia*; or perhaps the Writings were known collectively as *psalmoi* (*tᵉhillîm?*) simply because a number of them are poetic in character, much as the Fathers call the central section of the Greek canon *libri didactici* because that is the character of some of them.

(3) As we have already noted, Daniel, which appears among the prophets in Greek Bibles, is in Hebrew manuscripts and lists always one of the Writings. Given the importance of the book and its prophet-like character, it is difficult to believe that it would not have been placed in the Prophets if the Prophetic canon had still been open.[26]

(4) An important passage from Josephus's treatise *Against Apion*,

25

which like Baba Bathra 14b–15a is always cited by scholars discussing the canon, attests not only a tripartite canon but also a *closed* canon at the end of the first century AD:

It therefore naturally, or rather necessarily, follows (seeing that with us it is not open to everybody to write the records, and that there is no discrepancy in what is written; seeing that, on the contrary, the prophets alone had this privilege, obtaining their knowledge of the most remote and ancient history through the inspiration which they owed to God, and committing to writing a clear account of the events of their own time just as they occurred) – it follows, I say, that we do not possess myriads of inconsistent books, conflicting with each other. Our books, those which are justly accredited (*ta dikaiôs pepisteumena*), are but two and twenty, and contain the record of all time. Of these, five are the books of Moses, comprising the laws and the traditional history down to the death of the lawgiver. This period falls only a little short of three thousand years. From the death of Moses until Artaxerxes, who succeeded Xerxes as king of Persia, the prophets subsequent to Moses wrote the history of the events of their own times in thirteen books. The remaining four books contain hymns to God and precepts for the conduct of human life.

From Artaxerxes to our own time the complete history has been written, but has not been deemed worthy of equal credit with the earlier records, because of the failure of the exact succession of the prophets.

We have given practical proof of our reverence for our own Scriptures. For, although such long ages have now passed, no one has ventured either to add, or to remove, or to alter a syllable; and it is an instinct with every Jew, from the day of his birth, to regard them as the decrees of God, to abide by them, and, if need be, cheerfully to die for them. Time and again ere now the sight has been witnessed of prisoners enduring tortures and death in every form in the theatres, rather than utter a single word against the laws and the allied documents.[27]

Josephus's 'prophetic' section cannot be made to correspond to the Prophets of the present Hebrew canon – a point to which we shall return – and his count of twenty-two sacred books conflicts with the twenty-four traditional in later rabbinic lists; but there does

26

seem to be a good *prima facie* case for regarding him as a witness to an emergent tripartite canon. It is noteworthy, too, that his whole discussion takes place in the context of a polemic against the multiplicity of holy books recognized by pagan religions (in fact he has in mind the large number of books, both secular and sacred, of Greek literature, and his argument is entirely specious, since he is not comparing like with like).[28] In contrasting with this the modest compass of Jewish Scripture he can be seen as a witness to the sense that Scripture formed a *closed* corpus in Judaism as early as the first century AD.[29]

The picture drawn so far is, as I have said, relatively uncontroversial. Such controversy as there is concerns the absolute rather than the relative date of the various stages in the process of canonization. Nearly all scholars, that is, agree that the tripartite shape is a key to the order in which Scripture was canonized, but recent studies have brought a crop of different theories about the date at which each division was closed. The most 'conservative' theory is probably that of David Noel Freedman,[30] who regards not only the Torah but also the Prophets as already a fixed corpus by about 500 BC – by which date, according to most students of the prophets, substantial portions of the book of Isaiah and several complete books of the minor prophets had not even been written! At the other extreme is the thesis of A. C. Sundberg, which will be examined in detail in the next section, that the canon of the Writings was not fixed until well into the Christian era. A number of scholars still defend a pre-Christian date for the closing of the entire Hebrew canon. Thus Geza Vermes[31] speaks of all the books except Daniel as canonical by 200 BC, and S. Z. Leiman holds that 150 BC is the lowest possible date consistent with both biblical and rabbinic evidence. Leiman interestingly recycles the familiar argument that the Prophets must have been closed before the writing of Daniel to make it apply also to Chronicles. He suggests that since the very similar historical material in Kings is included in the Former Prophets, Chronicles would have been also had it existed when the Prophetic canon was closed. This produces in his view a *terminus ante quem* for the Prophets of about 400 BC.[32] Leiman has been followed in this by B. S. Childs, in his important attempt to ground the interpretation of the Old Testament in a 'canonical' perspective.[33]

But even this degree of disagreement may in reality be less serious

27

than it looks, since in some ways it masks a fundamental failure to agree on the meaning of the term 'canonical'. When scholars say that even as late as the second century AD there could still be dispute about the canonicity of a few of the books in the Writings, they usually mean by the 'canon' a closed list to which no books may be added – indeed, the idea of closure is integral to the idea of canonicity in most scholarly discussions. But when Leiman argues that the Prophets were already finished by 400 and the Writings very soon after the composition of Daniel, it is important to see that his definition of canonicity does not include this vital ingredient. According to his understanding of the term 'canonical', 'A canonical book is a book accepted by Jews as authoritative for religious practice and/or doctrine, and whose authority is binding upon the Jewish people for all generations'.[34] This apparently says nothing about the *closed* character of the canon at all, so that in claiming that all of the present Hebrew Bible was 'canonical' by 150 BC or thereabouts, Leiman is not implying that by that time it was universally agreed that no other books could ever be of equal authority. 150 BC is the *terminus ad quem* for the acceptance of all the books in the Hebrew Scriptures as authoritative, but not for what would usually be called the 'closing' of the canon.

My impression is that in practice Leiman often elides this point in his discussion, and treats the 'authoritative' books as having *exclusive* authority for Judaism just as do scholars whose definition of 'canon' does include the note of closure; but at least in principle, some of the disagreements between him and proponents of a later date for the fixing of the canon are disputes about words rather than about facts. It is consistent with his formal definition that Leiman speaks of the Mishnah and the Talmud as 'canonical', too, and argues that in a sense the canon never has been closed in Judaism, since authority attaches to the whole work of interpretation running without a break from biblical times to the present day.

In a way, of course, this merely shifts the weight of the question, for there is no doubt that subsequent tradition has distinguished between the Bible and other books, and indeed Leiman himself finds that a distinction needs to be drawn between 'inspired' and 'uninspired' canonical works. Once we ask at what date *this* crucial distinction was drawn, so that exactly the present corpus of the Hebrew Scriptures came to be on one side of the dividing-line, and the Mishnah, Talmud, and later traditions on the other; then we are back where we began, with the question which most scholars would call the question of the canon. In practice Leiman's answer to this question is probably closer to the mainstream consensus than a superficial reading of his rather polemically written book would suggest. He represents the more conservative end of the spectrum, and prefers high to low datings both for the completion of biblical books and for their acceptance as authoritative, but his basic assumptions do not diverge sharply from the general consensus.

Most scholars with no particular axe of their own to grind would probably agree with a summary such as the following. Biblical books became accepted as authoritative at different times during the post-exilic age, and firm datings for this process are not available. However, by the age of the Maccabees the Torah had long been regarded not only as authoritative but as exclusively so, in the sense that it formed a closed body of material to which nothing could be added. By the end of the second century BC a similar conclusion had been reached about the Prophets: not only were these books holy and inspired, they also constituted a closed corpus which did not permit of additions – thus Daniel, for all its claim to ancient origins, was unable to gain admission. Beside these two collections there was a third body of writings, not yet settled in either its authority or its extent, which had no name, but was referred to in terms that show it to have been on the way to becoming a third division of the 'canon'. By the end of the first century of the Christian era there was no serious doubt about the scriptural status of most of its component books, though a certain slight fuzziness at the edges persisted for a time. By the middle of the second century AD we can speak confidently of a tripartite Hebrew canon of Law, Prophets, and Writings, in the form and with the extent which is throughout presupposed by the Talmud.[35] If this is so, then by the first century BC the Prophets – our primary concern – were ordered in such a way, and had such a status, that they were well adapted to be read from the perspective we have already outlined, as the work of inspired commentators and tradents of the Torah.

V

Until comparatively recently the case which is being summarized in this chapter, that the Hebrew and Greek Scriptures of the Old Testament enshrine respectively Jewish and Christian conceptions of prophecy in the way that their contents are ordered, would have been difficult to sustain, because it was held that *both* canons were in origin Jewish. According to a theory which had held sway since the classic work of Francis Lee in 1719,[36] the LXX's longer and distinctively arranged canon did not come about (as the Reformers had thought) because the early Church wrongly permitted 'apocryphal' additions to be made to the shorter Hebrew canon of the Jews. On the contrary, the Greek Bible had just as good a pedigree within Judaism as the Hebrew, representing the Scriptures regarded as canonical by the Hellenized Jews of Alexandria, just as the Hebrew Bible preserved the canon accepted in Palestine. But since the work of A. C. Sundberg a new consensus about the Greek Old Testament has emerged, which makes it far easier to contrast the two canons as we have been doing. Again, I shall concentrate on features of this new approach which are specially relevant to our present inquiry, since it is easy to find elsewhere full accounts of the evidence on which Sundberg draws.

Sundberg's demolition of the Alexandrian canon hypothesis[37] has had so much success largely because it distinguished more clearly than had been customary between 'scripture' and 'canon', and also because it showed a keener awareness of the social realities to which abstract terms such as 'canonization' refer. First, Sundberg drew the crucial distinction which I have just been examining in my discussion of Leiman: the distinction between an agreement to regard *at least* a certain corpus of books as possessing some kind of official authorization (which is what turns 'writings' into 'Scriptures') and an agreement that Scripture comprises these books *at most*, thereby placing all others on a lower level (which is what turns 'Scriptures' into 'the canon of Scripture'). Sundberg is essentially in agreement with the theory for which Leiman has recently contended, that more or less all the books in the present Hebrew canon were regarded as authoritative Scripture (i.e. were what *Leiman* calls 'canonical') by about the second century BC. But he denies that there were any official lists of Scripture, such that it is possible to say that certain other books were *not* regarded as scriptural (i.e. were 'uncanonical' in the more usual, and stronger, sense of the term). According to him there was already agreement in both Palestine and Alexandria (and everywhere else, for that matter) that what we now call the Law and the Prophets were both scriptural and canonical: in other words, all Jews accepted *both* that these two collections had binding authority *and* that they each formed a closed corpus to which no other books could be admitted. But so far as the section which in the Hebrew Bible would come to be called the Writings was concerned, different communities in practice used different books and regarded them all as semi- or potentially inspired. The time had not yet come at which it had occurred to anyone to draw a line marking any particular book as the last of the Writings. Thus Judaism knew a bipartite canon of Law and Prophets, and in addition a category which we could call 'other Scriptures'. By the end of the first Christian century this category had still not been 'closed', and when the Church and the Synagogue eventually did come to draw sharp lines of demarcation around it, they opted for different selections from what Sundberg called, in a phrase that has become an identity-marker for those of his persuasion, 'a wide religious literature without definite bounds'.[38]

It was only after both canons had been closed by their respective communities that Christians began to learn of the shorter selection made in Judaism, and to wonder whether it did not represent a more 'primitive' list. Thus in the fourth century we find the well-known disagreement between Augustine and Jerome, the former preferring the traditional Christian canon but the latter, on the basis of his much more extensive acquaintance with Judaism, arguing for the primacy of the Hebrew canon.[39] But in reality the impression of greater antiquity in the Hebrew canon is spurious. Even though it is shorter and does not contain books with no Hebrew originals, as the LXX canon does, this does not mean that it is an older list: for in New Testament times it had not yet occurred to Jews (in Palestine or the diaspora) that books in Greek could not be 'Scripture', or that Scripture should be of modest compass. (Josephus's insistence on the brevity of the Jewish Scriptures belongs to his polemical purpose.)

Secondly, Sundberg's argument has commended itself because it takes account of the realities of life in Jewish and Christian communities in the early centuries. It is not to be supposed that

31

every synagogue will have possessed a copy of every book reckoned scriptural by the community that worshipped there nor, conversely, that people will have checked any book that came into their possession to see if it appeared on some official list of 'approved' books. As Sundberg sees it, no one in the period from about 100 BC to AD 100 would have needed such a list to form a judgement on the authority of the Law or the Prophets, which had not 'been closed' so much as closed themselves. Everyone knew that the books of Moses and of the Former and Latter Prophets (to give them their later names) were ancient and holy and had no equals: in other words, that they were both 'scriptural' and 'canonical'. But if a scroll of Ecclesiastes, or Daniel, or Enoch, appeared, most people would have assumed, from its ostensible authorship, that it should be received as 'Scripture', though they would recognize that it did not belong to the 'canonical' core of the Scriptures. To think of *all* the books in either the Hebrew or the Greek Bible as already constituting a canonical collection by the turn of the era seems, then, to Sundberg essentially an anachronism. And that being so, talk of 'the Alexandrian canon' or 'the Palestinian canon' is equally anachronistic. In New Testament times 'the other books', as Ben Sira's grandson calls them, were as yet an indeterminate collection. Furthermore, though in Judaism the final selection when it was at last fixed continued to constitute a corpus separate from the Law and the Prophets, the Church felt free to rearrange the canon and to mix Prophets and Writings together, so that even the shape of the Greek canon is different from that of the Hebrew. In short, the Greek Bible is a Christian Bible, and has never been anything else. Though the books of which it is composed are all Jewish in origin, the principles of the selection and arrangement of its contents follow Christian, not Jewish interests.

Sundberg's reconstruction of the history of the canon is sharply opposed by Leiman, because it implies that the *Hebrew* canon was not finalized until well on into the Christian era, and Leiman is keen to maintain that the Hebrew Scriptures already formed a closed corpus by the middle of the second century BC. But, despite the very harsh tone in which Leiman expresses his disagreement with Sundberg, it is not clear to me that a great deal separates them in reality. We have already seen that 'canonical' is a much weaker term for Leiman than for Sundberg and most other scholars. Similarly, on the fixing of the *Prophetic* canon there is little difference between them, and indeed it is scarcely possible to find a major scholar who does not share their common conviction that the Prophets were 'closed' well before the New Testament period. Again, even on Leiman's view the canonical status of a few books in what would become the Writings was at least still capable of being discussed in the first century AD, even if the outcome was more or less a foregone conclusion. Sundberg's position is novel in its suggestion that the Writings were not closed in Judaism before the Greek canon adopted its longer list, and in claiming therefore that the finished Greek Bible is a Christian work *wholly* independent of the Hebrew Scriptures, but it is not clear to me why Leiman regards the expression 'a wide religious literature without definite bounds' as so peculiarly loathsome a description of the books from which the Writings would eventually be selected. Especially for someone whose main interest is in the Prophetic part of the canon, there is not really such a great difference between Leiman and Sundberg.

It is easy to see that Sundberg's position on the Greek canon is both consonant with the general consensus about the formation of the Hebrew one, and highly congenial to the thesis about the Prophets that I have been presenting. Like most students of the Hebrew canon, Sundberg thinks that the Prophets were 'closed' by the end of the first century BC, but that the Writings were still 'open' for at least two centuries more. And like those who have thought about the presentation of prophecy in the two canons, he sees the Greek arrangement of both Prophets and Writings into a pattern different from that of the Hebrew Bible as dictated by Christian perceptions. It does not derive from a pre-Christian Jewish arrangement, and so it cannot be argued that the Christian idea of prophecy was already enshrined in the shape of the canonical text before the Church got to work on it.

The witness of Josephus is especially relevant here, for the ordering of the biblical books in *Against Apion* was one of the strongest trump-cards in the hands of proponents of the Alexandrian canon hypothesis.[40] Although they were right to point out that Josephus's list does have significant points of contact with the order in the LXX (e.g. in apparently distributing many of the Writings among the Prophets, placing Ruth in its chronological position, Lamentations with Jeremiah, and so on), in other respects it seems to have a characteristically 'Hebrew' flavour, and the clearest example of this is precisely in the way he treats the prophets. For him the prophets were inspired *historians*. This must imply, we may reasonably argue, that he drew no distinction between the 'Former' and the 'Latter' Prophets, and what is more that he did not see prediction as the essence of the prophetic task. Both these points give the clearest possible indication that Josephus's Bible, however unlike the eventual Jewish canon of Law, Prophets and Writings it may have been, lacked the essential feature of all Greek Old Testaments: it did not see the Latter Prophets, the books in which eschatology was emphasized, as forming a special category of their own, and one which determined the way in which Scripture as a whole was to be read. True, Josephus's view of Scripture does not entirely square with the later Jewish conception either, since it focuses on historiography rather than Torah. But that can be explained both by the fact that Josephus was himself a historian, and so naturally saw Scripture with a historian's eye, and also by the context of *Against Apion*, in which historical reliability is the very point at issue. His failure to point out, at this juncture in the argument, that prophets have inspired knowledge of the future as well as the past cannot be similarly accounted for, however, and is all the more striking in view of his own intense interest in the predictive side of prophecy, much in evidence in many other places in his works.[41] The simplest explanation is that the classic Hebrew model of Scripture, in which the Prophets are a second-order Torah rather than the climax of the whole canon, was normative even for this highly Hellenized Jew. Thus an examination of Josephus is a further help in establishing a thoroughly harmonious hypothesis, in which the history of the canon and the history of Jewish and Christian perceptions of prophecy march hand in hand.

Thus, it seems, we can end this presentation of the consensus that has established itself over the last twenty years or so about the canon, and especially about the place of the Prophets in it, with a contented sigh. Unfortunately the consensus view is in my judgement probably quite wrong. In the next chapter, therefore, we will start to dig up the road we have just finished so carefully surfacing.

2

'The Law and the Prophets'

I

The problem of the canon is like many other problems in biblical studies in that we probably already possess all the evidence we are ever likely to have. Certainly I have no fresh information that is not freely available elsewhere from which to argue for an explanation of the place of the Prophets in the canon different from that of the consensus view just summarized. I shall begin, however, by calling attention to seven facts which, though not in dispute, fit very uneasily into the framework established by the consensus, and then go on to present an alternative explanation which accommodates them as well as the evidence on which the consensus itself is based.[1]

(1)   In the New Testament by far the commonest way of referring to Scripture is as 'the law and the prophets': see, for example, Matthew 5:17; 7:12; 11:13; 16:16; 22:40; Acts 13:15; 24:14; 28:23; Romans 3:21. Compare also Luke 16:29–31, which speaks of 'Moses and the prophets', and Ignatius, *Smyrneans* 5:1 ('they have not been persuaded by the prophecies nor by the law of Moses'), which probably refers to this passage. By contrast the threefold designation 'the law of Moses, the prophets, and the psalms' in Luke 24:44 is without parallel in New Testament literature. We may therefore argue *ad hominem* that, if Luke 22:44 can legitimately be cited in support of the tripartite canon, a case could much more reasonably be made for a bipartite one on the basis of the far commoner designation 'law and prophets'. More seriously, it may be asked whether it is legitimate to appeal to Luke 22:44 at all when it represents such an exception to the general pattern of New Testament usage.[2]

(2)   Despite the fact that the book of Daniel now appears among the Writings, Daniel is frequently referred to as a 'prophet' in

35

literature of the New Testament period. Thus Matthew 24:15 makes explicit the allusion to Daniel 11:31 and 12:11 in the phrase 'the abomination of desolation' by adding 'spoken of by the prophet Daniel'; and the Qumran community appears to have regarded Daniel as a prophet.[3] Josephus is particularly clear on the point:

> For the books which he wrote and left behind are still read by us even now, and we are convinced by them that Daniel spoke with God, for he was not only wont to prophesy [*prophêteuôn*] future things, as did the other prophets, but he also fixed the time at which these would come to pass. And, whereas the other prophets foretold disasters and were for that reason in disfavour with kings and people, Daniel was a prophet of good tidings to them, so that through the auspiciousness of his predictions he attracted the goodwill of all . . . And he left behind writings in which he has made plain to us the accuracy and faithfulness of his prophecies [*tês prophêteias autou*].[4]

This passage is of interest for several reasons. It seems to show that Josephus thought of prophecy as essentially predictive in character; it also attests a tradition that there was more than one book by Daniel. But it leaves no doubt that 'prophet' is the correct designation for him – indeed he seems to be presented as superior to the other prophets.[5]

Nor is there any shortage of later evidence for Daniel as a prophet. In the Christian Fathers the designation is a matter of course,[6] but there is also rabbinic support for it despite the fact that Daniel's book is reckoned among the Writings in Jewish tradition. We may quote Ginzberg:

> [In Megillah 3a and Sanhedrin 94a] in reference to Dan. 10.7 it is remarked that the men who were with him were the prophets Haggai, Zechariah, and Malachi; yet it was he, though not a prophet, who was found worthy to behold the vision. Palestinian sources, however, tannaitic as well as amoraic, count Daniel among the prophets. Comp. Mekilta 1b [where Daniel is cited as one of the prophets to whom God spoke outside Palestine, the others being Jeremiah and Ezekiel]; PK 4, 36b; PR 14, 61 (where the anthropomorphism of the 'prophets' refers to certain anthropomorphic expressions used in Dan.); Seder 'Olam 20.[7]

Ginzberg's own explanation of this is that 'the old authorities spoke of the 'Book of Daniel' as belonging to the Hagiographa and not to the prophetical part of the Canon. Later, however, the 'book of Daniel' was confused with its author, and hence the statement that he was not a prophet. But the writing of a prophet is not necessarily a prophetic book, as may be seen from the Book of Psalms, which belongs to the Hagiographa, though David was a prophet'.[8] In the terms I have been using, this would mean that Daniel was a prophet but the book *Daniel* was not a Prophet. But this distinction, obvious as it is to us, is seldom clearly drawn in the literature of our period, and Ginzberg's explanation looks to me like special pleading. The simplest way of accounting for these traditions seems to me to be that at one time Daniel was thought of as a Prophetic book, and that though eventually it was assigned to the Writings, the habit of calling Daniel a prophet persisted in Judaism just as in Christianity. There is indeed a parallel with the case of David and the Psalms, but this raises precisely similar questions, and one usage cannot be invoked to explain the other.

This second point, then, bears on the argument that the Prophetic canon must have been closed before Daniel achieved scriptural status, or else Daniel would have been included in it. There is evidence that Daniel *was* regarded as a 'prophetic' book in some sense or other until quite a late period, and one can only conclude that his book was nevertheless not reckoned among the 'Prophets' if one already knows that the canon of the Prophets was closed by then. But that is the very point at issue.

(3)   Two further points arise from Josephus's discussion of the Jewish Scriptures in *Against Apion*. One is that the passage provides a clear criterion for deciding whether a book has the authoritative status of 'Scripture' (avoiding for the moment the word 'canonical'). This criterion is that books are authoritative only if they were written by a *prophet*. A prophet is apparently someone who followed Moses in a line of succession which ended in the days of 'Arta-xerxes'. It is true that strictly speaking prophetic authorship is said to be a necessary guarantee of authenticity only for historical narratives, but in its context historical accuracy is the only question with which the passage is really concerned anyway. Josephus seems to treat it as generally agreed that books written after the failure of the prophetic succession could not claim the allegiance of the Jews, much as in the famous saying in Tosefta Sotah 13:2 'When Haggai, Zechariah, and Malachi, the last prophets, had died, the holy spirit

disappeared from Israel, though she was allowed to hear the *bath-qol*.[9] The essential sources of 'Scripture' seem here to be 'Moses and the prophets', as in the New Testament; the third group of books Josephus mentions do not seem to be non-prophetic so much as non-historiographical – nothing is said about their authorship at all.

In the concluding words of the passage Josephus sums up the components of the Jewish Scriptures as 'the laws and the allied documents' (*tous nomous kai tas meta toutôn anagraphas*), much as in *Antiquities* 20:265 he speaks of 'those who have an exact knowledge of the law and who are capable of interpreting the meaning of the holy writings' (*tois ta nomima saphôs epistamenois kai tên tôn ierôn grammatôn dunamin hermeneusai dunamenois*). Like the New Testament's 'the law and the prophets' this sounds as if it refers to a bipartite rather than a tripartite canon, if we are to think in terms of the divisions of a canon at all.

(4) A second point that may be made about this passage in *Against Apion* is that it is hard to align it with either the Hebrew or the Greek canon as we know them. As we have already seen, Josephus shows some kinship with the Hebrew arrangement in not making any distinction between the Former and the Latter Prophets, as they have come to be known; though the reason why he is able to regard all the Prophetic books as the same sort of work is that he treats all their authors as historians, rather than that he sees them as tradents of the Torah as later rabbis were to do. But on the other hand the distribution of books between the 'thirteen books' containing the history of the prophets' own times and the 'remaining four books' seems if anything closer to the Greek canon, and was, as already noted, one of the arguments used to support the 'Alexandrian canon' hypothesis. There has been much discussion (competently surveyed in Leiman's work) of which books Josephus included among the 'thirteen', and how he counted them: whether Samuel and Kings were each reckoned as one book (as in the Hebrew) or two (as in the Greek), where Ezra, Nehemiah, and Chronicles fitted in, what he did with Ruth, and so on. For our present purpose all that needs to be noted is that he plainly speaks as if all the narrative books were arranged end to end, and does not, for example, reckon Chronicles among the 'four'. For what it is worth, the evidence of the *Antiquities* is consonant with such a scheme, for it tells the story of Ruth in its chronological position,

as in the Greek Bible, continues the history of Israel from the Exile into the age of Ezra and Nehemiah (and, of course, beyond), and even fits the prophets into their proper chronological places – proper, that is, according to the dates claimed by the books them-selves: thus Nahum and Jonah duly appear in the eighth century, and Daniel alongside Ezekiel in the sixth.

If we are to treat Josephus's statements in *Against Apion* as evidence for a particular way of ordering the canon, then, it would be logical to suppose that after the books of Moses it had all the narrative and prophetic books arranged in chronological sequence, followed by a short appendix consisting of the four books of 'hymns and precepts' (Psalms and Proverbs, no doubt, but what else? The Song of Songs? Ecclesiastes? The Wisdom of Solomon?) As will soon emerge, I do not make this suggestion seriously, but only to show that one cannot naturally find support for *either* the present Hebrew *or* the present Greek canon in Josephus. Even if his division is genuinely tripartite (which point 3 was meant to call in question) the three sections do not correspond to the three sections of any other system known to us. He can therefore be claimed as a witness to an emergent tripartite canon only if the fact that he mentions three divisions (supposing this to be a fair interpretation anyway) is felt to be significant quite apart from what he says the three divisions contained. It is misleading to say that from Josephus we can tell that the *Writings* were not yet fixed, since his 'Prophetic' division is equally at variance, on any conceivable distribution of the books, with the present Prophets of the Hebrew canon *and* with the 'prophetic books' of any Greek manuscripts known to us. *Against Apion* is thus much harder to reconcile with the consensus view of the history of the canon than is usually allowed.[10]

(5) We noted in chapter 1 that there is a good deal of rabbinic evidence for the use of *torah* as a catch-all term for the whole of Scripture, just as in Christian writings the whole Old Testament is sometimes called 'prophecy' without discrimination. It should be noted, however, that rabbinic texts also frequently use 'prophet' as the name for any scriptural book, at least for any book outside the Pentateuch. The fact that this happens with Daniel has already been discussed because it bears on a standard argument about the date at which 'the canon of the Prophets' was 'closed'. But in itself it is not surprising. One would as a matter of fact expect Daniel to be called a prophet, if one did not have a prior conviction that the

39

placing of his book in the Writings was important for the history of the canon. After all, Daniel could easily be mistaken for a prophetic book; it is precisely this that makes it possible for scholars to argue that his failure to make the grade can be accounted for only on the hypothesis that the Prophets were already 'closed'.

What is much more surprising is that some books which bear no resemblance at all to prophecy as represented in the Latter Prophets were also dubbed 'prophets' by the rabbis. Thus, as we saw under point 2, David is often called a prophet. When this occurs in the New Testament (Acts 2:25–31) we scarcely notice, even though this too may have implications for the canon; but it is more startling to find it in Jewish texts. Yet Sotah 48b, as already noted, describes David as one of the 'former prophets'. Josephus, for whom David's composition, the Psalms, is one of the few books that we can certainly assign to his 'four remaining books', nonetheless treats the king as a prophet, and a prophet of a definitely predictive type. Thus in *Antiquities* 8:109–10 we read:

> [Solomon] turned to address the multitude and made clear to them the power and providence of God in that most of the future events which he had revealed to David his father had actually come to pass, and the rest would also come about, and how God himself had given him his name even before he was born, and had foretold what he was to be called and that none but he should build him a temple . . . And now that they saw the fulfilment of these things in accordance with David's prophecies [*prophêteian*] he asked them to praise God and not despair of anything he had promised for their happiness.

Solomon himself was also regarded as a prophet. In Sifre Deuteronomy 1:1 the beginning of Qoheleth is described as what Solomon 'prophesied', and Song of Songs Rabbah 1:1, 6 says that the holy spirit rested on Solomon and made it possible for him to compose the Song.

It may be the need to find a 'prophetic' author for the scroll of Esther that leads to the curious tradition according to which Mordecai, who was supposed to have written the book, was identical with Malachi. This idea appears in Megillah 15a, in the same passage where Daniel is identified as one of the Restoration prophets:

40

R. Nahman said, Malachi is the same as Mordecai. Why was he called Malachi? Because he was next to the king. The following was cited in objection to this: 'Baruch the son of Neraiah and Serayah the son of Mahseyah and Daniel and Mordecai, Bilshan, Haggai, Zechariah and Malachi all prophesied in the second year of Darius!' – This is a refutation. It has been taught: R. Joshua b. Korha said: Malachi is the same as Ezra.[11]

The fact that Esther was certainly counted among the Writings by the time that this tradition arose does not seem to have militated against the idea that, since it was an inspired book, it must have had a prophet as its author.

Thus it does not seem that the distinction between Prophets and Writings necessarily implies that books reckoned among the Writings are not 'prophetic'. Just as Josephus can distinguish historiography from hymnody and didactic material, and yet hold that all authentic Scriptures have prophets as their authors, so we find that the authors of a number of the Writings are characterized in Jewish sources as 'prophets'. Unless we hold, with Ginzberg, that a clear distinction was drawn between books and their authors, this should make us uneasy about the suggestion that an entirely clear line separated Prophets from Writings by around the turn of the era.

(6) Closely allied to the previous point is the observation made in passing in chapter 1, that rabbinic terminology includes a category *qabbalah*, which means the Prophets and the Writings considered together.[12] This undoubtedly tells us, as we have already seen, that Scripture outside the Pentateuch was understood to have a secondary status in relation to the books of Moses; but it also suggests that for practical purposes there was little differentiation within the corpus of secondary books. When it is said that the *qabbalah* was revealed to Moses and handed down to subsequent *prophets* by a secret tradition, this is a theory not simply about the Prophets of the Hebrew canon but about the Writings too: it occurs, for example, in a discussion about the origins of the book of Esther.[13] It is easy to find contexts in which the distinction between Torah and Qabbalah is significant, but hard to find any in which the distinction between Prophets and Writings matters at all. Though it is assumed throughout the Talmud that Scripture is threefold, no practical consequences of any kind seem to follow from this.[14] Thus

41

the New Testament's 'law and prophets' and the rabbis' 'Torah and Qabbalah' seem roughly equivalent.

What then are we to make of the theory that Law, Prophets and Writings constitute three concentric circles of diminishing authority? As we have seen, this has been a customary way of describing the Hebrew Bible since medieval times; yet there seems to be no way of illustrating the principle in practice. The suspicion must arise that the theory is simply a theory: that instead of being a description, based on empirical examples, of how Scripture functions for the Jewish people, it is an attempt to make sense of an arrangement of the Bible which was traditional, but whose original purpose was no longer understood. In this it may be likened to many 'explanations' in Christian tradition in which an edifying meaning is extracted from a traditional practice whose origin is either unknown or no longer relevant to a community which none the less continues to observe the practice.[15] The medieval commentators, it may be suggested, were not describing how Scripture functioned, but constructing a theory to account for a feature of Scripture puzzling precisely because it had no known function. Leiman sees this point very clearly, and it is curious that his exposition of it does not seem to have had any effect on his general theory about the canon:

Scripture (Nu. 12:6–8 and Deut. 34:10) and the rabbis (Yebamoth 49b and Vayyikra Rabbah 1:14) assert that the manner of reception of Moses differed from that of all other prophets; a similar distinction between Prophets and Hagiographa does not appear in talmudic and midrashic literature. It was precisely because such a distinction was lacking that the medieval Jewish commentators had to wrestle with the problem as to why books such as Daniel and Psalms were classified among the Hagiographa.[16]

For decisions on matters of halakah, verses from the Prophets and the Writings appear to be of equal force: that is to say, one does not find arguments where a verse from the Prophets clinches an argument against a conflicting verse from the Writings, on the grounds that the latter is from a less authoritative division of Scripture.[17] In Sanhedrin 97b–98a, for example, a verse from Daniel is decisive in swinging an argument, and it is not suggested that it should yield to texts from the Prophets.[18]

For the New Testament writers as for Philo, the Psalms are

42

particularly important, and in practice are much more often used to clinch an argument than, say, Judges or Ezekiel. Philo, for instance, has some thirty citations from outside the Pentateuch; of these, twelve are from Psalms, and four from Proverbs. He does not give any indication whatever that the Writings are of less standing than the Prophets, and if we had to reconstruct his 'canon' on the basis of these citations, Psalms would follow the Pentateuch, and neither Joshua nor Ezekiel would appear at all. An examination of the Mishnah would yield a very similar conclusion: non-Pentateuchal citations there tend also to be from Psalms and Proverbs, hardly at all from the other books.[19]

The only important exception to the point being made here comes from the liturgical sphere. It is certainly now the case that no *haftaroth* are taken from the Writings, and though the five *megilloth* (Esther, Song of Songs, Lamentations, Ruth, and Ecclesiastes) now occupy a position of importance in the liturgy of the synagogue, there is no evidence for the liturgical use of any but Esther at an early enough date to be relevant for our purposes. The absence of liturgical readings from the Writings constitutes, in fact, the main ground on which Leiman continues to defend the antiquity of the tripartite canon in spite of his own argument that the distinction between Prophets and Writings was not significant for halakah. Here, however, it must suffice to say that there is no way of showing that in New Testament times *haftaroth* could never be taken from the Writings, or indeed that there was any established system of two lessons, one from the Torah and one from 'the Prophets', at all; but I shall return to this theme in more detail in trying to offer my own suggestion for the origin of the present tripartite canon.[20]

(7) Finally, even when we have modified the theory of a tripartite canon so as to allow for the equal status, from the point of view of halakah, of the second and third divisions, we are still to some extent misrepresenting the way the *qabbalah* functions in practice. While it is right to stress, for example, that for both Philo and the Mishnah the Psalms matter more than the Prophets, one's overwhelming impression is that neither is more than marginally significant in any case. The main nerve of the halakah runs through the Pentateuch and the traditions of the scribes, virtually bypassing the rest of Scripture. If by 'canon' one means that body of material which is actually functional for the religious system of Judaism, then the Prophets and the Writings should be excluded altogether:

43

the canon in that sense consists of the Pentateuch, the Mishnah, and the Talmud.[21] This point is stated with great clarity by L. B. Wolfenson, in a very important article to which I shall return:

> The term *Jewish Canon*, properly understood, means those writings which were adopted as legally and morally binding. Such writings are the Pentateuch, or 'Law', the Mishna and Gemara; and since the Pentateuch is properly the Hebrew Canon, the Jewish Canon is really the Mishna and Gemara.[22]

But this leads us into deeper waters, and it is time to try to present a positive alternative to the consensus view which these seven points tend to undermine.

II

The alternative view of the canon for which I shall argue in the rest of this chapter was in its essentials outlined by N. Schmidt in his article 'Bible Canon – Untraditional View' in the *Jewish Encyclopedia* of 1902, in which he dissented from the 'traditional' view of the main article by L. Blau. L. B. Wolfenson's article, just quoted, took much the same line in 1924, and much more recently J. N. Lightstone has raised many objections to the consensus which put him in the same camp.[23] Nevertheless it is only in James Barr's recent book *Holy Scripture* that one finds similar ideas in the mainstream of biblical scholarship, whilst the alliance of B. S. Childs's 'canonical method' with the very thorough research of Leiman's standard work seems likely to ensure that the consensus picture will continue to prevail.

An 'untraditional' view of the history of the canon in the age of the New Testament might be characterized by three essential theses:

(1) The classification of scriptural books was bipartite, not tripartite, and a 'Prophet' was any book with scriptural status outside the Pentateuch.

(2) The word 'canon' itself is a most inappropriate term to describe the Scriptures of Jews and Christians in the first few centuries of our era.

(3) The books of Scripture were not arranged in any particular order from which theological implications can be derived.

It should be fairly obvious that if these three points can be

44

sustained they involve considerable changes in our understanding of what 'prophecy' meant in our period, and that the conclusions to which the consensus view leads must be largely abandoned.

The first point, that Scripture in New Testament times was bipartite rather than tripartite, has already begun to emerge from the 'straws in the wind' set out in the first section of this chapter. The consensus that the canon of the Prophets must have been fixed by the time when Jewish and Christian writers speak of 'the law and the prophets' rests on the (usually unstated) assumption that 'prophets' refers to the same collection of books as it does now. Once this is accepted, it does of course follow that the present section of Scripture called 'the Prophets' was already fixed by then, and that the books which constitute the Writings were not yet canonical – since they had no name of their own – but were only in the process of becoming so. But in reality there are two quite separate questions: first, which books were regarded as authoritative? and second, what term or terms were used to refer to them? In principle it could be the case that every one of the books in the present Hebrew canon was already 'canonical' in New Testament times, but that all of them were included under the title 'Prophets'. The consensus view of the matter arises by allowing the answer to one of these questions to determine the answer to the other.

As Schmidt pointed out, writers in our period do not give us a list of the books they reckon as 'Prophets', and it is mere supposition that they meant the books now in the second division of the Hebrew Bible. We have already seen that Josephus's 'thirteen books' written by prophets cannot by any stretch of the imagination be made to coincide with the present Prophets. But what grounds do we have for supposing that he is *changing* some already conventional list for his own purposes, and not merely reporting a widely agreed convention (as on the 'Alexandrian canon' hypothesis) or even producing his own classification scheme where there was simply no conventional list at all? As I have written elsewhere, 'the issue has been . . . clouded by the assumption that he must have been working with *some* kind of canonical list arranged in a certain way, which he must be either following or deliberately varying'.[24] But we do not know that: and most of the available evidence suggests rather that 'the prophets' in his days meant 'scriptural' or 'inspired' books in general. Wolfenson sums the matter up well: 'The classification into Prophets and Hagiographa is late and artificial. We know that

45

Josephus counted 13 Prophets as late as about 100, . . . which proves conclusively that the Jews had no fixed classification as late as that time'.[25]

In the New Testament Luke 24:44 is the sole exception to what appears to be a bipartite scheme: the Law and the Prophets.[26] It seems overwhelmingly likely that this scheme is meant to cover all the Scripture there is, not to refer to only two sections of a canon already perceived as tripartite. No one, I suppose, really believes that when 'all the law and the prophets' are said to hang upon the twin commandments to love God and one's neighbour (Matthew 22:40), this means that the first two divisions of Scripture depend on them, but that the third, which was then just in the process of formation, may or may not. This saying is universally taken to mean that *the whole of Scripture* depends on these two commandments.[27] On the consensus view this is of course accepted, but it is usually implied that because the rest of Scripture at that time lacked a short name, 'law and prophets' had to be understood to refer to the Writings as well by extension. A rare exception to this appears in the new Schürer, where we read: 'In the New Testament, the two-part formula still prevails ['still', that is, as a leftover from a time when the Prophets were 'closed' but the Writings had not yet begun to take shape as a third section] . . . It should not of course be concluded from this that the third collection did not yet exist: in fact, there are good reasons to think that it was closed in the middle of the second century BC. But it was not felt to be a group possessing independent significance and of the same status as the other two'.[28] This does appear to imply that the formula explicitly excludes the Writings, but it seems to me hardly plausible. Most of the New Testament references to 'the law and the prophets' seem to include by implication everything that could be called Scripture, and there is really no question of the (still unnamed) Writings having a lower status than the Prophets. (We may recall once again that the Psalms appear in the Writings, and they could hardly be said to have a lower status in the eyes of the New Testament than Judges or 2 Kings.) The choice lies, surely, between saying that 'law and prophets' is allowed to apply by extension to the Writings as well, or thinking that this was simply the normal way of referring to Scripture as a whole; and the latter is much the simpler hypothesis. But this would imply that 'prophets' for the New Testament writers, just as for Josephus, included books which now appear among the

46

Writings, so that to speak of the closing of the canon of the Prophets in its present form before this period must be erroneous.

Once the possibility is admitted that 'the Prophets' in writings of our period may not refer to precisely the books that now bear that name, most of the other evidence that the Prophets had been 'closed' disappears in the same way. For example, Sundberg appeals to the passage in 2 Maccabees 15:9, where Judas encourages his troops with quotations from 'the law and the prophets'. This shows, he says, that the first two divisions had already been fixed by the time when 2 Maccabees was written: therefore there cannot have been an 'Alexandrian canon', organized along the lines of the present LXX; for if there had been, the Prophets would not have been distinguished from the Writings and consequently the phrase 'the law and the prophets' could not have been used. But in this argument everything depends on the assumption that 'the prophets' in this verse refers to precisely the books now included in the second division of the canon. How do we know that? It is, on the contrary, surely very unlikely that Judas did not regard the Psalms as authoritative Scripture: indeed, in 2 Maccabees 8:23 'he appointed Eleazar to read aloud from the holy book, and gave the watchword "God's help" ', which some have taken to mean that Eleazar read Psalm 46 and that Judas then picked out the phrase with which it begins as a motto to encourage the troops.[29]

Similarly, the Prologue to Ecclesiasticus does not provide unequivocal evidence for the tripartite character of Scripture. It *could* mean that Law and Prophets, in their present form, were already fixed, and the vague expressions 'the others that followed them', 'the other books of our fathers', and 'the rest of the books' might then imply that the third division had as yet no name and was not yet 'closed', as on the consensus view. But the passage makes better sense, and coheres better with the evidence of the main body of the text itself, if we assume that 'the law and the prophets' refers to Scripture, the holy books of Ben Sira's people, and 'the rest of the books' means simply 'all other books'. The author of the Prologue is arguing, after all, that books lose in translation: not just the Scriptures, but other books too – hence the reader should not expect the present work to be an exception; just as he is painting a picture of his grandfather as not simply learned in Scripture, in the sacred writings ('the law and the prophets'), but learned *tout court*, well versed not just in the holy books but in literature in general.

There is little to suggest that Ben Sira himself knew a canon in which the Prophetic division ended where it does now. His list of the heroes of Israel includes Nehemiah, and almost certainly also Job,[30] and he does not seem to make any distinction between Prophets and Writings as source material – nor, for that matter, between Prophets and Torah. Much the simplest hypothesis is that while both Ben Sira and his grandson recognized as Scripture more or less all the books that subsequently came to be included in both Prophets and Writings, they did not themselves assign them to different 'divisions', but called them all simply 'prophets'. The Prologue then gives us no information whatever as to which particular books were 'Prophets' for Judaism in this period: this can only be deduced from a consideration of which books seem to be cited or used in the body of the text.[31]

To revert to Josephus: we have already seen that his 'prophetic' division must include some of the Writings, and therefore is a poor ally for the consensus view. But we can go further, and ask whether Josephus really attests a tripartite canon at all. As I pointed out in the first section of this chapter, in summing up at the end of the famous passage in *Against Apion* he adopts a bipartite division: 'the law and the allied documents'. Although this is broken down in the central section of the text into three parts, not only do these parts not correspond exactly to any other known division of the canon, it is not even clear that the principles of the division have anything to do with authority, canonicity, or traditional listings. The division is, rather, a thematic one: laws, histories, hymns and precepts. The impression one gets is not that Josephus is attempting to describe how the Jewish canon is officially or usually divided by the Jews themselves, but that he is analysing the sacred books of the Jews in a way that will make them comprehensible (and convincing) to Gentile readers.

For Josephus, the authority of Scripture is defined in terms of its source, in the work of Moses and his duly authorized successors, the prophets; its contents, in terms of the genres it contains, with historiography highlighted as much as possible because of the need to stress accuracy and reliability. (The polemical context may also explain the strange silence about the predictive side of prophecy, which in any case is a problem for *any* use of Josephus in reconstructing the history of the canon – no one, after all, supposes that his Bible did not include the Latter Prophets.) It is, in fact, perfectly possible to read Josephus as saying that all books other than the Pentateuch are by prophets: thirteen of these are histories, four are poetic and didactic.[32] At all events the primary idea to which Josephus is a witness is not that the books of Scripture were organized in a tripartite form, but that they derived from either of *two* sources: Moses and the prophets. And in the end these two sources are really one, since the prophets are Moses' successors, and Moses himself was a prophet, the greatest of them all. In this Josephus accords completely with Philo, who has various ways of subdividing the books of Scripture[33] but is clear that they come from only two sources: Moses, or the 'disciples of Moses'. This second expression is used to designate the Psalmist,[34] Zechariah[35] and Solomon.[36] Such evidence as we have from Hellenistic Judaism thus confirms the essentially bipartite character of Scripture to which the New Testament and the sayings of the Tannaim bear witness.

Even the evidence of Baba Bathra 14b–15a is more ambivalent than it might seem. Despite the fact that in its present form it derives from a period in which the distinction between Prophets and Writings was well established, its suggestions about 'authorship' or 'transcription' (*ktb* has no clearly definable meaning) do not respect the boundary-lines between these two divisions. Thus we read:

> Who wrote the Scriptures? – Moses wrote his own book and the portion of Balaam and Job. Joshua wrote the book which bears his name and eight verses of the Pentateuch. Samuel wrote the book which bears his name and the book of Judges and Ruth. David wrote the book of Psalms including in it the work of the ten elders, namely, Adam, Melchizedek, Abraham, Moses, Heman, Jeduthun, Asaph, and the three sons of Korah. Jeremiah wrote the book which bears his name, the book of Kings, and Lamentations. Hezekiah and his colleagues wrote Isaiah, Proverbs, the Song of Songs and Ecclesiastes. The Men of the Great Assembly wrote Ezekiel, the Twelve Minor Prophets, Daniel and the scroll of Esther. Ezra wrote the book that bears his name and the genealogies of the book of Chronicles up to his own time . . . Who then finished it [sc. Chronicles]? Nehemiah the son of Hachaliah.[37]

It is easy to imagine the theories about the shape of the canon that would be put forward if we possessed this portion of the text without the preceding discussion, in which the books comprising the three divisions are in fact the familiar ones! Not even the equation Moses = Torah is respected here, for Job is assigned to him (probably on the traditional theory that Job was the same person as Jobab, a pre-Mosaic king of Edom according to Genesis 36:33–4 – cf. Testament of Job 1), together with those Psalms which are identified as his in the titles of the Psalter. Ezekiel, Daniel, the Twelve, and Esther make an interesting list, and none of them was 'written' by a prophet. From these fanciful suggestions nothing of importance follows, of course, but it is interesting to note how little influence the three divisions had even on a passage which takes them as a given.

The evidence of Christian writers may be thought too weak to be considered, so far as the history of the Hebrew Bible is concerned, since clearly very few of the Fathers had any first-hand acquaintance with Judaism. Even those who warn that some books in the Christian Old Testament are not considered canonical among the Jews not only continue in practice to use them, but also retain a way of ordering the Hebrew books which is essentially that of the LXX – just as do Protestant Christians to this day. Thus Cyril of Jerusalem advises his catechumens against reading the apocryphal books, but in listing the genuine Hebrew Scriptures he includes Baruch and the Epistle of Jeremiah; and he divides the canon into histories, verse books, and prophets like any good reader of the LXX, taking care to include Daniel as the last of the prophets.[38]

Similarly Epiphanius, who is aware of the *contents* of the Hebrew Scriptures, *divides* them in ways that bear little resemblance to the tripartite Hebrew canon. *Weights and Measures* 4 speaks of four 'Pentateuchs': five books of the law, five of poems (Job, Psalms, Proverbs, Ecclesiastes, Song of Songs), five 'hagiographa'(!) (Joshua, Judges + Ruth, Chronicles, Samuel, and Kings), five prophetic books (The Twelve, Isaiah, Jeremiah, Ezekiel, Daniel); and two 'extra' books (Ezra–Nehemiah and Esther). In §23 of the same work, however, we find an undifferentiated list in a different but almost equally eccentric order: Job appears between Joshua and Judges, and Chronicles precedes Kings.[39] Apart from a practically universal belief that Daniel belongs with the Prophets, little can be made of most patristic lists in the absence of evidence that they were obtained from Jewish authorities. Athanasius's Festal Letter of 367 is important as apparently containing precisely those books that are in the Hebrew canon with no additions, but it does not

50

provide us with any evidence of the *distribution* of books among the three divisions of Law, Prophets, and Writings.

The only really clear patristic attestation of the tripartite Hebrew canon is in Jerome, who had of course consulted Jewish opinion. In his *Preface to the Books of Samuel and Kings*[40] we find a clear recognition that the Writings are not, as many of the Fathers supposed, identical with the 'poetic' or 'didactic' books of the Greek Bible, but include such works as Chronicles and Ruth. Here Daniel is reckoned as one of the Writings,[41] and the Minor Prophets are placed last, following the Hebrew arrangement accurately. Yet in the *Epistle to Paulinus* of 395, when he comes to survey the contents of the Hebrew books, he reckons Daniel a prophet ('quartus . . . et extremus inter quatuor prophetas'), listing the four 'major' prophets in the LXX order (Isaiah, Jeremiah, Ezekiel, Daniel), places Ruth after Judges, and inserts Job between the Pentateuch and Joshua. Thus Jerome does not seem to regard the Hebrew classification into Law, Prophets and Writings as important for understanding the books, though he is certainly a witness to its existence by the fourth century.

Augustine, who was at least interested in the Hebrew Bible though not well-informed about it, seems to have known that the Hebrew tradition knew of two sorts of 'prophetic' books, though he wrongly identifies the 'Former' Prophets. After the 'histories', in which he includes Chronicles, and a group of 'aliae [sc. scripturae] ex diverso ordine', consisting of Job, Tobit, Esther, Judith, and Maccabees, Augustine thinks a Bible should next contain

> the prophets, in which there is one book of David, the psalms, and three of Solomon, Proverbs, the Song of Songs, and Ecclesiastes.

Then come Wisdom of Solomon and Ecclesiasticus, which are not to be called Solomonic since they were both (*sic*) written by Jesus Sirach, but

> since they have proved worthy to be accepted as authoritative, they are to be counted among the prophetic books.

Then come the books of those

> who are properly called prophets, the individual books of the twelve prophets, which being joined together and never divided

are reckoned as one book . . . then there are the four prophets with longer volumes, Isaiah, Jeremiah, Daniel, and Ezekiel.[42]

Thus Augustine seems to be aware of the existence of two kinds of prophetic books, though he garbles the distinction; but he is in no doubt about the prophetic status of Daniel, one of the prophets properly so called ('qui proprie prophetae appellantur').

The patristic evidence is, in fact, of little help in deciding on the state of the Hebrew canon even in the fourth century, but even where it does seem to represent some degree of contact between Christians and Jews it does not unequivocally support the present division, with Daniel firmly among the Writings; and it reflects a vagueness which may, of course, result from pure ignorance, about the character of this third division. When they are not discussing lists, it is common enough to find the Fathers continuing the New Testament usage, and calling the Old Testament 'the law and the prophets'.[43]

Much of the material which can be used to strengthen the case being argued here is collected, strangely enough, by Leiman, in an extended footnote which seems to me to undermine the thrust of his argument in the main text.[44] He writes: 'There is ample extra-rabbinic evidence that the term Prophets in the first centuries BC and CE referred to all non-Pentateuchal biblical books . . . See especially 4 Maccabees 18:10ff. where verses from Proverbs and Psalms are said to belong to the "Prophets".' And as we have already seen, he accepts that no distinction in authority is found between the Prophets and the Writings until after the closing of the Talmud.[45] He even produces a theory, which we shall examine later,[46] to explain how an originally unitary 'Prophets' came to be divided into Prophets and Writings. This makes it extremely strange that, in the body of the text, he continues to maintain that the present canon of the Prophets, excluding the Writings, was closed in early post-exilic times, and I have no explanation for this apparent contradiction.

Furthermore, according to Leiman (this time in the text itself, pp. 60–4) there are traditions preserved in two different forms in various parts of the literature of the rabbis, where one saying refers to *the Prophets* and the other to *the Prophets and the Writings*. In such cases, he argues, it may be reasonable to think that the form with simply *the Prophets* is the older of the pair. Clear examples may be found by comparing j. Megillah 73d–74a (=3:1) with Tosefta Megillah 4:20, where there are discussions of such matters as whether one kind of scriptural book may be bound in the wrappings of another, and whether the proceeds from the sale of one kind may be used to buy another kind. Thus:

> j. Megillah 73d: A Torah may be wrapped in Torah wrappings, *homashin* in *homashin* wrappings, Prophets in Prophets wrappings. Torah and *homashin* may be wrapped in Prophets and Hagiographa wrappings, but Prophets and Hagiographa may not be wrapped in Torah and *homashin* wrappings.
>
> Tosefta Megillah 4:20: A Torah may be wrapped in Torah wrappings, and *homashin* in *homashin* wrappings. Torah and *homashin* may be wrapped in Prophets wrappings, but Prophets may not be wrapped in Torah and *homashin* wrappings.

In each case, the Jerusalem Talmud speaks of all three divisions, Law, Prophets and Writings, whereas the Tosefta mentions only Law and Prophets (as does the mishnah in M. Megillah 3:1 to which these passages refer). Leiman is uneasy about drawing the conclusion he points towards, noting that in another example, Baba Bathra 13b (cf. j. Megillah 73d–74a), the parallel which lacks the explicit reference to the Writings is in Soferim 3:1, which is hardly likely to be earlier. He also holds that the shorter versions may be abbreviated from the longer, or that there may be other reasons for the difference which are now not recoverable. Naturally, in the absence of any sure way of dating talmudic passages, one can only agree that these examples do not *prove* the tripartite division to be late. Nevertheless the difference is suggestive, especially in view of the fact that the original mishnah thinks in terms of only two divisions; the way Leiman discounts this evidence which he himself has so scrupulously assembled looks a little lame to me. At all events he correctly concludes that 'the talmudic view . . . contrasts sharply with the medieval view that the three sections of the biblical canon represent three different degrees of inspired writing' and that 'the halakhic codes reflect the earlier, talmudic view'.[47] He should, I believe, have gone on to draw a more far-reaching conclusion from this accurate observation: that the distinction between Prophets and Writings is itself a late arrival, and that much material even in the Talmud reflects the same inability to find a function for the distinction that eventually led to the artificial 'concentric circles' theory of medieval commentators.

From the discussion in this section three important conclusions follow so far as 'prophecy' in our period is concerned. First, the tendency to think of the whole of Scripture as 'prophecy', which can easily be presented as a peculiarity of early Christianity, or at least of the eschatological sects among which the Christian move-ment was the most successful, turns out to be widely diffused among people of many different persuasions. In stressing that the Greek Old Testament is essentially a Christian creation, Sundberg over-states his case when he writes that in Christianity the Jewish distinc-tions between the different types of book were lost, and 'everything became "prophets" '.[48] On the contrary, when Christian writers speak of all the Old Testament authors as 'prophets' they are not thereby differentiating themselves from common Jewish practice. No one could be further from eschatological enthusiasm than Philo, who tells us that we do well to think of God as a shepherd *because we have the authority of a prophet*, whom we can trust, that 'The Lord shepherds me and nothing shall be lacking to me';[49] or who else-where describes David the Psalmist as 'a member of Moses' fellow-ship' who was 'moved . . . to an ecstasy by the love that is heavenly and divine'.[50] Blau no doubt exaggerated this tendency when he wrote 'Jewish tradition adopts the view that every word of Holy Writ was inspired by the Divine Spirit. This Spirit is believed, in every case, to have rested upon a prophet; and, consequently, every Biblical book was said to have been written by a prophet'.[51] But the exaggeration was not implausible.

But, secondly, this usage of course means that 'prophecy' is not being understood primarily as *eschatological prediction* in any case. Josephus is particularly instructive here, for he is not only extremely interested in predictions but also has a theory according to which authorship by a 'prophet' is of the essence of a scriptural book; and yet he does not connect the two ideas. Scripture is not 'prophetic' because it is about the future, but because its authors are the duly authorized successors of Moses – and it is expertise in the past, rather than in the future, which this guarantees. Prophets are essen-tially people who have a special, privileged relationship with God. In the next chapter we shall look more closely at the essential features of this relationship as it was conceived in our period.

Thirdly, from this reconstruction of a stage at which Scripture was essentially bipartite it must follow that nothing can be deduced about the way a book was read in earlier times from the fact that it *now* stands in the Prophets rather than the Writings (or vice versa). Thus it would be misleading to say that Daniel (to take the most crucial example) was *transferred* from the Writings to the Prophets when the Christian (Greek) Old Testament was being constituted, just as (conversely) it would be to say that the Hebrew tradition did not think of Daniel as a prophet on the grounds that it *assigned* his book to the Writings. The Church did not insist on the prophetic character of Daniel against the synagogue; Judaism did not try to deflect attention from that character by relegating it to the Writings. For one thing, these 'decisions' lie far in the future, and imply distinctions which were not drawn at all in New Testament times; for another, even when such decisions were taken they do not appear to have had any hermeneutical intention behind them. No one said 'This is a book of such-and-such a kind, and *therefore* it belongs in this division of the canon rather than that.' As we shall see, a good deal was implied in describing a book as the work of a 'prophet'; but the implications were not connected with the distinctive messages that 'prophetic' texts would later come to be thought to contain, in the divergent traditions of Jews and Christians. 'Prophet' is the most generalized term for any book written by a successor of Moses, who was himself a prophet – much as in the Western Christian liturgy any non-gospel reading from the New Testament came to be called *epistola* (even if it came from Acts or Revelation), and for that matter any Old Testament reading *prophetia*.[52]

III

In this section I shall pursue my second thesis, that 'canon' is an inappropriate term to describe the status of Scripture in the New Testament period. The argument will be somewhat complex, and it has two aspects: (1) the absence of any sense that Scripture formed a *closed* list, and (2) the equivocal status of many esoteric books. An excursus will deal with a residual problem.

(1) Discussion of the canon is frequently bedevilled by a failure to define what is meant by 'canonical'. We saw in the previous

Oracles of God

chapter that some of the disagreements among scholars prove on examination to be disputes about terms rather than about historical reality. This seems especially true of the differences between Leiman and Sundberg, who on the face of it seem to stand at opposite ends of the spectrum of opinion but who (in theory at least) are talking about different phenomena: Sundberg is interested in the point at which it was impossible for fresh works to gain admission to each division of the canon, Leiman in the moment when the authority of particular books ceased to be questioned. In fact, as we have seen, Leiman freely uses phrases such as 'the closing of the Prophets', which indicate that he does not himself sufficiently draw this distinction, and that is why my own argument has taken issue with him at some points. But if we take his own definition of 'canonicity' quite strictly, then little can be said against his position. The evidence clearly suggests that more or less every book that is now in the Hebrew canon was 'authoritative for religious practice and/or doctrine' in New Testament times. I am not sure that he has succeeded in demonstrating that there were absolutely no doubts about the marginal cases, Ecclesiastes and the Song of Songs, but for our purposes this matters very little. If by 'the closing of the Prophets' is meant merely the end of any doubts about the scriptural status of the present eight books of the Prophets (Joshua, Judges, Samuel, Kings, Isaiah, Jeremiah, Ezekiel, the Twelve), then nothing I have been saying offers any reason to reject the expression.

But in reality no one is likely to take such an expression in this minimalizing way. For most readers, to say that the Prophets were 'closed' by the New Testament period (or even by 400 BC, as Leiman does) immediately conveys an impression that no further books could be admitted into the corpus. The fact that Leiman can produce the usual argument about Daniel (it would have been included among the Prophets if the Prophets had still been open, therefore they must have been closed before the middle of the second century BC) shows that he fully shares this impression himself. To return to a way of formulating the crucial distinction which I have already used: to speak of 'scripture' is to say that there is a group of books such that *at least* those books have an authoritative status (however this is defined); but to speak of a 'canon' is to say that *at most* this particular group of books has authoritative status – or, to put it another way, that *only these books* have that status. Leiman uses 'canonical' where I should use 'scriptural', and thereby confuses not

56

only his readers but, I believe, himself as well. If we are to retain both terms, it seems sensible to keep 'canonical' for the second, narrower sense, and this accords with the usage of most scholars. Thus Sundberg suggests that we should understand 'by "scripture" religious writing that is in some sense authoritative, and by "canon" a closed collection of scripture'.[53] The same implication is present in Blau's comment: 'The idea of canonicity can only have been suggested at a period when the national literature had progressed far enough to possess a large number of works from which a selection might be made'.[54]

My thesis here is that there was no canon in this sense at all, for either Jews or Christians, until well into the Christian era. We may if we like speak of the Pentateuch as 'canonical'. People did not feel free to add to the Pentateuch, or to suggest that other books were equal to it in authority (though even this cannot be regarded as beyond dispute, as we shall see). But where other books are concerned, there was Scripture, but no canon. The argument of the previous section was that Scripture outside the Pentateuch formed not two collections with a clear line between them, but one single amorphous pool of material, often called 'Prophets'. Now I want to suggest that, though there was no doubt that some books were definitely *in* this pool, there was as yet no sense that others were definitely *out*.

Much of the evidence which is held to point to some stage or other in a process called 'canonization' seems to me to do nothing of the sort. This is particularly true of a good many passages cited by Leiman. For example, 2 Maccabees 2:13 says that Nehemiah 'collected the books about the kings and prophets, and the writings of David, and letters of kings about votive offerings'. Then in v. 14 we find that 'in the same way Judas also collected all the books that had been lost on account of the war which had come upon us'. Leiman comments (p. 28) on the first of these verses: 'What may very well be described here is a collection and canonization of biblical books'; and on the second (p. 29): 'The literary activity ascribed here to Judah Maccabee may, in fact, be a description of the closing of the Hagiographa, and with it, the entire biblical canon.' Surely this is a quite unnatural way of reading the passage, which is actually about a salvage operation on archival material of all kinds, including Scripture. It has nothing at all to do with a decision about the limits of the canon. As is often the case, Leiman's

57

footnote on the first suggestion is more cautious than the main text (p. 149, note 132): 'Uncertainties, however, abound and, when viewed independently, nothing conclusive can be derived from this passage . . . the activity ascribed to Nehemiah may reflect the formation of a private library rather than an act of canonization.' This is surely far more sensible. Anderson, too, can cite the passage as an attestation of a canon in which at least the Psalms were already canonical, if not the rest of the Writings.[55] 'Known', even 'venerated', perhaps: but not, I believe, 'canonical'.

Again, Philo's references to the holy books of the Therapeutae is sometimes cited as demonstrating not just the existence of Scripture but the acceptance of the tripartite *canon* with which we are now familiar. In *de vita contemplativa* 3:25, he says that the Therapeutae 'take nothing into their sanctuaries but laws and oracles delivered through the mouth of prophets, and psalms, and the other books'. 'The correspondence to the tripartite division of the canon is obvious', Leiman comments (p. 31).[56] But surely this, like Josephus's description of the Jewish Scriptures in *Against Apion*, is a list of the *kinds* of material the scriptures venerated by the Therapeutae contained, not a definition of the shape or structure of their 'canon'. If it were really justifiable to press the details of the list to this extent, we might more properly say that Philo was a witness to a *quadripartite* canon, consisting of (a) laws, (b) oracles, (c) psalms, and (d) other books; but this only serves to show how inappropriate such a reading is.

The unnaturalness of reading our sources in this way convinces me more than any other argument that in asking about the state of the *canon* in our period we are asking a question which the available literature cannot be made to answer, for the very good reason that no one had yet begun to think in such terms. More appropriate categories need to be found if we are to understand the status that certain books had in New Testament times. Perhaps we can make some progress towards this goal by concentrating on the questions that *are* asked in the literature, rather than on those that are not.

R. Meyer has argued that we can see in Josephus the beginnings of a desire to 'close' the canon,[57] against the prevailing tendency of his day (which Meyer sees very much as I have been presenting it) to set no bounds to the religious literature that could be regarded as 'holy' or 'inspired'. At Qumran, for example, there is evidence that the community prized Ecclesiasticus as highly as Proverbs, and

Tobit as highly as Ruth or Daniel.[58] Josephus, on the other hand, does wish to set some limits. He says that only twenty-two books are accepted by the Jews; and he specifies conditions as to the date of composition of sacred books. Meyer's point that other authorities are less concerned than Josephus to fix limits to the 'canon' is undoubtedly correct, and supports the present argument, but I am not sure that even Josephus should be read with later ideas of a strictly delimited canon in mind. He may indeed have wanted to exclude from Scripture some books that other Jews accepted – the passage in *Against Apion* could be read in that way; but it should be remembered that he is not writing for a Jewish readership, but rather to commend Judaism to people familiar with Greek literature. His argument that the Jews have only twenty-two sacred books is part of a polemic against what he chooses to see as the multitude of mutually inconsistent books believed in by Greeks. In maintaining the small compass of Jewish Scripture he does not, as a matter of fact, say that *no other book could conceivably be found* that would meet the criterion of prophetic authorship, only that no more than twenty-two have until now been found to do so. Even if we feel it is more natural to follow Meyer's reading of Josephus, however, we should certainly note as he does that in setting limits to the canon at all Josephus is out of step with his contemporaries.

But in any case I am less sure than Meyer that Josephus was unusual in maintaining that Scripture belongs to a special *period*. Even if he was original in thinking of a prophetic canon, I doubt if he was innovating in thinking in terms of a prophetic *age*. The idea recurs in the *Jewish War*, where Josephus proposes to begin his tale 'at the point where the historians of these events [sc. the course of Jewish history up to and including the Exile] and our prophets conclude'.[59] This seems to distinguish between 'historians' and 'prophets' as *Against Apion* does not, and to imply that just as the Histories in Scripture do not reach beyond the Persian period, nor do the Prophecies. This seems to me an assumption, rather than an empirical observation, about the books of the Latter Prophets, and it probably rests on a theory of the same kind as that in *Against Apion*. Once again, a good deal depends on the antiquity of the tradition that prophecy (in some sense or other) ceased with Malachi, which is discussed elsewhere.[60] But the idea of a prophetic age, whose exact cut-off point need not be precisely defined, but which is seen as closed, seems to be more widely diffused than the writings of Josephus. For Josephus's criterion does in fact tally quite well with what we know was widely believed about the supposed authors of all the books that ultimately found their way into *any* canon of Scripture. The criterion that a book shall have been written by an author living in the period before the death of Artaxerxes is probably to be understood as meaning that it must not postdate the age of Ezra, because it was in that period that prophets existed: since then the 'exact succession' of the prophets has ceased. This gives us few positive indications of how Josephus envisaged a prophet, and it fails to specify what is a sufficient condition for recognizing one; but at least it gives us a negative criterion, or necessary condition. If a book was written after the death of Artaxerxes, then it cannot by definition be the work of a prophet, and equally therefore it cannot be given the credence due to Scripture (which is not to say it need be worthless; after all, Josephus's own works were in his view among the most edifying books ever written).

Presumed antiquity, then, is a minimum condition for a book to be 'prophetic', i.e. scriptural. Judaism, for Josephus, stands or falls by traditions that have descended from the remote past. Such an idea was second nature to most people living in the Graeco-Roman world: it was by no means a distinguishing mark of the Jews. As David Aune points out in his important book on prophecy in the New Testament world, 'The revival of oracles that began in the first century AD was just one expression of a widespread nostalgia for the past. Part of the archaizing tendency of the era was expressed in attempts to copy and revive ancient conventions and forms of expression'.[61] The idea that divine wisdom had been communicated at some time in the past, in a special age which was now finished and complete, finds in Josephus's definition of a prophet its Jewish expression.

For not one of the books that appears in any canon known to us has as its putative author anyone living later than Ezra. The sole exception is Ecclesiasticus, about which there were many debates among the learned and which was clearly regarded from early times as a special case precisely on these grounds.[62] All the books of the Old Testament that we know or suspect to be late are furnished with an author or hero (the distinction is never clearly in focus) of the requisite antiquity. Jonah lived in the eighth century, Ruth in the days of the judges; Daniel was a contemporary of Ezekiel, Tobit of Isaiah; Judith lived in the days of 'Nebuchadnezzar, king of the Assyrians', a ruler little known to historians but certainly not to be dated after the Exile; Ecclesiastes and the Song of Songs were by Solomon himself, who also wrote a rather Hellenized wisdom book (as a prophet he could easily foresee the turns of expression that would be needed in Alexandria in the first century BC) and gave it his own name; Jubilees was one of the less widely-known works of Moses; and the Enoch literature was written only a few generations after the creation of the world. Even the Sibyl is said (Sibylline Oracle 3, lines 823–9) to be the daughter of Noah. There are no recent upstarts among the authors of books that were taken seriously as prophecy in the years around the turn of the era. And so far as I know there is no case before about the third century AD of a Jewish work pseudonymously attributed to anyone later than Ezra.

It may appear an irrelevance to bring pseudepigraphical works into the discussion, for are not most such works outside the canon in any case? But my point is that one of the effects of such pseudonymity is to confer on these books the same kind of potential authority that the books to which the canon was eventually limited were felt to possess. The same considerations apply to the Ezra or the Enoch literature as to Daniel. It is said that 'the canon of the Prophets' must have been closed before Daniel was written, or the book would have been included in it.[63] But if the canon of the Prophets was closed, what point can there have been in attributing the book to Daniel, rather than calling it by the name of its real author?[64] If the attribution confers no authority, it is pointless.[65] In the same way it makes good sense to attribute a book to Ezra, if it is known that any book by Ezra is bound to bear a seal of divine approval; but if it is held that all the genuine Ezra books have been found, and are in a closed canon, then the false attribution becomes an obvious confession of spuriousness.

This does not necessarily undercut the common observation that ancient ideas of 'authorship' were different from modern ones, and that people may have been willing to countenance such false attributions without accusing the author of 'forgery'; indeed, it is because 'authorship' was so much more fluid a concept that it is hard to believe in a canon, with its implication that certain books *claiming* the authority of some ancient worthy should be disregarded as 'inauthentic'. Pseudonymous writers were not trying to get their

61

works 'added to the canon': the whole idea is an anachronism. Questions about whether pseudepigraphy was an attempt to gain 'canonical' status for a book, whether sects that used particular pseudepigrapha regarded them as 'canonical', and so on, are in reality non-questions, proceeding from a misunderstanding of the attitude to ancient writings that prevailed in our period. All are agreed that *one* purpose at least of pseudonymous attribution was to confer on a book the authority of a figure from the past, from a time when divine wisdom was available to the great inspired figures whose names were held in honour; and that kind of authority was all there was to get, in a period which knew nothing of officially approved lists of canonical works.

Thus it seems to me that a theory such as that of Josephus probably was at least implicitly held by many. For a book to have a claim on one's attention as 'Scripture' it needed to be ancient: modern works, such as Ecclesiasticus, or the works of Josephus or Philo, were simply a different kind of thing. 'Ancient' might be variously defined, and no doubt Josephus's apparently precise dating of the cut-off point goes further than most people either would or could have gone in explicitness. But, in general, ancient books would be books that bore the name of some famous person from the time covered by those 'prophetic' books that had surely long been regarded as 'Scripture', the histories from Joshua to Kings. What such people had taught – even if their works had only recently been discovered – would have the authority of God himself, since they had enjoyed his special favour. Thus it is not surprising to find the epistle of Jude quoting from 1 Enoch (Jude 14–15); or Josephus, despite his theoretical 'canon' of twenty-two books, using what we call 1 Esdras and the apocryphal additions to Esther (*Antiquities* 11:216–19), or apparently referring to the fourth Sibylline Oracle as 'the records of the ancient prophets' in a speech (*Jewish War* 6:109). It is in the same spirit that the Christian Fathers often quote texts from the deuterocanonical books even though they may in theory already think in terms of a 'canon',[66] and will happily cite pseudepigraphical material too: cf. the citation of a non-canonical prophecy (perhaps from an apocalypse of Eldad and Medad) in 1 Clement 23:3 and '2 Clement' 11:2–4 with the formula 'The prophetic word says'. Any writing by an ancient 'prophet' is venerable and to be respected, whether or not it appears in some official list of holy books.

What we find in both Jewish and Christian writers of the New Testament age is in fact a common attitude towards ancient writings which was widely held in the past, and which has probably come to seem strange only since the Enlightenment: the belief that 'the ancients' knew more than people today. W. G. Lambert has shown that very similar attitudes prevailed in much Babylonian literature in many periods. 'There is', he writes, 'a Babylonian conception of canonicity . . . which is stated plainly by Berossus: that the sum of revealed knowledge was given once for all by the antediluvian sages'.[67] But, as he goes on to show, this did not imply that all the records of such revelation were already known. If a work was found which derived from these sages, it too would be accorded 'canonical' status. There are plenty of parallels to such a way of thinking about old literature in medieval Europe.[68] None of this is helpfully summed up in the term 'canon', with its implication of some authoritative body endowed with the power to include some books and exclude others. Indeed, I think it probable that Judaism would not have accepted the idea of a 'canon' at all if it had not been that Christians insisted in later times in talking in such terms. Even in Christianity the canon, as opposed to Scripture, has seldom been highly functional for the character of the religion, and it is not clear that it is really functional in Judaism at all, or ever has been.

If the word 'canon' is to be used at all, then it should probably be in the sense in which the term was sometimes used in the early Church, to denote a 'norm' or regulative standard rather than a closed body of texts. In this sense there is no doubt that the Pentateuch can very well be said to have been the 'canon' for post-exilic Judaism, at least from the time of Ezra. Almost all the ancient writers we have so far discussed make it clear that 'Moses' had a higher status than any other prophet, however venerable, and it is very unusual for the boundary between the Torah and the rest of the Scriptures to be blurred. Though I have been arguing that the distinction between 'Prophets' and 'Writings' is unattested in our period, the same can most certainly not be said of the boundary between the Prophets and the Law. While, as we have seen, Christian writers tend to see no divide between the end of Deuteronomy and the beginning of Joshua, this is not so in Judaism, where 'words of *qabbalah*' cannot overrule 'words of *torah*'.[69] But in the more common sense, even the Torah is not a 'canon', for it was never selected from any larger collection.

(2) So far we have uncovered one major reason for caution in using the word 'canon' to refer to Scripture in our period: the absence of the sense of exclusiveness. There is, however, a second reason, which is specially relevant to the pseudonymous books just discussed. An important source for understanding the reception of Scripture in some types of Jewish group is the passage often cited in discussions of the canon from 4 Ezra 14. Ezra laments (vv. 20–2) that 'the world lies in darkness, and its inhabitants are without light. For thy law has been burned, and so no one knows the things which have been done or will be done by thee.' He prays that he may receive God's holy spirit so that he may be able to 'write everything that has happened in the world from the beginning, the things which were written in thy law, that men may be able to find the path'. God agrees to this, and commissions five scribes to accomplish this task. When Ezra has completed the dictation, 'some things you shall make public, and some you shall deliver in secret to the wise' (v. 26). Ezra is then given a special drink, which inspires him to dictate ninety-four books. At the end of forty days, when the writing is complete, God says to him (vv. 45–7):

'Make public the twenty-four books that you wrote first and let the worthy and the unworthy read them; but keep the seventy that were written last, in order to give them to the wise among your people. For in them is the spring of understanding, the fountain of wisdom, and the river of knowledge.'

It is generally agreed that the twenty-four books are those of the present Hebrew canon, and that the seventy must be what we should call 'apocalyptic' works; and it is inferred that this passage is an explanation of why so many of the pseudepigrapha did not find their way into the canon of Scripture.[70] It can certainly be said of this passage that it does seem to envisage a canon, in the sense of a closed list beyond which nothing may be published, around the end of the first century AD. What is seldom noticed, however, is that God's words in the passage quoted seem to set the seventy books on a *higher* level than the twenty-four. The latter are to be available to everyone, but the former are meant for the initiates, 'the wise among your people'. This by no means suggests a sacred canon of twenty-four books from which apocalyptic works (if that is indeed how we should define the 'seventy') are excluded as of

64

inferior importance, but on the contrary a multiplicity of holy books of which only a few can safely be entrusted to all and sundry.[71]

This curious impression might make us think again about what is implied in 'excluding' books from a canon. It can only be a guess, but I wonder whether the attribution of so many of the works we call apocalyptic to *pre*-Mosaic figures may be meant to give them the same kind of superior authority (greater even than the Torah?) which seems to be implied for the seventy books in 4 Ezra. Anderson suggests that when Josephus lays down a prophetic period from Moses to Artaxerxes he is deliberately trying to devalue any works claiming to antedate Moses as well as those of (admittedly) recent origin.[72] I doubt however whether this is so, for Josephus nowhere shows any hesitation about the authority of pre-Mosaic prophets such as Jacob (*Antiquities* 2:194) or Abraham (*Antiquities* 1:57), any more than does Philo, who calls Noah a prophet (*quis heres* 260). But even if Josephus himself did have such an intention, majority opinion in New Testament times was surely in favour of regarding books older *even* than Moses as possessing the most superlative authority and inspiration.

What is particularly interesting about such books is that they frequently convey 'truths' which Moses had not openly divulged – details, for example, of the process of creation. Thus in Jubilees Moses himself learns much more about the creation and the history of the patriarchs than he was ever authorized to communicate in Genesis, just as Enoch, in 1 Enoch 6–14, proves to have the inside story of the sin of the sons of God and the daughters of men, and is shown a great deal more of the workings of the universe than was available in the Torah. In the prophecy of Cenez in Pseudo-Philo the patriarch is shown the very moment when the firmament was created, and learns how the sin of Adam will have consequences for the whole cosmos:

> I beheld and lo, a spark came up and as it were built for itself a floor under heaven, and the likeness of its floor was as a spider spins, in the fashion of a shield. And when the foundation was laid, I beheld, and from that spring there was stirred up as it were a boiling froth, and behold, it changed itself into another foundation, and between the two foundations, the upper and the lower, there drew near out of the light of the invisible place as it were forms of men, and they walked to and fro; and behold, a

voice saying: These shall be for a foundation to men, and they shall dwell therein for seven thousand years. And the lower foundation was a pavement and the upper was of froth, and they that came forth out of the light of the invisible place, they are those that shall dwell therein, and the name of that man is ‹Adam›. And it shall be, when he hath (*or* they have) sinned against me and the time is fulfilled, that the spark shall be quenched and the spring shall cease, and so they shall be changed. (*Biblical Antiquities* 28:8–9; compare the parallel passage in *Chronicles of Jerahmeel* 57:41).

Now for anyone who is at all impressed with literature of this kind, the Torah must seem tame and bald by comparison. The Pentateuch, it would seem, contains all that Moses was allowed to communicate to the common herd; precious jewels of more detailed information were reserved for the *cognoscenti*, those privileged to read Moses' private diaries or the memoirs, last testaments, and secret memoranda of those who lived even before his time. For anyone who believed that he was in possession of the very words of Enoch, the works of Moses and his successors would not seem like a 'canon' of unparalleled inspiration, but more like a piece of *haute vulgarisation* – all that could safely be allowed to get into the hands of the man in the street. If this is correct, then the evidence of 4 Ezra 14, while it confirms the status that the twenty-four books had by the end of the first century, does not tell us that they were the only books accounted holy. On the contrary, it suggests that they were rather ordinary by comparison with the 'hidden books' available to those in the know. I am aware, of course, that such books may have been the private hobby of specialized sectarian groups, and it may be only their opinions, not those of Judaism or Christianity as a whole, that 4 Ezra reports. But if that is so, then the book is in any case evidence only for the 'canon' of such groups, not for those in the mainstream.[73]

Evidence for a somewhat similar attitude towards certain books may be found at a later date in the rabbinic debates about the 'withdrawal' of certain books. There are five relevant passages, usefully assembled and discussed by Leiman,[74] in each of which the verb *gnz* is used of particular biblical books. Shabbat 13b tells of Hananiah b. Hezekiah, a sage of the first century AD, who consumed three hundred barrels of oil sitting up late to reconcile the book of

Ezekiel with the Torah (probably on matters relating to the Temple and the orders of priesthood), and so prevented it from being 'withdrawn'. Two other passages (both in Shabbat 30b) tell of a threatened 'withdrawal' of Proverbs and of Ecclesiastes, on the grounds that these books were *self*-contradictory. Ecclesiastes, we read, was spared because it 'begins with words of *torah* and ends with words of *torah*'; Proverbs, on the grounds that a good reason had been found for not withdrawing Ecclesiastes, so it was worth finding one for saving Proverbs, too. In Aboth de-Rabbi Nathan 1:4 a ground for withdrawing Proverbs, Ecclesiastes, and the Song of Songs is given: that they 'presented mere parables and were not part of scripture' (*hem 'ômerîm mᵉshalôth wᵉ'enan min ha-kᵉtûbîm*). Finally, Hagigah 13a again relates that Hananiah b. Hezekiah intervened to save Ezekiel from 'withdrawal' when a child read and understood 'the passage about amber (*hashmal*)', that is, the chariot-vision (the word occurs in 1:4), whereupon he was killed by the fire that came from the amber. Hananiah argued that the probability of other children having enough understanding to be at risk was very low.

The verb *gnz* in these passages has been interpreted to mean that the books in question risked 'de-canonization', 'withdrawal' from the official list of the Scriptures,[75] but Leiman argues, convincingly to my mind, that this is very unlikely. It is inherently improbable that Proverbs, for example, was ever considered to be of doubtful authority. As we have noted, it is one of the favourite non-Pentateuchal books both in the Mishnah and in the works of Philo.[76] It is far more probable that *gnz* is being used in the sense familiar from other rabbinic discussions about what is to be done with holy objects and scrolls of the law that are worn out or found to contain errors, which have to be 'stored away' in a sanctified storeroom – a *genizah*. One's initial expectation might be that these passages raise the question whether the books under discussion qualify for such treatment, that is, whether they are sufficiently *holy* to need 'storing', rather than whether they are so profane as to deserve removal from the canon. But this cannot be so, for the reason why they were considered for 'storing away' is their problematic character, and it is clearly a fate from which they have been rescued, not a status which they have failed to achieve in the eyes of the rabbinic writers. It is most likely, therefore, that *gnz* is being used figuratively, and means, not that there was a proposal either that these books should be literally placed in a *genizah* or that they should be held to qualify for such treatment when the scrolls on which they were written were discarded, but that they ought to be kept away from the eyes of those whom they might disturb. In other words, the debates *presuppose* that Proverbs, Ecclesiastes, the Song of Songs and Ezekiel are holy, scriptural books: the proposals which were eventually defeated would have entailed their being withdrawn from public availability to protect those of weak faith or at risk from accidental mystical states. This explanation was suggested fifty years ago by G. F. Moore: 'The question was not, Is this book sacred, or inspired, Scripture? but, assuming its prophetic authorship or inspiration, is it expedient to withdraw the books from public use?'[77]

If this is so, then the passages in question confirm, rather than casting doubts on, the scriptural status of the books concerned. I think it unlikely to have been seriously suggested that books by Solomon or Ezekiel *actually* contained material that was self-contradictory or at variance with the Torah. The point is not that the books are really in error in these ways, but that they will appear so to the unenlightened. The presence of problems of this sort in a book which is known to be inspired is probably seen as a sign to the learned that deep mysteries lie encoded within it, which it is perilous for the unlearned to attempt to pry into. Perhaps then the passage in Aboth de-Rabbi Nathan 1:4, which Leiman renders 'for they presented mere parables', should rather be translated 'for they spoke riddles'; we shall return to *'enan min ha-k^{e}tûbîm* in a moment. Hananiah b. Hezekiah did not save the canonical status of Ezekiel, but rather showed that it could be reconciled with the Torah in the ordinary ways in which the rabbis did reconcile Scripture with Scripture, and hence that it was not a book that would be dangerous to the average person.

A similar explanation may help to resolve the long-standing uncertainty over the meaning of rabbinic debates about whether or not certain books 'defile the hands'. The classic case is M. Yadaim 3:5, the passage on which the theory of the 'council of Jamnia' ultimately rested:

All the Holy Scriptures (*kitbe ha-qôdesh*) defile the hands (*m^{e}tam'îm 'eth ha-yadaim*). The Song of Songs and Ecclesiastes defile the hands. R. Judah said: The Song of Songs defiles the hands but there is a dispute concerning Ecclesiastes. R. Jose said: Ecclesiastes does not defile the hands but there is a dispute concerning the Song of Songs. R. Simeon said: Ecclesiastes is among the lenient decisions of the School of Shammai and among the stringent decisions of the School of Hillel. R. Simeon b. Azzai said: I have heard a tradition from the seventy-two elders on the day that R. Eleazar b. Azariah was appointed head of the Academy, that the Song of Songs and Ecclesiastes defile the hands. R. Akiba said: God forbid: No man in Israel ever disputed concerning the Song of Songs, saying that it does not defile the hands, for the whole world is not worth the day on which the Song of Songs was given to Israel, for all the scriptures [$k^e t\hat{u}b\hat{i}m$: Writings?[78]] are holy, but the Song of Songs is the holiest of the holy. If there was a dispute, it concerned Ecclesiastes. R. Johanan b. Joshua, the son of R. Akiba's father-in-law, said: Ben Azzai's version of what they disputed and decided is the correct one.

Leiman's discussion of this and the other passages in which this phrase occurs provides exhaustive coverage of the various theories that have been suggested, and I shall not attempt to summarize them here. I think, with Barr,[79] that the discussions among the rabbis about this issue do not relate to what we should call 'canonicity', nor even to what Leiman calls 'canonicity', that is, accepted authoritative status, but are what they appear to be: disputes about questions of purity relating to particular books which were in any case accepted as Scripture. None the less this issue may have something to contribute to the present discussion. It is interesting to notice that two other books are also mentioned about whose capacity to cause uncleanness there was some dispute: Ruth and Esther (Megillah 7a). This surely confirms that canonicity is not the point at issue: neither of these books was of doubtful authority. What it does bring out, however, is that the question about books which makes the hands unclean arises in the case of four of the *megilloth*. Unfortunately we do not know exactly when these books began to be read at the great festivals, though the association of Esther with Purim is certainly very old; but when the custom did arise, the *megilloth* came to share with the Torah the distinction of being read whole, rather than in selections as with the *haftaroth* from the Prophets. It is possible to imagine that the question may have arisen whether these scrolls conveyed uncleanness[80] in the same way as did the Torah: a question which did not arise for scrolls of other biblical books, since only excerpts from these were ever used in the service of the synagogue.

If this conjecture is accepted, we may build a little further on it, though here I can offer no more than a shot in the dark. Two further passages, both concerning Esther, suggest a further distinction within biblical literature, which again has nothing to do with 'canonicity' in any sense: the distinction between books which were composed to be written down (*lktwb*) and those composed to be recited (*lqrwt*). Thus again in Megillah 7a we find:

> Rab Judah said in the name of Samuel: The Scroll of Esther does not defile the hands. Are we to infer from this that Samuel was of the opinion that the Scroll of Esther was not composed under divine inspiration? How can this be, seeing that Samuel has said that the Scroll of Esther was composed under divine inspiration? It was composed to be recited but not to be written.

And in Yoma 29a:

> R. Assi said: Why was Esther compared to the dawn? To tell you that just as the dawn is the end of the whole night, so is the story of Esther the end of all the miracles. But there is Hanukkah? We refer to those [miracles] the account of which was authorized to be written down. This accords well with the view that Esther was authorized to be written down, but what can be said on behalf of the view that Esther was not authorized to be written down?[81]

The saying in the first of these passages suggests that for the later of the rabbis whose opinions are recorded in Megillah 7a (Rab Judah may be dated in the late third century AD) 'not defiling the hands' was already being misunderstood, as it has often been misunderstood in modern times, to mean 'being uncanonical'. This impression is corrected here, and it is explained that if the scroll of Esther was held by some not to defile the hands, the reason for this had nothing to do with any defect in its authority or inspiration, but was simply a function of its originally *oral* character. It was indeed divinely inspired, but it was intended to be recited, not written down: hence, one may perhaps deduce, a scroll containing it is not a sacred object, like a Torah scroll, but theoretically no more than an *aide-mémoire*, and therefore does not confer uncleanness (compare Sanhedrin 100a for a practical illustration of this, where

70

those repairing the mantles of scrolls hold (wrongly, according to R. Judah) that the scroll of Esther does not require a mantle).

The passage from Yoma accords well with this: Esther records the last of the 'miracles' (*ha-nisîm*) which are celebrated with a festival. The objection is that the miracle of deliverance celebrated at Hanukkah, which occurred later, is also recorded: to which it is replied that it is not recorded in any book authorized to be written, but (presumably) in Maccabees (thereby providing a slight corroboration for Josephus' theory of the cut-off point for holy Scripture). That is all very well, replies a third voice, on the view that Esther was intended to be written, but how would you deal with the objection on the view that Esther was not intended to be written either? How this is to be answered, we are not told.

What these examples strongly suggest is that the issue of whether or not books 'defile the hands' is concerned not with all use of Scripture, for example for study, but specifically with its *liturgical* use. The issue arises only with the Torah and the *megilloth*, because only those are used in their entirety in the liturgy in any case; and any doubts about the status of the *megilloth* as regards uncleanness arise from the view that they may not have been given as writings but as oral compositions to be recited, in principle, from memory.

My suggestion, then, is that the question of 'defiling the hands' arises only with books which are used in the liturgy, and unless a book was already regarded as Scripture no one would have thought of using it liturgically in any case. Now correspondingly it may be that 'withdrawal' also has a rather specific, liturgical reference, and does not mean 'withdrawal from public availability' – not an easy thing to enforce – but 'withdrawal from liturgical use'. Thus to have 'withdrawn' Ezekiel would have been to rule that lections could not be taken from it. We know that such rulings were in fact made with regard to certain portions in Ezekiel: cf. M. Megillah 4:10 and M. Hagigah 2:1. 'Withdrawal' would presumably have involved a similar interdict on using any of the book at all for *haftaroth*. The grounds are, as already suggested, to do with the arcane character of some of the material in Ezekiel, as well as the (to us more obviously problematic) obscenities in it. If my conjecture is accepted that the same reasoning led to the suggestion that Proverbs, Ecclesiastes, and the Song of Songs should be withdrawn (assuming that there is some historical foundation to the account in Aboth de-Rabbi Nathan 1:4), then we might understand the puzzling

71

expression 'and they were not *min ha-k*^e*tûbîm*' as meaning, not 'they were not part of Scripture' (which is nonsense in the case of Proverbs, whatever one may believe about the canonicity of the other two), nor 'they were not among the Writings' (which, even if not anachronistic, would contribute nothing to the argument), but 'they were not among the "written" (as opposed to the "recited") books'. The argument would then run as follows: certain sages held that Proverbs, Ecclesiastes, and the Song should not be used liturgically, since they taught mysteries. It could have been objected that holy writings, that is, scriptural books 'given to be written', may not be withdrawn from liturgical use, since they are like the Torah. But these books are not in that category; they are books 'given to be recited', just as was the scroll of Esther according to some learned opinion. Therefore it would have been in order to withdraw them, had there been good reason. However, this suggestion did not in fact prevail in any case, since 'the men of the Great Synagogue' were able to show that they did not contain arcane material after all.

The suggestions of the last four paragraphs have represented a detour whose conclusions, if accepted, slightly strengthen my main line of argument; but it does not depend on them. I do think it likely in any case that the issue of 'withdrawal' has to do with the belief that inconsistencies in Scripture are a danger to the simple; not because they show Scripture to be imperfect (God forbid!) but *because they are a signal that the text contains deeper meanings which are best left to the learned*. The inconsistencies 'float on the surface of the deep like buoys to mark the position of the sunken treasure', as J. A. Baker puts it (in an unpublished paper). Now – and here at last we reach the point of this lengthy discussion – this says something about the kind of information contained in holy books which is of a piece with the attitude evinced in 4 Ezra. There are some scriptural books which are meant for those who are more advanced in spiritual understanding, and others which all can be permitted to hear and meditate upon. And the Torah comes into the second class, not the first. For a thinker who adopts this way of thinking, a book such as Ezekiel thus has a higher status, in one very important sense, than the Law itself.

Thus we reach the paradoxical conclusion that the work which has the highest authority in matters of halakah, the Torah, is for some other purposes considerably less valuable. If one is seeking

'The Law and the Prophets'

the kind of 'advanced' wisdom which many in New Testament times longed for, then one should turn to various other books, which can provide information that the Torah itself does not contain, since God does not wish to reveal it to all and sundry. For some, the other books will have been books which fall outside the canon as we now know it; for others, works which are now in the canon had this esoteric quality, making them unwise choices for public reading. If we are to speak phenomenologically rather than theoretically, we should have to say that such books enjoyed a higher status for those of this frame of mind than did the books of Moses. The point can be well illustrated from another tradition preserved in Megillah, this time in 3a. It is clearly a late legend, which presupposes the distinction between Prophets and Writings; but it captures the mood I am trying to describe:

> R. Jeremiah – or some say R. Hiyya b. Abba – also said: The targum of the Pentateuch was composed by Onkelos the proselyte under the guidance of R. Eleazar and R. Joshua. The targum of the Prophets was composed by Jonathan ben Uzziel under the guidance of Haggai, Zechariah and Malachi; and the land of Israel quaked over an area of four hundred parasangs by four hundred parasangs, and a *bath qol* came forth and exclaimed, Who is this that has dared to reveal my secrets to mankind? Jonathan ben Uzziel arose and said, It is I who have revealed thy secrets to mankind. It is fully known to thee that I have not done this for my own honour or for the honour of my father's house, but for thy honour have I done it, that dissension may not increase in Israel. He further sought to reveal by a targum of the hagiographa, but a *bath qol* went forth and said, Enough. What was the reason? – the end of the Messiah is foretold in it.

Christopher Rowland has stressed the importance of this passage as an indication of the rabbinic belief that Scripture contained divine secrets which could be revealed to the learned, and this is an extremely important corrective to the impression one sometimes gets from books on rabbinic Judaism that halakah was the rabbis' only concern. But perhaps he does not sufficiently note the distinctions within the legend. It is not quite the case that it rests on a belief that 'the Torah is the repository of the secret things of God',[82] unless we take 'Torah' in its broad sense. More precisely, the Torah – the Pentateuch – apparently contains nothing that may not be

73

revealed freely in a targum. Objections begin when the Prophets are translated – and it may be significant that to complete this task it took the help, not of a rabbi, but of the three last prophets themselves – because in *them* God's secrets are to be found. And, to complete the curious role-reversal, the Writings contain such deep mysteries that Jonathan is not even given a chance to discuss the matter with the *bath qol*: enough is enough.

Perhaps one good way of defining the status of books, whether or not they are in our present canon, which were thought to provide additional, esoteric information about the mysteries of the universe, is to draw a parallel with the 'oral Law'. The oral Law, which was transmitted from Moses by word of mouth alongside the written Torah (see Pirqe Aboth 1:1) is in one sense less authoritative than the written Torah, but in another sense more authoritative. Less, because it was not recorded and might not be recorded until the time when it was eventually decided that a collection of mishnayoth should be committed to writing, and therefore it could not be cited in the same precise way as the written Law. More, because in a culture that venerated the living voice above the written word (as Judaism did in some phases) it belonged to the continuous historical identity of the Jewish people, and also because it provided a hermeneutical framework within which the written Law was read – and hermeneutical frameworks are notoriously more authoritative, for the group that embraces them, than the text to whose hidden meaning they purport to give access. This analogy is explicitly drawn by Patte:

> Just as besides the Written Torah there was the Oral Torah, which was received by Moses on Mt Sinai, so for the author of the *Book of Jubilees* besides the Written Scripture . . . was another revelation which was also given to Moses. Yet we find here not a distinction between written and oral revelations, but rather one between the common revelation (open to anybody) and the secret revelation which was to be found in 'secret books' like the *Book of Jubilees* and which was reserved for specific circles of people (viz. circles of especially pious people).[83]

I would qualify what Patte says here in one respect. He thinks of Jubilees and its like as para-scriptural: as the oral Law is to the written Pentateuch, so Jubilees and its like is to the written Scripture as a whole. I suppose that what he has in mind is that 'apocalyptic', pseudonymous works like Jubilees stand outside 'Scripture', including the Prophetic books which in some ways they resemble. Thus as the oral Law (now codified in Mishnah and Talmud, but originally unwritten) is to the written Pentateuch, so the 'secret books' for the inner circle of the pious are to the 'public books' of Torah, Prophets, and Writings. In the light of our discussion of the state of the canon in our period, I would suggest that Jubilees stood, for the groups that recognized its inspiration, within 'Scripture' rather than over against it, but in a direct relationship to the Pentateuch rather than to the rest of Scripture taken together. For me, therefore, the analogy is tidier than for Patte, and I would put it as follows: as the oral Law is to the Pentateuch in its character of halakah, so the 'prophetic' books, in so far as they are understood as 'secret' books, are to the Pentateuch in its character as the revelation of the divine nature and the origins and character of the universe. For, as we have seen, it is not only 'pseudepigraphical' works that are treated in our period as esoteric in character; the same was believed about Ezekiel and probably also about the Song of Songs and Ecclesiastes.

Once we eliminate the anachronistic category of 'canonicity', which drives an artificial wedge between Ezekiel and Jubilees, the picture that results is quite a simple one. Some 'scriptures' were thought by some to provide secret information that Moses had not thought it good to communicate to the generality of people, and this at one and the same time increased the prestige of such books and suggested that they should remain concealed from the general public – while also conveniently explaining the fact that no one had ever heard of them before.

EXCURSUS: THE DEVELOPMENT OF THE TRIPARTITE CANON

Since I have argued that the tripartite organization of the canon is considerably later than the time at which the books in it were recognized as Scripture, I have left a loose end in the discussion. Judaism does now have a tripartite canon, and certainly had one by the time of Baba Bathra 14b–15a or by the time of Jerome, whichever is the earlier; and this arrangement must have come from somewhere. Furthermore, though I have said that the distinction between Prophets and Writings has never been functional within

Judaism, there is one exception to this, which may be thought to undermine my whole hypothesis. Whereas *haftaroth* from the Prophets are read in the liturgy of the synagogue, there are no *haftaroth* from the Writings. Liturgical readings from these are restricted to the five *megilloth* and some of the Psalms. This point, therefore, also needs to be discussed. My thesis is that there is in fact a connection between the liturgical practice and the origins of the tripartite canon, so the two matters that call for explanation belong naturally together.

In the Jewish liturgy today there is a fixed list of *haftaroth*,[84] which are drawn from all eight books of the Prophets, but never from the Writings. In practice this means that only a very small portion of the Prophets is read in the course of the annual cycle, with some books, especially Isaiah, greatly predominating: thus *all* the *haftaroth* to Deuteronomy are drawn from Isaiah, with a marked preference for the sections known to critical scholarship as Deutero- and Trito-Isaiah. How far back can this arrangement be traced? There is good early attestation for the reading of 'the law and the prophets' in Acts 13:15, but here as always we have the difficulty of knowing just what 'the prophets' was deemed to contain. There is plenty of detailed evidence in the tractate Soferim, but this is hardly a reliable witness to the custom in the first century AD. The earliest explicit evidence is probably in material from the Cairo Genizah,[85] which includes lists of *haftaroth* differing in detail but confirming that the choice was restricted to what are now the Prophets, and that Isaiah was much the favourite book. The importance of Isaiah is confirmed by the number of scrolls of the prophet found at Qumran (twelve, more than any other biblical book), though there is no evidence for the community's liturgical practice so far as readings from the Prophets are concerned.

Apart from this we are dependent on the Mishnah, but here again the meaning of terms is uncertain. M. Megillah 4:2 stipulates that there shall be a reading 'from the Prophets' on the sabbath, after the reading of the Law, but it does not make it clear which books are to be understood by 'Prophets', any more than does Acts 13:15. I cannot see that Leiman is correct to hold that this mishnah prohibits the use of the Writings; even if 'Prophets' here has its later meaning (books from the second division), nothing is said to show that readings from the Writings were *forbidden*. This idea seems to derive from a comparison of this text with M. Shabbat 16:1, where we read: 'Any of the Holy Scriptures ($kit^ebe\ ha\text{-}q\hat{o}desh$] may be saved from burning, whether they are such that are read or not'. If we take the *gemara* on this to be correct in its interpretation, 'those that are read' are the Prophets, and 'those that are not read' are the Writings: thus Shabbat 115a, compare Soferim 15:2. This explanation finds its way into Danby's footnotes,[86] and Leiman takes it for granted that this is what the mishnah means; however, there is no way of knowing this for sure. Perrot thinks that the choice of *haftarah* was in early times left to the reader, though undoubtedly customs would soon have grown up which restricted his choice in practice.

One of our very few early descriptions of the reading of the *haftarah*, in Luke 4:17, might be thought to favour the view that *haftaroth* were already fixed, since Jesus is there 'given' the scroll of Isaiah rather than selecting it; and in view of the difficulty of turning the scroll all the way to chapter 61 while the congregation waits to hear the reading, one could perhaps suppose that the place was already found. However, I think that this impression should yield to other considerations.[87] One of the rules in M. Megillah stipulates that certain portions of Scripture are not to be read publicly, and we have already considered these when discussing the 'withdrawal' of books.[88] Thus the first portion of Ezekiel, with the chariot-vision, is not to be read, and chapter 16 is banned as too indecent (4:10). Similarly, it is ordered that the reader may skip verses in a reading from the Prophets so as to produce an abbreviated passage, but that this may not be done in reading the Torah (4:4). Both these rules make sense only on the supposition that the reader still had freedom of choice in general.[89]

Once again we need to apply common sense in trying to imagine the practice of the synagogue in our period. Probably a number of passages in scriptural books outside the Torah had established themselves as favourites, and some Torah-readings already had a widely-accepted companion piece. Paul's casual reference to what the scripture says 'in Elijah' (Romans 11:2) probably points to the existence of an excerpt from 1 Kings 18–19 which could be identified in this shorthand way, just as could Pentateuchal passages (cf. Mark 12:26 and parallels, 'in the bush'). Probably also not every synagogue possessed a very extensive set of biblical scrolls. Perrot speculates that, besides the Torah, most synagogues probably had Isaiah and the Psalms, but many may have lacked most others.[90]

Perhaps, if the story in Luke 4:16–30 has any basis in fact, the synagogue at Nazareth possessed no prophetic scroll apart from Isaiah – an accident of history which had a major effect on early Christianity, if it was truly so. A wide diversity of practice held together by a number of shared tendencies seems altogether likelier than an official list of passages whose authority was recognized by all: who in any case was competent to legislate for this kind of custom in the Graeco-Roman period?

This way of looking at the development of the *haftarah* system suggests some possible explanations for the emergence of the tripartite canon. Leiman, as we have seen more than once, often makes suggestions in his notes which are much less traditional than those of the main text, and on this question of the *haftaroth* he seems to me to have hit upon an attractive and economical explanation, which with some modifications will be adopted here. Beginning from the observation that Prophets and Writings were not distinguished in early times, he writes:

> Assuming that an original $n^e b\hat{\imath}\,'\hat{\imath}m$ developed into $n^e b\hat{\imath}\,'\hat{\imath}m\ \hat{u}k^e t\hat{u}b\hat{\imath}m$ – with no change in the extent of the biblical canon – , one must account for the change in nomenclature. Such an account is necessarily speculative, and is offered here only as a plausible working-hypothesis. In early Second Temple times, when the Torah was read aloud in the Temple and the synagogue, the growing canon of non-Pentateuchal biblical books was called 'Prophets' since it was the belief in their prophetic authorship which distinguished the biblical from ordinary books. When it became customary to read portions from the prophets in the synagogue, the readings were confined to those books which relate the national history of Israel . . . , thereby excluding readings from a large number of Prophetic books. Thus, a liturgical distinction was introduced which distinguished biblical books read publicly in the synagogue from the other biblical books. These latter were reduced to writing ($k^e t\hat{u}b\hat{\imath}m$) but were not read publicly in the synagogue. Hence the tripartite canon, and the introduction of the term $k^e t\hat{u}b\hat{\imath}m$ for the third section of the biblical canon.[91]

I do not think that the reason for restricting readings to the Prophets (in the later sense) had much to do with the *content* of these books, and in particular I do not find Leiman's attempt to see the Prophets as 'those books which relate the national history of Israel' convincing. The one ancient author to use this category, Josephus, included a number of the Writings in it, and it is hard to see how one could exclude Chronicles, Ezra and Nehemiah, or Esther. Much more probable, it seems to me, is that the books from which *haftaroth* were in practice taken tended to be those which a large number of synagogues happened to possess; and this means (here we return, with a paradoxical twist in the story, to the view that the three parts of the canon have something to do with the date of the books within them) those which were older – really older, not simply believed to be older. By New Testament times the scrolls of the 'Deuteronomistic History' and of the three great prophets and the Twelve were, we may suppose, widely known, and all synagogues would aspire to possess copies. Later books, such as Chronicles or Daniel, were becoming known but were not yet common property. This is the truth behind the theory that the 'third division' of the canon was still in process of formation: as it stands the idea is erroneous, but as a purely phenomenological description of the state of distribution and use of the scriptures – rather than as a statement about the theoretical beliefs that were held about them – it has a lot to be said for it.

All we have to do to make Leiman's suggestion convincing is to stand it on its head. It is not that, for some reason which we have to guess at, certain books were regarded as suitable for reading after the Torah, that these then formed the second division of the Bible, and that the remaining books were relegated to the third division. It is quite simply that over the years a traditional body of *haftaroth* grew up, drawn from those books which were most widely available. Eventually the books in question came to be distinguished from those which had not contributed any *haftaroth* to the common pool, and the latter were referred to as the 'written' books, as opposed to the 'read' books, just as Leiman suggests. We might imagine a stage (though it must be stressed that this is pure conjecture) at which people spoke of *nᵉbî'îm kᵉtûbîm* and *nᵉbî'îm qᵉrî'îm*, 'written prophets' and 'read prophets'. The reason why the selection of books in the two divisions seems to have no basis in content, genre, or function in any sphere other than liturgy is that the distinction never had any basis except in liturgical use, and even that for more or less adventitious reasons to do with the availability and popularity of particular books.

The purpose of this section has been to argue that the term 'canon' obscures more than it clarifies if we are trying to understand what Scripture – and in particular 'prophetic' Scripture – meant in Judaism in New Testament times; and to find ways of describing how Scripture functioned that would do more justice to the categories in which people at the time actually thought. We have seen good reason to endorse a number of the criticisms made by Lightstone of the assumptions on which scholarly discussion of 'the canon' seems often to rest. For example, we have seen that it is anachronistic to talk as though there was some kind of regulative authority within Judaism which could legislate on questions of canonicity, so that there was an 'official' canon, deviations from which may be labelled 'sectarian'.[92] On the contrary, 'Scripture' was a far vaguer concept than this model suggests, and the variety of ways of thinking about it that we have outlined are not deviations from a norm that was even theoretically acknowledged. Christians did in due course decide on questions of canonicity by the decrees of councils, but such a pattern should not be retrojected into New Testament times, nor foisted on Judaism as though not to have approached matters in the same way would argue some defect in the Jewish understanding of Scripture.

The picture that has emerged is of a number of books whose status had never been seriously in doubt, but with a very large penumbra of other books about which opinions varied widely and which were no doubt quite unknown to some communities even at periods when others valued them highly. As Lightstone rightly urges us to remember, it is quite anachronistic to assume that every Jew was familiar with every book that was 'extant' at a given time, and knew where it belonged in the canon and exactly how much authority it was officially held to possess. 'Arguments ... such as Leiman's that authorities closed the canon before ca. 200 BCE, because they would otherwise have included Daniel, suppose that a work was likely to become a 'best-seller' soon after the author's ink dried. Given a non-centralized milieu exhibiting a fair degree of diversity, I cannot imagine a less probable scenario.'[93]

The positive advantage of setting aside the notion that there was a 'canon' of Scripture in our period is that we are free to register various nuances of emphasis in the attitudes to Scripture that prevailed in various groups. First, there is the peculiar status of the Pentateuch. As we saw in the last section, Scripture was widely understood to consist of two kinds of documents: the Law, and other books, often called 'Prophets'; and there was no question that in all matters relating to conduct the Law was supreme. In one useful sense of the word *canon* the Law could therefore be said to be the canon in Judaism in our period. Distinctions within the other books are of quite secondary importance by comparison with this primary difference, between the Torah and everything else.

Secondly, however, there are aspects of the value attached, at least by some, to certain books outside the Pentateuch which do not fit a simple model of degrees of authority or inspiration. The 'prophetic' books, which might include books not now in the canon as well as those of whose status there had never been any doubt, were sometimes seen as communicating *higher* levels of truth than did the books of the Torah, which were available to all, and it was sometimes held that access to these books of arcane wisdom should be restricted to 'the wise' or 'the learned'. While this does not necessarily mean that the Torah was relegated to a second place in any formal way, in practice it must have implied that it was seen as lower in prestige for those who wished to embark on what might be seen as a perilous but heroic quest for a knowledge of the deeper truths about God and the universe. The supposedly esoteric character of much that the 'prophetic' books contain will concern us in more detail when we turn, in later chapters of this book, to study the ways in which they were read. I have argued that the rabbinic debates about the 'withdrawal' of certain books probably related to the perception that they contained such (dangerous) truths. When rabbinic authorities say that they risked being 'withdrawn' because they were thought to contain contradictions, passages at variance with the Torah, or unedifying sections, this does not mean that such 'defects' led to a questioning of their scriptural status, but rather that they conveyed to the rabbinic mind a suspicion that dark secrets, best kept from the attention of the unlearned, lay encoded within the text.

Thirdly, there was a widely-diffused belief, to which Josephus explicitly bears witness, that the kind of 'prophetic' activity that led to the production of holy books of law or wisdom was confined to a special age or ages in the past, with which present-day inspiration could not compete. No one knew for sure how many books had been written by prophets, and new ones were constantly being 'discovered' in our period: but it was widely agreed that it was in the works of such prophets that divine revelation could be found. From this point of view, the Torah represents the supreme example of prophetic inspiration, since it derived from the greatest of all the prophets of old, Moses. But there had been a chain of authorized successors to Moses, whose work ceased only in the time of Ezra; and before Moses there had been great sages and patriarchs, some of whom had left a written record of their visions and teachings. Such works deserved to be venerated and studied. Some of them may have been seen as representing a sort of authorized commentary on the written Torah as regards the historical and cosmological information that Moses had only hinted at there, just as the 'oral Law' (*torah she-be'al peh*) represented a secret tradition from Moses as regards the divine commandments about daily conduct. But whether pre- or post-Mosaic, they came from an age that was now over, and it was in their antiquity that the secret of their appeal lay, for the children of a deeply antiquarian culture which delighted in all that bore the marks of ancient tradition.

IV

So far all attempts to find a hermeneutical significance in the fact that certain books are 'in the canon', or in their assignment to one 'division' rather than another, have turned out to be a wild goose chase. If we turn now to the third thesis outlined in section II, it will hardly come as a surprise to the reader that the *order* in which the biblical books are arranged – an equally promising avenue, one might think – is equally devoid of importance. Again, once the canon was firmly established in its present form, significance could easily be found in the order of the books, but I think this has usually been a matter of making a virtue of necessity.

Blenkinsopp, for example, finds considerable significance in the last verses of Malachi.[94] These, he suggests, 'are intended to serve as the conclusion to the entire prophetic collection, perhaps even to Law and Prophets combined'.[95] He sees 'the last paragraph of *nebî'îm*'[96] as an attempt to reconcile 'prophetic' and 'priestly' strands in post-exilic Judaism: 'whoever added this coda to the Prophets intended to present them as inculcating an observance of Torah which would not exclude the millenarian hope'.[97] In principle there is of course no reason why such ideas should not have been

82

expressed in the way the Scriptures were ordered, and it has been an important contribution of 'canonical criticism' in its various forms to alert the reader of the Bible to this possibility. However, the question whether significance of this kind was in fact conveyed by the way texts were ordered in our period is a historical question that ought to be settled by looking for specific evidence, and (to my own regret, since I am greatly attracted by 'canonical' readings) I doubt if such evidence can be found.

The greatest single difficulty about the order of the biblical books in New Testament times is that, so far as we know, the codex had not yet been invented. In a codex 'order' has a clear meaning: as one turns the pages, one book follows another. Where each book is written on a single scroll, however, 'order' is a much less clear idea. On the whole I think Wolfenson was justified when he argued, as long ago as 1924, that the idea that there was any 'order' in Scripture at the beginning of our era was an entirely spurious one. He wrote:

> The idea that the Jewish Bible or Canon, *i.e.*, a collection of books in a single volume, was formed at an early date is due to Elias Levita, who states . . . that 'in Ezra's time the 24 books of the Old Test. were not yet united in a single volume: Ezra and his associates united them together, and divided them into three parts, the Law, the Prophets, and the Hagiographa'. There is, however, absolutely no evidence for this assertion. It is a fabrication pure and simple, and this idea of a single volume containing all the Scriptures at the time of Ezra is not met with before Elias Levita.[98]

The use of codices for the Hebrew Scriptures is only very sparsely attested before the eighth century AD,[99] and even then, as Wolfenson implies, not for the entire corpus of Scripture. What is more, even when codices do appear, they by no means agree in all respects with the printed Hebrew Bibles we are familiar with. It is well known that the Leningrad Codex, which forms the basis of most modern printed Bibles, places Chronicles before Ezra-Nehemiah, indeed, at the beginning of the Writings,[100] even though modern editors always depart from it in this one respect in order to produce the order Ezra–Nehemiah–Chronicles which is the received tradition.

But Wolfenson shows that even *printed* Hebrew Bibles were not until modern times uniform in their arrangement. Thus some Italian editions of the fifteenth and sixteenth centuries place the *megilloth* between the Pentateuch and the Prophets, presumably because thereby all the books read in their entirety in the liturgy are placed together.[101] In others, each of the *megilloth* is interpolated after the book of the Pentateuch read at the season during which the festival to which it is assigned usually falls, thus disrupting the 'order' even of the Torah.[102]

What can be meant by 'order' if one is thinking of a 'Bible' consisting of a set of scrolls? N. M. Sarna, in one of the few studies to take the sheer physical reality of the matter seriously, suggests that the only meaning the term can have is an order for labelling the pigeonholes in which scrolls were kept, which in effect amounts to a library classification scheme.[103] It is not beyond the bounds of possibility that rabbinic authorities should have legislated for the design and arrangement of book-rooms, but it is perhaps odd, if they did so, that the matter is not made more explicit in the literature. Sarna thinks that the 'order' (*seder*) in Baba Bathra 14b is to be understood in these terms, and this has at least the merit of providing an explanation of that passage that has some contact with conceivable realities. Even if we do understand there to have been some customs about the storage of biblical scrolls, however, we are obviously not in the same world of thought as 'holistic' readings of the canon, in which the arrangements of the books has an effect on the meaning analogous to the way the shape of a single work contributes to its interpretation. Furthermore, with individual scrolls the sense of a boundary between divisions of the Bible, or even between 'canonical' and 'non-canonical' works, cannot possibly be so clear as it is within the covers of a codex. An individual synagogue might not possess a full set of biblical scrolls, and it would tend to treat as 'Scripture' whatever scrolls it did possess. One may guess that whereas the books that make up the 'core' of the canon – the Torah, certain Prophets such as Isaiah, the Psalms, and the scroll of Esther – may have been almost universally available, towards the fringes the 'canon' or library may have varied widely. Maybe some communities possessed a scroll of Daniel, others of 1 Enoch, others again of Jeremiah, not necessarily all in the same recension; perhaps some scrolls contained a couple of shorter books, others half of a longer book; no doubt (since the rabbis discuss which combinations are permissible) shorter scrolls were joined together to make longer ones, producing all kinds of strange combinations. We do not know, and there is no point in pretending that we do. And any theory about the order of the books which requires us to prove that there was some kind of 'official' order from which it was irregular to deviate is asking the impossible.

It is not even clear that the 'order' *within* certain books was fixed in New Testament times. Of course in the narrative books the order is dictated by the nature of the contents, but many scriptural books are plainly anthological in character. The 'Book of the Twelve', for example, may have gone through a series of editions before it reached its present form. We might surmise that the linking of Joel and Amos is early enough to have left its mark on the text itself, in the form of the passage that occurs at the end of one and the beginning of the other in almost identical form (Joel 3:16 [Hebrew 4:16]//Amos 1:2); whereas the connection of Haggai, Zechariah and Malachi with the other nine may belong to a much later stage,[104] 'Malachi' even being seen as an artificial extra book split off from the (secondary) 'Deutero-Zechariah' in order to make the number up to twelve.[105] I do not say that I hold any of these suggestions to be true, but put them forward as the kinds of suggestion any biblical scholar would be prepared to consider. In such a case it would be entirely possible that some collections of biblical books may have retained old copies of one or other of the earlier editions at a time when others already possessed the later ones, so that the number and arrangement of the Minor Prophets could have been quite differently understood in different places. Greek Bibles do not follow the same arrangement of the Minor Prophets as Hebrew ones – the first six in particular regularly appear in a different order; and one does not have to be an adherent of an 'Alexandrian canon' hypothesis to think that there may have existed Hebrew manuscripts arranged in the order usual in the LXX. So far as we know, nothing was held to depend on any particular way of listing the Twelve.

Another case where the internal arrangement of an anthology may have varied until a late date is that of the Psalms. A good deal of discussion has been provoked by the discovery in Cave 11 at Qumran of a scroll of the psalms (11QPs^a) in which the order is radically different from that of the Masoretic Text. As well as including a Hebrew version of the LXX's Psalm 151, three of the Psalms otherwise known only in Syriac,[106] and the psalm from Ecclesiasticus 51:13–20, all ascribed to David, this scroll arranges many Psalms quite differently from other Psalters, as follows: 101, 102, 103, 109, 105, 146, 148, 121–32, 119, 135, 136, 118, 145, 139, 138, 93, 141, 133, 144, 142, 143, 149, 150, 140, 134.[107] There has been much discussion of whether this means that the Qumran community had a different canonical ordering of the Psalms from that which is now familiar, or whether the scroll is merely an arrangement for liturgical use of Psalms whose 'official' order was not disputed. My own impression is that Sanders, who published the scroll, is right to interpret it 'not as a deviation from a rigidly fixed canon of the latter third of the Psalter, but rather as a signpost in the multi-faceted history of the canonization of the Psalter'.[108] Since we have no other evidence at all for the order of the Psalms at that early period,[109] I cannot see how this interpretation of the evidence of 11QPs^a can be refuted. It is interesting to find Goshen-Gottstein understanding Sanders to mean that the Qumran community recognized a *different canon* of the Psalms from other groups in Judaism, and then rejecting his interpretation on the grounds that nothing in the scroll shows that its order, or the additional Psalms it contains, were regarded as *canonical*. What Sanders in fact said, as Meyer correctly sees, is that the evidence of this Psalm-scroll shows the idea of a *canonical* Psalter in this period (which Meyer takes to be the first century AD) to be simply an anachronism through and through. Goshen-Gottstein's comment on Sanders's theory is intended as a *reductio ad absurdum* of his position, but it seems to me that it accurately sums up the conclusion that 11QPs^a in fact forces on us:

> The sources known prior to the publication of 11QPs^a seemed quite abundant and reliable, and scholars had good reason to be more or less agreed on the picture to be drawn of the state of the 'canon' in the first century CE. If this picture now turns out to be basically wrong, if a rival 'canon' of Psalms could exist as late as the first century, *we must doubt whether any other view we hold with regard to questions of 'canon' is more than the result of lack of information.*[110]

The only qualification we need to make is to remove the expression 'a rival canon'. There was *no* canon of the Psalms in the first century AD: there were collections called 'The Book of Psalms',[111] and no one knows exactly what they contained or how they were arranged.

The earliest passage which gives us information about an 'order'

86

in the Hebrew Bible, so far as Jewish sources are concerned, is the discussion in Baba Bathra 14b to which we have referred so often already. This is particularly interesting because it does not seem to be thinking of a codex. Two features seem to me to imply this: the comments about Hosea, whose book is so small that 'it might be lost' if separated from the rest of the Twelve; and the fact that the order of books is not given as a description of the contents of a volume, but as a report of a tradition, parts of which are evidently contested. It seems clear to me that the passage envisages each of the books named as a separate scroll (Esther is actually called, as commonly in rabbinic literature, *megillath-Ester*, the scroll of Esther). The question then is, in what order should one list them? The objections to the proposed order seem generally to work on the principle that listing *ought* to be chronological: Hosea ought to come first, if he really was the first to prophesy (which is in fact disputed, but that is a separate issue); Job ought to come first, since he lived in the days of Moses. In each case the deviations from a chronological listing are justified. Isaiah and Ruth appear outside their proper places for reasons to do with their content; Hosea is (unfortunately) part of the Minor Prophets, and they come last because the latest books that comprise the corpus are later than anything else in the Prophets – so, in this case, the chronological principle is in fact being followed, but place in the order is determined by the latest rather than the earliest portion of a book.

Since these reasons are fairly obviously specious, concocted *ad hoc* in each case, we must assume that the 'order' being defended really is older than its justifications here. On the other hand, it is not the order which any existing codices actually follow, nor does it correspond to any other known listing of the books.[112] It is of course possible, with Lightstone, simply to deny the passage any evidential value at all, and to write it off as pure fantasy. Leiman, who allows it considerable weight, says that it 'is anonymous and cannot be dated',[113] though he suggests that 'its present form . . . suggests its relative antiquity'.[114] Sometimes such suggestions rest on the observation that the passage is a *baraita*; though Wolfenson was already contesting this: 'the whole passage is not a *B:raita*. Only the two lists of books and possibly the short passage beginning "And who wrote them?" . . . are *B:raita*, and the rest is *Gemara* discussion.'[115] It seems to me that, even if we give the passage the benefit of the doubt and regard it as having some historical value for our period, the order to which it refers is not presented *even within the passage itself* as functional in any way. Nothing hangs on the order in which the books are listed: the question seems to be an end in itself. When the suggested order is challenged, the challenge does not take the form of an appeal to a more familiar order, but exists in a vacuum of theory. The challenger does not say, 'The order *we* have learned is different from that suggested', but 'Would it not be more logical to list the books in some other way?' The theoretical nature of the discussion is well seen in the argument about the proper place of Hosea, for even the most ardent proponent of the view that the canon was not fixed at Jamnia will not want to argue that the book of the Twelve was still being seen as *twelve separate books* in New Testament times. No one, I imagine, seriously thought of lopping off Hosea from the Twelve and producing an individual scroll, to meet the point that 'God spoke first to Hosea'.

If we suppose that the 'order' of the Scriptures recorded here is not mere fantasy, however, in what context and for what purpose can it have arisen? My own impression is that it may be originally intended as a chronological listing of the books within each of the three divisions.[116] The four Former Prophets arrange themselves, since they tell the story of Israel in chronological sequence anyway. It is possible to think that the Latter Prophets are in chronological order, too, if one attends not to the date of the prophet himself but the date of the events with which his book *ends* (as suggested above): Jeremiah speaks of the Exile, Ezekiel of the rebuilding of Jerusalem, Isaiah of the gathering in of the Gentiles, and the Twelve of the coming of Elijah to prepare for the final triumph of the kingdom of God. So far as the Writings are concerned, the sequence is almost entirely satisfactory: Ruth tells of the birth of David, who wrote the Psalms; Solomon wrote the books of wisdom (Proverbs, Ecclesiastes, Song of Songs); Jeremiah wrote Lamentations; Daniel came after Jeremiah; Esther and Ezra, who wrote Chronicles, succeeded Daniel. Job is a problem for this theory, as it was for the commentator in Baba Bathra. David was held to have 'written' the Psalms and to have included in it the 'Psalms of Moses', according to the list in the second half of the passage, so it is conceivable that he was held to have 'written' also the book of Job, which Moses had originally composed. But this is the best explanation I can offer.

If the 'order' is not in origin a chronological one, then its significance seems to me quite obscure. Is it possible that at some stage children were expected to be able to reel off the names of the books of the Bible, and that the list was drawn up for that purpose? The lists of books with particular 'authors' in the second half of the list include mnemonics (*sîman*), which are useful for this kind of purpose, though the primary use of them known to us is as an aid to scribes, that is, they are a device of the Masoretes (compare the mnemonics in the Masorah which enable one to list the pre-Israelite inhabitants of Canaan in the correct order when copying such passages as Genesis 15:19–20 and Exodus 3:17).

At all events chronological order seems to be the commonest criterion for arranging the books in most other lists of the Hebrew Scriptures. This is surely the case with Josephus, for example. It is not, as is sometimes said, that Josephus counted Ruth (for instance) among the Prophets *rather than* the Writings, as though he had been either rearranging the 'canon' or using a different one (an Alexandrian canon, say); rather he places Ruth between Judges and Samuel because that is the order in which the history runs, taking the narratives at face value. Much the same can be said of Ben Sira. In chapters 44–9 he runs through the chief heroes of Jewish history, not in 'canonical' but in chronological order. There is no sign that for either Josephus or Ben Sira there was any 'canonical' order which had to be followed. Of course, like anyone else, they could see that Kings came 'after' Samuel; but there is no similar sense in which Ecclesiastes comes either before or after Proverbs. Given, as I have tried to show, that the distinction between Prophets and Writings is comparatively late, questions about the original place of Lamentations or Ruth in the canon are, as Wolfenson uncompromisingly put it, 'quite useless and absurd'.[117] There is no reason why some communities may not have possessed a scroll of Judges with Ruth appended, and others two separate scrolls, without either arrangement being thought to matter in the least.[118] But chronological order is one rational way of *listing* books, if for some reason that has to be done.

A number of the Fathers give lists of the books accepted by the Jewish communities of their day, the earliest being Melito (in Eusebius, *Ecclesiastical History* 6:25) and Origen (ibid.); note also the Bryennios list.[119] But in practically every case they list the Hebrew books in something close to the Greek order, not distinguishing the three Hebrew divisions of the canon. The same is true of Athanasius' *Festal Letter* 39: histories, poetical books, and prophets are collected together. Our only witness to the tripartite Hebrew canon, and hence the only one of the Fathers who may be expected to throw any light on the Hebrew order, is Jerome. The *prologus galeatus* follows the Hebrew order familiar to us for the Prophets, but says that the Jews include Ruth with Judges to make one book, and does not mention Lamentations in its list, treating it as simply part of Jeremiah; but Jerome adds the comment that 'some include Ruth and Lamentations amongst the Hagiographa, and think that these books ought to be reckoned separately'. His list of the Writings appears to be chronological: it begins with Job – which is the earliest if we understand it to be Mosaic – then moves on through David and Solomon (Psalms, Proverbs, Ecclesiastes, Song of Songs) to Daniel, Chronicles, Ezra–Nehemiah, and Esther.

With the Greek Bible, and the eventual dominance of the codex over the scroll, the idea of 'order' becomes much simpler to understand. If early Christian writers placed great emphasis on the correct order for the Greek Old Testament, we should at least know what they meant: the order in which one book should follow another inside the covers of a codex. The curious fact is, however, that whereas rabbinic literature has left us at least one detailed discussion of how the books ought to be arranged, and we cannot at all understand what can be meant by it, the Christian Fathers, for whom the concept would have been a perfectly clear one, do not seem to have thought that it mattered. None of the patristic listings of books seems to regard the order in which the books are listed as significant. There is some interest in arranging them so as to produce a certain total number, sometimes to agree with the number of letters in the Hebrew alphabet, or to make pleasing patterns, such as the 'Pentateuchs' of (one of) Epiphanius's lists.[120] But there is never any suggestion that any particular order is the 'proper' one or has any special authority, still less that the preferred arrangement has any hermeneutical importance. I still think it probable that there is some truth in the suggestion discussed in the first chapter, that the overall arrangement of many manuscripts of the LXX is meant to have an eschatological orientation: past history followed by present experience followed by future hope. But even this arrangement is by no means universal. It is the order of the Codex Vaticanus, whence modern printed Greek Bibles derive it. But both Sinaiticus and Alexandrinus place the prophetic books in the middle, between the histories and the poetical or didactic books – in this respect following an order which is closer to the Hebrew canon as we now know it. For Christian communites that used these codices or their descendants, the 'message' that we extracted from the arrangement of the LXX was simply not available, since they knew no Bible arranged in such a way as to make it plausible.

The 'order' of the books in Scripture turns out, then, to be of small importance. Once an order is fixed and agreed on, all sorts of theological ideas can be read into it; but these are rationalizing explanations of something which in fact arose in large measure by accident rather than design. In New Testament times there is very little evidence that 'order' was an issue at all, except in the most obvious, chronological sense in which, for example, Joshua is 'before' Judges. There is no clear evidence of lists before Josephus, and no list can have had much effect on the way the Scriptures were understood before the use of codices became usual.

V

In many respects the overall effect of this chapter is likely to seem negative to anyone who starts with a fairly traditional understanding of the history and development of the canon. Instead of a clear tripartite canon, with all the books in the order we are familiar with, and grades of authority appropriately assigned to each, Judaism in the New Testament period has here appeared relatively chaotic in its approach to the Scriptures. We have seen that no one had any doubts about the antiquity or compass of the Pentateuch; but for the rest, Sundberg's 'wide religious literature without definite bounds' has proved to be, if anything, an understatement. There was 'Scripture', but no canon; books other than the Torah were neither grouped together nor listed in any particular way, except for some specific purpose, apologetic or mnemonic; and almost any book could be referred to as the work of a 'prophet'. Sundberg's proposal that only Law and Prophets were fixed by the end of the first century AD, with the Writings still fluid – which seemed to many to be radical enough – does not go nearly as far as this. The reality is that only the Law was 'closed' in our period; the other divisions did not exist as such at all.

On the other hand, the picture presented here is in some other

91

respects more conservative than the conclusions of much recent scholarship, though in a way which will probably also appear negative rather than positive. I have been concerned to argue that the 'canon' was open for far longer than is generally supposed, indeed that 'canon' is a quite misleading term to use of Old Testament Scripture until well into the Christian era; but at the same time I have found little reason to support the common opinion that the status of some books which are now in the canon was disputed in our period. On the contrary, it seems to me most unlikely that anyone in the New Testament age had any doubts about the inspiration and authority even of such books as the Song of Songs or Ecclesiastes. The debates about these books which have traditionally been cited as throwing doubt on their 'canonicity' had quite different questions in mind, questions to do with the *character* of the information conveyed by such books rather than their scriptural *status*. So far from wanting to argue that the 'canon' was smaller than tradition has made it, it seems to me that the body of texts widely regarded as 'Scripture' in our period was probably a lot larger than the present limits of even the Greek canon allow. People were only too willing to accept the claims of ostensibly ancient books. Most of the books now in the Prophets and the Writings probably seemed to most to be of immemorial antiquity, and to have disputed their claims would have seemed mere folly.

To say this, however, is unlikely to appear a very positive contribution to the discussion of the canon. It is no great tribute to the books that Jews and Christians agree in accepting as canonical to say that they already had an undisputed status in the New Testament period, if at the same time we say that they shared this status with a great many more works which both communities were later to reject as dross. To put it bluntly, the value of saying that Isaiah was authoritative for the New Testament writers may seem to be considerably reduced, if we mean that it fully shared the authority of 1 Enoch! In arguing along these lines I may seem to be taking away with one hand what I have just given with the other.

The question whether these conclusions are or are not palatable from a religious point of view is not one I intend to go into here. But it seems to me that, at least from a historical standpoint, they are not at all negative in their implications, but open a number of doors which can lead to a more subtle and illuminating presentation of the perception of ancient 'prophecy' in our period. Some of this has been suggested already in the concluding parts of sections II and III, but it is worth risking a little repetition to make it as clear as possible.

The conclusion of the second section of this chapter was that in our period Scripture was bipartite rather than tripartite. This hardly sounds like a conclusion worth spending much ink on, when it is stated as baldly as that: does it really matter how many parts Scripture was divided into? The substance of the matter, however, is of considerable importance. The normal view of the 'canon' is that it had once consisted of only one element, the Law; then the Prophets were added; then, in New Testament times, the third division gradually formed. But, in the consensus view as it is usually presented, one misses any sense that there was any radical difference between one division and another: it is as though Scripture were like an old house, to which new wings were gradually added. The model I am suggesting is quite different from this. It seems to me that in an important sense the Torah was, and had been for a long time, the only corpus of material that was 'Scripture' in the fullest sense, the only set of documents on which the character and integrity of Judaism crucially depended; and in saying that other scriptures formed only one category rather than two my primary concern is to argue that all other holy books, of whatever precise kind, were equal in being of secondary rank by comparison with the Torah.

Within the corpus of such books, which might vary greatly in its compass according to the scrolls that a particular local community had managed to collect, there were no significant differences of rank. Some of these secondary books were in fact very old, others were quite new, but for those who valued them they all seemed ancient and venerable. On the other hand, they did not belong in the same class as the Torah at all. Whereas all Jews would cite the Torah and regard it as binding upon them in matters of halakah, the use made of these other books depended a good deal on the particular interests of one group or another. Philo, for example, and most of the authorities cited in the Mishnah, hardly take any interest in the second-rank books except for the Proverbs and the Psalms, which seem from the New Testament evidence too to have enjoyed widespread currency – perhaps because at least some of them were familiar from the synagogue liturgy in a way that most of the others were not. Groups who were especially interested in abstract theology, cosmology, and divine mysteries tended to gravitate towards certain books that seemed specially suited to their purposes, which included Ezekiel but also a number of books since excluded from the canon and dubbed 'pseudepigraphical'. Some people with these interests thought that the average man should not be exposed too much to books of this kind, and from time to time proposals were made that the public reading and even the private study of this potentially dangerous literature should be curbed. All this second-order literature, I have suggested, tended to be called 'prophets', and it was generally assumed that its authors lived long ago, in a period which some historians (such as Josephus) were prepared to give precise limits for, but which the ordinary person thought of simply as 'ancient times' – the times unlike today when God communicated directly with 'prophets' and revealed to them information which they could not otherwise have known. Moses indeed was the first such 'prophet', and the Torah was the supreme and unparalleled case of such revelation; the later works partook in some measure of the same sanctity. But they were not felt to form a definite or closed collection among themselves. There could not be a third 'division' of the canon, because there was not yet a second one: many holy, ancient, inspired works jostled for the attention of the pious reader, who believed that all such prophecies from the hallowed past were sacred and important, but had as yet no sense that they formed an ordered, coherent canon with a binding authority of the same sort as that exercised by the Torah.

The 'ancient prophecy' of the present book's subtitle, then, has a wider scope than might be expected by a reader who approaches it with the normal modern understanding that certain books in the Old Testament are 'prophets' while others are not – whether because they fall in a different part of the canon; or because they are not 'predictive'; or because they have been assigned by modern scholarship to a different category ('wisdom' or 'apocalyptic', for instance); or because they do not seem 'prophetic' in the sense that term bears in the Church today. Whatever the religious or intellectual background of the modern reader, he is unlikely to expect a book on prophecy in ancient Israel to concern itself with the whole Old Testament minus only the Pentateuch. Of course I have no wish to suggest that we *ought* to regard all this material as prophecy, or that it is 'really' prophecy. The various kinds of distinction between different books in the Old Testament which have been noted within Judaism, in Christian ways of ordering the canon, and by modern scholars with an eye for differences of genre within Scripture are all, in their different ways, real distinctions. But for the purposes of our present inquiry it is necessary to think ourselves back into the mentality of those for whom these distinctions had not yet been drawn: of those who could speak like St Paul, of 'the prophets in the holy scriptures' (Romans 1:2), or who could say in a vague, summarizing way, that 'God spoke of old to our fathers by the prophets' (Hebrews 1:1) and then go on to quote verses from the prophets, the psalms, the Pentateuch even, without any sense of incongruity.

To some small extent it is possible, if my contentions so far have been correct, to work out how 'the prophets' must have been read and understood in our period merely by thus blacking out our own critical and historical sense, and asking (for example) what meaning would be conveyed by Isaiah, Daniel, Jonah, and Jubilees to someone who thought of them all as the same kind of thing. This kind of historical (or rather, non-historical!) imagination will take us some way, and without it we shall certainly make no progress. Some help can be obtained in this by reading fundamentalist commentators, who often retain to a remarkable degree the kinds of perception of 'ancient prophecy' that characterized writers of the New Testament period; though care is needed here, for modern people who think in these ways adopt them polemically, and also have usually a very high sense of the unity of the present canon of Scripture – neither of which is true of their predecessors in the ancient world, whose 'fundamentalism' was of a more naive (because pre-, not post-critical) kind. But clearly the dangers of subjectivism are very great in proceeding as it were from first principles. Primarily we need to examine the views of prophecy either actively promoted or tacitly assumed by writers of our period, and I have already (in the Introduction) given some indications of who these are.

3

Prophets and their Message

Without prophets, there would have been no Scriptures: on that Josephus and most of his contemporaries were agreed. But what were these prophets like? Though their words came from God himself, they were more than mere copy-typists, their inspiration affected the kind of people they were in every way; and they did other things besides writing holy books. In this chapter we shall canvass the opinions of the varied witnesses in our period, and try to discover how different groups saw the ancient prophets whose writings were held in so much reverence. Who were they; what did they do; what did they have to say to the people of their own time? And when they received the inspiration to write their books, what kind of information were they being commissioned to convey, and whom was it supposed to benefit?

I

If 'prophets' wrote all the books in Scripture, not only those we now tend to think of as 'prophetic', then the definition of 'prophets' must have been vaguer than one might have expected. In the New Testament 'prophet' seems quite often to be not much more than an honorific, like 'saint' in later Christian usage. This is specially marked in the Lucan writings. When Jesus in Luke 13:28 says that those who try to enter the narrow door after the householder has locked it will 'see Abraham and Isaac and Jacob and all the prophets in the kingdom of God' but themselves 'thrust out', we are to understand 'prophets' to mean all the great figures of Israel's history.[1] Elsewhere in Luke and Acts we find a way of thinking about prophets which is not unlike modern uses of the term to mean people who make an impact on their contemporaries, and who are

96

God's envoys – so that in accepting or rejecting them people are accepting or rejecting God himself. See, for example, Luke 11:49: 'Therefore the Wisdom of God said, "I will send them prophets and apostles, some of whom they will kill and persecute", that the blood of all the prophets, shed from the foundation of the world, may be required of this generation, from the blood of Abel to the blood of Zechariah' – Abel, since he was a righteous man, is evidently also a prophet. (Matthew has 'all the righteous blood shed on earth' (23:35), though in the rest of the passage there are the same references to prophets as in Luke.)

A vague, honorific use of 'prophet' is also found in Luke 10:24 ('Many prophets and kings desired to see what you see, and did not see it') where the collocation with 'kings' presumably means that the two terms are being used to cover all the great men of the past; the Matthaean parallel (13:17) has 'prophets and righteous men' – though the association of prophets with hidden mysteries should be noted in passing, since it is a theme that will greatly concern us later.

Plenty of other New Testament examples share this usage, however. In John 8:52 'Abraham died, as did the prophets' seems to mean 'Abraham and everyone of that sort', that is, all the people with whom it is presumptuous of Jesus to compare himself; and in 7:52 'no prophet is to rise from Galilee' perhaps means 'no one of any consequence'. The list in Hebrews 11:32–8 speaks of Gideon, Barak, Samson, Jephthah, David, Samuel, 'and the prophets', treating all alike as heroes of the faith;[2] and in James 5:10 the prophets, though identified as those 'who spoke in the name of the Lord', are important not primarily for their words but for their 'suffering and patience', and it is not surprising to find Job among their number. The prophets as those who suffered through persecution, and who can therefore serve as an example to Christians in similar straits, make an appearance in Matthew 5:12 ('so men persecuted the prophets who were before you') and 1 Thessalonians 2:15 (the Jews 'killed both the Lord Jesus and the prophets'), as also in Stephen's speech (Acts 7:52) 'Which of the prophets did not your fathers persecute?'. Revelation continues to be interested in the prophets as heroes, especially suffering heroes: 'men have shed the blood of saints and prophets' (16:6); 'in her [sc. Babylon] was found the blood of prophets and of saints and of all

97

who have been slain on earth' (18:24); 'rejoice over her, O heaven, O saints and apostles and prophets!' (18:20).[3]

There is no great difficulty in seeing why the New Testament should on occasion use the designation 'prophet' for one of the great figures of the past, especially one of those who suffered or died for the sake of his commitment to the God of Israel (what the Church would later have called either a martyr or a confessor, in fact), regardless of whether the Old Testament formally designated him by one of the terms rendered *prophêtês* in the Greek Bible. There is plenty of evidence, after all, that *Jesus* was described as a prophet in much early Christian thought; and to a great extent the image of the prophets of old was adjusted to bring them into line with the one whom, in the eyes of Christians, they had prefigured. Luke, who seems to use 'prophet' in the present sense more than most, is also our primary witness to a 'prophet' Christology, if that is not too anachronistic a term. The saying 'it cannot be that a prophet should perish away from Jerusalem' (Luke 13:33) is peculiar to Luke; the disciples on the road to Emmaus describe Jesus as 'a prophet mighty in deed and word before God and all the people' (24:19) who was condemned and executed through the malice of 'chief priests and rulers'; and Peter, in Acts 3:17–26, presents him as the 'prophet like Moses', whom the Jews have been given the first chance of receiving but who, as Acts goes on to make clear, was on the whole rejected by his own people just as, according to Stephen, they had rejected Moses himself and all his prophetic successors (Acts 7:23–53).

It may well be the Christian assimilation of the Old Testament prophets to Jesus which produces the idea that the prophets are examples to be imitated. We shall go on to see plenty of evidence that in Judaism the prophets were revered as great teachers, but it is less often suggested that their *lives* are meant as a paradigm for later generations. In early Christianity, however, this is frequently the case, as may be seen from the passages just cited about the suffering of the prophets. This theme comes into its own in the Apostolic Fathers: thus 1 Clement 17:1 encourages its readers to 'be imitators [*mimêtai*]' of the prophets; cf. also Ignatius, *Magnesians* 8–9.[4] For Tertullian, the deeds of the prophets are valuable as a reminder of the power of prayer:[5] thus he cites the way in which Daniel's prayer was efficacious in causing another prophet, Habakkuk, to be transported to Babylon complete with his freshly-cooked dinner for Daniel to eat in the lions' den (Bel and the Dragon 33).

In general it is fair to say that Christians seem to have been interested in the prophets as *people*, in what they did and suffered in the name of God, rather than as the names of books or as rather featureless recipients of oracles – a tendency shared with Josephus and Philo. This produces some surprising judgements on who are the 'major' prophets. Habakkuk, to us a shadowy figure, was evidently a focus of some interest, not only for his exploits in airlifting food to the *golah*, but also as a hero of the faith who will appear with Christ in glory at the Second Coming: see Sibylline Oracle 2, lines 245–51, where he and Jonah are the only two of the writing prophets to be accorded this privilege. We know, of course, from the evidence of Qumran that Habakkuk's book was a focus of much interest around the turn of the era. Daniel, too, enjoyed a much higher status than he now has in mainstream Judaism or Christianity; as with Habakkuk and Jonah, this may reflect the fact that there were more stories about him in Scripture than about some other prophets, many of whom were little more than names.

In all these cases a prophet is an idealized hero around whom hagiographical legends are likely to cluster. This process was clearly already far advanced in earlier post-exilic literature. The prophet Zechariah, who perished for denouncing the idolatry of the reign of Joash and so served as an example of the sufferings of true prophets, is already presented as a noble martyr by the Chronicler (2 Chronicles 24:20–2), and indeed the ultimate model for this picture of the prophets is probably Jeremiah himself, in whose book the theme of the outcast, despised prophet is already thoroughly elaborated.[6] In the second century BC the sufferings of the righteous are epitomized in the three young men in the burning fiery furnace (Daniel 3), whom later tradition was to regard as prophets.[7] That prophets suffered for the sake of their divinely-given task was no invention of the Christian church or indeed of any other group in our period: the idea was firmly grounded in scriptures that were genuinely ancient. Elijah and even Moses had suffered because of their calling.

On the other hand, the tradition persisted that prophets had been men of power, with the ability to work wonders: there is of course plenty of biblical material about this, in the stories of Moses, Elijah, and Isaiah. The New Testament does not offer many examples of wonder-working as a sign of prophetic office, though it is interesting that the one reference in Mark to Jesus as a prophet associates the idea with his ability to work miracles: thus in Mark 6:14–16, where the power which goes forth from Jesus to enable even his disciples to heal the sick and cast out demons leads to the popular surmise that he is 'a prophet, like one of the prophets of old' (cf. Luke 9:7–9; in the Matthaean parallel (Matthew 14:1–5) too 'the people held him to be a prophet'). One of the few other New Testament references to this aspect of prophecy, Revelation 11:4–13, builds on the destructive power of prophecy: the two witnesses 'have power to shut the sky, that no rain may fall during the days of their prophesying', making them 'a torment to those who dwell on the earth'. Once again, there is probably some mutual influence between the biblical picture of prophecy and the exploits of contemporary prophets. Those who were believed to work miracles were described as prophets because there were plenty of prophets who did so in Scripture; on the other hand a knowledge of Scripture will have led people to expect that anyone who 'prophesied' in any sense should also be a wonder-worker. Salient examples of 'modern' prophets who validated their proclamation by working wonders are Theudas, who claimed the power to part the waters of the Jordan (Josephus, *Antiquities* 20:97–9) and 'the Egyptian', who said that he knew how to make the walls of Jerusalem collapse (ibid., 20:168–72; *Jewish War* 2:261–3).[8] It is not easy to say in which direction the influence chiefly worked – a difficulty which we shall often meet, and must be content to leave largely unresolved.

One Jewish writer for whom the historical activities of the prophets are as important as their message is Ben Sira, and in his work we accordingly find miracle-working high on the list of prophetic accomplishments. In Ecclesiasticus 48:1–14 Elijah and Elisha are prominent examples of this manifestation of prophetic powers. Elijah 'shut up the heavens, and three times brought down fire'; he 'raised a corpse from death', and 'brought kings down to destruction, and famous men from their beds'. How far wonder-working is the prophetic activity *par excellence* may be seen even more from Ben Sira's comments on Elisha: 'Nothing was too hard for him, and when he was dead his body prophesied. As in his life he did wonders, so in death his deeds were marvellous'. Here the miracle by which the dead man buried in Elisha's grave was revived when his corpse touched the prophet's bones (2 Kings 13:21) is in itself a 'prophecy', that is, an act of prophetic power.[9]

The same tendency can be seen in Ben Sira's assessment of Isaiah. For the modern critical reader Isaiah's miracles are usually seen as excrescences of the kind which hagiography naturally draws out of any tradition about great religious figures, and they tell us nothing about the real man: but for Ben Sira they are the thing that makes Isaiah so great, distinguishing him even from the other major prophets Jeremiah and Ezekiel, who receive less attention. Isaiah (Ecclesiasticus 48:20–5) was instrumental in having God smite the Assyrians, but (better still) 'in his days the sun went backward, and he lengthened the life of the king'. In this he was like that other great prophet, Joshua, who 'was the successor of Moses in prophesying' (Ecclesiasticus 46:1–6),[10] by whose hand 'the sun was held back, and did not one day become as long as two?' Joshua was not simply an 'inspired' leader in the sense that he fought valiantly but in the more literal sense that he had a special power to prevail with God: 'He called upon the Most High, the Mighty One, when enemies pressed him on every side, and the great Lord answered him with hailstones of mighty power . . . so that the nations might know . . . that he was fighting in the might of the Lord.' These meteorological skills certainly gave the prophets an advantage over their more pedestrian opponents, and we are not greatly surprised to find that they were among the distinctively prophetic endowments of Samuel, too: 'when his enemies pressed him on every side, he offered in sacrifice a sucking lamb; then the Lord thundered from heaven, and made his voice heard with a mighty sound' (Ecclesiasticus 46:16–17, cf. 1 Samuel 6:9–10).

All of these miracles were already in the tradition, and Ben Sira read of them in Scripture; but the importance he gives them, sometimes to the neglect of what we think of as the more important aspects of the prophets' work, justifies Hengel's comment: 'What marked out the wise men and prophets of Israel's earlier history were their "heroic" personalities, which manifested themselves above all in their astonishing miracles.'[11] Stadelmann is probably right to stress that the prophets are not *mere* wonder-workers for Ben Sira; their miracles prove their divine vocation, and hence give added force to their calls to repentance. Thus, after the reference to Elisha's posthumous miracle, he immediately adds (48:15) 'for all this, the people did not repent'.[12] It is also true, of course, that the form which Ben Sira is using, the *laus patrum*, naturally requires deeds rather than words to be recounted. Nonetheless the space devoted to the prophets' miracles speaks for itself: these were what marked them out as God's chosen ones.

II

For all the variety in detail, all the perceptions of prophecy discussed so far manifestly share a sense that prophets are people who are out of the ordinary because they have a special relationship with God. For most writers in our period it seems that the evidence of this special relationship was to be found in heroic or superhuman experiences, abilities, and tasks. They certainly did not share the modern belief that 'true' prophets need neither miracles nor supernatural knowledge to achieve their mission; on the contrary, it was simply taken for granted that a prophet would be able to do things impossible to normal people. One gift which a prophet's intimate relationship with God conferred on him was the power of effective intercession. He could carry messages from the human realm into the divine with the assurance of being heard.

This prophetic power is widely attested in the Old Testament itself: for example, it is because he is a *prophet* that Abraham can intercede for Abimelech (Genesis 20:7); Hezekiah asks Isaiah to pray for his deliverance from the Assyrians (2 Kings 19:4); and Jeremiah can convey the extreme sinfulness of Israel by saying that even the prayer of Moses or Samuel would not be able to turn God's heart towards them (Jeremiah 15:1). This seems to be the tradition the author of 4 Ezra has in mind when he lists the great intercessors of Israel's past: Abraham, Moses, Joshua, Samuel, David, Solomon, Elijah, and (rather surprisingly) Hezekiah (4 Ezra 7:36–40 (106–10)) – pronouncing that on the day of judgement the power of intercession will cease.[13] The heroes of the pseudo-prophetic books written in our period[14] are generally skilled in intercession. This is true of Daniel (Daniel 9), Judith (Judith 9), Tobit (Tobit 3), and Esther (Esther 13:8, Greek); Mordecai also prays for the Jews in the Greek Esther (13:8–17), and his credentials as a prophet are made clear in the vision of 11:2–12. 1 Enoch 89:61–5 appears to imply that the prophets of Israel had the function of acting as scribes who recorded all that the Gentiles had done to the detriment of Israel, so that they could then (as God's remembrancers) read it out to him and so induce him to punish them for these sins, and to vindicate his own people.[15] Enoch himself intercedes for the Watchers who sin with the daughters of men (1 Enoch 13:4–7), and in much the same way, by writing out their petition for forgiveness and reading it out before God.

But much more important than this is the prophets' ability to function as a channel for communications to pass in the opposite direction, from God to man. The prophet, in fact, is a spokesman for God: compare Philo's description of Moses (*quod deterius* 39–40) as the spokesman of God, using Aaron as his own 'mouth', 'spokesman', and 'prophet'. Philo explains that the relation of the prophet to God is like that of utterance to thought: 'Speech is the spokesman and prophet (*prophêtês kai theopropos*) of the oracles which the understanding never ceases to utter from depths unseen and unapproachable.' This semi-philosophical explanation is of course peculiar to Philo, but it catches an idea which most Jews of his day shared, that God's intentions and directives cannot be known to mankind without a human channel of communication, and it is this that prophets provide. Just as sin can lead God to suspend the prophetic function of intercession (cf. Jeremiah 7:16), so too it can make him decide not to reveal himself through the prophets. When God was angry with Israel, says the Mekhilta on Exodus 12:1, he did not speak to the prophets: thus it was only when the entire generation that had sinned in the wilderness was dead that he spoke to Moses and gave him further instructions, according to Deuteronomy 2:16; 'during all thirty-eight years in which he was angry with Israel, he did not speak with Moses'.

When writers of our period say that all the Scriptures were produced by prophets, it is this emphasis on the prophet as a channel of communication with the divine that they have in mind. To say that Scriptural books are 'prophetic' is not in itself to say anything about their *contents*, as is sometimes wrongly assumed – for example, that they are eschatological predictions; it is first and foremost to say that they come from God, and were not devised by the wit of man. To use the traditional terms of Christian theology, it is to say that what is in the books of Scripture is *revealed* truth, not truths of natural theology, still less merely human opinions. As we shall see, this emphasis on the revealed character of the contents of prophetic books easily leads to an assumption that they will be esoteric in much of the information they convey. But this is not implied automatically in calling the authors 'prophets', however natural a step it may be from that. What it does tend to imply is that the prophetic author himself played little part in composing the book, so that something approaching a 'dictation' theory of scriptural inspiration is often found. Much has been written about the blurring of distinctions between prophet, scribe, and wise man in late post-exilic literature, but however this may be described or accounted for, it is not hard to see that once a dictation theory gains a hold, the prophet becomes something very like a scribe in the divine court, taking down God's words to deliver them to his people – or else to seal them up for delivery to the chosen ones who will be able to appreciate them.

Thus Enoch is commissioned, in 1 Enoch 12, in a way very reminiscent of the Old Testament prophets, to go and proclaim God's judgement to the Watchers; but in doing so he acts as a scribe ('scribe of righteousness'), sent from his employer with a kind of memorandum for members of the divine hierarchy. On reflection, this may not differ so much from the normal Old Testament picture of a prophet as it seems to do; for in acting as *envoys* (the metaphor usually supposed to underlie the use of the 'messenger-formula' 'Thus says the LORD') the prophets are carrying out a task which essentially belonged, in ancient Near Eastern societies, to a senior civil servant, who is not so far from a scribe in the mould of Ezra or Enoch. Sometimes the study of later conceptions of the prophetic role can thus throw gleams of light back on to the earlier reality, however distortedly it was perceived.

There is no tension between the prophet as a spokesman and the prophet as a hero. The two aspects are united by the overarching concept of the person empowered and commissioned and instructed by God: whatever he does or says or writes bears the impress of divine, not human initiative. Indeed, one of the confusing things in the literature which discusses prophets is the failure to distinguish properly between the prophets who *performed* great deeds and the prophets who *chronicled* the deeds of others. Both, we might agree in the light of the foregoing discussion, deserve to be called prophets, but in the interests of clarity they should be kept distinct. It would be helpful, that is, to know whether the books of Samuel are books *by* Samuel or books *about* Samuel. Such material as we have, however, is singularly unhelpful on this sort of point. Josephus, in the passage from *Against Apion* which we have already analysed at such length, confirms the general point that to say Scripture comes from prophets is to say that it comes from God, not from man: but he seems unable to draw the elementary distinction that would enable one to ask, Does this mean that the deeds recorded in it were divinely-inspired, never mind how they came to be written about, or that the written record is divinely guaranteed, never mind how the events recorded came about?

Modern theological discussions of the inspiration of Scripture require this distinction to be kept clearly in mind. There is a great deal of difference between saying, on the one hand, that certain events are crucial for our understanding of God, and that Scripture contains human records which can be examined critically to help us reconstruct those events, and saying, on the other hand, that Scripture is a divinely-authenticated record of all the events it reports, whether those events are in themselves theologically signif-icant or not. One looks in vain for any sense of these distinctions in Josephus. When 'the prophets subsequent to Moses recorded the history of their own times in thirteen books', they were writing a holy history of holy events enacted by holy persons. The 'prophetic age', as we may well call the time from Moses to the death of Artaxerxes (as understood by Josephus) was something like the 'heroic age' of Greece: a time when heroes lived, and heroic tales were written by heroic bards. The books of Samuel are *about* Samuel, for he was a great prophet – that is, a great inspired hero and leader; they are also *by* Samuel, who was a great prophet – that is, he was given divinely-guaranteed information about the past and the future: for Samuel knew in advance what would happen to all the kings of Israel and wrote it out before ever it happened, hiding it in an archive against the day when it should all have come true.[16] There were not many prophetic gifts that were lacking to Samuel, and one cannot think up possible meanings for the term 'prophetic history' faster than Josephus can show that all found their full expression in his deeds, visions, and writings.

III

In the age of the prophets, then, there lived people specially inspired by God to perform great deeds and to write authentic records of them for posterity. Two questions arise at once. Was this prophetic inspiration *confined* to the prophetic age, or could it occur even today?

105

And how was the inspiration actually conveyed to the prophets – what were the mechanics of it, as we might say? This section will deal with the first question.

For Josephus it is evidently important to stress that true prophets lived only between Moses and the death of Artaxerxes. They formed a line of succession with Moses at its head, and the succession was broken off in the Persian period (probably, in effect, coming to an end with the work of Ezra). In this he agrees with a strong tradition that finds its way into rabbinic literature, according to which prophecy ended with the demise of Malachi. The classic statement of this belief is in Tosefta Sotah 13:2: 'When the last prophets, Haggai, Zechariah, and Malachi died, the holy spirit ceased in Israel, though she was allowed to hear the *bath-qol*'. This appears to mean that prophet-like oracles may still occur, but they are not in the same class as the utterances of the spirit through the 'real' prophets of long ago. It has been usual to find traces of this idea within the Old Testament itself. For example, Zechariah 13:2–6 is widely held to show that in the time when the collection of utterances in Zechariah 9–14 was being written, it was believed that true prophecy could no longer occur, and hence that *claims* to prophesy must be spurious. In the days to come, God would do away with all who thus falsely claimed to speak in his name. Similar things might be said of Jeremiah 23:33–40.[17] The demise of prophecy is variously explained, but most commonly it is thought that the decline in the quality of prophetic thought, which since the work of Wellhausen has been commonly regarded as a feature of the post-exilic community, finally reached such a low point that the institution was wholly discredited in the eyes of faithful Jews.

On the other hand, a number of scholars have suggested that the 'dogma'[18] of the demise of prophecy has been exaggerated. If people could describe Theudas and the Egyptian mentioned by Josephus, and also Jesus, as 'prophets' – or even if it could be reasonably thought that they had done so – then it cannot have been a universal assumption that prophecy had ceased.[19] As Leivestad argues, the rabbinic evidence on the subject may not reflect opinion in Second Temple Judaism in any case. Much of the biblical evidence commonly cited is at best ambiguous, and has in the past been somewhat too readily pressed into service. Thus Zechariah 13:2–6 certainly foretells a time when *false* claimants to prophetic inspiration will be rejected, but tells us little as to whether 'true'

106

prophecy had ceased. Legislation about how to deal with false prophets occurs as late as Sanhedrin 89a, presumably implying that a claim to prophecy was not *necessarily* spurious, that is, that true prophets could at least in principle still exist. Again, a number of biblical passages think of a future revival of prophecy, but do not thereby necessarily imply that it has altogether ceased, only that it has declined in quality or become rarer than is desirable: one might read Joel 2:28–9 (Hebrew 3:1–2) in this way, as implying that whereas prophetic gifts are at present limited to a few, in the future they will become the possession of many. Some passages that clearly do speak of the demise of prophecy may not mean to imply that it has gone for good. For example, in the Prayer of Azariah 15 the lament is raised that 'at this time there is no prince, or prophet, or leader, no burnt offering, or sacrifice, or oblation, or incense', but this is plainly a reference to the conditions of the exilic age, and is part of the fiction that this is the period in which Daniel and his friends lived; it says nothing about the demise of prophecy after its reappearance in Haggai and Zechariah.[20]

The evidence of Psalm 74, also frequently cited, does little to support the idea of a definitive end to prophecy in the early post-exilic age. Psalm 74:9 reads 'We do not see our signs; there is no longer any prophet'; but this again refers to a specific situation, probably the exilic period, and one might as well argue from Lamentations 2:6 ('the Lord has brought to an end in Zion appointed feast and sabbath') that the sabbath came to an end for all time.

Only 1 Maccabees offers real support to the theory under discussion. First, in chapter 4:44–7, Judas and his followers tear down the polluted altar and, at a loss to know how to dispose of the stones (which are both holy and defiled), they resolve to store them on the temple hill 'until there should come a prophet to tell what to do with them'. This is generally treated as referring to an 'eschatological' hope for the revival of prophecy in the time of the end.[21] I am not so sure that this is necessarily the case; the passage can be read so, but it can also be read as a realistic interim decision taken on the understanding that a prophetic word might well occur in the not-too-distant future, without implying any particular 'eschatological' framework of expectation. It does show, however, that there were not thought to be any prophets in Jerusalem at the time, so that if prophecy is thought of as a regular institution, rather than as an intermittent phenomenon, one would have to say that

107

it had 'ceased', at least temporarily. Secondly, 1 Maccabees 9:27 uses the phrase 'since the time that prophets ceased to appear among them' as the mark of a period, evidently already thought of as quite long ago: probably, in fact, the reference is to the Exile. This use of such an expression tends to support Josephus's presentation of common Jewish opinion. Thirdly, 1 Maccabees 14:41 reports that Simon was elected leader and high priest 'for ever, until a trust-worthy prophet should arise'. Here it is harder to avoid an 'eschato-logical' interpretation; but in any case it is plainly implied that there are at present no such prophets. Leivestad rightly stresses that this may be a set formula for the remote future (like 'till pigs fly'), but such formulas do not arise from nowhere, and if, as with our formulas of this kind, the event in question is used just because of its extreme improbability, then the prevalence of a belief that prophecy had ceased forever is convincingly demonstrated.

The evidence seems, then, somewhat obscure and difficult to interpret. Some people at various times between the Exile and the age of the Talmud believed that prophecy had ceased, either when the Temple was destroyed in 586, or with the death of the 'last prophet', Malachi. Others remained willing to dub contemporary charismatic preachers and teachers 'prophets'. Hopes for the future sometimes included the revival or the increase of prophecy, and while for some groups this may have formed part of an 'eschatolog-ical' package of beliefs, others may simply have thought that the present lack of prophets was a temporary aberration to be rectified shortly.[22] Is it possible, given this rather vague picture, to say anything about the question of a 'prophetic age' at all?

Perhaps it will be useful to draw three distinctions which do not always seem very clearly observed in the literature (though one at least is noted by Leivestad in his careful discussion). First, we should differentiate quite clearly between the two questions (1) Was prophecy thought, in the New Testament period, to have ceased at some date in the past? and (2) Did prophecy in fact cease at some date earlier than the age of the New Testament? The second of these questions cannot be answered without first defining 'prophecy', but it seems clear to me that *any* definition which is likely to be useful for characterizing the pre-exilic prophets will probably lead to the conclusion that prophecy did not cease, indeed that it never has ceased. The first question, on the other hand, is a question purely about the beliefs of people in our period and about their use of the terms 'prophet' and 'prophecy', and we may find that it should be answered either positively or negatively without that influencing to the smallest extent our own assessment of how far there continued to be what *we* should call prophets in post-exilic times. Failure to observe this distinction sometimes clouds the discussion.

Secondly, when our sources differ in the answer they give to the question of the demise of prophecy, they may not all be using the term 'prophet' in the same way. As I have already indicated, I believe it is sometimes too readily assumed that 1 Maccabees always means by 'a prophet' 'the great Prophet of the end-time', when in fact its usage may sometimes be more casual. But it is also worth noting that whereas some of the passages cited are referring to the great prophets whose books were already highly revered in New Testament times, others mean the sort of official who can be listed alongside priests and political leaders, on the one hand, and cultic institutions such as sacrifices and incense, on the other. The distinction between these two senses is of course still very far from clear to us: much of the continuing debate about the relation of the 'independent' prophets to the 'official' prophets in pre-exilic times testifies to the obscurity of the biblical evidence.[23] But already in the literature of our period it is clear that prophecy as an institution is at least partly distinguished from 'prophets' as great figures intermittently raised up to speak to Israel. Thus 1 Maccabees 14:42, for example, is surely not saying that Simon is to be high priest until the *institution* of temple prophecy (as presented, say, by Chronicles) is restored, but until the coming of a great Prophet. Conversely the Prayer of Azariah, or Psalm 74, do not mean to imply that the Exile deprived Israel of any great spokesmen for God (what about Jeremiah?) but rather that all the sacred institutions, including prophecy, came to an end. Certainly the distinction is not drawn at all neatly, but the texts do surely preserve an awareness that all 'prophets' are not quite the same kind of thing.

Thirdly, as Leivestad well argues, some of the texts are thinking primarily of prophecy as an *activity*, the delivery of oracles by men empowered by God to respond to a particular crisis, while others mean by prophecy a *body of texts*, 'prophetic scriptures'. This distinction is related to, but not identical with, the one just discussed. The rabbinic texts in particular are thinking of prophecy mainly in the second of these senses, as a collection of written documents. The 'holy spirit' by which prophets like Haggai, Zechariah and

109

Malachi prophesied is the spirit that inspires holy Scripture. The 'dogma of the demise of prophecy' is a doctrine about the inspiration of Scripture, closely akin to that in Josephus. It is not primarily designed to be applied to questions about the presence or absence, in a particular period, of people who can give 'oracles' on specific issues that may arise from time to time, but is a theory about the period during which inspired *writings* were produced.[24]

These distinctions may be useful in trying to settle a question which has long been linked with that of the alleged demise of prophecy: the question of the replacement of prophecy by the increasing authority of the Torah as a written Scripture in post-exilic times. That prophecy died out *because* the Law came to carry the divine authority prophecy had once had is widely believed. Indeed, this view is perhaps already propounded by Seder ʿOlam Rabbah 30: 'Until then, the prophets prophesied by means of the holy spirit. From then on, 'Give ear and listen to the words of the sages [*ḥᵃkamim*]' (Proverbs 22:17, probably understood to mean 'listen to interpreters of the Torah').

That the Torah did come to have a status that eliminated the need for fresh prophetic revelation there can be little doubt. A pleasant illustration of the extreme authority of the written Torah is the incident related in Baba Mezia 59b:

On that day R. Eliezer brought forward every imaginable argument, but they did not accept them. He said to them: If the halakhah agrees with me, let this carob-tree prove it! Thereupon the carob-tree was torn a hundred cubits out of its place . . . They replied, No proof can be brought from a carob-tree. Again he said to them: If the halakhah agrees with me, let the stream of water prove it. Whereupon the stream of water flowed backwards. They replied, No proof can be brought from a stream of water. Again he said: If the halakhah agrees with me, let the walls of the schoolhouse prove it! Whereupon the walls inclined to fall. But R. Joshua rebuked them, saying: When scholars are engaged in a dispute about halakhah, what have ye to interfere? Hence they did not fall, in honour of R. Joshua, nor did they resume the upright, in honour of R. Eliezer; and they are still standing thus inclined. Again he said to them: If the halakhah agrees with me, let it be proved from heaven! Whereupon a heavenly voice cried out, Why do ye dispute with R. Eliezer, seeing that in all

110

> matters the halakhah agrees with him? But R. Joshua arose and exclaimed 'It is not in heaven' [Deut. 30:12]. What did he mean by this? – R. Jeremiah said: That the Torah had already been given at Mount Sinai; we pay no attention to a heavenly voice, because thou hast long written in the Torah at Mount Sinai, 'After the majority must one incline' [Exod. 23:3].

In this story the principle of majority decision on matters of halakah, being enshrined in the written Torah, cannot yield even to apparently fresh revelations through a *bath-qol*. The revelation to the prophets is of course, in the talmudic view, superior to pronouncements of a *bath-qol*, but for all that, the principle that written Law prevails over inspired utterance seems to be well established. It is very natural to say, therefore, that prophecy died out, or at least was believed to have done so, precisely *because* the written Law acquired the authoritative status implied in passages such as this.

In recent years the implied contrast between the living voice of prophecy and the fixed and unalterable Law has lain at the root of influential theories about the growth of 'apocalyptic'. In the theory of Otto Plöger,[25] and still more in the work of Paul Hanson,[26] the contrast becomes the basis for understanding the sociology of Israel in the Second Temple period, seen as a polarized society in which eschatological expectation on the part of the successors of the prophets (apocalyptists) confronted a conservative attachment to a fixed code on the part of priests and other religious leaders, who wished to rule out any innovation or change even by the hand of God.

It is important to see, however, exactly what is being asserted in claiming that prophecy declined and was replaced by apocalyptic. When Wellhausen (from whom the idea essentially derives) said that the voice of prophecy was silenced by the growing prestige of the Law, he was not thinking primarily of the suppression of one *institution* by another, so much as expressing a theological evaluation of a change in Israel's understanding of its relationship with God. Instead of expecting to hear the voice of the living God, post-exilic Israel (so he believed) tied itself to a system of supposedly divine ordinance which ensured that nothing new could ever again be said or thought. If God had wished to communicate with his people, they would not have been able to hear him, since they had adopted a theory according to which there could never be any fresh revelation.

111

Figures like the great pre-exilic prophets could not have gained a hearing, even if they had appeared: in that sense, prophecy had ceased. This was not a theory about the demise of an institution, but a judgement about the spiritual quality of life in post-exilic times, for Wellhausen of course knew that there continued to be functionaries called 'prophets', as Chronicles shows.

For the line of thought which runs from Plöger to Hanson, prophecy as an institution was drained of its meaning by the dominant party in post-exilic times, those who wanted a secure theocratic state with no interference from charismatic figures trying to undermine the status quo. But because in every age and society there are non-establishment figures who will not be silenced, post-exilic Israel also had its radicals, who followed in the steps of the prophets but who changed prophecy into the new form that is now known as apocalyptic. This was a movement threatening to upset the kind of society that those who lived by the written Torah wanted to see established in perpetuity. Consequently it could not be admitted into the mainstream of Jewish life in the Second Temple period but remained always on the fringes, in much the same way as eschatological sects in modern times have been minority groups on the fringe of large-scale organized religion. Thus prophecy and its descendant, apocalyptic, moved out of the centre of Jewish life, and the writings produced by apocalyptists were not admitted into the canon of Scripture that derived from the dominant, theocratic establishment.

On one level Hanson's work, to which we shall return, represents a reaction against Wellhausen. Whereas for Wellhausen post-exilic religion was on the whole A Bad Thing, because it lacked the spontaneity of those creative geniuses, the pre-exilic prophets, for Hanson the badness is mitigated by the presence of minority groups who stood out against the religious establishment which had thus suppressed the Spirit. At least in small sects, the spirit of prophecy lived on, to protest against the petrification of tradition by scribes and priests. In another way, however, the underlying assumptions are essentially the same as Wellhausen's. Hanson's evaluation of what is good and bad in religion are very much the same; he differs simply in thinking that, as a matter of fact, 'good' spontaneous religion was not *totally* submerged beneath 'bad' institutional religion. The terms of reference remain substantially unchanged.

Thus one of the most influential modern assessments of the

relation of law and prophecy in post-exilic Judaism continues in essence to follow the traditional interpretation: *real* prophecy died out because the Law was promoted as a final revelation, beyond which nothing fresh could ever be revealed. Those who gave the Law its enhanced status gave the name 'prophecy' to aspects of the Temple liturgy, and so the real thing, when it spasmodically re-emerged, had to dress itself in new clothes: hence the 'apocalyptic' movement. The saying 'from then on, give ear and listen to the words of the sages'[27] sums up the attitude of the theocratic, Torah-centred party: prophecy has ceased, the Law is now the true source of enlightenment.

Many scholars have questioned aspects of the theories of Hanson and his followers, and we shall return to some of these in due course, especially as they bear on categories such as 'apocalyptic' and 'eschatology'. But for the moment, I shall confine myself to asking whether there may not be some confusion here about one of the distinctions discussed above. For what kind of information did people in pre- or post-exilic times turn to law or to prophecy? Hanson seems to assume that both covered all the aspects of life about which people might have questions, so that there was necessarily competition between them. But is this so? We have seen a number of contrasts already between Torah and prophecy which suggest a difference of role rather than a mutually exclusive claim. Thus, for example, there were certainly those in New Testament times for whom 'prophetic' books revealed arcane mysteries, whereas the Torah gave instruction on how to live. In this contrast the two sources of divine knowledge are meant for different kinds of reader (initiates on the one hand, ordinary Israelites on the other) and deal with different topics (secrets of cosmology and rules for conduct, respectively), but there is no suggestion of a conflict between them – indeed there is no common ground on which they can meet and clash.

Again, when the Maccabees postpone a decision on the polluted altarstones pending the arrival of a prophet, this is because they need a specific ruling on an unprecedented question. In later times, it may be, the doctrine arose that any question, however new, could be settled by an application of the proper hermeneutical rules to the Torah, but there is no evidence that people thought this in the Maccabean period. A prophet was needed, and the lack of one regretted, because prophets can impart *new* truth, whereas the Law, being fixed, cannot. There is no suspicion here that the Maccabees would have looked for a prophet to tell them how to live as observant Jews – they are not presented as wanting a prophet because they rejected the authority of the Law. Equally, there is no hint that their evident attachment to the Law meant that they regarded the raising up of a prophet to give fresh instructions on a doubtful matter as inherently impossible. The supposed contradictions between law-centred piety and belief in fresh revelation through prophets is surely a fiction – one of the less happy of Wellhausen's ideas, which has been artificially given a new lease of life when other ideas of his (often better ones) are widely rejected. There may of course have been *some* whose attachment to the written Torah was so great that it led them to think no prophet could ever exist again, but we have no clear evidence of this. On the whole it seems that acceptance of the Torah as the final authoritative guide in matter of halakah was entirely compatible with the belief that God could still, from time to time, speak through prophets. Oracles and halakoth are simply two different kinds of utterance, appropriate to solving different questions in different kinds of circumstances.

To my mind, therefore, it is very unlikely that the belief that prophets had ceased has much to do with the increased authority of the Torah in post-exilic Judaism. After all, most people thought in any case that the prophets of old had known the Torah: our sense that the great 'independent' prophets of the pre-exilic age had been unacquainted with the 'priestly' parts of the Pentateuch was entirely unknown to them, for they had not read Wellhausen. (On this point my own belief is that Wellhausen was completely right, but he was discovering a truth that had already been lost by the Persian period.) *We* see all kinds of tensions between 'prophecy' and 'law', because we know that the great classical prophets did not appeal to a written code; but, as should by now be clear, the perception of 'prophecy' that prevailed in Second Temple Judaism did not see these tensions at all. Prophets were the authorized successors of Moses; obviously they were not opposed to the law of Moses. I think it highly unlikely that any movement, whether we call it 'prophetic' or 'apocalyptic', could have taken as one of its ground assumptions a rejection of the Pentateuch as the ultimate authority in matters of conduct, for to have done so it would have had to know that the Pentateuch was not Mosaic and that the great prophets had not accepted its authority – surely a truth that was

114

unknowable in ancient times. And conversely, any theory of the actual or supposed demise of prophecy which thus links it to an antiprophetic promotion of the Law seems to me equally anachronistic.

As we have already seen, when we do encounter the doctrine that prophecy has ceased it does not mean that there is no longer anything at all that can be called 'prophecy', but rather that there are no longer 'great' prophets like those of old. Even for the rabbis, oracles still occur, but they are utterances of the *bath-qol*, not directly of the holy spirit which spoke to the prophets in times past. As we might put this in everyday English, there are still prophets with a small 'p' but no longer prophets with a capital 'P'. I cannot see that this has any logical connection at all with the establishment of the Torah as central to Judaism. Rather, it is part of the very same process to which the Torah also owes its own status: the increasing veneration of the past to the detriment of the present.[28] The 'old' prophets are revered above 'modern' ones for the *same* reason that the laws given by Moses are revered above the rulings of contemporary lawyers: because they are ancient. So far from there being a tension between the perceptions of prophecy and of Torah in post-exilic times, both are subject to exactly the same pressures. Old laws are better than new, old prophets are better than new. 'Who is left among you that saw this house in its former glory, and how do you see it now? Is it not in your sight as nothing?' (Haggai 2:3). Post-exilic Judaism felt about law and prophecy just as it felt about the Temple, or as Jacob felt about human life in general: 'few and evil have been the days of the years of my life, and they have not attained to the days of the years of the life of my fathers in the days of their sojourning' (Genesis 47:9). Nostalgia, not theocracy, was the death of prophecy.

All this confirms the suggestion made in connection with Josephus's theory about scriptural inspiration: that there was no prophetic *canon*, but there was a prophetic *age*. No one had any difficulty in believing that a previously unknown book could be inspired, provided it was old enough. Similarly, there might well have been inspired prophets who did not appear in any known list, but they would need to have lived well in the past. Contemporaries could conceivably receive divine revelations, but that would take more believing, and it was generally unsafe to suppose it. The very passage which gives us our classic formula for the demise of

115

prophecy, Tosefta Sotah 13:2, goes on to report an oracle given by a *bath-qol* which said that Hillel was worthy to have been a prophet, had his generation been worthy to be granted one. Nothing could better sum up the ambiguities and uncertainties which faced people who received what seemed like divine revelations in an age that deeply distrusted itself by comparison with the hallowed past.

There is no need, then, either to embrace a dogmatic theory ourselves about the demise of prophecy, or to suppose that all writers in our period did so. On the whole it was probably agreed that the really great prophets had lived in the past, and Josephus's definition of the lower limit of the 'prophetic age' represents roughly what most people would have had in mind: not long after the Exile, or at the latest not long after the rebuilding of the Temple and the work of Ezra (whenever that was). This did not mean that there could never again be prophets. Many people hoped for a great revival or extension of prophecy in the future, possibly as part of a whole set of 'eschatological' hopes, and others may have thought more vaguely that prophets arose from time to time, and that there just happened not to be any at the moment but there would be again in due course. The kind of prophets who wrote holy books, however, were most likely regarded as a rarer breed, and in that sense contemporaries could not be prophets; at least, no one seems to have risked claiming to be one until the author of Revelation. All Jewish prophecies in *writing* are fathered on someone living in the real prophetic period. There is no hope, of course, of our being able to say that such views were universal, or that there may not have been groups who took a radically different line. In particular, the early Christians' readiness to accept contemporaries as 'prophets' may represent a really new departure, though it may have parallels for which we happen now to lack evidence. But as a rough generalization it is safe to say that prophecy was widely believed to be a thing of the past; and all the more revered for that.

IV

How did the ancient prophets acquire the knowledge which they passed on in their writings? Prophetic inspiration often seems to be rather vaguely understood. The Old Testament itself provides little information about the mechanism by which the prophets acquired their supernatural knowledge, and though it has been customary to draw a distinction between different kinds of 'vision' and even to correlate them with the various Hebrew terms available (*ḥozeh, ro'eh, nabi'*, and so on), this remains very speculative.[29] A number of types of inspiration occur in the Old Testament – dreams,[30] auditions,[31] waking visions,[32] communications through angels[33] – but it is difficult to find any case where there is any great significance in the mode in which revelation comes.[34]

Only in the case of Moses is there any insistence on one kind of inspiration rather than another. Thus in Numbers 12:6–8 ordinary prophets are said to receive their revelations through dreams and visions whereas God speaks with Moses 'mouth to mouth, clearly, and not in dark speech'; cf. Deuteronomy 34:10. Exactly what is meant by this distinction is not entirely clear, since it is said of several prophets that they 'saw the LORD' – cf. 1 Kings 22:17, Isaiah 6:1, Amos 9:1 – though it plainly implies the same kind of difference in *status* between Moses and his prophetic successors that is involved in the distinction between Torah and Prophets. Whatever experiences the prophets had, one can be sure that they were less direct than that of Moses, but since Moses was therefore in a class of his own it is naturally impossible for anyone to imagine just how his experiences differed from theirs. It is in fact quite difficult to gain any insight into how prophets were generally supposed to receive their inspiration. For most of the classical prophets, we have little more than expressions such as 'the word of the LORD came to me', which insist on the fact of divine inspiration but say nothing at all about the manner of it. Even if the prevalence of 'word' imagery seems to us to imply audition rather than vision, it is by no means clear that this was understood by those ancient interpreters of the prophets who edited their books, for whom 'The word which Isaiah the son of Amoz *saw*' (Isaiah 2:1) was evidently a natural enough expression.

In our period, however, more interest was taken in the manner of inspiration, with both Josephus and Philo devoting space to the question. The most striking feature in Josephus's understanding of the Old Testament prophets is his assumption that most of them received their inspired messages through *dreams*. Not deterred by the adverse opinion of dreams expressed by Jeremiah (23:23–40), Josephus frequently adds a reference to dreams where the Old Testament itself is silent about the mode of a prophet's inspiration.

For example, in *Antiquities* 5:215 God appears to Gideon 'in his sleep', and in 7:147 the bald statement of 2 Samuel 12:1, 'The LORD sent Nathan to David', is glossed as meaning that God appeared to Nathan in a dream with instructions to go and confront David; cf. also 6:38 (Samuel) and 8:126 (Solomon). It seems that for Josephus there is simply no way of imagining inspiration except as something that occurs during sleep, and it is sometimes suggested that he regarded any other alleged sources of revelation as of doubtful authority. Thus he tends to eliminate *angels* even where they occur in the biblical text (see especially *Antiquities* 9:20, on God's communication with Elijah).[35]

For Philo, prophetic inspiration is a subject of intense interest. Again, we find a general assumption that dreams are the most natural means of revelation, and he devotes two entire books to the subject in dealing with the story of Jacob and Joseph (*de somniis*). Philo distinguishes three grades of dream.[36] The first contains clear and unambiguous oracles, and when such dreams are recorded in the Pentateuch Moses himself also records their meaning. In the second sort, the interpretation given is itself somewhat obscure, since the dreams themselves are not wholly clear, being the product of an ecstasy which is divinely-induced but owes something to the dreamer's own mind; and in the third the moving force is the human mind itself, which in an abnormal state is inherently capable of precognition without special divine inspiration. Accordingly dreams of this third kind are always, in the Pentateuch, interpreted by men: examples are the dreams of the baker and the butler in Genesis 40. The first kind, those given by direct divine inspiration, includes those in which the speaker heard in the dream is an angel: Philo, unlike Josephus, does not regard this distinction as significant, since in either case God, not the dreamer's own mind, is the moving force.[37] And to interpret dreams correctly is itself a form of 'prophecy': 'the interpreters of dreams must needs tell the truth, since they are prophets expounding divine oracles' (*theia logia diermeneuousi kai prophêteuousi*; *de Iosepho* 95).

The essential feature of prophetic inspiration for both Josephus and Philo is its difference from all natural human powers, and it is this that is most powerfully safeguarded by the assumption that it usually occurs when the conscious mind is asleep. Since one cannot control one's own dreams, they must come from some external source. Philo, in believing this, has the support of Plato:

Clear enough evidence that god gave this power [sc. divination] to man's irrational part is to be found in our incapacity for inspired and true prophecy when in our right minds; we only achieve it when the power of our understanding is inhibited in sleep, or when we are in an abnormal condition owing to disease or divine inspiration. It is the function of someone in his right mind to construe what is remembered of utterances made in dream or waking by those who have the gift of prophecy and divine inspiration (Timaeus 71E).

It is in dependence on this philosophical explanation of inspiration that Philo sees prophecy as the taking over of a man's natural powers by an exterior force – for him, of course, as a Jew, the God of Israel, not a *daimon*.

[When a prophet reveals the future] nothing of what he says will be his own, for he that is truly under the control of divine inspiration has no power of apprehension when he speaks but serves as the channel for the insistent words of Another's prompting. For prophets are the interpreters of God, who makes full use of their organs of speech to set forth what he wills (*de specialibus legibus* 1:65).

No pronouncement of a prophet is ever his own; he is an interpreter prompted by Another in all his utterances, when knowing not what he does he is filled with inspiration, as the reason withdraws and surrenders the citadel of the soul to a new visitor and tenant, the Divine spirit which plays upon the vocal organism and dictates words which clearly express its prophetic message (ibid., 4:49).

The mind is evicted at the arrival of the divine Spirit . . . mortal and immortal may not share the same home . . . The prophet, even when he seems to be speaking, really holds his peace, and his organs of speech, mouth and tongue, are wholly in the employ of Another (*quis rerum divinarum heres* 265–6).

Dreams, then, are in effect simply the commonest manifestation of the essential feature of prophetic activity: that it occurs only in abnormal mental states, in which the conscious rational mind is invaded by a power beyond itself. In this vein Philo will speak of prophecy as a form of ecstasy or madness: 'all whom Moses describes as just are pictured as *possessed and prophesying*'

119

(*katechomenous kai prophêteuontas, quis rerum divinarum heres* 260); Jeremiah was 'possessed by divine inspiration' (*katapneustheis enthousiôn, de confusione linguarum* 44); in dreams of the second kind the understanding 'becomes filled with a divinely-induced madness' (*theophorêtou manias anapimplamenês, de somniis* 2:2). One of the clearest descriptions of this can be found in the *Questions and Answers on Genesis* (extant only in Armenian):

> What is the meaning of the words, 'At sunset an ecstasy fell upon Abram and behold a great dark fear fell upon him' [Genesis 15:12]? A certain divine tranquillity came suddenly upon the virtuous man. For ecstasy, as its very name clearly shows, is nothing else than the departing and going out of the understanding. But the race of prophets is wont to suffer this. For when the mind is divinely possessed and becomes filled with God, it is no longer within itself, for it receives the divine spirit to dwell within it. Nay rather, as he himself has said, it fell upon (Abram), for it does not come upon one gently and softly but makes a sudden attack (*quaestiones in Genesin* 3:9).

Moses is the supreme example of the inspired prophet, for 'all things in the sacred books are oracles delivered (*chrêsthentes*) through him' (*de vita Mosis* 2:188). Strictly speaking, in recording the laws Moses acts as an interpreter rather than a prophet properly so called, since they are words which God spoke *to* him rather than *through* him, and in receiving them he is unlike his prophetic successors. His claim to be a prophet as well as a lawgiver rests more particularly on those utterances which involved him in an intimate union of mind with God: to some extent those which he elicited from God by question and answer, but most of all those in which his divine possession (*to tou legontos enthousiôdes*) is manifested. Philo understands this last category to comprise chiefly predictive prophecies.[38] It seems clear that Philo understands prophecy primarily in terms of a supernatural endowment in which the mind is taken over by divine power and so becomes the receptacle for information that it could not have discovered for itself; he has some difficulty in assimilating Moses to this model, because Moses' 'oracles' have to include everything in the Pentateuch, not just Moses' own speeches, and consequently he has to invent two categories of 'prophetic' utterance peculiar to him. Though Moses is thus in theory the greatest prophet and the fount of all prophecy, Philo's basic understanding of prophecy does not derive from taking him as the norm; rather he has to be fitted in to a model derived from elsewhere. There is obviously some difficulty, as Aune points out,[39] in understanding paranetic material as 'oracles', but Philo forges ahead none the less, treating even Moses' most straightforward exhortations to obey the Law as oracular utterances.

Dreams, ecstasies, visions, revelations through angels: all these manifestations of prophecy, rare in the genuinely old prophetic books of Israel, occur frequently in the pseudo-prophetic literature roughly contemporary with the age of Philo and Josephus. Violent frenzy is attributed to prophetic figures perhaps especially in works heavily influenced by Hellenistic thought-forms (just as it is in Philo, who draws on the Greek philosophical tradition in discussing prophecy). The most extreme examples occur in the Sibylline Oracles:

> I will speak the following with my whole person in ecstasy.
> For I do not know what I say, but God bids me utter each thing
> (2:1–4).
> . . . my spirit lashed by a whip, compelled from within to
> proclaim an oracle to all (3:4–6).
> He it is who drove a whip through my heart within (4:18).

We find similar language in Pseudo-Philo: 'The holy spirit that dwelt in Cenez leapt upon him and took away from him his bodily sense, and he began to prophesy' (*Biblical Antiquities* 28:6). Similarly Isaiah is seen as an ecstatic visionary of this sort in Ascension of Isaiah 6:10–12: 'While he was speaking in the Holy Spirit in the hearing of all, he (suddenly) became silent, and his spirit was caught up into heaven . . . Only his breath remained in him, for he was in a vision'. Justin Martyr would see Zechariah, with more plausibility, in the same way (*Trypho* 115:3).

The vision by night – which is not necessarily a dream, though often it seems to be so – appears as early as the accounts of Solomon's encounter with Yahweh at Gideon (1 Kings 3:4–15), Abram's nocturnal trance (Genesis 15:12–17), and Jacob's dream at Bethel (Genesis 28:11–18) – there is no need here to decide which of these is the oldest. But its full flowering begins only after the Exile, with the allegorical night-visions of Zechariah, and it comes into its own from the time of Daniel. Daniel 7, 4 Ezra 3, 5–6, 11 and 13, Testament of Naphtali 5–7 and Testament of Abraham 7 offer

121

lengthy examples of the genre; compare also Mordecai's dream in the Greek Esther (11:5–12).

It is important, however, not to assume that the use of dreams and visions was thought by the authors of these books to differentiate their heroes from the prophets. It is often said that the replacement of divine *speech* ('thus says the LORD') by *visions* is one of marks of the transition from prophecy to apocalyptic,[40] but it does not seem to me that the difference was so obvious to writers of our period as it is to us. As we have seen, writers such as Josephus and Philo often assumed that the Old Testament prophets received their oracles in dreams or other trance-like states, even though the Old Testament does not say so: in other words, they read the accounts of the prophets' divine commissioning as if the prophets were something much more like what we call 'apocalyptists' than what we call 'prophets'. Consequently, for them and their contemporaries to describe an inspired figure in the past as having dreams and visions was not, in their terms, to say that he was not a prophet. Much of the discussion of the shift from prophecy to 'apocalyptic' fails, it seems to me, to distinguish sharply enough between how prophets actually functioned in various periods and how they were *perceived* to function, and it is one main purpose of this book to try to be clear about this. The editors of 4 Ezra evidently saw no incongruity in prefacing the 'Apocalypse' of 3–14 with a book beginning 'The second book of the prophet Ezra', in which 'the word of the Lord' comes to Ezra (1:1–4), nor in concluding it with oracles headed 'Speak in the ears of my people the words of the prophecy which I will put into your mouth'. Similarly the Syriac Apocalypse of Baruch begins (1:1): 'The word of the Lord came to Baruch the son of Neraiah.' How else should the word of God come except in a vision, or, conversely, what is a true vision but the word of God?

Revelation by an angel, equally, is typical of the works produced in our period, but again it is important not to draw the wrong conclusions from this. It is widely held that Judaism began to take an interest in angels and other mediating figures as its theology developed in an increasingly 'transcendent' direction. Whereas the prophets had felt that God spoke to them directly, 'apocalyptists' could not approach so closely to the divine presence, and so thought of the unapproachable God as communicating with them by means of angelic guides and interpreters. As a statement about the development of theological assumptions in post-exilic Judaism this is quite possibly correct. But it does not follow that writers in our period were aware that they differed from their predecessors in this regard. Many probably held, as did Philo, that it was through an angel that God had spoken to the patriarchs,[41] and believed, with St Paul,[42] that angels had been involved in the transmission of the Law to Moses; small wonder if the prophets, too, had received their revelations at the hand of angels. It was by an angel that Noah was warned of the Flood, according to 1 Enoch 10, and through angels that Moses learned all the details of the creation and of the early history of the world, according to Jubilees 2: indeed, most of Jubilees is presented as the autobiography of the angel of the presence, who does not spare Moses the smallest detail of all that he and his companions did, not even in the events which Moses himself had witnessed. Other angels entertained the luckless patriarchs with similar recitals, according to the Testaments of Levi, Job, and Abraham.

In any case, the Old Testament itself speaks of 'the angel of Yahweh' as active from the days of the patriarchs onwards. Modern Old Testament scholarship is on the whole convinced that this figure is to be understood as Yahweh himself in an earthly theophany, not identified with 'an angel' in the later sense of one among the many denizens of the heavenly court;[43] but this distinction was certainly unknown to those who read the Old Testament in our period, and they did not see angel-interpreters as restricted to the post-prophetic period. (In any case, as we have already seen, the heroes of the apocalypses do not live in the post-prophetic period, but are supposed to be contemporaries of the prophets we meet in the Old Testament itself.)

Another characteristic mode of revelation in the pseudonymous books of New Testament times is the heavenly journey, discussed with a wealth of illustrative material by Rowland.[44] As he shows, the journey into the heavens is sometimes combined with revelation through an angel, but at other times the seer is admitted into the heavenly court where he hears the voice of God for himself and is permitted to look around his kingdom, rather than hearing about the secrets he is meant to learn through a messenger. The classic traveller on a heavenly journey is Enoch, who was admitted to heaven and allowed to see the heavenly books: 'I do know the mysteries of the holy ones; for he, the Lord, has revealed (them) to me and made me know – and I have read (them) in the heavenly tablets' (1 Enoch 106:19). All the Enoch literature presents Enoch as a traveller in the heavenly world, and Rowland points out that the same is true of 'apocalyptic' books attributed to Abraham (cf. Testament of Abraham 11, where Michael takes Abraham for a drive around the heavens in a chariot drawn by cherubim). These stories are the lineal descendants of the old tales about prophets who had been admitted to the council of Yahweh – for example. Micaiah ben Imlah, in 1 Kings 22, or Isaiah in Isaiah 6 – but they are immensely more complex and elaborate, reflecting the taste of a later time.

It is often said, in another familiar contrast between classical prophets and apocalyptists, that techniques of preparation for prophecy played no part in the experiences of men like Amos and Isaiah, whereas the seers in apocalypses frequently fast to encourage a trance-like condition. We can say little with certainty about the techniques of the classical prophets, though it is generally held that their 'ecstatic' predecessors and contemporaries went in for a good deal by way of preparatory exercises. Once again, however, it is clear that people of the sort who wrote and read the pseudo-prophecy of our period thought that a prophet would engage in various ascetic practices to prepare himself for his visions. Daniel may be taken as typical: anxious to understand the meaning of Jeremiah's 'seventy years' prophecy, he prays, fasts, and sits in sackcloth and ashes, and Gabriel duly flies in to provide the interpretation he seeks (Daniel 9; cf. 10:2–3, and other references provided by Rowland, *The Open Heaven*, p. 228: Apocalypse of Abraham 9; 4 Ezra 9:23ff; Syriac Baruch 5:7, 9:2, 12:5, 21:1, and 47:2). Not only the fasting, but also meditation on Scripture, probably belongs to the conception of the prophet, who is one learned in the holy writings and able, by proper self-preparation, to work out the correct interpretation of their obscurities – or rather, to become the vehicle through which God can reveal it.

It may seem rather odd to think of prophets in ancient times meditating on Scripture. By the time of Daniel, the book of Jeremiah was already 'scriptural', that is, it was an old and revered book; so it made sense for the author to think that the answer to his anxieties about what the future held could be found by meditating on its holy words. But of course at the time when the hero of Daniel is supposed to have lived, Jeremiah was still alive, and his book did not (presumably) exist in its present form; while to think of earlier prophets puzzling over the words of scriptural books many of which had not even begun to be written yet is even more obviously a deep anachronism. But none of this would have worried the (real) authors of books such as Daniel, nor even the writers who commented on and paraphrased the books of the (genuinely ancient) prophets. For them, it went without saying that the books of the Torah already existed before even the earliest prophet prophesied, so that Moses' words at least were available for meditation, and of course each prophet in turn wrote exactly the book which now bears his name. By the time the wise man Daniel was pondering on the words of Jeremiah, they believed, every one of the books in the present Torah and Prophets already existed in more or less the form we are familiar with, and were already 'the holy writings', whose meaning could be revealed to one who approached them with the proper preparation. For us this is of course wildly implausible. There is absolutely no reason to suppose that anyone in the exilic period read either the Torah or the Prophets in the way attributed to Daniel. But to people in the second century BC it seemed entirely natural: how else would Daniel have gone about enquiring into the future?

There is no great mystery about the reason for the conceptions of ancient prophetic inspiration just outlined. It is overwhelmingly probable that they result from a reading back of contemporary 'prophetic' experience and expectation into ancient times. In people with little historical sense it is the most natural thing in the world to assume that the past was in all essentials like the present, only longer ago. Whatever a contemporary visionary or holy man is or does is assumed to give a direct insight into what the prophets of old were like. This is not in the least difficult to reconcile with the equally firm conviction that there are no longer any prophets like those of old. The ancient prophets were holier, more profoundly inspired, in every way greater than anything we have today: but they were not of a radically different kind. When we are told, as in the rabbinic tradition cited earlier, that Hillel would have been a prophet if his generation had been worthy to receive prophets, it is certainly implied that prophecy has ceased; but it is just as certainly also implied that prophets were people who, when they still existed, did just the sorts of thing that Hillel did.

For this reason it seems to me eminently reasonable to think, as Rowland does, that 'apocalypses' may be able to provide us with information not only about conceptions of what visionary experience had been like in the past but also about its character at the time these books were being written. It is far too easy to dismiss apocalyptic visions as 'literary' in character, and to draw a simple contrast between prophetic books as the record of 'genuine' inspiration and apocalyptic as mere literary artifice. Of course apocalypses purport to relate the experiences of figures who cannot actually be their authors; but that is comparatively trivial, from this point of view. Why, after all, should just these experiences be attributed to Enoch and Abraham and the rest? The very fact that 'real' Old Testament prophecy is so different strongly argues against seeing the experiences described in the apocalypses as mere imitation of scriptural models. Rather, the ancient figures on whom the apocalypses are fathered are attributed with the kinds of experience they are, precisely because the authors could not imagine any other kind. That does not mean that they themselves had really undergone the experiences they ascribed to the old prophets: I say nothing about their veracity. But it does mean that such experiences must have been credible to their contemporaries, that they must have struck some familiar chord in people's ideas of what a religious experience would be like if one were to have one.

The same applies, even more obviously, to the preparations for revelation: fasting and meditation on Scripture. These were among the commonest ways of preparing oneself to receive a divine revelation in what Rowland calls the esoteric tradition in rabbinic Judaism, and it has long been well known that certain passages in Scripture, most notably the vision in the first two chapters of Ezekiel, were widely regarded as the most potent (but also therefore the most dangerous) texts on which to practise such meditation. What is ascribed to Daniel is an attempt to discover hidden meanings in Jeremiah which is similar to rabbinic meditation on Ezekiel. The ancient prophet is simply made in the image of the nearest thing to a prophet the contemporary scene afforded, the mystical sage. There is no question but that the Teacher of Righteousness was seen by the community at Qumran as having the power to pierce the mystery of the scriptures and discover the exact *time* at which various obscure prophetic oracles would find their fulfilment: 'God told Habakkuk to write down that which would happen to the final generation, but he did not make known to him when that time would come to consummation. And as for that which he said, *That he who runs may read it speedily*, interpreted this concerns the Teacher

126

of Righteousness, to whom God made known all the mysteries of the words of His servants the Prophets' (1 QpHab 7:1–4).

For this reason I believe that Lindblom was right to think that in principle, at least, it may be possible to discover which of the apocalypses, if any, record real experiences.[45] His own attempt to distinguish the records of real visions from purely literary conventions in Revelation may not always be convincing, but there is no reason why the attempt should not be made. Of course such an inquiry cannot establish that the contents of the revelation are *true*, only at best that the seer who recorded them really thought he had had them. The sharp dissimilarity between the sorts of experience ascribed to ancient prophets in New Testament times and the actual experience of these prophets as reconstructed by modern critical scholarship must greatly strengthen the contention that 'apocalyptists' were not merely drawing on a literary tradition, but reading back contemporary expectations about religious experience into the remote past.

One striking example of this, among a number cited by Lindblom, is the almost universal assumption (to which I have already drawn attention) that God speaks to prophetic persons through *dreams*. As we have seen, the classical prophets never speak of having revelatory dreams, and Jeremiah at least seems to despise them (23:25–32). Ben Sira shrewdly comments that a dream can be interpreted to mean anything ('The vision of dreams is this against that', Ecclesiasticus 34:3), and advises that they should be ignored 'unless they are sent as a visitation from the Most High' (34:6) – and how is one to know that? Yet in the New Testament the prophetic power of dreams is taken for granted: there are many examples in Acts (e.g. 10:10, 16:9) and in Matthew (1:20, 2:12, 13, 19, 27:19). There seems to be no awareness on the part of the New Testament authors that they are out of step with the traditions of Israel of old; indeed, the infancy narrative in Matthew shows every sign of being designed to read like a section of the Old Testament. The conclusion lies very close to hand that this was because many New Testament writers (and those whose traditions they were collecting) simply took it for granted that prophecy came through dreams because this was an accepted aspect of the society of their own day. There is, of course, plenty of evidence that this was indeed so.[46] Similarly, Josephus probably modelled his picture of prophetic activity on his own experience as a clairvoyant. As F. F. Bruce observes, 'When in *Ant.* x. 267, 277ff., he appeals to Daniel's visions as evidence that God does have a concern for human affairs and does reveal to his servants not only *what* must come to pass but *when* it must come to pass, we may surmise that he has in mind his own prophetic gift and what he describes as "the dreams by night in which God has foretold to him the impending fate of the Jews and the destinies of the Roman rulers".'[47]

V

Finally, we may ask what kind of information inspired prophets were thought to acquire through their privileged access to God; but the answer will by now already be apparent. The fact that special means of revelation were needed, that prophets were a special class of person, and that they were endowed with extraordinary abilities, all make it clear that the distinctive mark of the prophet was his possession of *esoteric* knowledge. Through their special inspiration prophets knew *things that could not be known by normal means*. Prophets are people who have insight into *mysteries*.

Lindblom presents this point with great clarity in relation to the New Testament, showing that the essence of prophecy is to reveal truths hidden from ordinary people. In 1 Corinthians 13:2 to have 'prophetic powers' is equivalent to understanding 'all mysteries and all knowledge';[48] similarly in 14:37 Paul argues that if anyone really does possess, as some claim, prophetic inspiration, then he will recognize that what Paul has written is a command of the Lord – a pleasant example of how one prophet can upstage another. The gospels seem to use the same definition of 'prophecy'. In Luke 7:39 we find the Pharisee who has invited Jesus to a meal, only to be scandalized by the behaviour of a woman who was a sinner, saying to himself: 'If this man were a prophet, he would have known who and what sort of woman this is who is touching him'; compare John 4:19, where Jesus tells the Samaritan woman something that he could not have known by natural means, and she at once replies, 'Sir, I perceive that you are a prophet', and Matthew 13:17, where the disciples are told that they have seen and heard things that many prophets and righteous men failed to see and hear – implying that seeing and hearing mysteries is a reasonable expectation for prophets. (Matthew 26:67–8 – 'Then they spat in his face, and

128

struck him; and some slapped him, saying, "Prophesy to us, you Christ! Who is it that struck you?' – implies the same conception that a prophet will know what cannot normally be known, though at a more trivial level. The parallel in Luke 22:64, but perhaps not that in Mark 14:65, bears the same implication.)[49]

In effect, this means that a prophet is a practitioner of what is sometimes called 'mantic wisdom':[50] someone who can understand a mystery, a 'wise man' in the sense defined in Daniel 2:21–2:

> He gives wisdom to the wise
> and knowledge to those who have understanding;
> he reveals deep and mysterious things;
> he knows what is in the darkness,
> and the light dwells with him.

Solomon, the archetypal wise man who was also widely regarded as a prophet in New Testament times, is presented in the Wisdom of Solomon as a 'mantic' of just this kind, as Müller rightly argues. In 7:17–22 he understands astronomical (and therefore astrological) secrets – very much the kinds of information, in fact, that were imparted to Enoch during his guided tour of the cosmos (cf. 1 Enoch 72–82); and in 8:8 the wisdom which inspires him, and which is itself spoken of as if it were a mantic, is said to 'understand the solutions of riddles (*luseis ainigmatôn*)' and to have 'foreknowledge of signs and wonders, and of the outcome of seasons and times'. No one can acquire such wisdom through his own labour: 'I perceived that I would not possess wisdom unless God gave her to me' (8:21). Only those to whom God chooses to impart wisdom are truly wise.

It may well be felt at this point that I am seeking not only to undermine the usual distinction between prophets and 'apocalyptists' – a tendency which should by now be clear – but even to blur that between prophets and 'wise men'. And indeed it seems to me that in our period neither distinction can easily be maintained. Like the visionaries depicted in apocalypses, the 'wise men' revered in New Testament times are *inspired* figures to whom insight into supernatural mysteries has been granted: and the practical difference between a wise man of this kind and a prophet is not clear to me. Just as prophets are by this time widely seen as mantic wise men, so wise men understand divine mysteries in a way possible only for those who have, to use the older expression, 'stood in the council of Yahweh': there is nothing to choose between the two titles. In Philo, for example, Abraham's *prophetic* inspiration makes him a worthy rival for the Chaldean *astrologers* (*de migratione Abrahami* 464), just as is the case with the 'wise man' Daniel in Daniel 2. As an initiate into 'the greater mysteries' under the guidance of Moses, Philo came to value Jeremiah (whom he saw in a vision) as 'not only himself enlightened, but a worthy minister of the holy secrets' (*ou monon mystês estin alla kai hierophantês hikanos, de cherubim* 49). Just as Judaism largely lost the sense that 'wisdom' could be the developed use of the natural reason to plumb the depths of human life and of the natural world, and came to use the term increasingly for mystical and quasi-magical experimentation, so 'prophecy' too lost any connection it may have had with natural insight (into political affairs, for example) and came to be seen as the passive reception of secret, even coded, information, the divinely-imparted knowledge of the otherwise unknowable.

Perhaps the most striking place to see this is in the work of Josephus. From the famous description of the Scriptures in *Against Apion* one can easily get the impression that the prophetic writings are highly rational and sensible works of sober historiography, far removed from ideas of 'inspiration' and certainly having nothing to do with the kind of mysteries into which people might need initiation. 'The prophets wrote the history of their own times': what could be more humdrum? The *Antiquities* contains long stretches of narrative which confirm this impression, but suddenly one is pulled up short by some stray reference that stands what one thought one had grasped completely on its head. Thus, as we have seen, in the middle of the account of the monarchy we suddenly learn that the history was written by Samuel, not because he had accurate records to refer to or simply had a good memory for the acts of his own long life, but because God had given him secret knowledge of all the future events of the kingdom, which he wrote out *in advance* and laid up in the tabernacle to be proved right in due course (6:66). The modern mind reels at such a suggestion, as the great judge and austere keeper of Saul's conscience turns before our eyes into a figure like Nostradamus. Yet for Josephus nothing has changed: he had thought of Samuel like this, we realize, all along. In Josephus's world a great military and political leader might well be a clairvoyant too: so much the better if he was. In such a world-view there is little point in trying to distinguish 'prophets' from 'wise men' and 'visionaries': it is all one.

Much of the evidence for contemporary prophecy in the period in which such works as Josephus's were being written comes from Christian sources. Other Jewish groups did not all share the Christian belief that prophecy of a kind comparable in stature with that of old had revived and, as we have seen, there was a widely-held doctrine that first-rank prophecy belonged unalterably to the past. Nevertheless the Christian evidence helps to fill out our picture by showing what was at least thinkable in the first and second centuries AD, even if not many outside the Christian Church actually thought it. There are many debates about the nature of 'prophecy' in early Christianity, but all are agreed, I think, that the distinguishing mark of prophetic utterances was their novelty. The claim to be able to *prophesy*, as opposed to the exercise of other ministries, was the claim to fresh inspiration which made one able to communicate truths that would otherwise remain unknown.

It is a reasonable supposition that Paul's citation of rulings 'from the Lord' (1 Corinthians 7:10) amounts to a claim of prophetic inspiration, and the same may be true of the decision of the 'council of Jerusalem' in Acts 15:28, where Lindblom plausibly argues that 'it seems good to the Holy Spirit and to us' is a reference to what is taken to be a specific revelation, not merely a tendentious way of referring to a human decision.[51] Aune usefully collects similar examples and discusses them at length in chapters 10 and 11 of his *Prophecy in Early Christianity*, and there is no need to attempt to duplicate his work: even if some of his material should be interpreted differently, enough remains to prove the point. There are particularly good illustrations from Ignatius of Antioch, to whom it was revealed, among other incomprehensible mysteries, that nothing should ever be decided without the consent of the bishop (*Philadelphians* 7:1).

VI

One of the great insights of modern critical study has been that the great classical prophets were not clairvoyants providing their devotees with arcane information about the future or about the mysteries of the universe, but spokesmen for a moral and demanding God who addressed themselves to the state of Israelite society in their own day and uttered rebukes and warnings of immediate

131

application. Nothing I have written is meant to detract in the least from the truth of that insight. But it is an insight that was more or less unavailable to people in New Testament times; and, as we have now seen, the image of a 'prophet' for them was much more likely to conform to just the picture which modern Old Testament study has been at pains to correct. The prophet was a seer, a visionary, more like what we call an 'apocalyptist', who had penetrated the secrets of the heavens and could impart them to those who heard or read his work. *Revelation* is the key word here: through prophets one could obtain secret information which was unknowable apart from revelation.[52]

This does not mean, as we have seen, that prophets were lifted entirely out of their original historical setting. People remained aware that Isaiah had worked in the days of Hezekiah and the Assyrian kings who had threatened Judah, or that Jeremiah and Ezekiel had experienced the Babylonian invasion – though they also 'knew' that Daniel had been Ezekiel's contemporary, and that Jonah had prophesied, like Amos, in the days of Jeroboam II (2 Kings 14:25), very much as a modern fundamentalist 'knows' these things. They realized that the prophets had indeed spoken to the people of their own day, just as they had worked miracles and interceded for them. What kind of 'message' was it supposed that the prophets had delivered in their own day? As we shall find, the writers in our period find it hard to keep their minds concentrated on this question, because their primary interest is always in what the prophets have to say to *them*, but a small amount of material is available to show that a 'natural' or historical reading of at least some of the prophets did not entirely disappear.

Of all our witnesses Ben Sira perhaps comes nearest to perceiving the prophets in something like the modern way, and it is no accident that he is less prone than nearly all other writers of his time to be interested in the arcane aspects of prophecy: he has little time for ecstasies and other extravagances of that sort. Stadelmann's carefully nuanced treatment of Ben Sira provides invaluable help in getting his idea of the prophets in just perspective. Whereas Hengel, whom he criticizes, tends to present Ben Sira as interested in the prophets principally as heroes, wonder-workers, and preachers of the Torah – in other words, as having a thoroughly anachronistic picture of them – for Stadelmann Ben Sira was considerably less in the grip of popular misunderstandings.[53] As he rightly stresses, Ben

132

Sira's emphasis on the *deeds* of the prophets is partly dictated by the genre of the *laus patrum* in which they appear (Ecclesiasticus 46:13–49:10), and (as we have already noted) at least one of the prophetic miracles, the raising of the dead man whose corpse touches Elisha's bones, is understood not primarily as a piece of wonder-working but as a prophetic sign intended to show the power of God and so win the people to repentance.[54] The transmission of Israel's religious heritage, says Stadelmann, is the first task of a prophet according to Ben Sira's perception of the matter, and that includes both positively the inculcation of righteousness and negatively the call to repent:

> As in his life he [sc. Elisha] did wonders, so in death his deeds were marvellous. For all this the people did not repent, and they did not forsake their sins, till they were carried away captive from their land and were scattered over all the earth (Ecclesiasticus 48:14–15).[55]

Similarly Samuel, as well as predicting the future and working miracles on the people's behalf, also 'lifted up his voice out of the earth in prophecy to blot out the wickedness of the people' (46:20); Elijah 'heard rebuke at Sinai and judgments of vengeance at Horeb' (48:7); Isaiah directed Hezekiah's conduct, so that he 'did what was pleasing to the Lord'; and Jeremiah predicted the destruction of Jerusalem because her kings 'forsook the law of the Most High' (49:4–7).

For the taste of most critical readers of the prophets Ben Sira says a great deal too much about their confidence and hope for the future of Israel, but even here he has some sense of their setting in specific periods, and seldom seems to think in terms of a general and standardized 'prophetic eschatology'. Isaiah, it is true, 'saw the last things' and 'revealed what was to occur to the end of time' (48:24–5), but Jeremiah specifically predicted the destruction of Jerusalem and the Exile (49:4–7), and Ezekiel saw the vision of a God who 'remembered his enemies with storm, and did good to those who directed their ways aright' (49:8–9) – which seems to have some particular events in mind, possibly the overthrow of Babylon by the Persians. It may fairly be said, in fact, that Ben Sira's picture of the prophets adheres closely to the 'biblical' presentation of them, understanding this to be the impression that the Old Testament taken as whole would make on a non-critical reader.

His belief that the prophets rebuked the people for sin and called them, often unsuccessfully, to repentance, is in effect that of the editor of Kings, who sums up his understanding of prophecy in 2 Kings 17:7–41:

> The LORD warned Israel and Judah by every prophet and every seer, saying, 'Turn from your evil ways and keep my commandments and my statutes, in accordance with all the law which I commanded your fathers, and which I sent to you by my servants the prophets.' But they would not listen, but were stubborn, as their fathers had been . . . The people of Israel walked in all the sins which Jeroboam did; they did not depart from them, until the LORD removed Israel out of his sight, as he had spoken by all his servants the prophets (2 Kings 17:13–14, 22–3).

But equally Ben Sira's conviction that the prophets believed in the long-term well-being of Israel and in the everlasting character of God's covenant with her can also be found at the redactional level of Old Testament historiography and prophecy:

> Who is a God like thee, pardoning iniquity and passing over transgression for the remnant of his inheritance? He does not retain his anger for ever because he delights in steadfast love. He will again have compassion upon us, he will tread our iniquities under foot. Thou wilt cast all our sins into the depths of the sea. Thou wilt show faithfulness to Jacob and steadfast love to Abraham, as thou hast sworn to our fathers from the days of old (Micah 7:18–20).

We do not find in Ben Sira – and it would be startling if we did find it – any sense that the prophets had foretold the end of the covenant, or utter and irreversible destruction for God's people; but he does at least present the Bible's own overall view of prophecy, not one wholly revised in the light of later experience of prophetic figures.

Josephus, since he is writing a history, also follows the biblical record in recording instances where the prophets spoke to the concerns of people in their own generation, and does not always think of them simply as clairvoyants. In *Antiquities* 7:321 he faithfully reports that 'the prophets' rebuked David for taking the census, just as 2 Samuel 24 and 1 Chronicles 21 had said: and he goes beyond the biblical record in making Noah a preacher of repentance to his contemporaries, thereby casting him as a prophet in the mould implied in 2 Kings 17 (*Antiquities* 1:74; compare 2 Peter 2:5 and Sibylline Oracle 1, lines 146–98). From our point of view it is perhaps a pity that the three prophets whose importance to their contemporaries Josephus most stresses are Jonah, Nahum, and Daniel, but at least he does follow the Bible in thinking of them as having had something to say which was relevant to the times in which they lived. Philo is also vaguely aware that the prophetic message included warnings of *imminent* punishment for sin as well as predictions of good things in the distant future and intimations of immortality, and in this vein he embellishes Joseph's speech to Pharaoh, interpreting his dreams (*de Iosepho* 107–10). But of course this is a message of coming judgement on a Gentile nation, not on Israel (compare Moses' prophecy at the Red Sea in *de vita Mosis* 2:251–2); and in fact Philo seems entirely to ignore all criticisms of Israel in the prophets. Even though the prophets did sometimes concern themselves with the immediate future, it was to reassure Israel, not to threaten her: compare Ben Sira's picture of the Twelve as those who 'comforted the people of Jacob, and delivered them with confident hope' (Ecclesiasticus 49:10).

There are a few other places in which the prophets' role is to rebuke and warn Israel. In 4 Ezra 7:59–60 (129–30) we read that 'Moses, while he was alive, spoke to the people, saying, "Choose for yourself life, that you may live!" But they did not believe him, or the prophets after him, or even myself [sc. the angel] who have spoken to them.' 1 Enoch also depicts the prophets as those who tried to warn Israel, but were rejected: 'The Lord of the sheep called some of the sheep and sent them to the sheep, but the sheep began to kill them . . . And he sent many other sheep to those sheep to testify (to them) and to lament over them' (1 Enoch 89:51–4), and in this is in line with Daniel 9:6: 'We have not listened to thy servants the prophets, who spoke in thy name.'

As would be expected in the light of what it records about the preaching of John the Baptist, the New Testament is generally sensitive to the note of judgement on sin in the message of the prophets. Matthew 12:41 speaks of Jonah as a preacher of repentance, and Matthew 15:7–10 (with the parallel in Mark 7:6–7) is a rare quotation of a piece of prophetic rebuke, though it understands Isaiah 29:13 as referring to the 'Pharisees and scribes' of Jesus' day rather than to the prohet's own contemporaries; compare the citation of Isaiah 6:9–10 in Acts 28:26–8. Even in the New Testament, however, there are striking cases of what we may call the non-use of prophetic oracles of judgement. In Stephen's speech in Acts 7, whose whole tenor concerns the persistent disobedience of Israel, the only prophecy of destruction which is quoted is Amos 5:25–7 (Acts 7:42–3), with Isaiah 66:1–2 (Acts 7:49–50) brought in to demonstrate that God does not dwell in temples made with hands, but not as a judgement-oracle. When Stephen refers to the persistent slaughter of the prophets it is as those who 'announced beforehand the coming of the Righteous One', not as preachers of a morality which the people were transgressing.

How far the prophetic message of judgement on Israel was blunted in later tradition may be seen very clearly from the Isaiah Targum, where oracles against Israel are consistently turned into condemnations of the Gentiles. Isaiah 1:24, against the sinners in Zion, becomes 'As for the city, Jerusalem, I am about to comfort her; but woe to the wicked, when I shall reveal myself to render just recompense to the enemies of the people, and shall repay vengeance to the adversary'. The remarkable oracles in 19:23–5 ('Israel will be the third with Egypt and Assyria, a blessing in the midst of the earth') – probably the most 'universalist' passage in the entire Old Testament – is turned into a prediction that the Egyptians and Assyrians will fight with each other, thus enabling Israel to be saved.[56] In the same vein Josephus notes that Daniel was greater than the other prophets, because 'whereas [they] foretold disasters, and were for that reason in disfavour with kings and people, Daniel was a prophet of good tidings to them, so that through the auspiciousness of his predictions he attracted the goodwill of all' (*Antiquities* 9:268).

There are occasional hints in our period of a dim awareness that prophecy had had something to do with reading the signs of the times. Jesus' reply to the messengers sent by John the Baptist (Matthew 11:2–6, cf. Luke 7:18–23) seems to rest on the assumption that John, who is described in the verses that now follow as a prophet, will be able to draw the right conclusions from the evidence of Jesus' deeds; though in practice this may mean that he will see that they fulfil the prophecies of Isaiah 61, rather than that he will be able to interpret them with direct prophetic insight. Knowledge of what the outcome of an immediate action will be is vouchsafed to Judith (11:19), though she is not explicitly called a prophet.

There can be little doubt that one of the functions of contemporary prophets in New Testament times was to predict immediately future events, not to speak only of the 'eschaton'. Mordecai's dream (Greek Esther 11:5–11), which we have already referred to, is an example of a prediction relating to events in which the dreamer himself is involved. But this kind of prediction, though it is certainly different from the long-term prognostications which ancient prophets were thought to have uttered, clearly belongs firmly within the esoteric conception of prophecy: it has nothing to do with the kind of enhanced skill in detecting the drift of current political events which is often held by scholars today to have characterized the great classical prophets.

On the whole, indeed, writers of our period regarded what may be called 'non-esoteric' prophecy as a lower, not a higher skill than supernatural knowledge of the remote future and of cosmic secrets. It is difficult to imagine a culture before the Enlightenment that would not have done so; for the direct inspiration from God which reveals mysteries is surely greater than the most sublime of natural skills. We may if we wish regard the political sensitivity of a prophet like Isaiah as greater than the visions of Enoch, but we should be clear that in doing so we are at variance with most of our predecessors in any religion. For the people of our period, if Isaiah was as great as Enoch that would have to mean that he too had journeyed through the heavens: *decuit, ergo factum est* – the Ascension of Isaiah tells us all about it. The Christian Fathers were generally in no doubt that the importance of the prophets lay in the secrets they revealed, not in their opinions about the current state of affairs in Israel or Judah, which are no more than a side-issue. Thus Eusebius insists on the eschatological scale of prophetic predictions, writing that Moses and the prophets 'were not concerned with predicting matters which were transient and of interest only for the immediate future' (*Demonstration of the Gospel* 5, praef. 20–4).[57] The prophets for him were like Enoch, who saw visions 'not for this generation, but for a distant generation which will come' (1 Enoch 1:2). Despite some evidence, then, that what we should call a 'historical' reading of the prophets still occurred occasionally, the primary concern of writers in our period was with the message of the prophetic books for their own day. In St Paul's words, 'Whatever was written in former days was written for our instruction' (Romans 15:4). What the secrets were held to be to which the prophetic writings could

137

give the reader of New Testament times access, it will be the task of the remainder of this book to discover.

Why were people so convinced that the prophets had something to say to their own situation? In some cases, as we shall see, the belief amounted to a claim to be living in the times specifically predicted by ancient prophecies, and the grounds for such a belief lay in a sense of inspired knowledge which did not fall far short of being 'prophetic' itself. But this does not by any means apply to all those who read the prophets in the conviction that their oracles were written 'for our instruction'; nor for that matter does it apply to most modern Jewish or Christian readers who turn to the Bible with an expectation that its words will be of more than antiquarian interest. It is worth briefly examining the reasons there can be for such a belief.

There are two explanations which at once suggest themselves, but which I think we should reject. The first we have already by implication ruled out: it is that the prophets were read in the expectation that they would illuminate the life and times of their readers because they were the official canonical Scriptures of Judaism. Certainly this is a factor which can be very influential today. Many Christians accept that the Bible will have something to say in their own situation because the Bible comes to them with the authority of generations of believers and with the official sanction of the Church. If passages in it appear not to be illuminating, that will be because they are not being properly understood or interpreted, not because they are in fact irrelevant to the reader's concerns. In a Christian Bible-study group it is not one of the acceptable options to declare that the passage being studied is false, meaningless, or irrelevant. But although something similar might be true of the Torah in our period, we have already seen that *canonical* status, in a strict sense, was not yet accorded to most of the Scriptures. If they were regarded as lively oracles of God, that was not because some authority had declared that they were the 'official' Scriptures of Judaism.

But secondly, and on the other hand, it cannot have been because a dispassionate reading simply led to a common recognition that these books were in fact illuminating – as one might 'discover' a great book one happened not to have read before, and come to see that it shed fresh light on one's own life. It is of course theoretically possible that this is how prophetic Scripture came to be venerated:

138

that it established its status through the appeal of its own inherent merit. This is perhaps seldom suggested where the Old Testament is concerned, but one does sometimes hear the converse given as a reason why, for example, the apocryphal gospels did *not* find their way into the canon: Christian readers simply saw that they were of inferior quality to the canonical four gospels, and so they died a natural death for lack of support.

It would be extremely comforting to believe that this is how the Church's judgement operated, and in general it seems to me that the quality of the canonical books in both Old and New Testament is indeed higher than that of much that was in time rejected. It would be a sore trial to have to listen to, still more to preach on, a series of readings from 1 Enoch 89 or the Ascension of Isaiah, and few Christians will be found to regret the loss of the Shepherd of Hermas from the New Testament canon. All the same, it is very doubtful whether inherent merit was a major factor in determining canonicity. Who would include Jude but exclude Ben Sira on such grounds, for example? In reality things seem to work the other way about: certain books are of (apparently) unimpeachable apostolic or prophetic authorship; therefore they are regarded as 'holy Scripture'; and therefore they are read in ways which cause them to yield a helpful and edifying message.[58] This continues to be the logic of much Christian Bible-reading, though sometimes glorified by the name of biblical hermeneutics: to find a way from a text which is not obviously helpful to the modern Christian to an interpretation which will be so, often insisting that this is the 'true' sense of the text and sometimes decrying a more 'historical' (i.e. more natural) reading as a falsification. The inherent quality of parts of the Bible does, as a matter of fact, sometimes produce converts among those who come to it fresh, but it is very rare for those who have grown up with the Bible, as Christians or Jews, to see any merits in it other than those which their community's tradition of interpretation has deemed to be present. For most people the high quality of Scripture is a function of its authoritative status, not the reason for that status, and there is every reason to think that this was equally true for most of those who read the prophetic books in our period and found in them words of life. These books were good and important *because* they were the 'holy writings': they were not granted that status because they were so good.

Thus the relevance of the Scriptures to contemporary concerns

139

in the New Testament era probably derived *neither* from their having been imposed by some competent authority *nor*, on the other hand, from their inherent merit: both these considerations, which may be encountered today (though seldom in the same person) cannot without anachronism be retrojected into our period. The true answer seems to me to lie in a feature of the Scriptures which we have already adduced as a potent part of their appeal. It was their very antiquity (real or supposed) that gave them their importance.

For the modern Christian the question is often posed 'How can such old writings possibly be relevant to today's concerns?' Certainly critics of Christianity ask this, and so do many ordinary Christians, perhaps especially those for whom the paradigm case of useful knowledge is provided by science. Biblical scholars are sometimes accused of *relegating* the Bible to the position of merely an 'old book' by insisting on trying to read it in its original historical context to the detriment of its authority for the present. ('Biblical Theology' and 'canonical criticism' are, in their different ways, attempts to respond to this charge.) Thus for many today, the antiquity of the Bible is a considerable problem. But for the people of New Testament times the antiquity of the holy writings was their strongest appeal. It was usual to think that all important issues bearing on human life and destiny had been settled definitively in ancient times, and that what had been said and written then could guide conduct in the present as well as providing, in oracular form, information about present and future events. This is how Greeks and others had long read Homer, and were beginning to read Plato. It was simply assumed that writers of the past were likely to be of more value than moderns in helping one to understand the present. When one adds that the 'prophecies' with which we are dealing were written by the most venerable ancestors of the race and by men who had talked with angels, then the possibility that they would have nothing to say to the reader's own situation becomes remote indeed. This will not explain why people thought that the prophets had revealed precisely the types of information they did; but it is more than adequate to account for the conviction that for true wisdom one should turn to these books, rather than to modern ones. All true wisdom was old wisdom; and, in the bookish intellectual cultures of the Graeco-Roman world, it was to be found in old books. The older the book, the more use it would be in the present.

4

Modes of Reading the Prophets

I

How does a *critical* reading of the Bible differ from pre-critical or non-critical readings? Many possibilities suggest themselves: an ability to question the accuracy of the text, an eye for inconsistencies, a concern for a book's original, historical setting, and so on. No doubt there is some truth in most such proposals. It seems to me, however, that one of the most crucial distinguishing marks of a critical approach to the Bible – or, indeed, to any book – is some attention to the genre of texts. Reading the Bible critically means knowing what kind of literature particular portions of the text are, and therefore what sort of question it makes sense to ask of it. Until we have assigned a text to some genre or other, we do not know how to understand its individual sections, sentences, even words.

To take an example which would be accepted even by a fundamentalist: Jotham's fable of the trees, in Judges 9:7–15, is misread if it is taken to show that there was a time when trees could speak and when they had forms of social organization akin to those of human beings. We recognize this at once, because we recognize that stories such as this do not belong to any historiographical genre, but are to be read as illustrative tales or parables. A 'literalistic' reading of the story is mistaken, not simply because as a matter of fact trees cannot talk, but because in this kind of fable it is not being asserted that they can, and to think so is to have misunderstood the type of literature one is reading. One might as well claim to have discovered the bones of the Good Samaritan's donkey or the ring worn by the Prodigal Son. Furthermore, our critical awareness of the genre to which particular texts belong is primarily based on the evidence of the texts themselves, and only to a very limited extent by external factors. It is true that we bring certain expectations to a text if we have already been told (through its title, for example) what kind of text it is: the fact that a book appears in the 'Fiction' section of a library, for instance, immediately activates in us certain sorts of expectation and suppresses others. But such 'pre-understandings' are always corrigible, and we are quite prepared after beginning to read the book to decide that it was wrongly classified, trusting the evidence of our own literary judgement more than the library's classification system.[1]

Now many people in the ancient world were just as aware of the importance of genre as we are. Aristotle's *Poetics*, with its constant consideration of what is *appropriate* in different types of literature, is about almost nothing else; and in our own period generic classifications can be found in texts describing the Bible, at least at a rudimentary level. The decision to group biblical books together as 'histories' or 'hymns and precepts', for example, as we find it in *Against Apion*, is certainly a decision about genre. But in general it must be said that an awareness of distinctions of genre is commonly inhibited, in the literature we are concerned with, by the overriding interest in the *source* of biblical books. As we have seen, for most people in New Testament times by far the most interesting and important feature of the 'holy books' that had come to them from the hallowed past was their divine origin. The Scriptures were not the words of men, but the oracles of God. As such they were not subject to the same constraints of literary form and genre as human books. Prior to the question 'What kind of text is this?' was the question 'Is this a sacred text?'; and if once this prior question was given an affirmative answer, the other question might well never get asked at all. Genre distinctions can never be of more than secondary importance if one is dealing with the direct utterances of God. It would have seemed very strange in our period to ask, of a book which was given by God himself, in just what sense it contained truth, or what sort of truth it contained. Obviously, if it was divine in origin, it must be true in every possible sense, and contain every kind of truth there is. Thus differences of genre, even when (as by Josephus) they are noticed, are not really allowed to become properly functional for reading the text.

One important consequence of this is a failure to see at what level a text can be meaningful, and to find meaning in what we should regard as sub-semantic portions of the text – in words taken out of context, even in details of spelling and grammar. One is tempted to support this by saying 'See Babylonian Talmud, *passim*'; but an obvious example may be cited from the New Testament, Paul's argument in Galatians 3:15–18, where it is shown that the promises made to Abraham in Genesis 12:7 refer to Christ because God swore to establish Abraham 'and his seed', not 'and his seed*s*'. The purely idiomatic character of the Hebrew phrase 'to your seed', meaning 'to your offspring' (singular or plural, but here by implication clearly plural) is interpreted as if it were deliberately chosen to point to one particular descendant, namely Jesus. Because Scripture is God-given, nothing in it is unintentional or redundant; no detail however incidental can be without meaning even when taken on its own. Since a language with no redundancy and no sub-semantic elements is more or less unimaginable, this logically implies that the language of Scripture is not actually ancient Hebrew but a special language all its own, but this logical implication was not seen by ancient writers (it ought, however, to be seen by their modern fundamentalist successors). Meaning can be found, they supposed, in every smallest feature of the divine speech which Scripture contains, but they did not integrate this with any larger theory about language, as we should have to do. But it is readily apparent that there is no point in worrying about the genre of a text which conveys its meaning at levels even lower than that of the individual word.

Thus the concept of genre, though theoretically available, was not in practice able to gain a foothold where the interpretation of Scripture was concerned. We have already seen the effects of this in the way the term 'prophecy' was used. This looks like the name of a genre, such that we could say that Jeremiah, for example, is 'prophecy' but the Psalms are 'hymnody'; but in fact it much more often expresses a judgement about the origin of a book. To call a book 'prophecy' is to say that God speaks through it – and thus the Psalms too can be 'prophecy' – rather than to say that it should be read with certain generic expectations in mind.

This point can be illustrated by returning for a moment to the question of the prophetic status of Daniel. Origen exchanged some letters with Africanus on this question,[2] which arose in connection with the problem raised for Christians by the exclusion from the Jewish canon, by that time, of the Additions to Daniel – Susanna, Bel and the Dragon, Azariah's prayer, and the Song of the Three Young Men. Africanus notes something that has interested

143

subsequent commentators, too, and has led to some of the arguments about the place of Daniel within the canon which we surveyed in chapters 1 and 2: Daniel is nowhere in the Hebrew text called a 'prophet', whereas in Susanna he is at least by implication treated as such, since the text says (v. 45) that 'God aroused the holy spirit of a young lad named Daniel'. As Africanus puts it, Daniel does 'prophesy' in 'another way' (*allô(i) tropô(i)*) in the Hebrew book, 'in visions and dreams' (*horamasi kai oneirois*), and also receives an angelophany; but he does not prophesy *epinoia(i) prophêtikê(i)*.

Now here, one might think, is a very startling anticipation of the distinction between prophecy and apocalyptic: prophetic utterance, on the one hand, and on the other visions and dreams. Whether Africanus really had hit on our modern distinction I should not like to say, but certainly Origen makes nothing of this insight at all. For him, the question is entirely one about the *status* of the book of Daniel and its various parts, and he argues, in effect, that even without the Greek additions Daniel can properly be treated as a prophetic book, because one need not be explicitly designated 'prophet' or utter prophetic oracles to qualify for the title. Think of Jacob, he says: no one surely doubts that Jacob was a prophet,[3] yet he received his inspiration only in dreams and visions, just like Daniel. Thus the overriding concern for questions of the authority and divine inspiration of scriptural books edges out questions about genre. If nothing had hung on Daniel's claim to be a prophet, and if it had not been necessary to show that the book's status did not depend on including within it the Greek additions, Origen might well have taken a lively interest in the contrast (blindingly obvious to us) between the experiences attributed to Daniel and those of the 'classical' prophets. But other concerns leave no leisure for such topics, no neutral ground on which they could be discussed.[4]

In reading writers of New Testament times, therefore, it is important to remember that our own classifications of the various different sorts of book in the Old Testament, Apocrypha, and Pseudepigrapha have little validity. To us it is immediately obvious that historiography is something quite different from prophecy, psalmody from didactic literature, apocalyptic from romantic fiction. But we have already seen, in studying the development of the canon, how little such distinctions mattered in our period. Josephus happily describes what are now Torah, Former Prophets, and Latter Prophets, along with some of the Writings, as 'history'. Baba Bathra

14b distinguishes between records of destruction and records of consolation, but cares nothing that some of these are records of the past and others of the future. Most of our witnesses see the Psalms as forming a distinct category of some kind, but are not in the least disturbed by the thought that David, who wrote them, was a prophet, so that as well as being hymns they are also oracles, revealing mysteries of one sort or another.

The difference between ourselves and these writers may, in fact, be summed up as follows. We have certain ideas about what would constitute a single and recognizable genre, and when we read the books of the Bible, we notice that some of them are composite (for example, a mixture of narrative and prophecy) and others puzzling (for example, Deuteronomy is hard to classify at all – is it law, or wisdom, or a collection of sermons?[5]). We are perfectly ready to adjust our ideas in the light of what we read – our expectations are not hard prejudices – but we are open to finding the texts we read problematic. By contrast, the readers of the Bible with whom this book is concerned took the biblical text as a given, and adjusted such ideas of genre as they had to what they found there. Rather than being puzzled that the Torah contained both laws and historical narratives, they simply took it as a given that the Torah was a coherent work (for it was given by God) and therefore assumed that the oscillation between two different 'genres' was an entirely normal way of writing.

To put it in terms which are in fact anachronistic, but may help to focus the point clearly: in our period there was felt to be a genre 'torah' (which happened to have only one member), which combined narrative and law, together with various other types of writing such as poetry and prediction. As a matter of historical fact such a genre had never existed, in the sense that anyone had sat down to write 'a Torah'; it was the adventitious product of a long and chaotic process of redaction, in which originally separate sources and fragments were woven together into a shapeless collection. But no one knew that.[6] Consequently the Torah was read with an assumption of coherence (though indeed little attention was actually paid to its whole sweep – it tended to be heard piecemeal), in rather the way we are urged to read it by Brevard Childs in his proposals for a 'canonical' reading of the Old Testament.[7]

Philo is specially interesting here, since he noticed the mixture of genres in the Pentateuch:

145

[The sacred books] consist of two parts: one the historical, the other concerned with commands and prohibitions. . . . We must give the reason why he began his law-book with the history, and put the commands and prohibitions in the second place . . . (*de vita Mosis* 1:45–7).

There follows a lengthy exposition of the construction of the Pentateuch, showing how skilfully Moses put all these materials together to make a harmonious whole (ibid., 48–65; compare *de praemiis* 1–3). The perception of generic differences, to which Philo's literary background made him sensitive, becomes simply an opening to argue for the carefully planned unity of the Torah. Just as meaning is found in elements which we should regard as sub-semantic, so it is also found in aspects of the arrangement of material which we should probably judge accidental. Both tendencies are widely found in the interpretation of sacred texts: paradoxically, the holier the text, the more likely one is to find edifying meanings in aspects which are really devoid of meaning, and thus to misinterpret it more seriously than one would if it were less holy. There are many modern parallels here, but that is another story.

Now what happened in Philo's work on the Torah no doubt happened also in the reading of 'the prophets', that is, other inspired ancient writings. It is possible that deliberate intention should be ascribed to the post-exilic redactors of the books of the classical prophets, who arranged them in such a way that they generally included not only oracles but narratives too: that is, it may be that these redactors sought to provide a kind of biography of the prophet, including his sayings in a narrative framework – a natural enough mode of composition, perhaps. But it is equally conceivable that they merely heaped together all the material which bore the particular prophet's name, without regard for whether it was narrative or direct speech, nor for whether the narrative was in the first or third person. Thus the book of Isaiah *may* represent an attempt at telling the story of Isaiah through narrative and oracles in what was assumed to be chronological order. But it may also be no more than an anthology, built up from previous smaller collections (themselves more or less chaotic) by simple addition. But we can be certain of one thing: no one in New Testament times had any knowledge whatever about the process. They had no particular theory about how a prophetic book *ought* to be compiled: they simply had a number of such books, all of which contained – just like the Torah – a variety of types of material. It is hopelessly anachronistic to think that they had any sort of idea that the different genres within the books of the prophets should be read in different ways, or even that the different prophetic books differed in the kinds of material they contained.

For us, there is a vast difference between (for example) Jonah – a typical post-exilic 'tale' – and Amos, a collection of prophetic oracles. But in our period the two books were seen merely as minor variants of the same thing, the 'prophetic book'. Somehow we need to find ways of sharing this perception, closing our minds to critical questions for a while, if we are to see how the prophets looked to people who thought like this. After all, it is *possible* to see Jonah and Amos as similar. Both contain some ethical teaching, some predictions, and some information about the prophet's life. For a reader in our period the differences were trivial, compared with this essential similarity of theme and contents. What is more, most other 'prophetic' books also contain these same elements, in different proportions: Samuel, for example, is also made up of narrative, teaching, and prediction. The fact that the last two elements appear only within direct speech and that the narrative provides the framework is quite unimportant – God, after all, is the true speaker in it all anyway. By the time one has remembered that every word in the book is, or is part of, a divine oracle; that 'there is no before and after in Scripture'; that the prophets who spoke in these books also wrote them; and that their knowledge of both future and past was alike guaranteed by divine inspiration: little remains of any critical perception about genre!

No one in our period, if asked to define a 'prophetic book', would have said anything about genre: one would have heard only about the book's divine origin, and the inspiration of the author which made it possible for him to write down the divine oracles he was given. And – to come now to the point – the kind of information that the reader would expect to obtain from the book would not be determined by any internal criteria, based on a judgement about its genre, but solely on his conception of the kind of information prophetic inspiration had existed to impart. As we have already seen, for a great many writers in our period that meant arcane information. Prophetic scriptures existed to teach truths that one

147

could not know otherwise. What literary genres they adopted in doing so was quite beside the point.

One consequence of this which should not be controversial is the very obvious fact that our witnesses do not turn to different kinds of scriptural book for different kinds of information. If one wants predictions, they are quite as likely to be found in the Psalms or the wisdom books as in the Latter Prophets; if one is looking for history, the Latter Prophets are as likely a source as the Former; if one seeks wisdom, one may consult Prophets or Psalms just as well as Proverbs or Ecclesiastes: and cosmic secrets are encoded in the Song of Songs just as much as in Ezekiel. There may be a slight tendency for particular groups to favour particular books, as the early Christians obviously favoured Isaiah, the source of so many messianic predictions. But even that will not explain why they also took such an interest in the Psalms, whose messianic character does not in the least depend on their genre or overt contents, but only on the fiction of Davidic authorship. The horribly simple explanation that their preference had something to do with the distribution of scrolls of these two books – worse still, that these were the only two non-Torah scrolls that happened to be in the book-cupboard of the synagogue at Nazareth or Capernaum – cannot be discounted.

There is, however, another consequence which may be less obvious, but is important for thinking ourselves back into the frame of mind of our period. I have been suggesting that many of the pseudonymous works of Second Temple Judaism are, as one might say, pastiche 'Prophets': artificially produced 'holy books', put into circulation under the fiction that they dated back to the 'prophetic age'. If one tries to imagine how one might go about writing such a book, the immediate question will arise: what type of book is one trying to write? – or, in other words, with what conventions is the book to work? In our terms this is a question about genre. But for people in our period, as we have seen, genre is not a central concern in reading Scripture. In their context, the kind of book a would-be 'scriptural' or 'prophetic' author will produce will have to be merely an imitation of whichever of the (genuinely old) prophetic books he has read and values most. And since most of these are composite, heavily redacted, inconsistent works, it will not be surprising if a pastiche of them manifests the same characteristics.

This explains, it seems to me, many of the puzzling features in works from the Second Temple period, which cause such agonies when scholars have to produce classified anthologies of them. Is Jubilees 'apocalyptic'? Are the Testaments of the Twelve Patriarchs wisdom or apocalyptic? Are the Psalms of Solomon hymnody, oracles, or apocalypses? And so on. The difficult and complex titles of the two volumes in Charlesworth's recent *Old Testament Pseudepigrapha*[8] bear eloquent testimony to the gravity of the problem. The fact is that the people who wrote most of these works did not trouble their heads about genre at all, but simply looked at their scriptures and wrote more of the same. Because we read Isaiah, or Proverbs, or Job, as reconstructed by critical scholarship, we tend not to notice that *in their present form* these books are just as formless as the Pseudepigrapha. One of the few virtues of a 'canonical' approach might be to help us see with fresh eyes how they looked to a generation which had no critical knowledge of their origin at all.

II

So far we have established a number of negatives. The books of the 'prophets' were not on the whole read in what we should think of as their 'natural' or 'historical' sense in New Testament times. They were assumed to be addressed primarily to the contemporary reader, not to those who happened to live in the prophets' own day. Thus the normal methods of biblical criticism, which have been so successful in penetrating to the heart of the message of the prophets through the accumulated accretions of the centuries, are powerless to show us how these books looked to a reader in the time of Philo or Josephus.

Secondly, however, we have also seen that the very formlessness of so many of these books prevents us from being able to tell how they 'must have been' read in our period by simply attending to their 'canonical' form. The canonical approach to Scripture recommended especially by Childs looks as if it should amount to a return to reading biblical books as they were read at the time when the canon was forming: treating the book of Isaiah as a continuous series of oracles by the prophet of that name, the Pentateuch as a single and coherent work with a simple narrative thread, and so on. But this is really quite anachronistic. A reading which tries to treat a large and complex book such as Isaiah as forming a closed, unitary whole bears little resemblance at all to the way scriptural books were read in ancient times, and owes much more to modern literary criticism than to ancient modes of understanding Scripture.[9] We might put it like this: in ancient times everyone assumed that the whole book of Isaiah was by that prophet, but no one read the book as a unity. On the contrary, Isaiah (like the rest of Scripture) was read as if it were a collection of innumerable fragments, a book not unlike Proverbs, in which every pericope, indeed every sentence or even every word, had a meaning independent of its context. The perception of Isaiah as part of 'the holy books' inhibited any attempt to find unity within the book itself, since it was not seen as a work with its own internal integrity but as a more or less arbitrary length cut from a longer roll, the seamless fabric of the oracles of God.

This is why no one in New Testament times was at all troubled by the existence of the 'Book of the Twelve', which to us seems a most effective barrier to understanding any of the books of the Minor Prophets properly. It really does not matter how one amalgamates or divides prophetic material, since its meaning does not depend on the boundaries of a particular book, section, or even phrase. From this vantage-point we can see, I believe, that a 'canonical reading' will often be even further from capturing the way the Bible was read in our period than a 'historical-critical' reading. This does not matter, of course, so long as the canonical approach is not being recommended for its greater faithfulness to the tradition of the Church or the synagogue; but if canonical critics start to say that normal critical readings are anachronistic, we should reply 'So are yours (if not more so)'.

Neither critical nor anti-critical approaches, then, can show us how people of New Testament times must have read the prophetic scriptures; for they did not derive their understanding of Scripture either from studying it with a critical eye or by reading it with expectations of unity, closure, and the like, but (to speak frankly) from *preconceptions* about what divine oracles were likely to contain. To some small extent, no doubt, the Bible itself and the traditions within Israel which it represented helped to form these preconceptions. Perhaps no one would have expected the Bible to provide accurate information about the future if the ancient texts had contained absolutely no passages that were obviously predictions; perhaps no one would have expected it to yield secrets about the nature of God if there had been no sections like Ezekiel 1–2; perhaps, to take the most extreme possibility, no one would have thought to gain guidance about conduct from the Pentateuch if it had been entirely devoid of legal material. Perhaps: when one sees what the Hellenistic intelligentsia made of Homer, one may wonder whether even so much is certain.

But it is quite clear that even the preconceptions about Scripture that did have some foundation in the text itself were drastically altered in becoming hermeneutical tools to prise open the text's secret treasuries. Certainly, there is a vision of the throne of God in Ezekiel 1–2, and hints of the same sort elsewhere; but it could hardly be said that such passages constitute the central nerve of the Old Testament. To read the Bible as principally a repository of coded messages about the constitution of the cosmos and the orders of the heavenly hierarchies is scarcely a natural way of reading it; indeed, it would not be too much to say that it is a radically *unbiblical* way of reading it. The theology and thought-forms of Second Temple Judaism are not just slightly different from the theology and thought-forms of the Old Testament, they represent a radically different system articulated on quite fresh lines. Wellhausen was right about that, however much one may disapprove of his adverse value-judgements on Judaism. The startling difference between the genuinely old books in the Old Testament and the later works which were evidently thought to be of very much the same kind makes this point abundantly clear, without any recourse to Wellhausen's theories about the Pentateuch. Anyone who thinks 1 Enoch, or even Daniel, is anything like Isaiah or Amos *must* be living in a quite different world of thought from that of the Israel of the prophets. All this means that there cannot be any *a priori* way of establishing what the 'prophetic' books meant to those who read them in our period: one can discover the meaning they were thought to have only by seeing what kinds of information people in fact turned to them to discover, and what content they poured into their own imitations of these books.

III

It seems to me that the various kinds of information for which people in New Testament times turned to 'the prophets' can be classified under four headings; and I shall refer to these as four 'modes' of reading prophetic scripture. Each of the four chapters that follow will be devoted to one of them, but it will be as well to sketch them briefly in a preliminary way so that it can be seen how they are related to each other.

In the first mode what was revealed to the prophets is understood to have been halakah: directions on how life is to be lived to be pleasing to God. This is a way of reading Scripture which has obviously been central in most branches of Judaism, and it corresponds more or less to the view of 'prophets' that can, as we saw earlier, be thought to underlie the arrangement of the Hebrew canon, though I have questioned the antiquity of this. A major issue which this first mode raises is the relation of the prophets to the Torah: something that has already been discussed in various contexts, and which will require still further treatment before we can get a fully rounded view of it.

The second mode reads the prophets as predicting a divine intervention in history of a more or less decisive kind, within the lifetime of the reader. This is the 'eschatological' way of reading prophecy which we saw to have been common in Christianity, and which (with the same reservations as those just noted) can be correlated in some way with the arrangement the Greek Old Testament has in a large number of manuscripts. Those who read the prophets in this way believed that the Scriptures were 'written for our instruction' in an extremely direct sense: it was to foretell precisely the events that were about to take place *now* that God had commissioned and inspired the prophets of old. Ancient scripture has often been read in this way by those who expect the end of the present order to break in upon them soon, and indeed the Bible continues to be read in this way by many in our own day.

So far the reader will have needed no prophetic powers (in any sense) to predict the modes of reading Scripture with which we shall be dealing. The prophets as teachers of halakah and of consistent eschatology have already figured largely in our discussion. The remaining modes are not quite so easily foreseeable and will need to be described at more length before it can be seen that they are equally important. The third in particular looks like little more than a sub-type of the second, and it may be difficult for me to convince the reader that it is really distinct. In this third mode, the prophets are seen just as much as prognosticators of future events as in the second; but the sense that the decisive stage in the future they predicted is about to break in on the world is lacking. The function of prophecy here is to reveal the shape and consistency of God's plan for human history, not to awaken expectations of the imminent fulfilment of ancient promises. The recognition that this is a mode of reading prophecy independent of (in fact logically prior to) the imminently eschatological mode can, I believe, help to resolve some long-standing problems about the relation of prophecy to 'apocalyptic', as well as cutting through the tangle created by theories which postulate an opposition between 'theocracy' and 'eschatology' in post-exilic Judaism.

Finally, in our fourth mode the secret information revealed to the prophet is seen as consisting in truths which for us might best be classified as speculative theology: truths about the eternal being and character of God, and about the realm in which he dwells, which go far beyond what natural reason or the commonplaces of Jewish belief can tell us. In this mode the prophet is seen as a mystic who has approached the inner mystery of God himself, and has communicated it to those with eyes to see and ears to hear the wonders that lie concealed beneath the surface of his text. Here, too, we shall find that some of the problems associated with the term 'apocalyptic' find a resolution somewhat different from what is customarily argued; though here, as in all that follows, my concern is far less to settle old disputes than to introduce some fresh categories that may make these disputes less troublesome than they sometimes seem. There must be many ways of drawing a map of the thought-world of Second Temple Judaism and early Christianity, all with their own merits. My aim is not to carp at other people's maps, but to offer a new projection which may draw attention to some features that the more familiar maps allow one to overlook, and soften some contrasts they perhaps exaggerate. But all projections distort in some way or other, and mine is naturally no exception.

5

Prophecy as Ethical Instruction

I

The 'prophetic' books of the Old Testament contain, in various blends, narrative, prediction, and ethical pronouncements. The critical reader will often want to ask which was uppermost in the mind of a particular author. Thus we perceive Ecclesiastes primarily as a wisdom book, that is, a book of ethical instruction and reflection on the meaning of life and its moral coherence; the 'autobiographical' material about the author (1:1; 2:1–11) we see as merely a fictitious frame.[1] On the other hand, we read Kings as a historical narrative. We notice that in 'prophetic' speeches, and in the occasional passage where the compiler speaks *in propria persona*, there is ethical instruction, but on the whole we use historiographical models to grasp the work's unity. In other words, when we read the Old Testament we ask which of the various kinds of material in a particular book is 'foregrounded', because this is the only way we have of deciding on the book's genre, and thus knowing how to read it intelligently.

But, as we have seen, this has little in common with the way Scripture was read in New Testament times. Writers in that period seem not to have been aware of generic distinctions between the scriptural books, or if they were that awareness had few practical consequences for interpretation. On the whole they adopted some uniform model of what an 'inspired' book could be expected to contain, and applied this as a hermeneutical key to whatever book they might be reading. Since for many Jews the essence of the revelation contained in the Pentateuch was *torah* – detailed instruction on living within the covenant – it is not surprising that 'prophetic' literature was often seen in the same way. By the time of the Talmud there can be little doubt that this is the major

154

hermeneutical model for reading all non-Pentateuchal Scripture. For a verse of Scripture to be cited in support of some particular piece of halakah it makes no difference what kind of scriptural book it stands in. Whether in its natural sense it is history, prediction, or teaching is a matter of indifference. The dominance of the Torah is demonstrated, in any case, by the comparatively small use made in the Mishnah of books outside the Pentateuch,[2] but even where other books are quoted the halakic interest is clear. For example:

> Whence do we learn of a ship that it is not susceptible to unclean-ness? Because it is written, 'The way of a ship in the midst of the sea' [Proverbs 30:19] . . . Whence do we learn that they are to tie a strip of crimson on the head of the scapegoat? Because it is written, 'Though your sins be as scarlet, they shall be as white as snow' [Isaiah 1:18] (M. Shabbat 9:2–3).

It is clear in any case that for the rabbis a prophet was conceived as the same kind of person as Moses had been and as the sages of their own day were; and that means that the primary function of prophets was to provide inspired guidance in matters of conduct. Thus 'the prophets' appear in the chain of tradition for the oral Torah in Aboth 1:1: 'Moses received the Law from Sinai and committed it to Joshua, and Joshua to the elders, and the elders to the prophets, and the prophets committed it to the men of the Great Synagogue.' The same assimilation of prophetic teaching to halakah is implied in the belief that each of the prophets received his own words from God at the same time as the revelation of the Torah at Sinai:

> R. Isaac said, The Prophets drew from Sinai the inspiration of all their future utterances, for God spoke 'with him that stands here with us this day' (Dt 29:15) that is, with those who were already created, 'and also with him that is not here with us this day'; these are the souls which are destined to be created. So, too, it does not say, 'The burden of the Lord to Malachi' but 'by the hand of Malachi', to show that the prophecy was already in his hand at Mount Sinai. So, too, in Isaiah XLVIII, 16, it says, 'From the time that it was, there am I'; that is, 'From the hour when the Torah was given, I received this prophecy'. Not only to the Prophets alone does this apply, but to all the sages that are destined to arise in after days, for the Decalogue is described

in Deut v, 22, as 'One great voice', and this was divided into seven, and then into seventy tongues for all mankind.[3]

We may say that the rabbis assimilated prophetic scripture to the Torah in thus treating it primarily as a source for halakah; but it would of course be equally fair to point out that a similar shift has occurred with the Pentateuch itself. The books of Moses are no more obviously *torah* than the Prophets are. They, too, consist of a wide variety of genres, and the decision to read them primarily as a source of ethical or juridical rulings is scarcely more unnatural (if we are to adopt a modern critical outlook) than the parallel decision to treat the Prophets in this way. The shift had, however, occurred much earlier in the case of the Pentateuch. Indeed, a halakic understanding is already present in the latest stratum of material within the Pentateuch, the 'P' source, with its strong aetiological interest in the origins of festivals and religious observances: what is Genesis 1:1–2:4a but an aetiology of the sabbath? As Wellhausen pointed out, the post-exilic redaction of the Pentateuch was a deliberate attempt to turn it from a collection of stories and laws into the foundation document of Judaism, which could act as a guide to every aspect of life within the covenant. But in the process the narratives were not suppressed, but given a new function: to serve as exemplars for later generations of conduct which accords with the Torah.[4]

It is not surprising that a similar interpretative practice should have grown up around the books of the 'prophets'. The Former Prophets or 'Deuteronomistic History' was probably already understood in this way well before the New Testament era, as Martin Noth observed: 'When this [sc. the post-exilic] community preserved and maintained the ancient narrative tradition of the history of Israel along with it [sc. the Law], it was understood as a collection of historical examples of the attitude of man to the law and its consequences'.[5]

Already at the latest redactional stages of the work we find the tendency to treat particular incidents as exemplary, so that many of the stories about prophets, for instance, become object-lessons in how one should respond to the word of God, and warnings of the dreadful consequences that ensue if one does not. A good case of this, taken from many possible ones, is the story of Naaman and Elisha in 2 Kings 5. Whatever may have been the original form of this tale, as it stands it inculcates exact obedience to the demands of God (however apparently irrational), the worship of Yahweh alone, and the importance of humility, and it warns against any attempt to profit from spiritual gifts. It is even possible, as generations of Sunday-school teachers can witness, to extract an improving moral from the fact that the mighty Naaman owed his cure to the timely words of an insignificant Aramean captive, his wife's slave-girl. Whatever the uncertainties of traditio-historical criticism (and they are many), it is surely not unreasonable to think that the 'original' story was told for the greater glory of Elisha (or even of some other prophet, named or unnamed), not as an *exemplum* for the preacher. Its transformation into what we now find presumably owes much to just the trend we are at present investigating: the growing tendency in post-exilic Judaism to treat old stories as important primarily for their witness to the merits of keeping the Torah, in the widest sense.

Indeed, the redaction of the Deuteronomistic History exhibits this tendency not simply in individual stories but in its overall shape. The whole history of the kings of Israel and Judah is a story with a moral. Like *1066 and All That* it is a tale of Good Kings and Bad Kings, the Bad greatly predominating, and it goes to show that for nations as well as individuals the wages of sin is death. If Noth was right in seeing the work in its present form as the product of the desolate community that remained in Judah after Jerusalem had fallen to the Babylonians, then this didactic note will have been present in it from the first; for the chief purpose in recalling the history of sin and failure that was the sum-total of Israel's time in the promised land must have been to provide material for penitence and thence for reform.[6] It is highly likely that the same is true of the Book of Jeremiah, which bears the stamp of the same 'deuteronomistic' theology.[7]

By the time of Chronicles it is plain that a moralizing, didactic purpose could be taken for granted in writing 'history'. The Chronicler considerably increases the number of set-piece speeches on the theme of faithfulness to God and reliance on his help, and sharpens the emphasis on exact and immediate retribution for sin. His 'prophets' are usually presented as preachers of repentance, urging kings and people to good works and threatening that the wrath of God will strike the disobedient and godless. For example, in 2 Chronicles 15:2-7 the prophet Azariah ben Oded appeals to Asa to be loyal to Yahweh, pointing to the past history of the nation as affording examples of obedience to be imitated and of disobedience to be shunned:

> The LORD is with you, while you are with him. If you seek him, he will be found by you, but if you forsake him, he will forsake you. For a long time Israel was without the true God, and without a teaching priest, and without law; but when in their distress they turned to the LORD, the God of Israel, and sought him, he was found by them . . . Take courage! Do not let your hands be weak, for your work shall be rewarded.[8]

The same tendency to take earlier incidents already recounted in existing writings as *exempla* has been found in the redaction of the prophetic books proper by R. A. Mason, in an important article on 'sermons' in the Second Temple.[9] He suggests that material which already counted as 'Scripture', along with earlier well-known sayings of the pre- and early post-exilic prophets, were treated as the 'text' which preaching (a term that need not be too pedantically defined) expounded for each new generation. 'The preaching exhorts them to live lives of ethical and cultic purity; to avoid the sins of their fathers of the pre-exilic age, while showing a like response to those who heard Zechariah himself' (the redaction of Zechariah is Mason's particular example of this process).[10] There is probably no book in the Latter Prophets that lacks some evidence of this desire of the redactors to show the relevance of older prophecy and history to contemporary ethical needs.[11]

The perception of prophecy as teaching persists in the later books of the Old Testament. Daniel 9:10 takes for granted the picture of prophets that one can get from a straightforward reading of the Deuteronomistic History: 'we have not obeyed the voice of the LORD our God by following his laws, which he set before us by his servants the prophets'. 2 Maccabees 2:1–4 explicitly identifies Jeremiah's work as centred on the Torah:

> One finds in the records that Jeremiah the prophet ordered those who were being deported to take some of the fire, as has been told, and that the prophet after giving them the law instructed those who were being deported not to forget the commandments of the Lord, nor to be led astray in their thoughts upon seeing the gold and silver statues and their adornment. And with other

similar words he exhorted them that the law should not depart from their hearts.

People had thus come to read Scripture as a collection of examples of righteous conduct, and of exhortations to live well, long before our period. There can be no doubt that this continued to be a major hermeneutical key to Scripture, as it has been, indeed, down to our own day. Josephus on the whole has little interest in matters of halakah, and although he certainly sees the overall sweep of Israel's history as illustrating the general moral principles according to which God directs human affairs, he seldom treats individual passages from the historical or other non-Pentateuchal books from the point of view of their possible ethical implications. An exception, perhaps, is the life of his favourite prophet, Daniel, to which he makes some moralizing additions. For example, after Daniel's escape from the lions' den the lions are fed before Daniel's enemies are thrown to them, so that it may not be thought that mere hunger drives them to consume the victims. The lions well understand that they have a divine vocation, and the wickedness of those who opposed Daniel is so apparent that even they can see it, forcing themselves to wreak the appointed vengeance in spite of the risk of indigestion.[12] But, odd as it seems to us, Josephus altogether overlooks the ethical element in Amos and Hosea (whom he does not even mention), and in the case of Isaiah he concentrates most of his attention on the prophet's historical importance and wonder-working powers, saying little of his denunciations of sin. Where he does treat characters and incidents in the history of Israel as exemplary his choices are at times unexpected. Thus the witch of Endor is held up as a shining example of generosity and selflessness in being prepared to risk death (as she believed) in order to bring help to the disguised Saul.[13]

In Philo, on the other hand, prophetic Scripture is routinely treated as in later rabbinic texts, and regarded as essentially supportive of the Torah. N. Walter is certainly right to say that in Philo 'passages from the non-Pentateuchal books are never given an exegesis of their own in the true sense, but are simply adduced in the course of expounding sections of the Torah';[14] Philo's major work is, of course, a section by section exposition of the Pentateuch. As we shall see later, these expositions do not concentrate greatly on ethical matters, but more often find a 'mystical' sense in Moses' words. But Philo is nevertheless well aware that prophecy had a close concern with ethics, and indeed sees this as one of the aspects of the *prophetic* task of Moses: Moses' decisions in the case of the man who gathered sticks on the sabbath (Numbers 15:32–6) and of the daughters of Zelophehad (Numbers 27:1–11) are the result of an oracle (see *de vita Mosis* 2:213–18 and 233–41).

Philo at times uses characters in the Prophets as examples, and has a particular fondness for Hannah, to whom he refers about five times – perhaps because her silent prayer, mistaken for drunkenness, seemed to him particularly apt as an example of the spiritual experience in which he himself was an adept. He treats of her at length in *de ebrietate* 144–53, presenting her as a model to be imitated by those who are willing to pursue the way of virtue that leads to mystical ecstasy, by practising austerity and seeking only the intoxication that comes from contact with the divine.[15] It is clear that the actual historical reality of the characters who appear in the pages of Scripture matters little to him, if they can be pressed into service as examples of piety. Thus in this same passage we read 'probably there was an actual man called Samuel; but we conceive of the Samuel of the scripture, not as a living compound of soul and body, but as a mind which rejoices in the service and worship of God and that only'.[16] It is in Philo that we find the clearest account of the way of reading historical narratives that looks for *exempla* rather than 'mere' history:

These are such men as lived good and blameless lives, whose virtues stand permanently recorded in the most holy scriptures, not merely to sound their praises but for the instruction of the reader and as an inducement to him to aspire to the same; for in these men *we have laws endowed with life and reason* [*hoi gar empsuchoi kai logikoi nomoi andres ekeinoi gegonasin*], and Moses extolled them for two reasons. First he wished to show that the enacted ordinances are not inconsistent with nature; and secondly that those who wish to live in accordance with the laws as they stand have no difficult task, seeing that the first generations before any at all of the particular statutes was set in writing followed the unwritten law with perfect ease, so that one might properly say that the enacted laws are nothing else than memorials of the lives of the ancients, preserving to a later generation their actual words and deeds (*de migratione Abrahami* 4–5).[17]

160

Although this refers primarily to the pre-Mosaic patriarchs, the implication is clear: it is worth studying the heroes of the past, because in them we have the Law enfleshed, living examples for us to imitate.[18]

II

When we turn to the New Testament it is not too great a surprise to find that the use of 'prophetic' texts to provide either comment or supporting examples for the practice of the Torah is much less common than in later rabbinic texts, and even than in Philo. This is just what we might expect from our knowledge that most New Testament writers are heavily committed to a primarily 'eschatological' understanding of prophetic Scripture, and it accords well with the evidence of Qumran, where I have not been able to find a single example of a non-Pentateuchal text read in the first mode. Such New Testament material as there is, however, strikingly confirms the general scholarly consensus about the date and character of the New Testament writings, as will soon be apparent.

So far as I can see, the gospels of Mark and Luke are almost entirely lacking in any halakic use of non-Pentateuchal books. A marginal exception might be Luke 16:29–31 (the parable of Dives and Lazarus), where 'Moses and the prophets' ought to give the rich man's family enough encouragement to repent, which I suppose could be said to portray the rest of Scripture in the same guise as the Torah; though one could just as well argue that it is the scriptural predictions of God's impending judgement on sinners that are what should lead them to mend their ways.

Both Acts and John have enough material to show that what was to become the normal perception of prophecy in Tannaitic times was already current, but little more. Thus in John 4:19–20 the Samaritan woman, convinced by Jesus' supernatural knowledge of her marital state that he is 'a prophet', immediately assumes that he is therefore the right person to give a ruling in a matter of halakah: which is the proper mountain on which to worship God? Acts 3:22 (in Stephen's speech) similarly speaks of the eschatological prophet promised by Moses in Deuteronomy 18:15–16 as one whom men must *obey* – but in this, of course, it does no more than quote the words of Scripture. Verse 26, however ('God . . . sent him to you

161

first, to bless you in turning every one of you from your wickedness'), clearly perceives the Prophet as a preacher of repentance, probably with Malachi's Elijah in mind. Again, 'the law and the prophets' are evidently thought of chiefly in their character of *torah* in Paul's speech before Felix in Acts 24:14: 'I worship the God of our fathers, believing everything laid down by the law or written in the prophets' (cf. Romans 3:21). But these three examples are all I can find, and in two of them at least there could be some accommodation to what the writer perceived as a common Jewish view.

In Matthew, predictably enough, we find explicit references to 'the law and the prophets' as authoritative for conduct, in the Sermon on the Mount (5:17 and 7:12) and in the conclusion to the question about the 'greatest commandment' (22:34–40), where Jesus summarizes his teaching in the form 'On these two commandments depend all the law and the prophets' (unsupported in the parallels in Mark and Luke). The 'false prophets' of 7:15 may be false *teachers* (like the 'false prophet' of Revelation 16:3, 19:20 and 20:10) leading people into wrong paths, like those against whom the Didache warns (chapters 11 and 12). But even in Matthew there is extremely little use of non-Pentateuchal material in support of instructions about conduct. It is tempting to appeal to the principle of dissimilarity here, and to argue that if *even Matthew* does not attribute to Jesus many appeals to prophetic Scripture as support for his ethical teaching, this probably means that Jesus did not in fact make use of Scripture in this way. This contrasts with his reported use of the Pentateuch, where he is said to have pressed the detailed wording of the text: thus in Mark 10:2–9 and parallels (appealing to Genesis 1:27 and 5:2 in support of his prohibition of divorce)[19] and 12:26 and parallels (proving the resurrection from Exodus 3:6).

There is, in fact, only one passage in the synoptic gospels in which an incident outside the Pentateuch is cited as having implications for halakah: the controversy about the disciples plucking corn on the sabbath (Mark 2:23–8 and Luke 6:1–5). Here David's example in eating and sharing the shewbread (1 Samuel 21:1–6) is adduced in support of what is presented as an irregularity in Jesus' own conduct, with perhaps an implied Christological claim. Matthew here (12:1–8) intensifies the claim ('something greater than the temple is here') but also improves the argument by adding a reference to a Pentateuchal precedent (Numbers 28:9–10, which shows that the priests 'work' on the sabbath). The incident gives the impression that Jesus may often have argued in this way from precedents outside the Torah; but if he did, the evangelists record no other instance of it.

Paul's epistles are not much more productive of examples. None of those I have found uses scriptural allusions with any sense of binding force; usually texts are used more by way of underscoring a point already well made on other grounds. Romans yields two cases. In 12:20 Christians are encouraged to follow the advice of Proverbs: 'If your enemy is hungry, feed him; if he is thirsty, give him drink; for by so doing you will heap burning coals upon his head' (cf. Proverbs 25:21–2) – but first Paul has cited the Torah (Deuteronomy 32:35), and the quotation from Proverbs seems little more than a well-turned phrase chosen for its aptness. In 14:11 the readers are urged to be tolerant because all alike will be judged by God, and Isaiah (45:23) is quoted in support: 'As I live, says the Lord, every knee shall bow to me, and every tongue shall give praise to God.'

The same impression, that quotations from outside the Pentateuch are chosen for their apt phrasing rather than with any thought of strengthening the argument in a material way, is made by the four examples I can find in the Corinthian correspondence: 1 Corinthians 3:19 and 2 Corinthians 6:2, 6:17, and 9:9. In the first of these, sentences from Job 5:13 ('He catches the wise in their craftiness') and Psalm 94:11 ('The Lord knows that the thoughts of the wise are futile') are used to clinch Paul's cumulative argument against the pretensions of human wisdom in chapters 1–3; but the argument is in no way determined by them, not even ostensibly. It has already been fully established that no one should boast in his wisdom, by expounding the folly of the cross – for which Paul does not cite any scriptural proof, but only texts which show that God has secrets to reveal which will defeat human expectation. (Paul's use of Scripture in these chapters is in fact much closer to our fourth mode, and will be treated later.) He is not arguing that one should not boast of wisdom *because* Job and the Psalmist forbid it, but that when one has realized how wisdom and folly appear in the light of the paradox of the cross, then one will see how right Job and David were. This is a 'halakic' use of Scripture in appearance only.

Much the same may be said of the three examples from 2 Corinthians. In 2 Corinthians 6:2 and 6:17 exhortations are supported by tags from the prophets and the Psalms, but again Paul does not claim to be deriving the exhortation from the passages quoted; these come in, rather, as providing a fitting vocabulary with which to describe the weighty matters he is concerned with. Similarly, in 2 Corinthians 9:9 the readers are exhorted to be liberal just as God is liberal, and a Psalm verse (112:9) is quoted as a description of that liberality (though in fact, in its original context, it plainly refers to the liberality of 'the man who fears the Lord'). No one could suppose that Paul thought the obligation to give generously to his collection *depended on* Psalm 112:9, in the way that rulings on matters of halakah are formally derived from verses in the Pentateuch. The Psalm provides, to put it negatively, no more than a fine-sounding scriptural phrase to add sonority to the appeal or (to put it less dismissively) a confirmation that Paul's particular request is in line with the scriptural witness to the character of God and the kinds of demands he makes on his chosen people.

Neither in the gospels nor in Paul, then, do we find more than hints of the use of non-Pentateuchal material to support ethical decisions, which was to be such a marked feature of later Jewish use of the Prophets and the Writings. This contrasts with the use made of the Torah in the New Testament. In the gospels – not just in Matthew, but in the other synoptics – we do find questions of halakah decided on the basis of Pentateuchal proof-texts in something like the rabbinic manner. Thus in Mark 1:44 Jesus expects the cleansed leper to obey the law of Leviticus 13–14; in 7:9–13 he disputes over the correct interpretation of the fifth commandment; in 10:2–9 he compares one *torah* with another in order to rule against divorce; and in 10:17–22 and 12:28–34 he discusses what is involved in keeping the commandments. I say nothing as to the authenticity of any of this material, but simply note that it occurs in the gospels. Similarly Paul can on occasion discuss the application of the Law like any rabbi. Like the Jesus of the synoptic gospels, he is interested in the essence of the commandments (Romans 13:8–10); like Jesus again, he cites the saying in Genesis 2:24 'the two shall become one' in order to justify the view that sexual intercourse in itself constitutes an unbreakable bond – a stricter decision than any found in rabbinic literature, so far as I know. He can explicitly appeal to the Law as decisively closing a question, as in 1 Corinthians 9:9, where Deuteronomy 25:4 ('You shall not muzzle an ox when it is treading out the grain') is interpreted so as to prove that apostles are entitled to be supported by those to whom they preach.

No doubt with Paul as with Jesus it is significant that even appeals to the Torah are not plentiful, and many ethical injunctions are not justified by reference to any written authority but rather as direct divine imperatives, sometimes with a basis in natural rather than revealed law. But for our present purposes it is enough to note that the status of the Pentateuch for questions of halakah is at least acknowledged, and sometimes invoked. Where non-Pentateuchal books are concerned, the picture that emerges from the gospels and Pauline epistles is far more like that in Philo, or in the Mishnah. These books were useful in providing illustrative material, but one has the impression that they were very much secondary to the Pentateuch when it came to arriving at binding decisions. So far as it goes, in fact, this observation largely confirms the argument of chapter 2 above, that the Pentateuch was not seen as the 'first division' of a multipartite canon but rather as *the* canon. On matters of halakah the books that would come to be called the Prophets and the Writings had little standing. They were certainly 'Scripture', but they did not really belong in the world in which disputes about conduct were settled.

It is only in the Epistle to the Hebrews and the Catholic Epistles that the 'prophetic' books come into their own as a source of moral instruction, and where one senses that little distinction was perceived among the various books of Scripture. These books stand at the very beginning of the period in which Christians would stop speaking of 'the law and the prophets' and begin to think of the 'Old Testament', meaning *all* the old Jewish books by contrast with Christian writings. The use of the Old Testament as a whole for ethical instruction is explicitly mentioned in the famous passage about 'the inspiration of Scripture' in 2 Timothy 3:16–17: 'All Scripture is inspired by God and [*or* Every Scripture which is inspired by God is also] profitable for teaching, for reproof, for correction, and for training in righteousness, that the man of God may be complete, equipped for every good work'. Hebrews provides a fine instance of the tendency to read Old Testament history as a catalogue of moral *exempla* (Hebrews 11:4–38), and does not seem conscious of any break between Moses and Joshua, though the heroes after Joshua receive more summary treatment. Perhaps we have here the earliest clear evidence of a Christian 'Hexateuch', with the book of Joshua ('Jesus' in Greek) promoted, as it were, to Pentateuchal status. Unusual choices appear among the exemplars of righteous conduct, just as they do in Josephus. Hebrews (11:31) and James (2:25) alike single out Rahab the harlot (who also infiltrated the Matthaean genealogy (1:5) along with the almost equally improbable Tamar) and James, who is specially fond of finding examples to commend for imitation, names Elijah, Job, and the other prophets (5:10–11, 17).

It is to the Epistle of Jude that we owe the proposal that Christians should imitate the restraint of the archangel Michael, who was so fastidiously polite that he would not revile even the devil himself (Jude 9: the only case known to me of ethics as an *imitatio archangelorum*). Jude also perhaps treats Zechariah 3:3–4 as embodying a binding halakah when he exhorts his readers to 'save some, by snatching them out of the fire', though this must remain uncertain. Other passages which use non-Pentateuchal texts in our first mode are Hebrews 12:5–8 and 12; James 4:6; and 1 Peter 3:10–12 – though these are all a matter of moral *exhortation* rather than authoritative *ruling*, and in this resemble the cases in the Corinthian epistles.

The few examples to be found in the Apostolic Fathers add little to what we have already seen. 1 Clement recognizes that the prophets taught the Law: 'And him [sc. Moses] also the rest of the holy prophets followed, bearing witness with him to the laws that were ordained by him' (43:1); Barnabas (9:5) refers to Jeremiah 4:3–4 as an *entolê*, 'commandment'. On the whole it may be said that early Christian writers, while in theory seeing little importance in the distinction between 'Moses' and the other books of Scripture, tend even so to follow older Jewish practice in relying on the Pentateuch for ethical material, when they get it from Scripture at all. Like Paul, they often provide catalogues of vices and virtues which do not derive from the Bible anyway; but when they do seek scriptural support, they tend as if by instinct to turn to Moses first, for all that they sometimes describe him as 'the prophet' (cf. Barnabas 6:8).

III

The extent to which prophetic Scripture was actually used in taking ethical decisions and offering moral exhortation is thus quite variable in our period. Among the New Testament writers only those of the second generation appeal in this way to the Prophets with anything more than a casual interest; and in Philo and Josephus other interests tend to predominate – historical interests in Josephus, mystical in Philo. The heyday of such a use of prophecy still lies in the future, in later rabbinic citations. Nevertheless the principle that prophecy *can* be appealed to in much the same way, and for the same purposes, as the Torah, is well established, and it would surely have surprised any of the writers we have examined to be asked to justify it. Throughout the post-exilic age it had been entirely natural to see prophets as teachers, preachers of repentance, guides on matters of morality and heirs of Moses. Such a picture is firmly grounded in the work of the Deuteronomists and of the Chronicler, and it is presupposed in Daniel and in redactional passages in the prophetic books which we may suppose to come from the last few centuries BC. It was certainly not controversial. How did it arise?

Even to ask this question is of course to presuppose certain things about what the prophets had really been like. It presupposes, in fact, that prophets were not really what the Deuteronomists made of them. Whether this is the case is a question to which I shall return at the end of this book. But for the moment let us assume that at least some distortion of the truth was involved in presenting the prophets as teachers of morality and defenders of the Torah. It is then necessary to look for some explanation of this development: and at least since the work of Wellhausen there has been, broadly speaking, one main explanation available. For Wellhausen, the primary change within the religion of Israel, which began as early as the promulgation of Deuteronomy in the seventh century but was greatly hastened by the experience of Exile, was the replacement of the living voice of prophecy by the dead letter of the Law. It was the ascendancy of the Law that killed prophecy; and one result of this was that the writings of the old prophets came to be seen through the distorting lens of later assumptions about the primacy of Moses and of the system that was thought to derive from him.

It seems to me, as I have already suggested,[20] that this explanation lives on in the theories of Plöger and Hanson about the tensions between theocracy and eschatology in post-exilic Judaism, where the basic model established by Wellhausen is assumed, but it is then asserted that even after the Law had established its dominance there continued to be dissident groups, championing the free motions of the Spirit against the theocracy based on the eternal

Torah. From this starting point it becomes relatively easy to provide a background for the first mode of reading the ancient prophets. People who read them in this way will be those who were aligned with the mainstream, theocratic assumptions of those who formed the character of Second Temple Judaism. By reading prophecy as if it were 'a hedge about the Law', they effectively (though for the most part unconsciously) drew the sting of the old prophetic message and ensured that no prophetic outbursts would be able to threaten the stability of the religion they had established. Those who continued to have a truly 'prophetic' vocation had henceforth to exercise it outside the official religion, and such people became the founders of 'the apocalyptic movement'.

This explanation has many attractions, and in pointing to tensions between 'radicals' and 'conservatives' in Judaism it has an obvious plausibility, since we know that such (partly temperamental) oppositions are the stuff of which the history of many religions is made. Nevertheless I think it is too simple. We have found differences in the degree to which various writers adopted a first-mode reading of prophecy, but nothing at all to suggest either that it was vigorously promulgated against some rival theory or that it was angrily rejected as a travesty of the true prophetic spirit. The deuteronomists, the Chronicler, the redactors of Zechariah, and their like, may have falsified the message of the 'real' prophets, but there is no sign at all that anyone realized this, nor, on the other hand, that they were seen as 'saving' the prophetic books from annexation by wild extremist groups. The author of Daniel, who is not supposed to have been much attached to the ideas of the theocrats, presents the prophets in just the same light as the Chronicler; highly 'orthodox' figures such as Philo and Josephus, on the other hand, do not much insist on the halakic perception of prophecy, though they are perfectly happy with it and use it when it suits them. So far from being the subject of hot controversy, prophecy seems to have been an issue on which perfect peace reigned. This leads me to think that an explanation of our first mode in terms of the thinking of one group over against another is unlikely, and that the reasons behind the shift towards such a perception of the prophets may have been more general, related to features of the broad cultural and religious climate of the Persian and Hellenistic ages.

Mason interestingly suggests that one reason for the repeated processes of redaction and updating through which most of the prophetic books have passed is a result, not of the failure of the original prophets' oracles,[21] but of their success. It was not that post-exilic Jews were committed to the words of the pre-exilic prophets, and therefore had to find ways of making them palatable by inserting passages designed to remove the taint of unfulfilled predictions. On the contrary, prophetic oracles which had not proved themselves to be true were simply abandoned, following the sort of criterion proposed in Deuteronomy 18:22 and Jeremiah 28:9. Certain pre- and early post-exilic prophecies survived precisely because they had 'come true' (though admittedly not always in the most obvious sense), and it was for this reason that the books enshrining them were treasured, copied, and read. But of course there is a practical problem with fulfilled prophecies: they threaten to become empty in the very moment of fulfilment. Once the prophet has been proved right, the reader of his oracles is faced with a dilemma. On the one hand, the oracles are of no further interest: they are yesterday's news; on the other, they are obviously divinely inspired, since history has confirmed them.

What can one do with such oracles? Well, it is highly probable that a prophet who can accurately foresee the future will be a reliable guide on other subjects, too. Once his credit is established, it becomes only natural to turn to him for advice on conduct – the more so, as the predictions of the future which earlier prophets had uttered nearly always had a close connection with the way of life of those they addressed. In fact, since prophets demonstrate by the accuracy of their oracles that they are truly inspired, and have access to secrets otherwise known only to God and his heavenly court, there is no subject on which they are not a potential source of information and advice. Thus, it seems to me, one would *expect* ancient prophetic books to be regarded as a source of teaching about how one should behave in the present. This is the natural consequence of venerating old writings whose prestige results from their success in prediction. Even though they may contain little overt teaching about conduct, they will be read as if they do.

To put this another way, we may return to the question discussed at the end of the last chapter about the continuing relevance of old books. Just as the modern critical reader brings to texts various expectations about their probable content which rest on a perception of, or external information about, the genre to which the texts belong, so ancient readers of holy books brought an expectation of contemporary relevance and applicability. Like the modern Christian at a Bible-study group, these readers asked: 'What is the prophet saying to me?'; 'What privileged information does the prophet have, to which I can gain admittance by reading his words in the proper frame of mind?' The step from this to 'What then must I do?' is extremely short, and scarcely perceptible as a step at all to most readers. Because this is so, I am suspicious of theories about the shift in understanding prophecy just outlined that depend on finding *special* reasons linked to the distinctive character of Judaism, and still more of those that depend on reconstructions of the particular social groupings current in one short period. On the contrary, it seems to me that a first-mode reading is a practically inevitable consequence of recognizing a category of books as 'Holy Scripture', and it is not in the least surprising that the Koran, the Granth, various Hindu Scriptures, and indeed the books of the New Testament, are all read within the religions to which they belong as what in our terms may be called halakic prophecy. The same thing happened to the books of Homer in ancient times. The exaltation of the Pentateuch as a source of inspired teaching about the conduct of life, relevant in every age, is in reality not to be set over against the veneration of ancient prophecy, nor regarded as either an influence on or a reaction against such veneration, but is merely a parallel development of exactly the same kind. From a functional point of view, Torah and Prophets are titles for two bodies of material which have identical types of use; the difference between them is simply one of status.

How universal this tendency is may be seen from what happened to 'wisdom' texts, not only in Israel but in the other cultures of the ancient Near East. A detailed examination of this would take us too far afield, but H. H. Schmid's fascinating study *Wesen und Geschichte der Weisheit* is full of illustrations of the point. Schmid shows how the sharply contextualized teaching of old wisdom in Egypt, for example, came to be understood as the expression of timeless truths about the nature of man and of the good life which were valid, and could be made 'contemporary', for every generation. The teacher who originally delivered such teaching soon ceased to be thought of in realistic historical terms, and was turned into a sage who had revealed, not his own shrewd perceptions of what was appropriate to the conditions of life in his own day, but eternal insights into the character of man in general, such that no time could ever come when they would be out of date, still less untrue. 'What had originally – in the context of the perception of the world then current – been an "empirical" description of reality which could be verified from experience, became a postulate: a picture of reality that is applied in an unhistorical way to whatever situation one is in, and which makes a strenuous attempt to match reality exactly'.[22] This, Schmid argues, does not reflect a change of thought-forms, nor show that later teachers were actually out of touch with the realities of their own day: precisely because they were still in touch with those realities, they had to resort to all manner of hermeneutical devices to make the old texts say what they wanted them to say. The change is simply and solely a function of the fact that the texts were old, but were held in such esteem that they were being read, and treated as having contemporary relevance, in a quite different context from that which gave them birth. 'Books which had once been intended specifically for the training of officials, and therefore were meant (like all education in that period) only for the children of princes, later came to be used as school-books for teaching reading and writing'.[23]

As Schmid sees it, the act of putting originally time-bound sayings in writing, and preserving them for posterity, *automatically* (given the expectations about old books normal in ancient cultures) leads to a tendency to treat them as eternally relevant to the conduct of life. 'Once maxims come to be handed down in a fixed wording – which implies a claim to universal validity – they are stripped of their historical location and their particularity. Their context, which originally was immediately experienced and understood, comes to be objectivized, and thus becomes unhistorical. They lose their direct reference to real situations as they arise, and instead stand around in the linguistic lumber-room, ready to be employed in a new situation and to make themselves useful there. In this sense all wisdom literature *qua* literature – words learned by heart, fixed in writing, or in some other way conserved – is unhistorical'.[24]

What happened to prophecy in the post-exilic age, then, is essentially no different from what happened to the Law, or from what happens to any other body of ancient texts that come to be venerated as classics in any religious system. People assumed that they would provide guidance for daily conduct in the present. The dominance of the Torah did not affect the way prophetic texts *functioned*, though

171

it did determine the status they had: as second-rank religious literature, prophecy could not in mainstream Judaism countermand principles laid down in the Torah, but only illustrate and amplify them. Of course in practice this is a matter of how a particular ethical decision is dressed up, rather than telling us anything about its substance. Cases where a dictum of a prophet is formally opposed to a ruling in the Torah are very rare. Even in the New Testament Matthew 12:1–7, setting the authority of Hosea 6:6 and 1 Samuel 21:6 *above* that of the Torah, is a great rarity.[25] But it is not difficult so to interpret the Torah that it is taken to mean what one wants it to mean, in the light of a favourite passage from the Prophets; or, indeed, to read both Torah and Prophets through spectacles provided by some wholly external source. In the hands of a skilled interpreter Scripture can always be made to issue the rulings one wants to obey.[26]

IV

The pseudonymous works produced in our period confirm that prophets and their books were thought of as concerned with ethical conduct, by providing both precept and example. 'Wisdom' books continued to be written, but only in the case of Ben Sira do we have a self-conscious example of the old genre: on the whole 'wisdom' is communicated by attributing proverbial sayings to an ancient prophet; so that although the Wisdom of Solomon, for example, is recognizable to us as (just about) continuous with the tradition represented in Proverbs, in its own day it will have made a very different impression from Ecclesiasticus. Ben Sira was writing a book for publication in his own name – like Josephus or Philo: the author of Wisdom produced what most contemporaries will not have hesitated to think of as 'prophecy', the work of the inspired prophet-philosopher-king Solomon, who had learned 'both what is secret and what is manifest' (7:21). Much of what had been the concern of 'the wise' passes into the testament literature, and is placed on the lips of dying patriarchs who, as we have seen, were thought to have had 'prophetic' inspiration. In these works exhortation often mingles with prognostication to produce works that probably seemed harmonious at the time, though to us they are a horrible mixture of genres. Consequently the concerns of their

172

ethical teaching often diverge sharply from those of the older wisdom books, and the patriarchs or other worthies are presented as preaching obedience to the Torah and commending other pious Jewish practices, much as people believed the prophets to have done.

It seems to me that the ethical instruction fathered on famous figures from the past in pseudo-prophecy contains two somewhat different strands. The great majority of the works in question presuppose an ethical system which is not that of the older portions of the Old Testament, perhaps, but is certainly in line with the broad consensus of the late Persian and Hellenistic periods. The heroes and heroines of the shorter books of the Old Testament and Apocrypha are paragons of virtue, conceived as consisting in an observant Jewish life, honouring the written Law but also well-established pious customs, against a Gentile environment. Tobit and his family, Daniel and his companions, Esther, Judith, and all the minor characters who are commended in these books are good examples of how to live a well-regulated life within the covenant and to face death, if loyalty to the Torah demands it, with fortitude. As Noth rightly observed, 'New narratives from the late period, like the Daniel legends of *Dan.* II–VII, quite expressly have the aim of providing examples of correct fulfilment of the law'.[27]

Within these works, as well as in many other writings of our period, there are summaries, most commonly in the testament form, of the ethical standards which are both commended and exemplified by the hero or heroine. These frequently interweave words of comfort and promise with exhortation, and it would be a hard task to separate inculcation of the Torah (which is supposed to go with theocracy) from hopes for the restoration of Israel (which is commonly called eschatology) within almost any of them. So much is this interweaving the norm that it seems perverse to ask, as is sometimes done, how 'apocalyptic' comes to include passages of 'ethics': it is more of a surprise when one finds the two strands separately. Tobit's advice to Tobias when he sends him to Media, not expecting to see him again (which therefore is virtually a testament) is one of the best examples of the exhortation to righteousness, paralleled many times over in the literature of our period.

My son, when I die, bury me, and do not neglect your mother ... Remember the Lord our God all your days, and refuse to sin

173

or to transgress his commandments ... Give alms from your possessions to all who live uprightly, and do not let your eye begrudge the gift when you make it. Do not turn your face away from any poor man, and the face of God will not be turned away from you ... Beware of all immorality. First of all take a wife from among the descendants of your fathers and do not marry a foreign woman, who is not of your father's tribe; for we are the sons of the prophets. Remember, my son, that Noah, Abraham, Isaac, and Jacob, our fathers of old, all took wives from among their brethren. They were blessed in their children, and their posterity will inherit the land ... Do not hold over till the next day the wages of any man who works for you, but pay him at once; and if you serve God you will receive payment ... What you hate, do not do to any one. Do not drink wine to excess or let drunkenness go with you on your way. Give of your bread to the hungry, and of your clothing to the naked ... Place your bread on the grave of the righteous, but give none to sinners ... Bless the Lord on every occasion; ask him that your ways may be made straight and that all your paths and plans may prosper (Tobit 4:3–19).

Features which we recognize as characteristic of Judaism in many periods are clearly to be seen here, and they are found in innumerable other passages of the same kind in the pseudonymous books of our period. The more specific teaching stands in a framework urging the hearer to live a generally God-fearing life: compare Psalms of Solomon 3 and 4, pointing out the contrast between the godly and the wicked in similarly general terms, on the model of older biblical Psalms such as Psalm 37 or Psalm 112. Enoch's advice to Methuselah and his brothers (1 Enoch 91:3–4) is of a similar order of vagueness: 'Love uprightness and walk in it. And do not draw near to uprightness with a double heart ... but walk in righteousness ... and it will lead you in good paths, and righteousness will be your companion.' Whereas in Tobit the 'eschatological' teaching is to be found in a separate section (Tobit 13–14), in this instance the moral exhortation leads straight into an immensely detailed description of the divine plan for history, and then proceeds to the so-called 'Apocalypse of Weeks'.

Almsgiving and charity, one of the three 'pillars' of Judaism (compare also Tobit 12:8) is also commended elsewhere in our texts. Thus the Testament of Zebulun is concerned chiefly with compassion and kindness to one's neighbour, and indeed even to foreigners (6:5–8), and speaks of sympathy from the heart, not merely formal charity: 'If you have nothing at the time to give a man in need, have a fellow-feeling for him, and show him compassion and mercy' (7:3). Honesty and straightforwardness in one's dealings are similarly widely mentioned: double-dealing and hypocrisy are the primary topic in the Testament of Asher. Again, the evils of drunkenness, a favourite topic in Old Testament wisdom literature and also in the prophets (see especially Isaiah 5:11–12 and 28:1–4) are condemned in the Testament of Judah (12–16) with cautionary tales, while the Testament of Issachar holds its hero up as an example of temperance and hard work. In all this there is little that diverges from the ethos of much of the Old Testament wisdom literature.

We soon notice, however, that our texts concentrate their attention on other features which are less in evidence in the 'real' Prophets. Tobit's concern that his son should avoid marrying outside the tribe and should shun 'immorality' is paralleled by a great deal of material in other pseudonymous works. The Testaments of Judah and Joseph are to a great extent taken up with warnings against sexual immorality and licence, and are not quite free of the suspicion of making these vices seem more interesting than the corresponding virtues: no doubt the reader needed to be given detailed directions on what to avoid. But other features shift the emphasis still more from what we tend to think of as the typical concerns of the classical prophets. Paramount is the concern to preserve Jewish identity by *separation* from all things foreign: and it is quite clear that worship of other gods, which in the great prophets is forbidden as disloyalty, ingratitude, or even stupidity,[28] becomes essentially a matter of preserving the purity of Judaism. In the Wisdom of Solomon (13–14) we meet the scheme which was evidently crucial in forming St Paul's understanding of sin, whereby apostasy from the God of Israel and the consequent idolatry lead first to sexual offences and thence to the other sins which afflict mankind, especially the Gentiles: compare Romans 1:18–32.

The concern for separation is so normal a part of Second Temple Judaism that it is not at all surprising that people should have believed that ancient teachers like the patriarchs and prophets had insisted on it. In Jubilees 30:7–17 the rape of Dinah (Genesis 34)

175

becomes an awful warning against the dire consequences of mixed marriages: 'To this law there is no time limit, neither can there be any relaxation of it or atonement for it; but the man who has defiled his daughter shall be rooted out before the whole people of Israel, because he has given of his offspring to Moloch, and acted profanely and so defiled it.' The Greek Esther feels similarly about marriage to a Gentile: 'Thou knowest that I hate the splendour of the wicked and abhor the bed of the uncircumcised and of any alien' (14:15).

In all this there is nothing that conflicts with the conclusions drawn from a study of the way genuinely old prophetic books were read in New Testament times. The prophets were treated as ethical teachers, and the ethics which these teachers were thought to have expounded were the normal ethics of Second Temple Judaism: different in many respects from what the ethics of the prophets had actually been, in all probability, but not in any way consciously or deliberately so. To treat the old prophets as teachers of the Torah came naturally to everyone, and was not by any means the preserve of one particular group. In the material we have just been examining, from the pseudonymous tales, Testaments, and wisdom books which are roughly contemporary with the works that expound the older prophets, much the same general impression is created. There is, however – and this is the second, and much thinner strand in pseudo-prophecy – a small amount of material in which prophetic figures do not simply give teaching which is fully consonant with the Torah (even if not actually derived from it) but issue halakoth that represent a tendentious interpretation which not all would have shared. This, I think, is a rather different matter.

A good example of what I have in mind is the book of Jubilees. Here, one could say, we have not so much mock-prophecy as mock-Torah; or perhaps it would be better to say that the prophet who is being imitated is Moses himself, rather than any of his successors. Moses is here given halakoth, especially on calendrical matters (6:32–8), which represent the practices of one particular group, not of Judaism at large. It is perhaps too much to say that Jubilees proceeds from a desire to change 'Judaism', since the probability is that it was written before the 364-day lunar calendar was outlawed by 'official' Judaism. But there can be little doubt that the work is polemical in intention.

Now we have already seen that there is no reason at all to think that the distinction between 'ethical' prophecies and 'eschatological' prophecies can be correlated with the supposed tension between 'theocracy' and 'eschatology', for both 'ethics' and 'eschatology' belong to the normal perception of prophecy in our period, and neither was in itself in the least controversial. But there really is an opposition between 'ethical' pseudo-prophecy that respects and inculcates the Torah as understood by those who controlled the Temple, and 'ethical' pseudo-prophecy that seeks to expound the Torah in such a way as to fit its authors' own predilections. It is natural to conclude, on these grounds alone, that Jubilees derives from a minority sect. In its intense interest in eschatology, which Jubilees is at times concerned with, this sect was not unusual: no doubt it had its own special doctrines in this area, but there was nothing in that to make it stand in opposition to any other group, and certainly no reason why the ruling party should have objected to it. Indeed, as we shall see, the eschatology of Jubilees is noticeably less 'violent' than that of many apocalypses, and has no air of fanaticism about it. What marks out the community that produced Jubilees as distinctive is that, in sharing the common assumption that ancient 'prophets' such as Moses had delivered laws to Israel, it had its own opinion of what those laws were, and even a theory which could explain why they had not been understood before: Moses had handed them down by a secret tradition, and only to the sect had they been made known. All this, I think, could be deduced from a simple reading of Jubilees within the context provided by our model for 'first-mode' interpretation of ancient prophecy. But of course so much deduction is actually unnecessary, since it is now generally agreed that Jubilees derives from the circles that were eventually to lead to the creation of the Qumran community, which fits perfectly the description just derived from first principles.

For the disagreement between the Qumran covenanters and the Jerusalem authorities was not about eschatology, a speculative subject on which there were many opinions at the time; it was about halakah. One, could believe that the world was to end next week, and still worship in the Temple in the meantime, and no one need have the slightest objection. But one could not go to the Temple believing that what went on in it was contrary to the express will of God. Alternative eschatologies might abound, but there could not be more than one Torah. In practice, even in Christianity (which is notoriously much more concerned with people's inner

177

doctrinal beliefs that Judaism) most schisms have had to do with halakah, as it might be called, that is, with disputes about what Christians should *do*, either in public worship or in private practice, and above all with the question of who has the authority to tell them. Doctrinal disagreement alone seldom leads to schism; the doctrine in question needs to have clear ecclesiological implications, so that continued communion is rendered impossible.

In the pseudo-prophecy of our period there are just a few texts that belong to the literature of religious schism. Anyone who had a taste for pseudepigraphy and loved the Torah might have written Tobit or the Testaments of most of the Patriarchs; but only someone who knew better than Moses can have written Jubilees, and that means someone who could justly be called a sectarian. The great 'learning' which most of the pseudonymous books contain – additional embroidery to stories, lists of names and places, and so on – is mostly a pleasant revelling in words and patterns, like the border of a medieval manuscript: it is not to most modern readers' taste, but we can understand even if we cannot share the delight in intricacy that produced it. But the detail in Jubilees is in deadly earnest. Though its year of 364 days makes the seasons come at the wrong times, that is the fault of the sinners whose failure to reckon aright has put things out of true; Passover may fall in autumn before the author will acknowledge any falsehood in the secret revelation to Moses which he alone, with his community, has inherited. This is no playful embroidery: it is the learning of obsession, the scholarship of monomania.

6

Prophetic Foreknowledge of the Present Day

I

The prophets who prophesied of the grace that was to be yours searched and inquired about this salvation; they inquired what person or time was indicated by the Spirit of Christ within them when predicting the sufferings of Christ and the subsequent glory. It was revealed to them that they were serving not themselves but you, in the things which have now been announced to you by those who preached the good news to you through the Holy Spirit sent from heaven, things into which angels long to look (1 Peter 1:10–12).

For the author of 1 Peter as for most of his contemporaries, the prophets were people who enjoyed access to privileged information ('things into which angels long to look'): this was a commonplace. But the particular type of prophetic information that interested him concerned the events of his own day, the sufferings and glorification of Jesus, who was 'destined before the foundation of the world but was made manifest at the end of the times' (1:20), the establishment of the Church, and the imminent consummation of the age ('the end of all things is at hand', 4:7). Probably no one in New Testament times would have doubted that the ancient prophets *might* have predicted the events which were even then taking place, since there is no subject that prophets might not have been told about; but not everyone thought that this was so in fact, or regarded the contemporary relevance of prophecy (on which all agreed) as consisting in their foreknowledge of the present times. But many did, and in this chapter we shall be looking at this special foreknowledge which such people attributed to the prophets of old.

We have already seen that there was surprisingly little awareness

179

in our period that the prophets had been charged with a message of immediate concern to their own contemporaries. To warn one's own generation of coming disaster or to assure them of divine aid was, it was felt, an important task but not one that necessarily required supernatural inspiration; whereas to possess accurate knowledge of events that were far distant (whether past or future) was explicable only as a divine gift. It is very unusual to find the prediction of an imminent event by a contemporary described as 'prophecy' in post-exilic literature, even in authors who firmly believe that some people do have the gift of predicting events just before they happen. Josephus, as is well known, normally avoids the title 'prophet' when referring to the predictive powers of his contemporaries or of himself – possibly because of the theory that 'prophecy' in the strict sense had ceased but more probably, I think, because he did not feel that 'psychic' premonitions of the immediate future were rare and special enough to qualify for such a high-flown description. The usage in Nehemiah 6:12, where a (false) warning to Nehemiah akin to the soothsayer's warning to Caesar about the Ides of March is called 'this prophecy', is scarcely paralleled in other post-exilic writings.

What made the old prophets special was that they spoke of a time so distant that they could not possibly have known about it by natural means nor even, if we can put it like this, by *everyday* paranormal means (for even quite average people sometimes have true premonitions): prophets are in quite a different class from this. And what made them so important, in the eyes of many, was that the distant age of which they had spoken was the very age in which the reader was living, so that their predictions were coming true before the reader's eyes. 'Whatever was written in former days was written for *our* instruction' (Romans 15:4). With this conviction certain people in our period began to practise what Aune calls 'charismatic exegesis', which rests on the conviction that 'the true meaning of the text concerns eschatological prophecies which the interpreter believes are being fulfilled in the events and persons connected with the religious movement to which he belongs'.[1]

This mode of reading the biblical prophecies is already attested in Daniel 9:1–2, where Daniel reflects on Jeremiah's prophecy that 'seventy years' would pass 'before the end of the desolations of Jerusalem', and it is revealed to him by an angel that the prophecy is to be read as meaning seventy *weeks* of years, that is, 490 years

180

(9:24). On the assumption that Daniel 9 was written in the Macca-bean era, this means that Jeremiah is being seen as having predicted the events of the age in which the readers (and the actual author) of Daniel were living. Indeed, Daniel himself is presented as a prophet of the same kind. Though his prophecies may seem to us rather derivative in depending on those of Jeremiah, it is not clear that this would have struck the book's first readers as a disadvan-tage;[2] and in any case (as Josephus notes) the accuracy with which he pinpoints the events the prophecies refer to gives him an edge over most other prophets, including his older contemporary. The 'seventy weeks' prophecy became a classic for numerological interpretation of all sorts, and crops up again in 4 Ezra 12:10–39, where Ezra reinterprets Daniel's reinterpretation. (Moses is seen as a prophet of exactly the same sort in 4 Ezra 14:5.)

It is perhaps surprising to find that this perception of prophecy is shared by Josephus, if one approaches him with expectations based on *Against Apion*, where so much emphasis is laid on the soberly historiographical function of prophets. But we have already seen that for him the ability to record history accurately is not a matter of human ability to handle historical sources, but of guidance by the infallible spirit of God.[3] Past or future is all one to God, and the same inspiration can guarantee both historical records and future predictions. Josephus's high opinion of Daniel is strengthened by the fact that the prophet foresaw not only the Maccabean age but also the Roman occupation of Palestine, that is, events of Jose-phus's own time (*Antiquities* 9:276); and Jeremiah equally is esteemed because he wrote of 'the misfortunes that were to come upon our city, and left behind writings concerning the recent capture of our city, as well as the capture of Babylon' (10:78). Balaam (4:125) and Isaiah (13:64) receive the same accolade: when Onias IV asked Ptolemy Philometor and Cleopatra to build a temple in Egypt, 'he was encouraged chiefly by the words of the prophet Isaiah, who had lived more than six hundred years before and had foretold that a temple to the Most High God was surely to be built in Egypt by a Jew' (the reference is to Isaiah 19:19). In the *Jewish War* Josephus records a speech of his own, arguing that the Romans are God's instrument of punishment on the sins of Jerusalem, in which he asks, 'Who knows not the records of the ancient prophets and that oracle which threatens this poor city and is even now coming true? For they foretold that it would then be

181

taken whensoever one should begin to slaughter his own countrymen' (6:109, possibly referring to Sibylline Oracle 4, lines 115–29 – an oracle written in all likelihood at about the same time as the *Jewish War*, though Josephus was not to know that).

Our major evidence for 'charismatic exegesis' of Old Testament prophecy comes, however, from the New Testament and other early Christian writings, and from the Qumran community. Almost any passage in the Habakkuk commentary from Qumran will illustrate the community's conviction that ancient prophecies referred to events of the recent past or the immediate future with a direct bearing on the community and its relation to the rest of Judaism. Typical is the following:

'Behold the nations and see, marvel and be astonished; for I accomplish a deed in your days but you will not believe it when told' (Hab 1:5).

[Interpreted, this concerns] those who were unfaithful together with the Liar, in that they [did] not [listen to the word received by] the Teacher of Righteousness from the mouth of God. And it concerns the unfaithful of the New [Covenant] in that they have not believed in the covenant of God [and have profaned] his holy Name. And likewise, this saying is to be interpreted [as concerning those who] will be unfaithful at the end of days. They, the men of violence and the breakers of the covenant, will not believe when they hear all that [is to happen to] the final generation from the Priest [in whose heart] God set [understanding] that he might interpret all the words of his servants the prophets, through whom he foretold all that would happen to his people and [his land] (1QpHab 2).

To say that the community saw the text of prophetic books as pregnant with hidden meanings is a considerable understatement, but in that they did not differ from most readers of ancient scriptures in our period. What makes this kind of interpretation distinctive is the assumption that the hidden meanings concern the minutiae of the community's history. To extract such meanings requires the interpreter to treat the text as an elaborately coded message, in which none of the normal conventions of language and literature are relevant in establishing the sense: indeed, one might almost say that the text is no longer treated as a piece of continuous Hebrew at all, but as a cryptogram whose real meaning is, for the uninitiated, entirely veiled by the fact that it has a surface meaning which deflects the simple reader from guessing that there is anything mysterious about it. Without inside information it is unthinkable that anyone could have decoded the text. In the following passage, for example, one could never *guess* that the true meaning of 'Lebanon' was 'the Council of the Community':

'For the violence done to Lebanon shall overwhelm you, and the destruction of the beasts shall terrify you, because of the blood of men and the violence done to the land, the city, and all its inhabitants' (Habakkuk 2:17).

Interpreted, this saying concerns the Wicked Priest, inasmuch as he shall be paid the reward which he himself tendered to the poor. For Lebanon is the Council of the Community; and the beasts are the Simple of Judah who keep the Law. As he himself plotted the destruction of the Poor, so will God condemn him to destruction. And as for that which he said, Because of the blood of the city and the violence done to the land: interpreted, the city is Jerusalem where the Wicked Priest committed abominable deeds and defiled the Temple of God. The violence done to the land: these are the cities of Judah where he robbed the Poor of their possessions (1QpHab 12).

The New Testament remains by far the most important source for this mode of reading prophecy. The clearest theoretical statement of the way New Testament writers see ancient prophecy is the quotation from 1 Peter with which this chapter began, but the books where we find the greatest concentration of scriptural references interpreted in the second mode are Matthew and Hebrews, together with the speeches in Acts, which in this as in other ways differ from the book in which they appear. Mark, Luke and John, though they provide some instances, seem less concerned with the fulfilment of prophecy, while in Paul's letters appeals to prophecy of this kind cluster in a few passages, and are otherwise uncommon. Revelation presents a rather special case, being described as 'prophecy' itself, and will be looked at later.

Matthew's 'formula quotations' are the obvious place to begin: ten references to Old Testament prophecies, introduced with the formula 'this took place to fulfil what the Lord had spoken by the prophet', or similar words. The generally agreed list is 1:22; 2:15; 2:17; 2:23; 4:14; 8:17; 12:17; 13:35; 21:4; and 27:9. As would be expected from our earlier discussion of the 'canon', not all of the passages said to be 'fulfilled' come from the Prophets: 13:35 quotes Psalm 78:2, and the origin of the sentence 'He shall be called a Nazarene' has never been agreed. In one place, Matthew 20:18–19 (paralleled in Mark 10:33–4) we find that Matthew omits any reference to the fulfilment of Scripture but Luke uncharacteristically includes one ('everything that is written of the Son of man by the prophets will be accomplished', Luke 18:31). In addition to the 'formula quotations' proper[4] there are other references to the fulfilment of prophecy: see, for example, Matthew 13:14; 15:7; 24:15; and 26:56.

In some cases an event seems to have led Christians to interpret as predictions passages which originally had no such sense: the classic case is the quotation of Hosea 11:1 ('Out of Egypt have I called my son') in Matthew 2:15. Whatever problems this may raise for modern Christians, there is nothing in the least odd about it in its own time, since the belief that prophecy is prediction of events contemporary with the reader blocks any perception of the 'original sense' of the prophets' utterances – as the second example above from 1QpHab shows all too clearly. In other cases, apparent predictions in passages which happen to have caught the eye of the evangelist or his source for some other reason may have generated incidents that could be presented as their fulfilment. This may have happened, for example, in John 19:24, where the soldiers at the cross share out most of Jesus' clothing, but cast lots for the seamless tunic, in order to fulfil Psalm 22:18 ('They parted my garments among them, and for my clothing they cast lots'). Psalm 22 had probably been 'discovered' to be predictive prophecy on account of its apparent reference to crucifixion in verse 16 ('they pierced my hands and feet'), having in any case provided the cry of dereliction, 'My God, my God, why hast thou forsaken me?'; it then became natural to look for other verses which might have been 'fulfilled' at the crucifixion, and the scene in John 19:23–4 was one result.[5]

Luke has one particularly important passage about the fulfilment of prophecy in 4:16–30, the scene in the synagogue at Nazareth, which well illustrates the way in which oracles and incidents from the prophets' lives can have equal 'predictive' power – just as we saw in the first mode that both injunctions and recorded actions can be treated as having halakic force. After claiming that Isaiah 61:1–2 is fulfilled 'today . . . in your hearing', Jesus goes on to remind the congregation of the example of Elijah and Elisha, whose ministry was rejected by their own people but accepted by Gentiles. The clear implication, which they are not slow to realize, is that his own life will 'fulfil' theirs just as it will fulfil the oracle in Isaiah. The eventual Gentile mission is thus hinted at as early as the very beginning of Jesus' ministry: in Luke's presentation Jesus and Paul are ultimately victims of the same nationalistic opposition to the evangelization of the Gentiles.

This incident, so 'Matthaean' in its interest in the fulfilment of prophecy but so 'Lucan' in its implications about the eventual role of the Gentiles, may be seen as typical in three ways of references to ancient prophecies in the New Testament.

(1) First, in its combination of a kind of *pesher* interpretation of prophetic oracles with what we might call a *typological* use of incidents from the Old Testament Luke 4:16–30 is close both to Matthew and to the speeches in Acts. One does not need to subscribe to a lectionary theory (that *bête noire* of mainstream New Testament scholarship) to think that all the evangelists had a generally typological cast of mind, and were happy to present Jesus as paralleling more or less closely the actions of Moses, Elijah, or other Old Testament heroes. 'New Moses' images in particular abound in the New Testament, from Matthew's presentation of Jesus delivering his teaching on a mountain to Stephen's unwelcome reminder that Moses, too, was rejected by his own people (Acts 7:35–44).[6] Just as the oracular predictions of the prophets (including, of course, David) had been fulfilled in Jesus' life, death and resurrection, so all the essential characters and incidents in the Old Testament story were woven by him into a single pattern, so that with hindsight one could see them as fragmentary adumbrations of him.

Once typological interpretation gets under way, it becomes compulsive, and in the second and third generations of Christians we find not just the major figures (Moses, Elijah, Joshua and so on) fuelling the typological appetite, but apparently trivial incidents in the Biblical narrative being drawn into what ends as a total synthesis of the whole of Scripture, turning it into a kind of wardrobe of clothes with which the central figure of Christian devotion may be dressed. To pursue this further lies beyond our present brief,[7]

185

but it is worth pointing out what a strong conviction of the absolute cruciality of Jesus in the scheme of salvation is required to enable such a process to begin.

Paul Ricoeur has suggested that the enormous importance attached in early Christianity to the argument that Jesus fulfilled ancient prophecies shows that Christianity was essentially a hermeneutic of the Old Testament: 'The Christ-event is already an interpretation of a pre-existing Scripture'.[8] But the dominance of typology seems to me to point in a different and opposed direction. The concern of the New Testament writers who use typology most is not to validate Christian faith by showing that Christianity is acceptably continuous with the Old Testament, but on the contrary to show that Jesus is the one factor which makes sense of the Old Testament, perceived as in itself incoherent and unsatisfactory. For Matthew or for those who wrote the speeches in Acts,[9] the Old Testament is the repository of a great mass of obscure, inconsistent, even cryptic sayings and incidents, which Judaism at large struggles for the most part unsuccessfully to find any coherent meaning in: as Paul puts it, 'whenever Moses is read a veil lies over their minds' (2 Corinthians 3:15), for 'the god of this world has blinded the minds of the unbelievers, to keep them from seeing the light of the gospel of the glory of Christ' (4:4). Once Jesus is accepted as the key, light dawns: 'when a man turns to the Lord, the veil is removed' (3:16).

Quite evidently it is Jesus (as understood by early Christians, of course), not the Old Testament, that is calling the tune here, just as in Qumran it was the accepted teachings of the community which determined the meaning that was found in Scripture. It was not as if everyone already believed that Hosea 11:1, for example, was a messianic prophecy, and the point at issue was whether or not Jesus fulfilled it. Rather, the fact that an incident related of Jesus made it possible to take the passage as a messianic reference enabled it to be fruitful for Christians, rather than remaining as an unsolved riddle in the great lumber-room full of puzzles that the prophetic books seemed to many to be. It is quite anachronistic to think that the Old Testament was a given *with an agreed meaning*, which Christians had to shift as best they could to prove themselves in continuity with. Even if the Old Testament was a given, it was not perceived as having a unified and agreed 'message', certainly not so far as its predictive value was concerned. The very obscurity of the text for anyone trying to read the future with its help made it in effect a *tabula rasa*, on which fresh perceptions of meaning could be written at will. For Christians such as Matthew and the authors of the speeches in Acts, the key to the riddle had been revealed, and they exercised their virtuosity in turning it in as many unpromising keyholes as possible.

There is one concession to the surface meaning of the text: to be really satisfactory an interpretation has first to show why the surface meaning cannot be the true one. For an author composing freely, it is always possible to *invent* a riddle which anyone can see must be cryptic: 'This calls for wisdom: let him who has understanding reckon the number of the beast, for it is the number of a man; its number is six hundred and sixty-six' (Revelation 13:18). Small chance that anyone could rest content with the surface meaning of this riddle, for it has none; it exists to be cryptic. But some parts of the Old Testament do seem, to the uninitiated, to be perfectly intelligible. Here, therefore, the interpreter must first induce a sense of dissatisfaction in the reader, and so whet the appetite for deeper meanings which it will then be his task to satisfy.

A good example of this procedure at work is another passage that combines a *pesher* approach to prophecy with a strong typological interest, Peter's speech in Acts 2:14–36. The first prophecy he discusses is Joel 2:28–32 (in Hebrew 3:1–5), and here matters are straightforward. This is manifestly a prediction of something that will occur 'in the last days', and all Peter needs to do is to point out that what his audience can see and hear all around them tallies closely enough with the prophecy to justify the conclusion that the last days have arrived. But he continues with two quotations from the Psalms: 16:8–11 and 110:1. Here he has to meet the obvious objection that neither passage is obviously predictive at all, or if it is, it need not refer to Jesus. At Qumran they would not have stopped to argue about this, but Peter (or Luke, or Luke's source) is addressing, not the already converted, but those he is trying to convert, and so we are allowed to see the intermediate stages in the argument. Since both Psalms speak in the first person, one would expect them to provide information about David. But if they do, then they are false, since David's body did not remain uncorrupted (compare Acts 13:35), nor did he sit at God's right hand in heaven. But Scripture cannot be false. Therefore the Psalms must in reality be cryptic predictions of one whose flesh would not see corruption,

187

and who would be seated at God's right hand. The resurrection of Jesus shows that these two things are indeed true of him; therefore the true meaning of the Psalms is now revealed.

On its own terms this is an entirely sound and watertight form of argument, and it is not surprising that it occurs elsewhere in the New Testament.[10] One cannot discover by using it anything one does not essentially know already, and while this may be accounted a weakness from an apologetic point of view, it strikingly confirms the point already made about the primacy of the interpreter's key (in this case, Jesus and what he was believed to be and to have done) over the text being interpreted.

(2) This highlights the second major feature of the argument from prophecy in the New Testament of which Luke 4:16–30 provides an example: the emphasis on the fact that the present, the time in which the interpreter is living, is the time of fulfilment. It is not just that passages which might not have been thought of as predictions really do refer to the future, but that the future to which they refer is *now*. This is interestingly seen in a passage in Hebrews which makes use of exactly the same style of argument as Peter's speech on the day of Pentecost, in a situation where there may have been some danger that the time of fulfilment was coming to be seen as past – a belief that characterizes the transition to the third mode, as we shall see in the next chapter.

In Hebrews 3:7–4:11 the author wishes to warn his readers against the complacency of assuming that salvation is assured and can be taken for granted. To do this he mobilizes Psalm 95:7–8: 'Today, when you hear his voice, do not harden your hearts as in the rebellion, on the day of testing in the wilderness.' Again, it is necessary to show that this text has a meaning not exhausted by the past history of Israel. This the author does by pointing out that it was written *after* the settlement, and therefore cannot have been merely a warning to those who were left after the first rebellious generation in the wilderness had died off: for if it were that, then the fact that Joshua did achieve the 'rest' which was denied to the rebels would make it nonsensical to *threaten* anyone with failing to find rest. 'Entering into my rest' cannot therefore, as might super-ficially be supposed, be a synonym for 'settling in the land': it must refer to some other kind of rest, and relate to some period later than the settlement under Joshua. At this point one stage in the argument is, I think, suppressed: since there is another 'Joshua' (Jesus) who has even more right to succeed Moses than the first Joshua had, the call of the Psalmist must refer to the need not to be disobedient to *his* leadership. 'Let *us* therefore strive to enter that rest . . . Since we have a great high priest . . . Jesus, the Son of God [rather than of Nun], let *us* hold fast our confession' (4:11, 14). The relevance of the Psalm is not the general relevance of Scripture to conduct, as in the first mode, but the specific reference of prophecy to the time which the prophets predicted, and which is now upon us. David not only warned, he also *foresaw*: and Jesus and his people are the only satisfactory candidates that fit the specifications of what he foresaw.

It is clearly apparent throughout Hebrews that the author believes himself to be living in the days to which the prophets looked forward, just as Jesus did according to Luke 4:21; but for him 'these last days' (1:2) are lasting long enough for people to begin to feel that the act of salvation foretold by the prophets now lies behind them, rather than being upon them or just ahead of them. The author uses all his powers of persuasion to show that Jesus represents the final and decisive stage in world history, summing up all the types in the Old Testament in such a way that there cannot be any further fulfilment beyond him. Even if some acts in the cosmic drama remain still to be played, Christians already belong in the 'kingdom that cannot be shaken' (12:28). Yet he too is sufficiently aware of a sense of distance from the beginning of the fulfilment of prophecy to worry about the possibility of falling away and finding oneself outside the kingdom again.

My reason for discussing Hebrews, which in most respects represents, like Matthew, a very high form of the belief that Jesus is the ultimate key to the mysteries in Scripture, is to make it clear how fragile, for all its assurance, a doctrine of the fulfilment of ancient prophecies in one's own day really is. It is not of any great importance whether one thinks that fulfilment has just happened, is in the process of happening, or is about to happen; what is important is that one should be sufficiently close to the crucial events in which prophecy comes true to have no sense that the prophetic words will ever again need *another* interpretation as fresh as that which one is in the process of working out oneself. It is essential that no one should ever again be able to argue in the same way as Peter, by saying that since Jesus is now far in the past, the words of the Psalmist must apply to some future figure different

189

again from him and from David; or in the same way as Hebrews, that since Jesus by 'passing through the heavens' gave his people their rest, and yet we still go on singing Psalm 95, there must be yet a further 'rest' which we still await. Hebrews is poised at the moment when such possibilities are beginning to occur to people. By the time of 2 Peter the awful possibility has become a reality, and has to be staved off with vilifications of those who have thought of it, and with numerological fantasies designed to show that God-sized days are a little longer than the unenlightened would have us think (3:3–10).

(3) A third aspect of Jesus' sermon at Nazareth has points of connection with Paul's use of the argument from prophecy. All readers of Paul have the impression that he sees in Jesus and in the mission of the Church a fulfilment of the predictions of the prophets. He certainly says this in general terms: he speaks at the beginning of Romans of 'the gospel of God which he promised beforehand through his prophets in the holy scriptures concerning his Son' (Romans 1:2–3), and he treats the Psalms (like Peter in Acts and like the author to the Hebrews) as predictions of the glorification of Jesus (1 Corinthians 15:27–8).

But on closer inspection Paul does not spend a great deal of time showing exact correspondences between Jesus and specific Old Testament prophecies, just as he does not take much trouble to derive his ethical teaching from Scripture. The impression that his understanding of Jesus is much more important to him than scriptural proof texts is very clear; though he can provide interpretations of the encoded mysteries of Scripture well enough when it suits his purpose, and there are people with a taste for the cryptic to be countered on their own ground (1 Corinthians 1–3, perhaps). There is only one area in which Paul does not stint in using proofs from prophetic Scripture, and that is over the conversion of the Gentiles, which we saw to be also a strong theme of Luke 4:16–30. Thus, for example, there is a large concentration of verses from the Prophets in Romans 9–11, and again in Romans 15, on this theme.

One may speculate on the reasons for this. It was, perhaps, one of the stronger suits in the hands of Christians in controversy with Jews of other persuasions, since the gathering in of the Gentiles may well have been thought a likely part of the complex of events of the last days,[11] and the Christian movement could point unequivocally to the inclusion of Gentiles in its ranks as evidence that this expectation, at least, was being fulfilled. Equally one could argue that the degree of innovation involved made it necessary to provide scriptural support; though my own impression is that since Paul so comparatively rarely appeals to Scripture to justify much more radical ideas, this is not particularly probable. It is worth noting that the plethora of prophetic quotations about the salvation of the Gentiles is found in those places where Paul is discussing the divine plan for history and the role in it of his own mission. There is a positive need to demonstrate that old prophecies are coming true if he is to show that these really are the last days, not an insignificant interlude. The possibility cannot of course be ruled out that Gentile Christians had themselves already been specially assiduous in collecting *testimonia* with which to convince their Jewish fellow-Christians of their right to a place in the Church; or that the Christian community in Rome had been the scene of disputes which Paul needed to meet on squarely Jewish terms. But my main concern is merely to note the interesting fact that it is around this issue, more than any other, that Paul assembles what he sees as predictive prophecies that are coming true in his own work.

There is ample evidence, then, that early Christians saw their own experiences as the key to the predictions of the 'prophets', that is, those who wrote the old Scriptures.[12] These 'predictions' must be taken as including *incidents* recorded in the narrative books, since many of these are also presented as 'fulfilled', by means of typological reflections on features of Jesus and the Church that were prefigured in the Old Testament. One's immediate instinct, in the light of later Christian practice (especially in controversy with Judaism) is to see the use of old prophecies as a way of proving the credentials of the Christian movement, but that, I have suggested, is probably to stand things on their head. Rather, Christians regarded ultimate authority as resting with the experiences of the earthly and risen Christ to which they laid claim and which seemed to them to provide the key to much that was otherwise puzzling in Scripture.

Thus the Christian argument does not run, as it would sometimes run in later times: Jesus fulfils the prophecies in Scripture, therefore he is the Messiah, despite appearances to the contrary. That is to say, the claims of Christian faith are not 'proved' from their correspondence with prophetic predictions. On the contrary, the argument runs: The life, death and resurrection of Christ are a fresh and unexpected revelation of truth and the inauguration of a new order. In the light of this, much that was unclear in Scripture is now made plain, and older traditional interpretations are shown in many cases to be false. Consequently the Scriptures belong from now on to Christians, and their true meaning is veiled from everyone else.[13] This is essentially the same position, from a formal point of view, that was held by the Qumran community. It leads to a mode of reading ancient prophecy in which it is held that everything the prophets predicted had a bearing on one particular time in the history of the world: the time in which the interpreter is now living.

II

It is not necessary to search far for an explanation of second-mode readings of the kind we find in Josephus and, indeed, in much ancient literature outside Israel. In a culture where the continued relevance of holy books is taken for granted, it does not seem far-fetched to see a correspondence between an old prediction (or even a text that was not predictive at all in its original setting) and some contemporary event, and to claim that the ancient prophecy has been 'fulfilled'. As Aune shows, the Mediterranean world in New Testament times was highly hospitable to such ideas, and not much can be discovered about the other beliefs of people who thus claimed that prophecy was coming true, nor can they be assigned to any particular social group.

Anyone who accepted the claim of Old Testament material to be old and venerable might notice that an incident in his experience had some similarity, even if only verbally, to words in the sacred text, very much as a moral teacher might draw on words or incidents in Scripture to reinforce his teaching. In the last chapter I argued that the tendency to reapply prophetic utterances to new situations, as though the prophet had foreseen some moral dilemma that a future generation would face and had ruled on it, does not necessarily argue that prophecy had 'failed'; it can also suggest that the prophet had proved so successful that people expected his book to be endlessly pregnant with new meanings. Much the same may be said of the predictive side of prophecy. In a culture which believes that those inspired by God are likely to have supernatural knowledge, then there will be no difficulty at all in believing that a prophet whose predictions have (in their most obvious sense) already been fulfilled meant them to contain, in addition to the surface meaning, veiled allusions to far distant events. Thus for Josephus the observation that Jeremiah had correctly foretold the capture of Jerusalem by the Babylonians, or that Daniel had predicted the Maccabean crisis, is not (as it would be in a modern critical study) an argument *against* the view that they were looking into the even more remote future as well; on the contrary, it establishes the prophets' credit, and makes the reader *more* ready to expect contemporary fulfilments of their oracles.

This is not to say that the failure of prophecy did not also produce various hermeneutical moves designed to preserve the failed message and reinterpret it, as R. P. Carroll argues. It is quite likely that some glosses within the prophetic books have precisely this function; see, for example, the cases discussed by Fishbane in *Biblical Interpretation in Ancient Israel*, pp. 467–74 (on Isaiah 16:13 and Ezekiel 29:17–18 and 38:17). But once the prophetic books existed as finished texts of unimpeachable antiquity and authority, the notion that contemporary events might count as 'fulfilments' of them tells us nothing about the success or failure of the *original* prophets' message, for no one any longer perceived this as distinct from whatever meanings could be found in the book as it stood. Thus any verse or phrase, taken out of context, might suddenly light up, for someone who knew the text well, because of an incident that seemed to fit it so well that it 'must' be what the prophet 'really meant'. The more obscure the oracle, the more fruitful it was likely to prove for such an interpretation: hence, perhaps, some of the attraction of Zechariah 9–14 for certain New Testament writers.

Our second mode of reading prophecy, therefore, like the first, does not require an explanation in terms of minority sects' with 'eschatological' or 'apocalyptic' expectations. One need have no coherent set of beliefs about the end-time to think that one has discovered fulfilments of ancient prophecy in contemporary events. All one needs is a belief that prescience is possible, and this belief was pretty well universal in New Testament times. In any case, in seeing some event as the fulfilment of a particular prophecy one is not necessarily claiming that a new or decisive or final era in world history has arrived. *There is no necessary connection between the second mode of reading prophecy and eschatology.* Premonitions, omens and mysterious oracles from the past were the stock-in-trade of the religious culture of our period, as indeed they remain for much

193

popular thinking about religion in our own day, when many 'ancient prophecies' are available in paperback and Old Moore's Almanack still makes a profit. But most people who were attracted by them probably did not have any particular theory about how they all fitted together, nor any coherent set of expectations about the end-time. One could have an entirely cyclical view of history and still believe in prophecy in this sense.

Of course matters stand rather differently for the two groups for whom a second-mode reading of prophecy was a central part of their whole religious system, the Qumran covenanters and the Christians who wrote the New Testament. Their distinctiveness lies not in the mere fact that they read prophecy as predicting events of their own day, but in two claims that go well beyond this basic point. The first is the claim that *all* ancient prophecy pointed to the *same* age as being the time when it would be fulfilled. '*Whatever* was written in former days was written for our instruction'; all the prophets alike pointed to Christ, or to the Qumran community and its troubles. This does of course imply that the prophets are perceived as providing a coherent scheme of future predictions; since all their predictions refer to the same events, they must all be mutually compatible, so that it is possible in principle to extract from their writings a scheme of the time of salvation inaugurated by the events which are supposed to have fulfilled them. In this way of reading the prophets any 'original' reference of their predictions tends to be devalued or suppressed, and it becomes crucial to show that scriptural texts did *not* have any bearing on events contemporary with the writer. We have seen that arguments of considerable subtlety were produced with precisely this aim.

In presenting the details of the new age which has dawned or is about to dawn there is a very complex interrelationship between the prior beliefs of the community that is reading the prophets for its own purpose, and the surface meaning of the prophetic text. Thus, for example, many Old Testament texts would probably never have been read as predicting the age of salvation at all, had the group in question not found within them coded references to the events they were experiencing. It is hard to imagine that many Jews would have expected to find details of God's way of inaugurating the final drama in Psalm 22, for example, or indeed in Isaiah 53. In these cases the events which Christians believed were crucial generated a predictive prophecy where none had been seen before;

the same may be true of the use of Habakkuk at Qumran. On the other hand, once it had been grasped that the Old Testament text was in reality one great compendium of prophecies about the new age brought in through the work of God in Jesus, expectations about how the new age was likely to unfold began to be derived from Old Testament texts that *were* obviously predictive in character, and which therefore had to be taken into account even though the earliest Christian faith had not been much interested in them.

One might speculate, for instance, that the elaborate descriptions of the relationship of John the Baptist to Jesus in the Lucan Infancy Narrative came about because a need was felt to accommodate the prophecy of Elijah's return (Malachi 4:5–6 (Hebrew 3:23–4)) within the divine plan that Jesus was seen as fulfilling. The biblical text demanded a Forerunner; and since Jesus was now being interpreted not as God's forerunner but as himself the 'Lord', that role had to be transferred to John. There was no structural reason why Christian belief about the details of the events that inaugurated the new salvation in Christ should have included a Forerunner at all, but by the time the gospels were written all the important Old Testament prophecies of the end-time had to be somehow fitted into the new pattern.

Thus the belief that the series of events in the midst of which the Christian community found itself living was the one key to *all* ancient prophecy both simplified and complicated the reading of Scripture. It simplified it, because it provided a universal hermeneutical key making it possible to interpret *any* passage, however obscure; for the reader knew in advance what sorts of meaning, at least, he could expect to find in Scripture. On the other hand, it had the effect of making it compulsory to attend to books and passages which might otherwise have been left out of account. The belief that Christ had fulfilled all the Scriptures (and was therefore the only true key to their meaning) in one sense dethroned Scripture, for nothing Scripture contained could have any authority unless it fitted with what was believed about him (a principle grasped with admirable clarity by Luther); but at the same time it raised the status of that same Scripture by implying that Scripture had been vindicated. Prophets who had foreseen so remarkable and unexpected a thing as the death and resurrection of Jesus could not be wrong about anything. Thus, while this notion of 'fulfilment' insulated the reader from finding anything in Scripture that contradicted what he already believed, it also, on the other hand, made it imperative to discover a way of fitting *every* prediction that Scripture appeared to contain into a single consistent scheme.

It is this need for Scripture to be internally coherent in its predictions, a need which did not exist for types of Judaism lacking the belief in one particular set of events and no other as the definitive fulfilment of the prophecies, that began to make questions about exactly which books should be classed as 'Scripture' so important for Christianity. I would even hazard the guess that this was a major factor in making it inevitable that eventually there would need to be a 'canon'.

The second implication of consistently reading all the prophecies as fulfilled in contemporary (or imminently expected) events is that it implies a very high view of the interpretative process itself. New Testament writers, it is true, sometimes seem to imply that the prophets not only predicted Jesus and the Church but knew that they were doing so, although their meaning was veiled from their contemporaries. Thus in John 12:41 we read that Isaiah 'saw his glory and spoke of him', much as in 8:56 Jesus says 'Your father Abraham rejoiced that he was to see my day; he saw it and was glad'; and according to 1 Peter 1:10–12 the prophets 'searched and inquired about this salvation', and 'it was revealed to them that they were serving not themselves but you'. At Qumran, however, it was held that the prophets did not know the hidden meaning of the words they uttered, which was only now revealed to the Teacher of Righteousness and his followers:

> God told Habakkuk to write the things that were to come upon the last generation, but he did not inform him when that period would come to consummation. And as for the phrase, 'that he may run who reads', the interpretation concerns the Teacher of Righteousness, to whom God made known all the mysteries of the words of his servants the prophets (1QpHab 7:1–5).

As Longenecker rightly comments, 'Central in the consciousness of the covenanters of Qumran was what might be called the *raz*(mystery)-*pesher*(interpretation) revelational motif.'[14] He goes on to quote F. F. Bruce: 'In the book of Daniel it is clear that the *raz*, the mystery, is directly communicated to one party, and the *pesher*, the interpretation, to another. Not until the mystery and the interpretation are brought together can the divine communication be understood.'[15] In practice there is little difference between the approach found in Daniel and at Qumran, on the one hand, and in the New Testament on the other; for, whatever may have been known to the prophets themselves, their contemporaries had certainly not been given knowledge of the mystery which their words enshrined. Even if they themselves knew what the words they uttered really meant, they taught (like Mark's Jesus) in dark phrases lest their hearers should understand too. Only in the light of the direct revelation vouchsafed to the community in which the prophecies were coming true could their inner meaning be apprehended.

Indeed, it is tempting to say that the gift of interpreting prophecies is a *higher* gift than that required to deliver them in the first place: one would not be surprised to find someone who had it, such as the Teacher of Righteousness, described as a 'prophet'! If this does not happen, it is perhaps precisely because 'prophecy' is understood to be, not the interpretation of old oracles, but the utterance or writing of oracles whose fulfilment lies in the far distant future. As we have seen, this is one of the features of Daniel in virtue of which Josephus regards him as a peculiarly gifted prophet: not that he could interpret older prophecies (even though, in chapter 9, that is just what he does), but that he could foresee and write down for posterity events that would happen long after his own day. Our second mode of reading prophecy thus entirely reverses the way in which modern scholarship has taught us (rightly, I am sure) to think about the essence of prophecy in earlier times. The very feature that for us distinguishes the real prophets from later figures, such as those who added to the prophetic books or wrote 'apocalyptic' works, is the fact that they did *not* look into the distant future but spoke to the situation of their own day. For the Qumran community, on the contrary, the one thing a prophet did *not* do was to speak to his contemporaries; and consequently the Teacher of Righteousness, inspired as he was, was no prophet. Josephus's usage accords with this.

We thus find a distinction between different examples of a second-mode reading of prophecy. Where a fresh inspiration, reflecting a belief that a new and crucial stage in world history has arrived, dictates the kinds of meaning that are found in the prophetic texts, and all those texts are held to point to this one moment, we can fairly say that we have the exegesis of a sect: the kind of sect that biblical scholars usually call an 'apocalyptic' or 'eschatological' sect,

197

and sociologists a 'messianic' sect.[16] Where these features are not present, on the other hand, such a reading need not indicate anything more than the common belief that many future events were already known to inspired people in days of old, and that important deeds (and sometimes even trivial ones) cast a shadow before them, traces of which may be seen in ancient writings. We recall again that there was a widespread conviction in our period that the true content of prophetic books was arcane. Even where there is a straightforward surface meaning (and it has not been obscured by textual corruption), the true sense lies deeply buried. A reader who thought like this might well be on the look-out for incidents that revealed this sense, and as soon as one occurred, the 'eureka!' feeling engendered by it would be likely to leave no room for scepticism.

It is important, I believe, to note that the impression of a prophet as someone who predicted the remote future is very largely a result of second-mode reading or at least of the culture within which it made sense. It is a matter of the *perception* of ancient prophecy in our period, not a change in the actual practice of those who were conscious of a divine inspiration to utter a message from God. In discussions of the transition from prophecy to 'apocalyptic' it is quite common to speak of a lengthening of historical perspective in post-exilic prophecy, which eventually led to such features as the periodization of history, the belief in several 'world-ages', often of considerable duration, leading up to the eschaton.[17] Now such periodization is indeed a very marked feature of post-exilic thought about history: but there is nothing specially *prophetic* about it. The idea that there is some kind of divine plan, maybe of a deterministic kind, according to which the history of the world is mapped out from creation to consummation is an idea widely diffused in the ancient world, but specially common in Judaism of the Second Temple period. Post-exilic prophecy, along with a number of apocalypses, bears witness to its prevalence, as does the Pentateuch. But there is, I believe, no evidence at all that *prophets* in Israel were ever interested in predicting the whole sweep of the divine plan. Prophets always spoke to their contemporaries, in order to tell them not what God would be doing in the next age of the world, still long distant, but what God was about to do in their own day. There is no verifiable record of any prophet in Israel (nor, I suspect, elsewhere) uttering oracles that concerned the far distant future.

The impression that the prophets did utter such oracles is produced by two factors. First, the prophetic books of the Old Testament are for the most part anthologies of material from a number of different periods. If one thinks of the author of the book of Isaiah (to take the most extreme example) as the prophet of that name who lived in the days of Hezekiah, then one is bound to conclude that he had an interest not only in eighth century Judah but in the affairs of many nations down into the Persian or even the Hellenistic age. Readers in our period had, of course, no access to the critical study that enables us to see that this picture is an illusion, indeed possibly even an accident of the book's compilation: consequently they naturally assumed that a prophet would foresee the whole progress of world history from his own time into the far distant future.

Secondly, the very belief that the old prophetic writings foretold events in one's own day logically implied the same thing. If the book of Isaiah referred to events in the New Testament period, then Isaiah must have been able to see history unfolding over much of its length (remembering that the creation itself was only about four or five times as long ago as the age of Isaiah). If Isaiah had gifts of that sort, then obviously they were of the essence of being a prophet. To put it as strikingly as possible, a 'prophet' for many people in our period meant what much modern scholarship would describe as an apocalyptist: someone who had a long-term view of world history, whose details had been revealed to him supernaturally by God. But there is no reason to think that any such person ever existed. The real writers of eschatological apocalypses (there are other kinds, as Rowland has reminded us[18]) were not looking into the distant future; on the contrary, their whole effort was directed to convincing their readers that the decisive divine intervention in world affairs was on the very point of happening. Whatever the nature of their inspiration, however different their view of the righteousness of Israel, in this respect they were no different at all from the prophets. The people who looked into the distant future in ecstatic vision are all fictional characters: the seers whose names the authors of apocalypses assumed, and the eponymous authors of the prophetic books who, unlike the real prophets whose names they bear and with whose (genuine) oracles they are credited, are

199

presented as possessing insight into the deepest recesses of the future.

The whole notion that prophecy gradually developed a longer perspective as the post-exilic age advanced is no more than a trick of the light. It is a function of attributing to ancient figures predictions which people believed to apply to their own time. No one ever promoted predictive prophecies, old or new, whose import was that the crucial event in world history would happen after his hearers were all dead and buried. Many people, including a large number in our period, have promoted works which say that such an event will happen at a date well after their *supposed* author is in his grave; but only because that date turns out on inspection to be within the lifetime of those to whom the promotion is addressed. An 'apocalyptic sect' that assiduously peddled the information that the end of the world would arrive in several thousand years' time would quickly find itself short of converts.

In effect this means that the 'transition from prophecy to apocalyptic' is the title of a process that never occurred. Rowland has striven to show that prophecy did not 'turn into' apocalyptic because the two 'movements' have a different subject-matter: prophecy is concerned with the future (not in a crystal-gazing way, but as the consequence of present action), whereas apocalyptic is literature that concerns itself with the disclosure of secrets.[19] So far as it goes, this is quite compatible with my own argument, but I should want to go further. What happened was that prophecy, which (in the sense just defined) continued to exist even when the word was no longer used to describe the activity of contemporaries, came to be seen as essentially the disclosure of secrets. Sometimes these secrets were seen as concerning the future, and then the prophets of old were conceived of in exactly the same way as the seers on whom apocalypses were being fathered. But prophets in the true sense continued to speak to people about the likely consequences of present conduct, and to assure them (either as a promise or as a threat) that God was about to act in vindication of his purposes. Sometimes these prophets did this by writing apocalypses (of the kind where the secrets revealed to the seer concern 'what will be hereafter').[20] They used the convention that these secrets had been shown to a prophetic figure long ago, because that is what they thought 'prophetic' inspiration had been like: their own kind of vocation (which Amos or Isaiah would as a matter of fact have

200

recognized instantly as prophetic, being concerned with contemporary problems and God's imminent solution to them) they did not describe in those terms. Indeed, we do not know how they did describe themselves, since they hide completely behind the persona of the seer who is the subject of the apocalypse; but a reasonable guess would be that they described themselves in language drawn from the old wisdom tradition: 'wise', 'teachers', 'learned'. Phenomenologically, however, they were prophets. What had changed was the vehicle through which it was deemed appropriate to express a prophetic message, that is, a message about what God is about to do in view of the parlous condition his people find themselves in.

It will be seen, as I said in the Introduction, that this has the effect of abolishing the noun 'apocalyptic'. As the name of a literary genre, 'apocalypse' is indispensable. But Rowland seems to me already to have shown that the attempt to find any unifying theme among all the apocalypses that are extant is doomed to failure. Apocalypses were certainly all written to describe the disclosure of secrets, but what the secrets had as their subject matter varies widely. We could of course use the adjective 'apocalyptic' to mean 'concerned with the disclosure of secrets' and it would then make sense to say that there is 'apocalyptic literature' which is not in the apocalypse form. But if we are serious about including under that heading all the works that were so considered in the period when apocalypses were being written, we shall have to include the whole of the prophetic literature, and perhaps the whole of the Old Testament, Apocrypha, and Pseudepigrapha, for we have seen that all this material was widely regarded as 'apocalyptic' in that sense. The adjective is therefore defensible but, if strictly used, not very useful. In our period it would make no sense, for example, to speak of an apocalyptic *movement*. But the *noun* 'apocalyptic' seems on this showing as devoid of content as it is lacking in any ancient pedigree. 'Apocalyptists' (or even, if you insist, 'apocalypticists') will be those who wrote apocalypses, but nothing will thereby be implied about what we expect to find in their books in terms of content (as we saw in the last chapter, at least one apocalypse – Jubilees – is mainly devoted to sectarian halakah). We could use 'apocalyptist' to mean 'one who believes that God revealed secrets to prophets in antiquity' – but that would mean just about everyone in the world

201

of the New Testament. On the whole it seems better to abandon all the terms except 'apocalypse'.

III

With this in mind we may look at some of the pseudonymous 'prophecies', many of them apocalypses, that presuppose a second-mode understanding of prophecy. When all necessary allowance has been made for the fact that many apocalypses are concerned not with prediction but with secrets of other kinds, it remains true that the traditional association of 'apocalyptic' with eschatology, muddled as it was, was not surprising. Prediction of events contemporary with the actual writer and intended readers plays a large part in a great many apocalypses and also, of course, in works (such as two of the Psalms of Solomon) that are certainly not apocalypses. Daniel, Noah, Enoch, Ezra, Baruch, Zephaniah and many others are plainly conceived in the role of prognosticators of events far distant for them, but destined to come true in the period when the works bearing their names were meant to be read.

Sometimes, in line with the ideas of the Qumran Habakkuk commentary, the seer in question receives prophecies whose meaning is not made plain to him, but will become apparent to those who live in the time of their fulfilment. This is certainly true of Daniel's visions in chapter 12, where he is told to 'shut up the words, and seal the book, until the time of the end' (12:4). When he hears the final prophecy 'I heard, but I did not understand. Then I said, "O my lord, what shall be the issue of these things?" He said, "Go your way, Daniel, for the words are shut up and sealed until the time of the end' (12:8–9). Elsewhere it seems to be assumed that the visionary's predictions do make sense to him, and he knows that they refer to a specific time in the future well beyond the lifetime of his own generation. Thus in 1 Enoch 1:2:

> There was a righteous man whose eyes were opened by the Lord, and he saw a holy vision in the heavens, which the angels showed to me. And I heard everything from them, and I understood what I saw, but not for this generation but for a distant one which will come.

Similarly the Testament of Levi contains the record of everything his descendants would do 'and what was going to happen to them until the day of judgement' (1:1).

The details of the events predicted so long in advance through such prophetic figures vary a great deal from book to book, and it would take us too far afield to attempt a sketch of the various schemes that are extant. In any case the standard works on eschatology and apocalyptic provide all that is needed here. I shall single out three matters for discussion: (1) the relation of what is expected to the kinds of predictions that had been made by the classical prophets; (2) the question of whether the coming age of salvation is 'thisworldly' or 'otherworldly'; and (3) the use of codes of a symbolic kind in describing what is expected. These considerations all call in question still further common distinctions between prophecy and 'apocalyptic'.

(1) The writers of the works we are considering here believed, just as the prophets had done, that world affairs had reached a crucial point in their day, and that before long God would surely intervene – or that he had indeed already begun to do so – to punish the wicked and vindicate the righteous. It is difficult to find any difference between the writers of second-mode pseudonymous prophecy and their prophetic predecessors on this matter. It is sometimes argued that there is a difference in the *scale* of the coming judgement in the 'apocalyptists'. For example, it may be noted that judgement on all the nations of the world, not just on Israel or her immediate oppressors, is predicted.[21] But my own impression is that there is little to choose between the various books in ancient Israel predicting the intervention of God, so far as the scale of his judgement is concerned. One could hardly say that the book of Amos, for example, limits judgement to Israel and her current enemies; indeed, some long time before our pseudo-prophecies were being composed it seems to have come to be thought normal, even obligatory, for prophetic books to include oracles against a variety of foreign nations.

It may be said that the expected intervention of God in 'apocalyptic' has not merely international but cosmic dimensions: the whole universe is involved in the divine judgement. But it is hard to know how to distinguish between prophecies of cosmic disturbances in the two types of literature. Certainly we do meet such language in the literature usually called apocalyptic:

The earth will tremble:
It will be shaken to its farthest bounds;
And high mountains will collapse
And hills be shaken and fall.
And the sun will not give its light;
And the horns of the moon will be turned into darkness,
And they will be broken,
And it will be turned wholly into blood;
And the orbit of the stars will be disturbed.
And the sea will retire into the abyss,
And the fountains of waters will fail,
And the rivers dry up   (Assumption of Moses 10:4–6).

But we also meet the same sort of language in prophecy. Joel 2:30–1 (Hebrew 3:3–4), on which this passage presumably depends, may be thought late enough to mark the beginning of the shift that is supposed to have occurred (hence it is sometimes called 'proto-apocalyptic'); but what about Jeremiah 4:23–6?

I looked on the earth, and lo, it was waste and void;
and to the heavens, and they had no light.
I looked on the mountains, and lo, they were quaking,
and all the hills moved to and fro.

Or even Amos 8:9:

I will make the sun go down at noon,
and darken the earth in broad daylight.

It may be said that such language is meant 'metaphorically' in the prophets but 'literally' in the apocalyptists; but this seems to me a very difficult case to prove.[22] Granted that language about cosmic disturbances becomes commoner in post-exilic texts, it is not at all clear to me that it signals a more literal belief in a cosmic judgement than was held by the pre-exilic prophets. The problem can be seen acutely by considering Isaiah 34, where there are predictions that would not be out of place in the most 'cosmic' apocalypse:

All the host of heaven shall rot away,
and the skies roll up like a scroll.
All their host shall fall,
as leaves fall from the vine,
like leaves falling from the fig tree

204

– yet the 'cash value' of all this turns out to be the destruction of the Edomites:

> For my sword has drunk its fill in the heavens;
> behold, it descends for judgement upon Edom,
> upon the people I have doomed   (34:3–5).

For all this there is something different about the pre-exilic classical prophets; but I do not think it has much to do with the scale of the judgement they were concerned with. In them as in many apocalypses *interest* centres on the consequences of judgement for Israel, but *imagery* suggesting cosmic destruction appears, and it is very hard to know where to strike the balance between them.

One contrast that does seem generally valid is that the authors of artificial prophecies nearly always see the coming judgement as effecting the salvation of Israel, whereas the great pre-exilic prophets of course foresaw mainly her destruction. Again, however, this is more a contrast between pre- and post-exilic prophecy than between prophecy and 'apocalyptic': Daniel is no more convinced of the imminent vindication of God's people than is Deutero-Isaiah. How 'Israel' is defined for this purpose varies, and it may be that works from our period take it to mean the 'righteous remnant' rather than the whole population of Palestine or all those who would have called themselves Jews. But, of course, it is usually held that post-exilic prophets did the same: compare Isaiah 65:8–10:

> Thus says the LORD:
> 'As the wine is found in the cluster,
> and they say, "Do not destroy it,
> for there is a blessing in it,"
> so I will do for my servants' sake,
> and not destroy them all.
> I will bring forth descendants from Jacob,
> and from Judah inheritors of my mountains;
> my chosen shall inherit it,
> and my servants shall dwell there.
> Sharon shall become a pasture for flocks,
> and the Valley of Achor a place for herds to lie down,
> for my people who have sought me.'

I suspect that the impression that expectations are on a greater scale in 'apocalyptic' has something to do with the fact that longer sweeps of history are surveyed than was the case in the genuine oracles of the older prophets. But we have seen that this is an effect of the (mis)reading of prophecy itself as having a long-term character. It does not mean that the *real* authors of apocalypses thought of God's judgement as lasting longer or covering a wider area than the prophets had actually taught. The difference of scale is, in fact, another trick of the light.

(2) Linked with all this is the widespread impression that the imminent intervention of God often expected by writers in our period was seen as the supervention of an otherworldly kingdom, as opposed to the concretely historical and thisworldly expectations of the classical prophets. There is an excellent discussion of this question in Rowland's work,[23] where the great variety in the extant works is stressed. As he points out, 'the future hope in Jubilees is . . . entirely concerned with the renewal of this world and the return to a situation where man can live in obedience to God',[24] and the same can be said of many other texts dealing with the future hope.

It may well be that our common picture of 'apocalyptic' as implying that the earthly order is to be replaced by a heavenly one has been excessively influenced by Revelation and 4 Ezra, in both of which there is undoubtedly a shift to a more 'heavenly' hope. It is not uncommon for Jewish writers to suggest that 'otherworld-liness' is a peculiarity of *Christian* hope,[25] and while we should be aware that Judaism was much more pluriform in New Testament times than such a straightforward contrast between 'Jewish' and 'Christian' expectations tends to suggest, there is something in the point. Certainly it is in the pseudepigraphical literature where Christian interpolation is either proved or suspected that many of the 'heavenly' features figure most clearly;[26] and commentators who find references to a new heavenly order in other material may sometimes be reading such ideas into texts which really lack them simply because they are approaching the matter with assumptions influenced by later Christian tradition. Rowland shows, for example, that this may be the case in R. H. Charles's view that the new temple predicted in 1 Enoch 90:29 is a *heavenly* Temple, when in fact it may be meant quite realistically as a renovated Temple which it would become possible to build, in the literal sense, in the new age.[27]

One of the strongest criticisms of the idea that the 'apocalyptic' hope implied a new age of an otherworldly kind can be found in an article by T. F. Glasson, published in 1977.[28] Glasson, rightly to my mind, points out that passages which are often said to move messianic or other 'eschatological' hopes onto a new, heavenly plane in fact do no such thing. For example, the prophecies of a new David in Psalms of Solomon 17 have nothing otherworldly about them at all: they merely reiterate themes from the Psalms and Isaiah. Bultmann, who saw this clearly enough, nevertheless argued, in a passage which Glasson quotes, that alongside such 'thisworldly' hopes there were the hopes to be found in genuinely 'apocalyptic literature', which he characterized as follows:

> [a hope] for a blissful future which is no longer of this earth and which shall not be realized by an historical crisis brought about by God, but by a cosmic catastrophe, the end of which will be the resurrection of the dead and the Last Judgment.[29]

On the contrary, says Glasson, the contrast is a false one. Almost all Jewish apocalypses, and the other pseudepigraphical literature which is normally classed with them, speak in quite literal, thisworldly terms. In Jubilees, for example (just as noted by Rowland), the new age is marked by renewed study of the Torah and enhanced longevity (23:26–9): a renewed earth is what is hoped for, not the replacement of earth by heaven.

In fact, once the details of prophetic visions begin to be pressed in this way, it turns out to be quite difficult to know just what is meant by 'thisworldly' and 'otherworldly'. Is a world in which (as already in Isaiah 65:20) 'the child shall die a hundred years old' and 'the wolf and the lamb shall feed together' this world greatly improved, or a new world so different from this that it might just as well be called 'heaven'? Obviously one can so define 'heaven' that it is nowhere to be found in Jewish works, but our understanding is not thereby much advanced.

I suspect, in fact, that the issue here really concerns, not the *locus* of the new age, if I can put it like that, but its *cause*. What makes the new age new is that it is brought in by God, without the need for human agency. The disjunction between the present age and the age to come, which the imminent divine intervention will initiate, can certainly be seen as crucial, and it is interesting that this contrast appears in the quotation above, from Bultmann: 'not a historical crisis . . . but a cosmic catastrophe . . .'. It is the same contrast that is intended in Rowley's famous dictum: 'The prophets foretold the future that should arise out of the present, while the apocalyptists foretold the future that should break into the present.'[30] What is different about 'apocalyptic' has less to do with whether the coming age will be on earth or in heaven than with what brings it into being: historical causes (though under God) or a direct divine act cutting across human history. Though this can be exaggerated, it is surely fair to say that *direct* divine intervention plays a greater role in some of the pseudepigraphical works than in the prophets, to an extent that might justify the description 'deterministic'.

(3) Thirdly, it is interesting to observe the difference in the language used to describe the divine events that the authors of some pseudepigraphs felt themselves to be caught up in. In some cases they make the eponymous hero of the book foresee and foretell the future in more or less 'literal' terms, in others they communicate it through a web of complex symbolism, often involving animals.

An example of the first type would be the revelation of the future state of blessedness in Jubilees 23; whether or not this is meant 'literally' in the sense that every detail of it is to be fulfilled exactly, it is certainly 'literal' in the sense that it is not an allegory. The same is true of the expectations expressed in Psalms of Solomon 2, 8, and 17: the 'righteous king' (17:32) whom the psalmist expects is a real king, however different from kings that have lived before him. By contrast, the second type of prediction can be illustrated from Daniel 8, where animals symbolically represent kingdoms, and the struggles out of which the final kingdom of God is to arise are presented in an allegorical tale of fights between the various animals.

1 Enoch has plenty of material of both sorts. In the visions of chapters 83–90, each event in the history of Israel, including the final events which are expected as the eventual vindication of the righteous (90:6–42), is encoded according to a scheme in which different sorts of animal stand for different nations. Without the key, the visions are gibberish: with it, they can (in principle) be interpreted easily enough. In other sections of 1 Enoch prediction of the future is, by contrast, perfectly straightforward. When Enoch tells us that 'for the righteous he [sc. God] will make peace, and he will keep safe the chosen, and mercy will be upon them' (1:8), he means exactly what he says: there is nothing cryptic about the message, however difficult it may be to say exactly what would

constitute its fulfilment, whether it is 'thisworldly' or 'otherworldly', and so on.

It is hard to discover why certain prophecies were so carefully presented as complicated allegories, while others were written in a readily comprehensible form. The difference cannot, for example, be shown to correlate with the difference between sealed and open prophecies, for the message which Daniel is told to seal up in 12:4 is not an oblique, encoded one like that of chapter 8, but a straightforward description of the wars preceding the Maccabean age; while conversely Enoch is not instructed to keep his highly symbolic animal-vision to himself. Equally, there is no correlation between the use of symbolism and pseudonymity. Zechariah 1–8 is full of little 'apocalypses' in which a symbolic tableau is interpreted for the prophet by the angel, but it is not a pseudonymous work; while many pseudepigraphs – 1 Enoch again would be a case in point – make only occasional use of the vocabulary of symbolism.

Such correlation as can be found seems to be between symbolism and the literary genre of the apocalypse (not the same as 'apocalyptic', as I argued above). This correlation goes back into pre-exilic times: Amos and Jeremiah both 'saw' natural objects (whether literally or in a vision it is hard to tell) whose meaning was then revealed to them by God (Amos 7:1–2, 4, 7; 8:1–2; Jeremiah 1:11, 13). There has been, of course, a great deal of debate among scholars about possible differences between these visions and those of 'apocalyptists', but for our purpose it is necessary only to note that they are *formally* similar to apocalypses (though there is no angel-interpreter between the prophet and God).[31] The more frequent occurrence of what I call 'encoded' prophecies in our period is thus linked with the preference of the writers we are considering for the apocalypse as the vehicle of their prophecy. In an age which enjoyed the sense of having access to arcane knowledge, writing in code was all part of the mystique. It also has the advantage, one may more cynically observe, that symbols can be endlessly reinterpreted if the event they were initially intended to refer to does not materialize. As with so much else in the literature of New Testament times, the cultural expectations at large in the Mediterranean world as a whole, not just in Israel, must be taken into account. Hengel provides much of the material needed for this in his excursus ' "Higher wisdom through revelation" as a characteristic of religion in late antiquity' in *Judaism and Hellenism* I, pp. 210–18, showing that many in the

209

Hellenistic period valued 'wisdom' all the more if it was to be found in obscure writings from a remote culture.

Although there is such a large body of material using symbols, especially drawn from the animal world, to convey the expectations current in our period, there is so far as I know no comprehensive study of what may be called the symbolic lexicon of the time – an account of which symbols are most commonly used for which purpose. Northrop Frye's book *The Great Code* goes some of the way towards providing this, but the fact that it concentrates on a 'synchronic' reading of the whole Bible makes its usefulness for this kind of historical inquiry rather limited. Such a study would be of great value to the student of the intertestamental period.

What this does not explain is why some pseudonymous prophecies do *not* employ symbolic visions, but are couched in other prophetic forms. This, rather than the fact that some works *do* draw on a system of symbols, seems to me the puzzling phenomenon. But since classical prophecy itself contains both types, symbolic visions and direct prediction, it may be that we should expect its imitators to include both, too. If one is writing a book that is meant to make an impression similar to Ezekiel or Zechariah, a judicious mixture of mysterious visions, needing interpretation, and direct oracles from God will no doubt be best.

IV

We have already in effect answered the question why people in New Testament times wrote pseudo-prophecies whose import was that some great event, crucial in the history of the world, had begun to happen or very soon would happen, so that the readers for whom they intended their work would get to know about it. Like those who interpreted all of existing prophecy as pointing to events happening around them, such people had a strong conviction that they had received a special revelation of the cruciality of the times in which they were living – the sort of revelation that in earlier times would have led them to be called 'prophets'. Rowland comes rather close to this way of looking at the matter when he presents the book of Revelation as an attempt to confront the reader with the terrible reality of human injustice and misery, and so pave the way for the realization that God will soon – must soon – step in to establish his reign of righteousness.[32] This is indeed the kind of task that we associate with *prophecy* in earlier times, and it is clear that the sense of vocation which would lead someone to write a book with that purpose is what in other periods of Israel's history we should unhesitatingly call a prophetic vocation. Revelation, of course, is in many ways a special case, since its own author describes it directly as 'prophecy' (1:3, 22:18), and it is not pseudonymous in the same sense as all Jewish apocalypses: even if the real author was not called John, he has attributed his book to a contemporary, not to some ancient figure.

Still Rowland's suggestion is a fruitful one for the study of other works that resemble Revelation. They were surely written not by people in whom the fire of prophecy had almost died, as the consensus on 'apocalyptic' long held,[33] but on the contrary by those who had a burning conviction that events unparalleled in the history of the world were happening in their own day; and they used as a means of convincing others of this the literary form that would be most likely to carry conviction with their readers, who would believe a message of this solemn kind only if it came to them with the authority of one of the prophets or sages of old. In thus exploiting the possibilities of literary forms current in their own day these writers showed themselves true heirs of the great prophets, even though they may have been wholly mistaken in what they predicted.[34]

To put the matter in this way, however, may sound like a return to the old idea of pseudonymity as a kind of forgery: for surely there is a complete lack of fit between the conviction that one has a true message from God and a decision to communicate that message by a literary trick? The common reply to this objection, as we have seen already, relies on pointing to the difference between ideas of authorship in antiquity and our own strict notions about originality and plagiarism.[35] It seems to me, however, that there can have been little point in pseudepigraphy unless one's probable readers could understand a claim to authorship and thought that it mattered who the author of a book was. This ground has already been traversed in the discussion of the 'closing of the canon'.

Authors of pseudonymous works, then, were making a claim that was capable of being true or false, and it was in fact false. It is, however, perfectly conceivable that they were themselves convinced that it was true. If ordinary ancient attitudes to authorship have some features that seem alien to us, it is even harder for us to get inside the mind of someone who believes that a revelation he has just received from God was in reality made to a prophet who lived many hundreds of years ago; but such ideas are by no means without parallel even in the modern world. If, as Rowland very plausibly argues, the sorts of psychic experiences attributed to the seers after whom pseudonymous books are named are in reality the experiences of the real authors of those books – or at least are modelled on similar experiences which the authors knew about at second hand from their own contemporaries – then there is no reason why these authors should not have believed that God was recreating in them experiences that had really occurred to the ancient worthies whom they venerated. The authors of the Enoch literature, that is, may by their special devotion to the figure of Enoch have come to feel that the inspiration which God had given them was a sort of photographic image of the inspiration Enoch himself had received, and so may have genuinely believed that the visions which they reported were Enoch's own visions. Thus, in saying that they exploited the assumptions about the authorship and character of prophetic literature which their contemporaries held, we are not necessarily saying that they did so consciously. Subjectively they may well have felt themselves to be no more than amanuenses for the ancient patriarch, and they may have been no more aware than their readers that they were attributing to Enoch experiences which no one before the second century BC could have had.[36]

Maybe (and it can be no more than a conjecture) this is the reason why pseudonymous apocalypses *began* to be written. This does not, of course, preclude the possibility that very many other pseudonymous works, apocalypses or not, are simply examples of a literary convention, on the one hand, or quite deliberate forgeries, on the other. Tobit would be an example, surely, of the first kind: no one was being deceived when this tale was written. As for the second, it seems gratuitously disagreeable to suggest candidates, but there are plenty of them from later periods.[37] We may conclude with some words of Keith Thomas, which refer to examples from the sixteenth and seventeenth centuries but which seem to me to be equally appropriate to the 'ancient prophecies' of our period:

The truth seems to be that at the heart of the belief in prophecies

212

there lay an urge to believe that even the most revolutionary doings of contemporaries had been foreseen by the sages of the past. For what these predictions did was to demonstrate that there was a link between contemporary aspirations and those of remote antiquity. Their function was to persuade men that some proposed change was not so radical that it had not been foreseen by their ancestors . . . The appeal to ancient prophecy was therefore but one aspect of [a] concern to discover precedents for every radical step.[38]

Ancient prophecies which can fairly be called 'forgeries' are thus similar to those prophecies in the first mode that seek to *change* the halakah by which people should live; they justify innovation by turning it into tradition. It is not surprising that the Qumran community, which produced halakic prophecy of this second kind, also invented ancient predictions of its own history. There is plenty of evidence that early Christians followed a similar course.

7

Prophecy and the Divine Plan for History

I

The exegetical and pseudonymous literature that works in our second mode usually appears to have an interest in the whole sweep of world history, but the appearance is very often deceptive. Though a scheme of historical prediction and fulfilment reaching back into the remote past, sometimes as far as the creation, provides the vehicle for commentator or pseudepigraphist to convey his message, the substance of that message is concerned with the present and the immediate future; the grand historical scale is little more than stage machinery.

However, those who thought in our second mode could hardly have used such schemes if their readers had not been predisposed to think that God had indeed a plan for his creation on a vast scale, and that each episode in it unfolded in a sufficiently ordered way to make prediction of stages that still lay in the future possible. It is quite clear from many indications in our period that a belief in a divine plan, working itself out in the history of Israel, of the world, indeed of the universe was widely believed in by many who had no sense that its end was about to arrive. Such people, whose heirs are Jews and Christians in the mainstream of their respective religions, regarded prophetic writings as bearing witness to God's plan just as much as did those with expectations of a more 'imminent' kind. The contention of this chapter will be that their perception of the message of the ancient prophets ought to be considered a separate 'mode' from either of those discussed so far, and that to treat it as such introduces some important clarifications into our understanding of the thought of the New Testament period.

'The consummation of the age has long been forecast in the sacred books', wrote Origen, who certainly did not suppose that this

214

consummation was about to take place at any moment.[1] Christian tradition has in fact always regarded the Bible as containing not only the history of the world from the creation till the times in which the books were written, but also all that is still to take place: a fact represented most obviously in the arrangement of Christian Bibles which, whatever the variation in order, always agree in beginning with Genesis and ending with Revelation. This belief has existed quite independently of the fact that particular groups from time to time have believed that the end of the whole process was about to occur. As Eusebius put it, 'inspired by God, [the prophets] gained a vision of what was destined to happen as if it was present, and prophesied all things that were to happen to the race of men'.[2]

In much the same way Judaism has always believed that history manifests the operation of divine providence and that God had a plan in creation which will come to fulfilment in due time, even though this may not be in a way that would imply a deterministic understanding of events. Older writers on rabbinic thought, such as Moore and Schechter, rightly stressed that the absence of expectations of *imminent* divine intervention, which distinguishes the rabbis from the thinking of sects such as the Qumran community or the early Christians, must not be taken to imply that there is no 'eschatological' belief in the sense of a package of expectations about what the end-time will be like when it eventually does arrive. In Schechter's presentation, most rabbis represented in Mishnah and Talmud would have expected the events of the last days to include the coming of the Messiah, a battle between the forces of good and evil, the conversion of the Gentiles, and the general resurrection.[3] More recent scholarship is rightly cautious of generalizing in this way, and it is widely recognized that both messianism and expectations about the status of the Gentiles are more problematic than this.[4] But it is important to see that the question of what the component parts of people's expectations about the end-time may have been is quite separate from the question whether they expected that time to arrive soon. Failure to draw this distinction produces many confusions.

A good example of a passage which treats ancient prophecy as presenting a programmatic picture of what the future holds, but without any apparent sense that most of the events will occur within the speaker's own lifetime, is provided by Tobit 14. In v. 4 Tobit is presented as believing that one at least of the old prophecies

(Jonah's proclamation of the downfall of Nineveh!) will come true soon enough to make it sensible to take avoiding action: 'Go to Media, my son, for I fully believe what Jonah the prophet said about Nineveh, that it will be overthrown.' (According to 2 Kings 14:25, Jonah lived at about the same time as Amos, so that in Tobit's day his prophecies had not been uttered so very long ago.) But the rest of the events which for Tobit can be deduced from the writings of the prophets lie in a future which neither he nor his sons will see, but which God has carefully mapped out in advance:

Our brethren will be scattered over the earth from the good land, and Jerusalem will be desolate. The house of God in it will be burned down and will be in ruins for a time. But God will again have mercy on them and bring them back into their land; and they will rebuild the house of God, though it will not be like the former one until the times of the age are completed. After this they will return from the places of their captivity, and will rebuild Jerusalem in splendour. And the house of God will be rebuilt there with a glorious building for all generations for ever, just as the prophets said of it. Then all the Gentiles will turn to fear the Lord God in truth, and will bury their idols. All the Gentiles will praise the Lord, and his people will give thanks to God (Tobit 14:4b–7).

All the themes of 'Jewish eschatology' are to be found here: the new Temple, the conversion of the Gentiles, the return of the diaspora. But there is no reason at all to think that (as is the case in Daniel, for example) the various events in Jewish history which lead up to the end are 'foretold' by Tobit because the real author of the book expected them to come about in his readers' own lifetime. These events are imminent neither for the intended readers nor for the characters in the book, and this differentiates Tobit sharply from the works discussed in the preceding chapter. The message which, for this author, a faithful Jew should carry away from his reading of the prophets is most emphatically *not* that God is about to do a new thing, which will cut right across the expectations of his contemporaries and which, therefore, he has an urgent call to communicate to them. On the contrary, the readers of Tobit are intended to rest assured that, however little may seem to be happening towards the fulfilment of God's promises through the prophets in their generation, God is nevertheless still in command,

and his plan for the world is gradually coming to its fulfilment. It has to pass through a number of stages, and cannot be hurried. But its eventual fulfilment is assured; God is faithful; there is no cause to abandon the covenant. When we read the prophets, according to Tobit himself and the author of the book, we can work out what the stages in the divine plan are, and so be content to accept the constraints of whichever stage is being implemented in our own day.

This kind of interest in what the future holds, not because of a sense that one is among those 'upon whom the end of the ages has come' (1 Corinthians 10:11), but because a knowledge of what God has in store for his people in the end helps to make sense of the present and encourages piety and faith, can also be found in the Mekhilta. I make no comment on the date of any of its material, but cite it simply as an example of the attitude which became common among both Jews and Christians, that there were 'last things' which should be remembered as both an incentive to virtue and a warning against vice, but which were not expected particularly soon. In a comment on Exodus 16:25 ('And Moses said, "Eat it today, for today is a sabbath to the LORD" ') we read:

> R. Joshua says: If you will succeed in keeping the sabbath, the Holy One, blessed be he, will give you three festivals, Passover, Pentecost, and Tabernacles. In this sense it is said, 'And Moses said . . .'. R. Eleazar of Modi'im says: If you will succeed in keeping the sabbath, the Holy One, blessed be he, will give you six good portions: the land of Israel, the future world (*'olam ha-ba'*), the new world (*'olam ḥadash*), the kingdom of the house of David, the priesthood, the levites' offices . . . R. Eliezer says: If you will succeed in keeping the sabbath, you will escape the three visitations: the day of Gog, the suffering preceding the advent of the Messiah, and the great judgment day (*ha-dîn ha-gadol*).

Here we have a selection of items from an encyclopedic set of 'last things', which can be used as sticks and carrots in encouraging obedience to the Torah. Many of the rabbis cited presumably had a more or less coherent picture of the stages into which the events of the end-time were divided. But one receives no impression of any excitement, or any sense that this great final drama was about to begin. The unlikelihood that Israel really will 'keep the sabbath' with the requisite rigour and devotion is almost automatically implied in sayings of this kind. Certainly there is absolutely no danger that 'predictions' like this will ever be empirically falsified, for the non-arrival of the end can always be accounted for by arguing that sabbath-keeping is still not up to scratch. But whereas the 'disconfirmation' of expectations of imminent divine intervention generates various face-saving ploys (of the kind studied so usefully by R. P. Carroll), the sayings in *this* passage are not, I believe, really true 'predictions' at all. The scheme for the last things may well be seriously meant – there is no need to deny that – but the atmosphere is not one of ardent, bated-breath expectancy, waiting in fear lest one single transgressor should spoil the perfect sabbath which will bring up the curtain on the final act. The promise of end-time blessings if the sabbath is kept are surely of a far more routine kind, part of the stock-in-trade of the preacher who knows how to impress on his congregation the seriousness of breaking the Torah and the joy in heaven when it is kept. This is a different world from that of Paul or the Teacher of Righteousness.[5]

It should now be clear why I have been uneasy about using the word 'eschatology', and have generally written it in inverted commas. For it seems to me that the term does duty for two ideas which are often found together but are in fact distinct, and can easily occur apart. One can be said to have an 'eschatological' belief if one thinks that history (national, international, or even cosmic) has an end or goal which will one day arrive, and the path towards which passes through various distinct phases or epochs. In this sense 'eschatological' interpretations of history can be distinguished from cyclical interpretations, as well as from those which refuse to see any pattern, consistency, or direction in the historical process, and think of history as just 'one damned thing after another'. But among people who think in this way, there is a much smaller number who expect the end at any moment and think that they have read the signs that show it is about to arrive: and one can equally well use 'eschatological' to designate this, much more specific belief.

Both these uses seem to me equally valid. Indeed we can even add a third. In the study of pre-exilic prophecy 'eschatology' is sometimes used to describe, in the words of E. W. Heaton's excellent summary, 'that complex of teaching which arose from the prophets' conviction that Yahweh, the living God, was inaugurating a new action in history in relation to his people and to the consummation

218

of his purpose'.[6] In this third use there is not even an implication that God has a plan for the whole of human history, only that some events are crucial or heavy with meaning, as opposed to others which are casual or unimportant. When the eighth-century prophets are said to use a phrase like 'the day of Yahweh' in an *eschatological* sense, this then does not mean that they thought the Assyrian invasion would mark the end of the world or even the end of Israel, but it does mean that they did not see it merely as one in a series of alternating reverses and victories for Israel; it marked a decisive turning-point which made it stand out from the continuum of events, so that God's longer-term intentions and God's attitude to his people could be read off from it in a way that it could not be from previous, more ambiguous happenings.

Now it seems to me that we may use 'eschatology' for any of these three phenomena, but that it is a great aid to clarity not to use it for all three at once. My impression is that New Testament scholars tend to prefer the first sense, so that to say, for example, that Jesus' proclamation was an eschatological one is to say that he spoke of the imminence of the end. Terms such as 'realized', 'inaugurated', and 'consistent' can be added to spell out more precisely what is meant, but all depend on the primary sense that 'eschatology' implies 'urgent expectation'. In Old Testament studies the other two senses probably predominate; to speak of the 'eschatology' of pre-exilic prophecy, as we have just seen, is usually to say something about urgency, but not necessarily to imply the cosmic *scale* of the expected event that one finds in most New Testament scholars; while quite often the term is used to point to the Old Testament belief that history is not aimless but goal-directed, in other words, in the first of the senses outlined above.

My point is that this use, though entirely acceptable in itself, can mislead us, because it is seldom made clear whether the second sense is or is not also present. For example, in the debate about 'theocracy' and 'eschatology', it is customary to cite all prophetic passages which deal with the future as 'eschatological' by contrast with those that urge their hearers to live by the Torah. Any work which contains an interest in pre-ordained 'schemes' for history, or records 'apocalyptic' visions about the future is similarly placed on the 'eschatological' side of the scales. This fails to notice a really crucial difference of mentality between what we may call 'imminent' and 'non-imminent' eschatology. For many of those who firmly believed in the divine plan controlling history a sense that this plan was on the point of reaching its fulfilment could not have been further from their thoughts. Having an 'eschatological' faith in the sense of finding direction and purpose, even predetermined stages, in world history, was not by any means the prerogative of those special groups who thought that the time of fulfilment had been specifically revealed to them. The reverse (believing in the imminence of the end without thinking that there is a divine plan) is a more unlikely state of affairs, though not impossible; it is thinkable that someone who had no prior commitment to an eschatological scheme of history could none the less believe that God was about to do something so crucial that it must imply, retrospectively, that he had had a plan all along. But no doubt most of those who were convinced that 'the end' was near already believed that there would be an end; what was new was the conviction that its time had arrived.

Thus a third-mode reading of the prophets is perfectly possible without any commitment to a second-mode reading, but most second-mode readings do at least in practice presuppose a third-mode reading. As we noted, however, not all second-mode reading is 'eschatological' in *any* sense: it is possible in the case of more trivial predictions to become convinced that the moment of their 'fulfilment' has come without that having any large-scale theological consequences at all – as when Josephus mentions that some old prophecy seemed to 'come true' in a contemporary event, without drawing any particular conclusions from this about an overarching divine plan. For the most part, though, both ways of looking at prophecy do imply a theological commitment; but it is not the same kind of commitment in the two cases. Because the risk of confusion is so great, I prefer not to use the term 'eschatology' at all for my own purposes.

Though I doubt whether they are correct, I can see why those who follow P. D. Hanson's theories think that there was a conflict between people who believed in eschatology in the second sense just discussed – expectation that the new age was about to dawn – and groups committed to 'theocracy'. This is simply a conflict between those committed to the existing order and those with a divine mandate to change it, or at least to despise it in the light of their 'knowledge' that God is about to overthrow it. But there is no reason why there should have been any similar conflict between 'theocrats' and people who took the predictions in ancient prophecy to be speaking of times hardly less distant from the modern world than from the prophets themselves. One can believe that the present world-order is proof against any short-term dangers, and that God will not destroy it while it remains set on what, as a 'theocrat', one thinks is its God-given course, without therefore believing that it is actually eternal or timeless. Medieval Catholicism rested on the belief that God had established his Church in such a way not only that the gates of hell would never prevail against it, but that he himself would not suddenly uproot it or change its constitution. Any claim to have received a 'revelation' to the effect that the Pope should be deposed or the sacraments abolished would have appeared self-evidently false to the 'theocrats' who controlled the Church. Such claims were of course made, but by groups of a clearly 'sectarian' character. But that does not mean that the medieval Church had no 'eschatology' in the other sense, that is, that it did not look for patterns of providential guidance in history and for an eventual consummation of all things. Most certainly it had an 'eschatology' in this sense. It saw past, present and future as a tightly-organized and coherent unity, with a beginning and an end, and a well-ordered history leading from one to the other. In just the same way hardly any forms of post-exilic Judaism can be called anti-eschatological. There was a strong sense that history developed under God's guidance, and that he could and did reveal in advance through prophets what his future plans were for the nation and for the world.

Josephus provides a good example of belief in the divine providence revealed through the accuracy of prophetic prediction, without this implying that he thought the prophets had all been looking to events of his own day as the moment when their words would come true (even though there may be signs that he *also* believed this). When Solomon has finished his prayer at the dedication of the Temple, he makes much (according to Josephus) of the accuracy of God's predictions through David as providing a sure foundation for future confidence; for they show that God guides his people's history providentially. But there is no suggestion that this means that 'the end' is coming, either for Solomon's hearers or for Josephus's readers:

He turned to address the multitude and made clear to them the

221

power and providence of God in that most of the future events which he had revealed to David, his father, had actually come to pass, and the rest would also come about, and how God himself had given him his name even before he was born, and had foretold what he was to be called and that none but he should build him a temple . . . And now they saw the fulfilment of these things in accordance with David's prophecies (*prophêteian*) he asked them to praise God and not despair of anything he had promised for their happiness, as if it were not to be, but to have faith because of what they had already seen (*Antiquities* 8:109–10).

It is not surprising that there are few examples of this way of understanding prophecy in the New Testament or the Qumran texts, where 'imminent eschatology' tends to predominate, and that we find it on the whole in writers one might describe as 'sensible' – not given to 'end-of-the-world' enthusiasm, yet anxious to draw out edifying principles from the prophetic writings.

This is the place to observe that such third-mode reading of old prophecy, while it sometimes provides the system of assumptions within which people come to think that particular prophecies are about to be fulfilled, can also occur at times when the events which constituted that fulfilment are *past*, and have to be integrated into a larger pattern of continuing history. Just as 'fulfilled' or 'successful' prophecies can be kept alive by turning them into moral exhortation (mode 1) or by reinterpreting them as about to have a still more spectacular fulfilment (mode 2), so they can be fed back into the pool of prophecies from which a long-term scheme of history can be read off (mode 3). We can see this process happening in the second-generation books in the New Testament, just as we saw there the use of prophets as ethical examples. Jude 5–16 argues as follows: the pattern of God's action is that he saves his people in mercy, but punishes those who disbelieve. This can be seen from three examples: those who fell in the wilderness (compare Hebrews 3:17); the angels who rebelled; and Sodom and Gomorrah. In each case God said he would destroy them, and he did. We should take heed from this that God is not mocked by sinners, and so should believe that he will just as surely fulfil his prophecy of judgement uttered through Enoch. The same argument appears, of course, in the parallel passage in 2 Peter (2:4–22), where the readers are warned that they should 'remember the predictions of the holy prophets' (3:2) in spite of the apparent delay in their fulfilment. As subsequent preachers have discovered, constant vigilance is hard to maintain as a positive reaction to divine delay (3:8–10); but such is the attitude this epistle tries to inculcate.

To decide whether to call the theology of 2 Peter and Jude 'eschatological' or not is quite difficult. On the one hand, all the themes we associate with the term are here: judgement by fire, new heavens and new earth, punishment of the wicked, rewards for the righteous. On the other hand, these works are emphatically *not* saying that the time is short, but that it is long, much longer than anyone had expected. We have slipped from mode 2 into mode 3, where there is just as high a doctrine of prophetic inspiration and foreknowledge of God's plans for the future, but the loss of the sense that 'now is the acceptable time, now is the day of salvation' (2 Corinthians 6:2). There is no difficulty whatever in reconciling this sort of 'eschatology' with a theocratic ideal: Jude and 2 Peter fit well enough into 'early Catholicism'. Prophecy here becomes the revelation of God's consistent purposes in a long, planned historical scheme, and we are ready for summaries like those quoted above from Origen and Eusebius, or this, from the Epistle of Barnabas: 'The Lord made known to us by his prophets things past and present, and has given us the firstfruits of the taste of things future' (1:7).

II

One of the marks that distinguishes our third mode from the second is clearly its concern with the entire sweep of history, not simply with the impending events in which the divine purposes will find their fulfilment. In the second mode we found that there is often an *apparent* interest in long stretches of history, but this is little more than part of the fiction that the coming events were predicted long ago by a prophet, whose credit can be established by showing how right he was in his visions of all that has happened since his day. In reading prophecy as concerned with the whole divine purpose, rather than merely with its final stages, there is more room for a genuine interest in earlier events, which do not need to be reduced to the role of mere infill to join the end with the prophet who foretold it so long ago.

In this mode, therefore, there is more inclination to take seriously the *historiographical* function of the prophet. It is not surprising that we find a close correlation between a tendency to adopt a third-mode reading of prophecy and the picture of prophets as chroniclers as much of past events as of future ones. For if their task is to show that all times and seasons are in God's hands they can do this just as well by recounting the past as by foretelling things to come: divine inspiration is needed to perform either task adequately, for there is little sense that the past can be recaptured merely by consulting archives. It will be remembered that Josephus thinks of Samuel's knowledge of history as *fore*knowledge,[7] just as many other writers report that ancient prophets knew supernaturally about events which were past by the time these writers were commenting on them. In this mode an event does not have to be part of the complex of the end-time to be a worthy subject for prophetic fore-knowledge. But recounting details about the past which had not been recorded elsewhere is an equally suitable task for a prophet, since it too requires supernatural illumination. Thus Josephus also speaks of chroniclers as prophets, in this following the lead given by the Chronicler in such passage as 1 Chronicles 26:29–30 and 2 Chronicles 9:29, 20:34, 32:32 and 33:19.[8] 1 Enoch similarly presents Enoch as passing on to his descendants details of the early history of mankind, which could not have been known by any other means (see, for example, 1:6–9), and of course Jubilees casts Moses more or less entirely in this role, the more important since some of the secret information has implications for halakah.

The point is this. Since interest in the future, in this third mode, is part of a desire to present God as perfectly in control of history, which he directs according to his own plans and wisdom, it is almost a matter of indifference exactly when the predicted events are to come about. (This is diametrically opposed to the interest in mode 2, where the fact that fulfilment of prophecy will take place in the immediate future is all-important, and the overall plan of which the future events form the climax matters little.) Since the future is not of interest *as future* but because it bears witness to divine providence, it makes perfect sense to be just as interested in the past, from which the same point can be read off. Neither past nor future is of interest for its own sake, but because both point to the constancy of divine providence.

It is this, I think, that explains the idea which to us is so strange, that the same inspiration is needed to look into the past as into the future, and that the difference between narratives about the past and predictions of the future is of quite minor importance by comparison with other distinctions, such as that between optimism and pessimism in interpreting the meaning of events, whether past or future. Hence the extraordinary lack of attention in Baba Bathra 14b to the distinction between the Former and the Latter Prophets in respect of genre, which we discussed fully above.[9] This point can be made well by noting some words of James Barr:

> Narratives are not necessarily written because of a primary interest in the past. They can be written for a quite different reason: they can be written to provide pictures of the promises of God which will come to pass in the future. Even if their literal purport concerns the past, their theological function and purpose may be directed towards the future . . . In general, for much of the Old Testament material, even when past events are being narrated this is not necessarily out of an interest in past history but because of patterns of future hope . . . It is wrong to think of scripture as a 'record': it is not in essence a record, though in places it may incidentally be so. Even in its past narratives its function is often not to be a record of past events but to present paradigms for thinking about the present or hoping for the future.[10]

Now, equally, the same may be said of predictive prophecies, standing Barr's argument on its head. Just as narratives about the past are, as Barr rightly says, important not primarily as a historical record but for their paradigmatic quality, directed to present and future, so predictions are valued not only for their future reference but also (and in the third mode chiefly) for their paradigmatic quality in the present, and for the sense they make of the recorded past by telling the reader where ultimately this past was leading.[11] Extrapolating into the future the direction history took in the past gives one confidence about God's control of events: it does not provide direct 'predictions' which make it possible to know in detail what will happen next, as in the second mode.

Order and *pattern* are the crucial elements in all this. It is less important to know what God is going to do and when he will do it then to believe that his actions are regular and purposive and are going somewhere. Past and future obey the same patterns. Compare the following from the Mekhilta:

'The horse and rider he has thrown into the sea' [Exodus 15:1]. As soon as the Israelites saw the guardian angel of the Egyptian kingdom falling down into the sea, they began to render praise. In this sense it is said 'he hath thrown down' from on high. And you will find that in the future also the Holy One, blessed be he, will punish the kingdoms only after he has first punished their guardian angels, as it is said [Isaiah 24:21]: 'On that day the LORD will punish the host of heaven, in heaven, and the kings of the earth, on the earth.'[12]

There is plainly the potential for a deterministic view of history here, nowhere more attractively presented than in Judith 9:5–6: 'Thou hast done these things and those that went before and those that followed; thou hast designed the things that are now, and those that are to come. Yea, the things thou didst intend came to pass, and the things thou didst will presented themselves and said, "Lo, we are here"; for all thy ways are prepared in advance, and thy judgement is with foreknowledge.' In this world of thought prophecy of the future and historiography are simply two sides of the same coin, the recording of all that God has planned and performed in such a way as to bear witness to his wisdom and providence.

III

If the exegetical literature of our period is rich in third-mode interpretations of old prophecy, there is no less evidence of it in the pseudo-prophetic books that were composed at the same time. Of course the fiction of 'prophetic' authorship is sometimes used to give authority to a surprising message about the imminent arrival of the day of the Lord, but this is not the only use of pseudonymity, and there is no shortage of books which make an ancient figure the vehicle for conveying an 'eschatological' scheme in the non-imminent sense of that term. Tobit is a good example. Just as the author of Tobit reads the older prophets in the third mode, so the prophecies he ascribes to Tobit himself equally convey confidence that the whole of history is in God's hands, rather than any impression that its end is to arrive in the reader's day.

Thus the scheme of prediction in chapter 14 only partly derives from already existing prophecy, and is itself partly an 'original' utterance of Tobit himself; but there is no sense that most of the events Tobit predicts, such as the rebuilding of the glorious ('eschatological') Temple, the gathering-in of the dispersed, and the conversion of the Gentiles, are expected by the author to be nearing their fulfilment. The same is true of Tobit's 'prayer' in the preceding chapter: 'Jerusalem will be rebuilt with sapphires and emeralds, her walls with precious stones, and her towers and battlements with pure gold' (13:16), but it is not to be thought that the (real) author of this prayer imagined that this was destined to occur in his own lifetime. Rather, the promises of the prophets have here become the basis for never-ceasing confidence in God even though the consummation of his promises delays.

Much the same appears to me to be true of other 'eschatological' prophecies from our period. The Testaments of the Twelve Patriarchs, for example, contain a number of passages in which the future is predicted, but often it appears that there is a studied vagueness about the date when particular events will occur. Thus the Testament of Issachar foretells a time when 'your sons will ... attach themselves to Beliar ... and follow their own wicked inclinations; and they will be dispersed among the Gentiles and enslaved by their enemies' (6:1–3). But the purpose of Issachar's passing on this information is not to enable the reader to calculate the time of the end, but 'so that, if they sin, they may the more quickly return to the Lord; for he is merciful, and will deliver them' (6:4); compare also Testament of Zebulun 9, Testament of Dan 5, and Testament of Benjamin 10–11, where such specific references as there are may derive from Christian interpolation.

The essential point here is that 'eschatology' can be recorded, like history, for other purposes than to whip up expectations of imminent divine intervention. The (very late) Christian prologue to the Sibylline oracles sums it up in these words: '[These oracles] clearly recount the things which are expounded in the Mosaic writings and the books of the prophets, about the creation of the world, the fashioning of man and the expulsion from the garden and again the new formation. *In manifold ways they tell of certain past history, and equally, foretell future events and, to speak simply, they can profit those who read them in no small way.*' Such prophecies belong to the desire to have encyclopedic knowledge of the whole course of world

227

history from beginning to end, because this knowledge gives one a firm spiritual foundation: knowing what God is set on achieving in the world, one can fit oneself better to his plans. A similar perspective can perhaps be found in 4 Ezra, which is noticeably coy about just when the end will arrive despite the detail in which it foretells the events that will precede it. Here again the reason is that prediction is not really the book's primary concern; theodicy is the author's object, and in order to justify God's ways (especially given the destruction of AD 70) one has certainly to show that a just end is in store for the world, but there is no need to specify when it will arrive.

A further marked feature of pseudonymous prophecies in New Testament times is a sharp periodization of history – one of the clearest ways of signalling the divine control over events. Within the Old Testament the most obvious representative of such a tendency is Daniel, with its four world-empires. In post-biblical material we find it in 1 Enoch and of course in Jubilees, where the whole history of the world is arranged schematically to fit the cycles of jubilees. Moses is commanded to 'write down everything I tell you on this mountain, the first *things* and the last *things* that shall come to pass in all the divisions of the days, in the law and in the testimony, and in all the weeks of the jubilees till eternity, till I descend and dwell with them through all eternity' (1:26). In Daniel, which was written to convince the reader that the consummation of God's promises is at hand, the point of periodization is to suggest that the reader is living almost at the end of the final period; but in Jubilees, as we saw earlier, the main concern is with halakah, and much of the periodization serves the calendrical interests of the writer, as well as greatly intensifying the sense that history has been mapped out by God in every detail.

The organization of past history here is thus not a mere device designed to serve a belief in imminent divine action, but an important theme in its own right. Rowland has rightly stressed that 'apocalyptic' works are as frequently concerned with 'what was beforetime' as with 'what will be hereafter', and he resists the suggestion that one interest is subordinate to the other:

It has been argued that the records of past history are included mainly to show that, if the information about the history up to the present has been correct, the same is also likely to be true about the future predictions as well. The detail which is often included in the review of the past suggests more than a mere device to bolster eschatological teaching . . . There appears to be an interest in history for its own sake and not merely as a backdrop for the eschatological predictions which were to follow.[13]

Rowland goes on to discuss in detail the following major 'historiographical' sections in pseudonymous literature: Daniel 2; 7; 8–9; 10–12; 1 Enoch 85–90; 91:12–17; 93; 4 Ezra 11–12; Syriac Baruch 36–40; 53–74; Apocalypse of Abraham 27ff.; and Assumption of Moses 2–10. His conclusions are in general consonant with the position I have been arguing for: thus, on Syriac Baruch 53–74 he notes, much as I have done in the case of Tobit, that 'there is no evidence to suggest that the inauguration of the Last Things within a short time is the issue to which the whole of history has been leading'.[14] And he argues that the reality of divine control over the world, despite apparent breaks in its pattern, was the truth such surveys of history were written to assert. 'The Jew needed to be shown that the God who existed in glory in the world above had not abandoned his creation or his people and that the present, just as much as the past and the future, fitted into the overall pattern of God's purposes for mankind.'[15]

Since I am inclined to treat many works which do not fall under Rowland's definition of 'apocalyptic' as none the less constituting 'pseudo-prophecy', there is no reason why we should not take account of the retelling of history that occurs in them, too; and here we find very much the same features. Two books which may be regarded as midrash on biblical histories are Jubilees, an expanded version of Genesis, and Pseudo-Philo, which retells much of the Old Testament history, in both cases by means of recounting how the seers (respectively Moses and Cenez) were shown visions of past events with detail additional to that provided in the biblical account. Again, neither of these works contains prophecies of the end-time: Jubilees has an interest in halakah, Pseudo-Philo in heavenly secrets of a kind we shall be considering in the next chapter; but both strive to present the history of Israel as it should have happened, thereby making manifest more clearly than in the received version in Scripture the providence and goodness of God.

The same may be said of most of the retellings of history in the Testaments of the Twelve Patriarchs, and in the Testament of

229

Abraham, which (in so far as it connects with the biblical story at all) presents what happened to Abraham without ever embarking on speculations about what would happen after him. Retelling biblical stories to bring out a moral begins within Scripture itself, of course. Chronicles is sometimes described as a midrash on Samuel and Kings, implying a similar intention, and one may even say that there are passages within Kings that amount to a midrash on other passages: for example, the account of the Assyrian crisis in 2 Kings 19:8–35 may be treated as a midrashic expansion of the preceding account of the deliverance of Jerusalem, designed to bring out more fully the providential character of the events.[16]

IV

We are now already moving in the direction of asking *why* prophecies were both read and written in the third mode, and finding the answer in the desire to make both past record and future predictions fruitful for religion in the present – a present which those who used this mode did *not* think was 'the last days'. If prophecy in the second mode forces the reader to adjust his whole understanding of past history so as to accommodate the radically new event which is shortly expected or even already experienced, third-mode writings and interpretations have almost the opposite effect. They reassure the reader that whatever happens, and however startling it is, it is part of the history that God has already foreseen and even determined. Though God may delay to assert his control over history by leading it to its close, a proper understanding of past, present and future together will bring the conviction that he is still in control. 'Though the fig tree do not blossom, nor fruit be on the vines, the produce of the olive fail, and the fields yield no food, the flock be cut off from the fold, and there be no herd in the stalls, yet I will rejoice in the LORD, I will joy in the God of my salvation' (Habakkuk 3:17–18).

Such a message is eminently compatible with 'established' religion, and there is no reason whatever to suspect that those who produced pseudonymous works ('apocalypses' or not) in this mode belonged to 'millenarian' sects. On the contrary, they stood in what was to become the mainstream of Judaism and, in due course, of Christianity, encouraging calm and unshaken faith, not end-of-the-world enthusiasm. However, there are some more specific reasons for certain aspects of this mode of understanding prophecy, two of which must be briefly mentioned.

First, the idea that God can and does reveal to chosen people not merely events which concern them and their own generation, but secrets of the far distant future, is well established as a perception of ancient prophecy long before our period. I argued in the last chapter that such prophecy probably never occurs in fact, but there is no doubt that it was widely thought to have done so: 'I look not for this generation but for the distant one that is coming' (1 Enoch 1:2). Such a belief may arise for a variety of reasons: in particular, it may be a *conclusion* following from the sudden observation that a contemporary event strikingly 'fulfils' some remembered words of an old prophet, or it may be a *presupposition* for reading prophecies, derived from what is in effect a hermeneutical decision to read them as if they were texts of perennial validity. The very existence of a codified body of prophetic texts makes it likely that they will be read in this way, as surveying a wide sweep of history. At all events such a perception of prophecy seems to have existed outside Israel, too. It may even be implied in Plutarch's report of Heraclitus's comment on the Sibyl, who 'reaches to a thousand years with her voice through the god', if we take the thousand years to be the length of time her prophecies cover rather than the length of time they had already existed in his day.[17] Many texts which are not concerned with the end-time nevertheless see prophetic figures as predicting events which for them lay far in the future, even though for the real authors of the texts they now lie in the past. This is clearly so, for example, in 1 Enoch, where Enoch is shown many things as lying in the future which for the writer were a matter of record in Scripture – thus, for example, in 1 Enoch 10, Enoch foresees the coming of the Flood.

There are, in fact, a number of examples of predictive prophecies with no 'eschatological' implications at all in both exegetical and creative literature of our period. A good example is to be found in the Greek Esther. Here Mordecai (Mardocheus) foresees the events that will occur in the story in a dream, which interestingly presents the actors in the drama in the guise of animals, in the manner of the visions in Daniel 7 and 8. This is thus formally like much of what is called 'apocalyptic':

231

Behold, two great dragons came forward, both ready to fight, and they roared terribly. And at their roaring every nation prepared for war, to fight against the nation of the righteous . . . And the whole righteous nation was troubled; they feared the evils that threatened them, and were ready to perish. Then they cried to God; and from their cry, as though from a tiny spring, there came a great river, with abundant water; light came, and the sun rose, and the lowly were exalted and consumed those held in honour. Mordecai saw in this dream what God had determined to do, and after he awoke he had it on his mind and sought all day to understand it in every detail (Esther 11:6–12).

Once the story is ended, the Greek version adds a section giving a point by point interpretation of the dream, and showing that it has been exactly fulfilled in what has happened (10:4–13). Thus the 'apocalypse' of Mordecai, as we may call it, forms a frame around the original story of Esther and presents it as the fulfilment of prophecy. But in this arrangement the dream and its interpretation alike apply to a closed and completed set of events now in the past: there is no sense that they have any 'eschatological' significance. Prophecy is here prediction, but not eschatological prediction.

Much the same may be said of the dream of Amram, the father of Moses, recorded by Josephus in *Antiquities* 2:210–16 (which is also mentioned in the Mekhilta). Here God appears to Amram in a dream (*opsis*) and recalls the past history of his people, reminding Amram of his providential guidance of Abraham, Isaac and Jacob; and then he reveals that a child will be born 'to deliver the Hebrew race from their bondage in Egypt, and be remembered as long as the universe shall endure, not by Hebrews alone but even by alien nations'. This vision is fulfilled in the birth and subsequent career of Moses, whose miraculous deliverance from death at the hand of Pharaoh's daughter confirms 'that all that [God] wills to accomplish reaches its perfect end'.

We may also note a similar divine communication in a dream to Job, according to the Testament of Job 3–5, in which God tells Job that if he cleanses a neighbouring idol-temple, Satan (who is worshipped there) will afflict him, but that if he endures such sufferings his name will become famous, he will have his possessions restored fourfold, and he will be raised from the dead at the last; all of which duly comes about. Here again there is no suggestion that the dream has a significance beyond the story in which it stands. The same may be said of the midrash on Genesis 12:10–19 found in the Genesis Apocryphon, where Abraham is forewarned of Abimelech's designs on Sarah in a symbolic dream similar to that of Mordecai in Esther (1QGA 19:14–17).[18] In all these cases we have the fulfilment of prophecy detached from any interest in the end-time, which is not a concern of the works in question.

Secondly, the periodization of history, which is such a common way of understanding the progression of history in prophecy of this kind, is a very common feature of post-exilic Jewish thought in any case, quite apart from any ideas of prophecy. It certainly has no necessary connection with the sorts of groups widely held to be responsible for 'apocalyptic', but on the contrary is ingrained in literature which on any showing is not the work of fringe groups or disaffected sects. Its beginnings go back at least to the Deuteronomistic History,[19] and it is general in historiography from the Exile onwards.[20]

There seems little doubt that the chronological scheme of the Pentateuch in all its various recensions represents a general agreement that history should be divided up into periods, along with disputes over the exact duration of each and sometimes about the principles of division. The priestly school of thought from which the dating system in the Pentateuch and the historical books probably derives, works predominantly with a threefold division of history: a pre-Abrahamic era, a second age running from Abraham to the building of Solomon's Temple, and a third running from then down to the present, but probably expected to end with the inauguration of a new age at some point in the future, whose date is variously calculated.[21] This implies, of course, that 'P' (that monument to 'static', 'theocratic' religion and polity) had an 'eschatology', and this is a further difficulty for the 'theocracy *versus* eschatology' point of view – though the 'eschatology' is surely an example of mode 3, not mode 2, in our scheme. By adjusting the dates given for various events it is naturally possible to turn the Priestly Document, and thereby the whole Pentateuch or even the whole Old Testament, into a cryptic prophecy of the imminence of the eschaton in one's own day; even without changing the text one can get the same result by numerological devices, since there is never any great difficulty in calculating dates once one knows what the answer is meant to be. Groups that thought of prophecy in our second mode spent much

233

labour on tasks of this sort, and may well have left their mark on various recensions of the Hebrew text. But it does not seem very likely that the Priestly writers *originally* meant their dating scheme to be taken in this way: rather, it represented a periodization of history for its own sake, rationalizing the historical process much as the system of festivals rationalized the cycles of the year and made the seasons serve the interests of a theology of divine order and beauty.

Again, periodization is certainly not peculiar to Jewish texts, but has a venerable history in the ancient Near East, appearing for example in Mesopotamian king-lists and other elementary historiographical works.[22] There is also a good deal of evidence from Greek texts that periodization was a common feature of prophetic presentations of history, and it is implied in Virgil's fourth Eclogue as a commonplace that the world passes through various 'ages'. The idea is sometimes ascribed to Persian sources, but the matter is very complex.[23] At all events periodization in itself is clearly not an invention of Jewish thinkers, and special explanations for its occurrence in Jewish 'apocalyptic' are inherently implausible, since they ignore its widespread occurrence elsewhere.[24]

V

The distinction between the second and third modes of reading and writing prophecy is, I hope, now established. So far from one being a subtype of the other, they are in certain important respects incompatible, and express a quite different kind of religious consciousness. My hope is that the typology of interpretations of prophecy which I have sketched in this chapter and the preceding one will provide a clearer and more satisfactory map than existing categories such as 'eschatology', 'apocalyptic', and 'theocracy' afford. These terms highlight certain questions which appear to me to be really nonquestions, while making it very difficult to find words to draw other, more important distinctions. In speaking of 'mode 2' and 'mode 3' readings I am aware of not contributing any useful fresh terms, but for the time being I think some circumlocution is better than a premature invention of special terms that might prove equally unsatisfactory. Shorthand terms have, I believe, seriously hindered the study of our period and its literature.

8

The Prophet as Theologian and Mystic

I

It is not a great step from being interested in the history of Israel, past and future, because it manifests the consistency of God's purposes, to treating particular events within it as examples of how God acts in any and every circumstance. Once attention has been concentrated more on the theological meaning of the historical process than on the details of particular episodes within it, it becomes natural to read history as an illustration of principles that in themselves are timeless, rather than to be greatly concerned with the particularity of specific events. Just as characters in the Pentateuch and in the histories are seen as paradigms for human conduct in the first mode, so their fate comes to be seen as paradigmatic for understanding *God*'s ways of acting in the world. This gives us our fourth mode of reading 'prophecy', in which a prophet is seen as someone with special insights into theological truths.

As we shall see, this has two major aspects: insight into the way God acts in human affairs, and insight into what he is like in himself. There is no clear-cut point of division between these two questions, but rather a spectrum, approximating at one end to the third mode, but with more concern for recurrent patterns of divine activity than for discerning a single direction in historical events, and at the other end moving into the realms of speculative and mystical theology, where history becomes more or less irrelevant to the vision of God in his eternal glory. What unites all the conceptions of prophecy in the fourth mode, however, is that they represent what may be called a 'philosophical' interest in the nature and character of God.

Many of the works from our period that make a conscious appeal to older prophetic literature clearly operate in this fourth mode. For

235

example, both past history and predictive prophecy are appealed to to illuminate the present. In the Vulgate version of Tobit, Sarah's prayer in chapter 3 reflects on God's providence shown in the history of Israel, and concludes that 'all who revere you know that if they have been tested they will be crowned; if in distress, delivered; if punished, free to come to your mercy. For you take no pleasure in our fall, but after the storm bring the calm, after tears and weeping you give abounding joy'. In similar vein in Esther 3:15 the Old Latin adds a prayer uttered by the Jews when the decree has gone out that they are to be annihilated, in which they say: 'O Lord, thou alone art God in heaven above, and there is no God beside thee. For if we had performed thy law and thy precepts we might have lived in peace for all the duration of our life; but now, because we have not kept thy precepts, all this tribulation has come upon us. Thou Lord art just and tranquil, great and exalted, and all thy ways are just; now, O God, do not give thy children to captivity nor our wives to be violated and destroyed, thou who wast merciful to us from Egypt until now.' The past record of God's dealing with Israel is here regarded as a clue to his eternal character, and forms the basis of an appeal to him to be equally gracious in the future: not with any sense that history forms a predetermined pattern, as often in the third mode, nor that it is working towards a goal, but simply on the principle that God's actions will always exhibit the same pattern as in the past.

There is of course nothing new in this way of interpreting the past. It reaches back into the age of the Exile, at least, when writers of laments and prophets alike asserted that God's character was consistent and reliable, and therefore he could be expected to show the same faithfulness to his people in the future as he had shown in the 'mighty acts' of the past, especially in the whole complex of events we refer to for short as the Exodus. Such is the appeal of Isaiah 63:7–17, Psalm 44, and Jeremiah 14:17–22; it is presupposed by Deutero-Isaiah, and expressed in many prayers in post-exilic texts, such as Nehemiah 9 and Daniel 9. One might say that these texts point to the history of Israel as providing evidence that God does indeed have the character that such texts as Psalms 145–47 ascribe to him, and so justifies those in trouble in calling on him to reassert that character in the face of the challenge to it which their present condition represents.

Thus in this aspect our fourth mode is the application to ancient

236

texts, and the story they tell, of a way of looking at the past which in earlier times had been applied to the ancient *traditions* of God's salvation of Israel. In Exile people had already looked back to a kind of 'canonical' version of Israel's history; now they could appeal to this in written form, and see all the old books which enshrined it as bearing witness to the love of God for his people, which would be manifested anew in each generation. It could be argued that this is already the message of the Deuteronomistic History,[1] and it is attractively summed up in Psalm 107, with its catalogue of disasters and punishments which can from time to time afflict God's people, but out of which he always delivers them. The pattern of divine activity here is closely akin to that in the book of Judges:

He turns rivers into a desert, springs of water into thirsty ground, a fruitful land into a salty waste, because of the wickedness of its inhabitants.

He turns a desert into pools of water, a parched land into springs of water. And there he lets the hungry dwell, and they establish a city to live in . . .

When they are diminished and brought low through oppression, trouble, and sorrow, he pours contempt upon princes and makes them wander in trackless wastes; but he raises up the needy out of affliction, and makes their families like flocks . . .

Whoever is wise, let him give heed to these things; let men consider the steadfast love of the LORD (Psalm 107:33–43).

As the last verse shows, the Psalmist's reflection on Israel's history has here turned into a generalization about God's way with the world: that is, it has become a piece of 'wisdom'. In our period it was quite normal to read the record of the past in this way. Where older wisdom had drawn conclusions about the moral character of the world and its creator from empirical observations of nature and of human society, in New Testament times it was just as common to use the recorded history of Israel for this purpose. The Wisdom of Solomon is rich in examples, for it contains a lengthy retelling of the history of salvation deliberately generalized in just this way, to serve as an illustration of general principles about the way true 'wisdom' protects those who love her (10–19). One example may serve for many: according to 16:24–9, the manna was given to show

237

Israel that 'the creation ... exerts itself to punish the unrighteous, but in kindness relaxes on behalf of those who trust in thee', and that 'it is not the production of crops that feeds man, but that thy word preserves those who trust in thee'. The fact that the sun melted the manna was 'to make it known that one must rise before the sun to give thee thanks, and must pray to thee at the dawning of the light; for the hope of an ungrateful man will melt like wintry frost, and flow away like waste water'. Our fourth mode here joins hands with the first; for the lessons one learns from history about the nature of God have consequences for human conduct.

Josephus saw the story he was retelling in exactly this light:

> The main lesson to be learnt from this history by any who care to peruse it is that men who conform to the will of God, and do not venture to transgress laws that have been excellently laid down, prosper in all things beyond belief, and for their reward are offered by God felicity; whereas, in proportion as they depart from the strict observance of these laws, things else practicable become impracticable, and whatever good thing they strive to do ends in irretrievable disasters (*Antiquities* 1:14).[2]

Josephus's work itself provides many cases where historical events are thus 'moralized'. One of the most striking occurs in Antiquities 6:262–8, where almost the whole *raison d'être* of Saul is understood to consist in his being available to the author of Samuel (who, of course, is the prophet Samuel himself) as an example of sinfulness and the divine retribution that falls upon it. A very similar idea may well lie behind St Paul's reference to those who sinned in the wilderness, in 1 Corinthians 10, to which we have already referred in other connections: 'these things are warnings to us, not to sin as they did ... these things happened to them as a warning, but they were written down for our instruction' (10:6, 11).

What is perhaps more surprising in the literature of our period is the tendency to treat predictive prophecy in the same way as the prophetic record of the past. When prophecies are said to be 'fulfilled' in the New Testament, this generally means that specific predictions have 'come true'; but the same is not necessarily the case in other works from New Testament times. For example, Tobit 2:5–6 quotes Amos 8:10 when Tobit finds a murdered man on the day of Tabernacles: 'Then I remembered the prophecy of Amos, how he said, "Your feasts shall be turned into mourning, and all your festivities into lamentation". And I wept.' I doubt if this is meant to suggest that Amos, consciously or unconsciously, had foretold this particular event; the sense is rather that the words of Amos came into Tobit's mind as peculiarly appropriate for the occasion. This was the *kind* of event Amos had had in mind.

The same might be said of a text such as 1 Maccabees 14:4–15, a eulogy of Simon, in whose days 'they tilled their land in peace; the ground gave its increase, and the trees of the plain their fruits'; 'old men sat in the streets'; 'each man sat under his vine and his fig tree, and there was none to make them afraid'. Obviously this passage is full of reminiscences of the prophets, whose words 'came true' in Simon's day; but there does not seem to be any implication either that 'the last days' had arrived, or that the prophets actually foresaw the coming of Simon. It is simply that his reign was a period of blessing, and so corresponded, more or less, to times of prosperity as foretold by the prophets.

A third example might be 1 Maccabees 7:16–17. Alcimus here treacherously kills sixty men who have come to him to make terms, 'in accordance with the word which was written, "The flesh of thy saints and their blood they poured out round about Jerusalem, and there was none to bury them" '. The prophecy here 'fulfilled' is from Psalm 79:2–3. There is room for disagreement here, but for my part I doubt whether the author wants us to think that Alcimus 'fulfilled' an ancient prophecy in the way that Jesus in Matthew fulfils certain scriptural texts. More probably the Psalm is taken as describing in a classic way what happens whenever lawlessness gains the upper hand: as it was then, so it was also in the days of Alcimus, and so it will be again whenever God is despised.

It seems to me that a similar process of thought is often at work in the Targums. In the Targum of Jonathan, for example, the predictive aspect of the teaching of Isaiah is well to the fore; but it seldom appears that he is interpreted as looking forward to any single era of salvation. More often, the targumist assumes that Isaiah foresaw the regular pattern which all Israel's history would exhibit: a pattern of sin and humiliation, followed as the night the day by forgiveness and restoration. In this Targum we find the beginnings of the particular indomitable quality of the Jewish people which never ceases to astound Gentiles. National suffering is accepted as part of the lot of God's people, yet there is an assurance that he will never abandon his covenant: 'weeping may tarry for the night, but joy comes with the morning' (Psalm 30:5). Thus prophecies of the future have the same essential role as prophecies (that is, inspired records) of the past: to bring comfort and consolation by stressing that God remains in control, and that present suffering is simply part of another cycle which, like all its predecessors, will end in joy and salvation. As in other modes, so here, the distinction between past and future in prophetic utterances is barely functional. What is all-important is the witness borne by both alike to God's ways of dealing with his recalcitrant yet beloved people.

Some of the clearest illustrations of this tendency can be found in the Mekhilta on Exodus 15:6, where the principle that 'there is no before and after in the Torah' comes into its own and helps to produce many examples of the consistency of divine action:

When the Israelites do the will of God, they make his left hand, as it were, to be like a right hand, as it is said: Thy right hand, O Lord, thy right hand [Exodus 15:6] – twice. And when the Israelites fail to do the will of God, they make his right hand to be like a left hand, as it is said: He hath drawn back his right hand [Lamentations 2:3].

When the Israelites do the will of God there is no sleep unto him, as it is said: Behold, he that keepeth Israel doth neither slumber nor sleep [Psalm 121:4]. But when the Israelites fail to do his will, there is, as it were, sleep unto him, as it is said: Then the Lord awaked as one asleep [Psalm 78:65].

When the Israelites do the will of God, there is no anger unto him, as it is said: Fury is not in me [Isaiah 27:4]. But when the Israelites fail to do the will of God, there is, as it were, anger unto him, as it is said: And the anger of the Lord be kindled [Deuteronomy 11:17].

When the Israelites do the will of God he fights for them, as it is said: The Lord will fight for you [Exodus 14:14]. But when the Israelites fail to do the will of God, he fights against them, as it is said: Therefore he was turned to be their enemy [Isaiah 63:10]. And what is more, they make the Merciful One cruel, as it is said: The Lord is become as an enemy [Lamentations 2:5].

A still more striking example of the indifference as between past, present and future may be seen in the comment on Exodus 14:24, 'it came to pass in the morning watch':

> You find that the prayers of the righteous are heard in the morning. Whence do we know about Abraham's morning? It is said: And Abraham arose early in the morning [Genesis 22:3; other examples from the past follow] . . . Whence do we know about the mornings of the prophets destined to arise in the future? It is said: O Lord, in the morning shalt thou hear my voice; in the morning will I order my prayer unto thee, and will look forward [Psalm 5:4; other examples follow from passages taken to be predictions]. Whence do we know about the mornings of the world in general? It is said: They are new every morning; great is thy faithfulness [Lamentations 3:23].

Thus Scripture witnesses to the providence of God, who acts, has acted, and always will act according to the same principles; and this is ultimately good news for Israel, who has a God on which it can rely.

It is not surprising, therefore, that the synagogue in selecting prophetic passages to serve as *haftaroth* normally ensured that they would speak of God's ultimate blessing, and not contain words of judgement alone. As Mann puts it, 'The haftarah was supposed to bring consolation and encouragement for Israel by leading down to a conclusion that was heartening and foretelling the ultimate redemption.'[3] Sometimes this leads to the need to jump verses in order to produce a lesson which conveys the right message without being excessively long. For example, the *haftarah* to Genesis 18:1ff. is now Isaiah 33:17–24 *plus* 35:10, which brings the reading to a rousing conclusion. In some cases it may be suspected that this or some similar kind of liturgical use has actually influenced the redaction of the prophetic books themselves.[4] At any rate the regular alternation of judgement and blessing in a collection such as Isaiah 1–12 might lead one to think that the arrangement has been dictated by a similar motive, to ensure that any substantial section will include both poles of the prophetic message, and so ensure that people's expectations of God will in every generation embrace both sorrow and consolation. In their present form almost any one of the prophetic books (both Former and Latter) can be read as eloquent reminders of the truth summed up by Blake:

Man was made for Joy and Woe;
And when this we rightly know
Thro' the world we safely go.[5]

Any slice of history one cares to take, be it past or future, will have the same shape. Those Jewish thinkers who see in the history of European Jewry the pattern of destruction, in the horrors of the Holocaust, followed by rebirth in the foundation of the state of Israel, stand in the tradition of those who compiled and selected readings from the prophets of past and future to capture what Paul called 'the kindness and the severity of God'. Those on the other hand who see in the Holocaust an absolute end, which it is something approaching blasphemy to assimilate to *any* conceivable pattern in which God could have a part, are declaring that the carefully shaped mould, designed by the Deuteronomistic Historians, perfected by the Chronicler, and copied from generation to generation as the prophets were read and re-read, has been decisively broken, and cannot be remade unless God remakes the world. In their own way, early Christians were saying something not dissimilar when they declared that after the Cross things must begin anew: the history and the predictions of prophets had come to a crucial point, after which nothing would be the same again.

From either of these more absolute standpoints, there begins to be something a little too glib about the simplicities of our fourth mode of reading prophecy, which looks in that perspective like the banality that life has its ups and downs. Certainly in our period there is more cutting edge to the belief in divine providence than that, for all that we may want to argue that it is not up to the task of coping with the unimaginable scale of suffering seen in the present century. Few, however, would now be found to defend the simple moralism of Josephus, or to share the assurance with which prophets in Chronicles can declare that 'the Lord is with you, while you are with him' (2 Chronicles 15:2).[6]

Despite their sense that the old pattern had been broken, some early Christian writers continued to see the prophets as important because they had taught general theological principles, or illustrated such principles through what they had predicted or recorded. There are few examples in the synoptic gospels, and such as there are seem designed to show that the character of God revealed in the prophetic records has been widely misinterpreted – thus disturbing, rather than consoling, the hearers. In Luke 4:25–7 Jesus, in the synagogue at Nazareth, is presented as arguing from the examples of Elijah feeding the widow of Zarephath and Elisha healing the Syrian Naaman to the conclusion that God's primary concern lies outside Israel – an argument reminiscent of Paul's in Romans 9:13, where Malachi 1:2–3 ('Jacob I loved, but Esau I hated') is turned against the Jewish people by casting them as the elder son, Esau, and arguing that God has a fixed policy of choosing the less likely candidate in preference to the more likely. Similarly, in Luke 9:54 the disciples appeal to the example of Elijah in calling down fire from heaven on those who do not receive their master, but only to be told by Jesus that that is *not* how God chooses to work through him.[7] Stephen's speech in Acts 7, which we have already discussed, represents a similar case. Where the prophetic books are indeed taken to disclose truths about God's way of acting in the world, that way is redefined in the light of Christian convictions about the supersession of the Temple by Jesus and the conversion of the Gentiles as preceding that of the Jews.

For examples of 'normal' fourth-mode interpretation of prophecy we must turn to Paul. We have already seen that 1 Corinthians 10 preserves a clear case of this way of reading Scripture, though admittedly the incidents that illustrate God's dealings with man are taken from the Pentateuch. Chapters 1 and 2, however, show clearly that Paul could also use the prophetic books in the same way, since he there grounds his argument that 'God chose what is foolish in the world to shame the wise' (1:27) in the prophecy of Isaiah 29:14, 'I will destroy the wisdom of the wise, and the cleverness of the clever I will thwart'. Again, how we understand the force of the quotation is a matter of judgement. One could take it as a prediction which has been fulfilled uniquely in Christ (mode 2); but I am inclined to think that it is intended more as a general truth about God's attitude to human wisdom, of which the cross of Christ is the supreme but not the unique expression. The crucifixion demonstrates the truth of the prophetic saying – just as, in its own way, does the divine choice at Corinth of 'not many' who are 'wise . . . powerful . . . of noble birth' (1:26). Jeremiah 9:24 ('Let him who boasts, boast of the Lord', 1:30) is pulled in to make the same point, without, indeed, any violence to its sense in its original context. That the *true* wisdom, which belongs to God alone, is hidden from normal human sight, is proved by quotations from Isaiah 64:4 and

243

65:17 (2:9) and from Isaiah 40:13 (2:16), which Paul so glosses as to make the point that this hidden wisdom has now been revealed to those who have 'the mind of Christ'.[8]

The prophets, in these chapters, are clearly presented as having understood mysterious truths about God which are only now revealed to a wider audience: these mysteries are the fact that God works through what men account folly rather than through what they account wisdom, and that unimaginable treasures await those to whom God is prepared to disclose them. These are general truths about God, though they are revealed only to those (the early Christians, and the prophets themselves) who are their beneficiaries. We begin here to glimpse the other major aspect of a fourth-mode reading of prophecy: the revelation of hidden mysteries. About this there will be more to say shortly.

Paul's other uses of the fourth mode appear in Romans. We have already looked at Romans 9:13; other simple cases are 4:6–8, where Psalm 32:1–2 is adduced to show that God does not 'impute' sin – in other words, the Psalm is treated as an authority for defining the meaning of 'reckoned to him as righteousness' in Genesis 15:6, not as a prediction but as evidence of scriptural word-usage; and 14:11, where Isaiah 45:23 is said to show that God judges each person according to his own conscience, and therefore that human judgements on others are to be avoided. In neither of these cases does the scriptural tag do more than prop up an argument whose internal logic plainly does not depend upon it, but on Paul's own system of thought.

More problematic is the general case of the use of Scripture in Romans 1–8. To put a common dispute about the meaning of Romans in terms of 'modes of reading', we may say that one of the great difficulties in interpreting the epistle is to decide whether Paul is operating in mode 2 or mode 4 in these chapters. When he quotes Habakkuk 2:4, 'The righteous shall live by faith' (or however we are to translate it) in 1:17, we may take this in either of two ways. We may say that Paul regarded this verse as a prophecy of the end-time: *the day would come* when the qualification for acceptance by God would be 'faith' rather than, let us say, membership of the covenant community of Israel. Read in this way, Romans 1–8 is an assertion that this time has now arrived: it is a treatise on the totally changed conditions which obtain now that the day foretold by the prophets has dawned, and Gentiles are preceding Jews into the kingdom.[9]

On the other hand, we may follow the traditional Lutheran interpretation of Romans as expressing a *general truth* about how people 'qualify' for God's acceptance, and see the quotation from Habakkuk as stating an insight which had always been true, but had only come to be realized through the ministry of Jesus and the teaching of Paul himself. The one who is 'righteous through his faith' is then any Christian who turns to the Lord without relying on 'works', and the message of Romans has an existential rather than an eschatological import.[10] I think it probable that the former explanation is to be preferred, but suspend judgement in so weighty a dispute, on which whole schools of experts differ. I note, however, that the acceptance of the second opinion implies that Paul read Habakkuk 2:4 in our fourth mode – not as a prediction which was just in the process of coming true, but as a statement about God's manner of behaving towards man. In either case, it is fair to point out, there is little likelihood that Paul has reproduced the meaning Habakkuk had in mind; his interpretation of this prophet, however much it differs from that current at Qumran, is no less the product of his own *prior* convictions about theological truth.

II

If by reading prophecy we can learn how God acts in the world and what character he reveals in doing so, it will be natural to think that we can also learn something about what he is like in himself. Traditionally Old Testament study has been chary of suggestions that Israelite prophets or writers were interested in the 'attributes' of God, which suggests the God of philosophical theology and hence of the 'Greek' strand in Christian thought; and Jewish thinkers have often also been unwilling to speak of Jewish 'theology', judging this to be a speculative concern alien to the religion of the Torah, which is a *task* rather than a speculative system. I think, however, that these reservations, though they may be valid for modern Judaism (I am not entitled to an opinion on that) and of the earlier strands of Old Testament thought, do not really apply to the situation in New Testament times. Much study of the Old Testament in modern times has stressed the *historical* character of 'revelation' in ancient

245

Israel; but Judaism in our period is not part of 'ancient Israel'. From this point of view there is, just as Wellhausen saw so acutely, a point of transition in the early post-exilic period, when Judaism ceased to depend on 'God's acts in history' and became a religion with a far more 'static' conception of God, not so far removed from 'philosophical' concerns. It came to stress the eternal and unchanging character of the divine nature, and God's utter transcendence and separation from all that is transitory or earth-bound. This did not necessarily produce, as it has sometimes done in Christianity, a religion which was world-renouncing or 'spiritual' in the negative way disliked by the Biblical Theology movement, but it did open the door for questions about the nature of God in his exalted splendour which are not far from the concerns of philosophical theology.

The lines of thought I have been trying to tease out so far in this chapter lead, in fact, naturally in such a direction. Once people begin to see the record of both past and future in the prophetic books as important mainly for the light they shed on the eternal or unchanging character of God and his consistent purposes, it does not need much contact with the Greek philosophical tradition – perhaps none at all – to sever the connection with real history almost entirely. Interest then comes to focus on what the prophets can teach us about God in his own inner nature, and on the relation to him of the individual human soul. In any case, earlier Israelite tradition had not, as I see it, lacked such an interest as completely as is sometimes implied. The pre-exilic prophets were no doubt concerned primarily with God's imminent *actions*; but they, and their predecessors in guilds at sanctuaries and in prophetic bands, seem to have had just as firm a conviction that they had 'stood in the council of Yahweh' as any later 'mystic'. The heavenly realm into which they believed they had been admitted was not conceived after the model of the Platonic world of Forms, of course, but according to ancient Near Eastern models of the world of the gods, itself modelled on royal courts. Still it represented the reality of divine life which existed independently of the human world, and an interest in it could easily lead into a kind of speculative theology, as we see well enough in Ezekiel, the prologue to Job, and even the vision of Micaiah ben Imlah in 1 Kings 22 – though this may not of course really go back into the ninth century, as it claims. The prototypes for such scenes in Israelite literature may well be found in Ugaritic texts which themselves are not the fountainhead of thinking about 'heaven' and the private life of the gods.[11] I cannot see any reason, unless one has a prior conviction that speculation about such things *cannot* have occurred in Israel, for denying the antiquity of an interest in what God is like 'in himself' even before the Exile.[12]

Thus there are at least two lines of thought – the interpretation of history and prediction as conveying universal truths, and the old Israelite interest in the divine realm – which converge to make possible a reading of prophecy in which speculative or mystical theology becomes a serious pursuit for Jewish writers.

Pride of place here must certainly go to Philo, in whom 'indigenous' Israelite traditions are heavily afforced by conceptions that unquestionably do derive from Greek philosophy as he had encountered it. For Philo, just as for the texts we have been examining until now, the distinction between past record and future prediction is scarcely functional by comparison with the witness borne by both to essentially timeless truth. The titles of his expositions of the various Pentateuchal sections already alert us to this: 'On the Immutability of God'; 'On the Virtues'; 'On the Contemplative Life'. He frequently takes the biblical text, which to the uninitiated reader seems to tell a very particular story, as the key to general truths about God and the soul, and in his 'Allegorical Interpretation' produces a detailed hermeneutical theory, as it would now be called, to justify his practice. As we have already seen, Philo's quotations from books outside the Pentateuch, which are our proper concern, are comparatively few, but such as do occur accord entirely with his use of the Pentateuchal text in being treated as windows onto eternal truth, philosophically conceived. Here is a typical example:

I was moved a few pages above to praise the virtues of those who say that 'We are all sons of one man' [Genesis 42:11]. For if we have not yet become fit to be thought sons of God yet we may be sons of his invisible image, the most holy Word. For the Word is the eldest-born image of God ... I bow, too, in admiration before the mysteries revealed in the books of Kings, where it does not offend us to find described as sons of God's psalmist David those who lived and flourished many generations afterwards, though in David's lifetime probably not even their great-

247

grandparents had been born. For the paternity we find ascribed to the standard-bearers of noble living, whom we think of as the fathers who begat us, is the paternity of souls raised to immortality by virtues, not of corruptible bodies (*de confusione linguarum* 147–9).

But if the histories are thus seen as teaching truths which are really timeless, so too are texts such as the Psalms, which lend themselves more naturally (to our minds) to such treatment:

So good a thing is shepherding that it is justly ascribed not to kings only and wise men but also to God the all-Sovereign. The authority for this ascription is not any ordinary one but a prophet, whom we do well to trust. This is the way in which the Psalmist speaks: 'The Lord shepherds me and nothing shall be lacking to me' [Psalm 23:1]. It well befits every lover of God to rehearse this Psalm. But for the Universe it is a still more fitting theme. For land and water and air and fire, and all plants and animals which are in these, whether mortal or divine, yea and the sky, and the circuits of sun and moon, and the revolutions and rhythmic movements of the other heavenly bodies, are like some flock under the hand of God its King and Shepherd . . . Therefore let even the whole universe, that greatest and most perfect flock of the God who is [*tou ontos theou*, cf. Exodus 3:14] say, 'The Lord shepherds me, and nothing shall fail me' (*de agricultura* 50–2).

The prophetic texts which we are likely to see as least amenable to such treatment, however, are probably those that Philo cites most in support of general theological truths and divine mysteries revealed to the prophets (whom, as we saw in chapter 4, he consistently presents as mystics). Thus in *quis rerum divinarum heres* 267–70 the promises made to Abraham in Genesis 15:3–21 are presented not as predictions of the future but enunciations of truths about the enlightened soul. The prediction that 'thy seed shall be sojourners in a land that is not their own' (Genesis 15:3) teaches (it is described as a *paideuma*, a 'lesson') that 'God does not grant as a gift to the lover of virtue that he should dwell in the body as a homeland, but only permits him to sojourn there, as in a foreign country'. The warning that 'the slavery is for four hundred years' (Genesis 15:13) 'shows the powers exercised by the four passions'.

In a similar vein the prophecy of the 'Branch' in Zechariah 6:12

is taken to be, not the prediction of a human successor to David, but a reference in code to the Logos, 'that Incorporeal One, who differs not a whit from the divine image . . . the eldest son, whom the Father of all raised up' (*de confusione linguarum* 62–3, following the LXX *anatolê*, 'rising' or 'daystar' for 'branch'). Prophetic denunciations fare the same as predictions: Jeremiah's withering attack 'They have forsaken me, the fountain of living waters, and hewed out cisterns for themselves, broken cisterns, that can hold no water' (2:13) interests Philo not for its condemnation of idolatry but for the light it sheds on the divine nature as the source and cause of all life, and the consequent futility of all merely human effort:

> God . . . is the chiefest spring, and well may he be so called, for this whole universe is a rain that fell from him. But I bow in awe when I hear that this spring is one of life: for God alone is the cause of soul and life, and pre-eminently of the rational soul, and of the life that is united with wisdom . . . All the receptacles of the ill-conditioned soul are crushed and leaking, unable to hold in and keep the inflow of what might do them good (*de fuga* 198, 201).

One of Philo's clearest references to the prophets as mystagogues has already been cited in chapter 4: *de cherubim* 48–50, where he speaks of becoming a disciple of Jeremiah because he was 'himself enlightened, and a worthy minister of the holy secrets (*ou monon mystês alla kai ierophantês hikanos*)'. One of the things Philo learned from Jeremiah was, he believed, conveyed through his oracle in 3:4 (LXX): 'Didst thou not call upon me as thy house, thy father and the husband of thy virginity?' 'Thus,' says Philo, 'he implies clearly that God is a house, the incorporeal dwelling-place of incorporeal ideas, that he is the father of all things, for he begat them, and the husband of Wisdom, dropping the seed of happiness for the race of mortals into good and virgin soil.' Such ideas are treated by Philo as arcane truths about God, reserved for the initiated: 'Ye initiates (*ô mystai*), whose ears are purified, receive these thoughts into your souls as holy mysteries indeed and babble not of them to any of the profane . . . But if ye meet with anyone of the initiated, press him closely, cling to him, lest knowing of some still newer secret he hide it from you; stay not till you have learnt its full lesson.' Thus prophets can reveal *fresh* truths about God, even beyond what has been revealed through Moses: and when they do so, the kind of truth of which they speak will have to do with God's eternal nature and perhaps with relationships within the divine realm, as in this example.

In another place we find a typical feature of Philo's allegorical method: its tendency to look for mystical teaching of this kind in places where the literal sense of the text is difficult or self-contradictory.[13] In Philo's text Psalm 75:8 (LXX 74:8) runs *potêrion en cheiri kuriou, oinou akratou plêrês kerasmatos*: 'In the hand of the Lord there is a cup of unmixed wine, full of mixture'. This provides the cue for an interpretation in terms of the 'powers' through which God acts upon the world. 'The powers which God employs are unmixed in respect of himself, but mixed to created beings. For it cannot be that mortal nature should have room for the unmixed. We cannot look even upon the sun's flame untempered . . . and can you think it possible that your understanding should be able to grasp in their unmixed purity those uncreated potencies, which stand forth around him and flash forth light of surpassing splendour?' (*quod deus immutabilis sit* 77–8). We are here in a world infinitely remote from that of the Psalmist, in a Platonist heaven: that is what a reading of Scripture in mode 4 can do for us. Compare also *de somniis* 2:246–8, where further verses from the Psalms are given a similarly mystical interpretation.

I have dwelt on Philo because he represents the fourth mode in its most characteristic form, in which all those texts which in their original setting are so serious about *time* – histories and predictive prophecies – come to be seen as important for precisely the opposite property: their ability to open a window into heaven, and show the reader God in his timeless nature. But similar ideas, strange as they may seem to the modern reader, can be found in less obviously 'Hellenized' forms even in writers whose concerns are not so philosophical or mystical as Philo's.

The most immediately obvious case of this would be the rabbinic texts dealing with Ezekiel's chariot-vision, in which all manner of mysteries concerning the heavenly world were thought to lie hidden. As with so much rabbinic material, it is extremely hard to feel any confidence about dating the various descriptions of meditation on the *merkabah* and its (sometimes highly dangerous) consequences, but we are lucky now to have Rowland's extended discussion of the texts, one of the few attempts made so far to suggest a relative chronology for the traditions and to reconstruct the earliest version of the most famous incident related in connection with *merkabah*-mysticism.[14] But in any case we are not told in detail what were the mysteries which meditation on the chariot revealed, though one peculiarity was that in this case, unlike most other texts on which one might meditate, there was a chance that the original vision might reproduce itself in the one meditating – hence the value, but also the danger, of the exercise.[15] Undoubtedly Ezekiel 1 was regarded by the circles around Johanan ben Zakkai as one of the most concentrated bodies of esoteric information to be found anywhere in Scripture, though the secrets were so ineffable that we still do not know just what they were.

The New Testament, however, provides more evidence of the mystical type of fourth-mode reading of older prophecy than one might, perhaps, expect. In the story about Jesus' dispute with the Sadducees over the resurrection (Mark 12:18–27; Matthew 22:23–33; Luke 20:27–40) a passage from the Pentateuch is treated in this mode: 'that the dead are raised, have you not read in the book of Moses, in the passage about the bush, how God said to him, "I am the God of Abraham, and the God of Isaac, and the God of Jacob"? He is not God of the dead, but of the living.' The resurrection is a mystery – not here an 'eschatological' mystery, for the implication is surely that Abraham, Isaac, and Jacob have been raised already, and were alive with resurrection life when God spoke to Moses – in so far as the question is clearly in focus at all. It is, rather, a mystery about the nature of man and God's intentions for him. The truth, that the dead rise again, is not revealed in a direct way in Scripture, but through God's own self-description which (as might be expected) is pregnant with meaning.

The resurrection of Jesus himself, as well as his passion and his birth, are treated as 'mysteries' in rather the same way in the Apostolic Fathers, and the prophets are said to have understood them: here the idea that the prophets *predicted* the events is certainly present (mode 2 or 3), but there is also a sense of plans long hidden in what Ignatius called 'the silence of God' (*hêsychia theou, Ephesians* 19:1) to which the prophets had privileged access.[16]

Several other passages in the gospels speak of God revealing mysteries, and adduce quotations from the prophets in support of this. Matthew 13:17 (compare Luke 10:24) says that things are revealed to the disciples which were hidden from the eyes of 'many prophets and righteous men' ('kings' in Luke); by contrast, the

251

multitudes fulfil the prophecy of Isaiah 6:9–10, to the effect that 'this people' has closed its eyes and ears. This may be taken as a predictive prophecy, in the second mode; but it is also a general statement about the way God hides his mysteries from the many and reveals them to the few. Compare Matthew 21:16, where Jesus rebukes the 'chief priests and scribes', when they are indignant about children hailing him as Son of David, by quoting Psalm 8:2: 'Out of the mouth of babes and sucklings hast thou brought perfect praise.' The line of thought here is akin to that in 1 Corinthians 1–3: those despised by the traditionally 'wise' have been given privileged access to God's mysteries. Whether Jesus' practice of teaching in parables was meant to reveal or to conceal God's secrets is, of course, a point of difference between Mark and Matthew (compare Matthew 13:10–13 with Mark 4:10–12);[17] we cannot go into this here, but note merely that in Mark at least the cryptic nature of Jesus' teaching plainly belongs in the same world as our fourth mode of prophecy.

We see in these passages an essential point about the New Testament understanding of old prophecy. Whereas for a commentator like Philo the prophets of old were initiated into the mysteries (freely understood after the model of the Greek mysteries) and so had knowledge which we need to labour to recapture, for the New Testament it is on the whole assumed that the prophets were granted only partial, flickering pictures of the truth: true illumination comes only with Christ (compare Ephesians 5:14).

This theory receives its fullest elaboration in the Epistle to the Hebrews, where the Son reveals not only 'eschatological' secrets but also the hidden realities of the heavenly world.[18] The best example of this is perhaps the extended interpretation of the Old Testament references to Melchizedek; for Hebrews, as evidently for the Qumran community, Melchizedek was a type of the access to God's court granted to his specially favoured servants. Though he is a priest, the fact that the sanctuary into which his antitype, Jesus, has been admitted is a heavenly one means that images of *vision* and revelation appear alongside those of sacrifice, and those whom Christ has associated with himself in entering the sanctuary are described as 'those who have been enlightened' (6:4). We are here clearly in the world of journeys through the heavens in which mysterious truth is imparted to the seer, as well as in that of atonement-theories: hence much of the complexity of Hebrews.

252

Moses, who is also a type of Jesus, is predominantly seen as a visionary prophet, as he is by Philo: not only did he 'testify to the things that were to be spoken later' (3:5), but he also saw the heavenly archetype of the Temple (8:5). But Moses and all the other prophets did not receive the knowledge that God has now imparted in his Son, for they all had only partial and fragmentary truth to impart (1:1). On the whole, then, though the New Testament thought of prophets as having taught in the fourth mode, it saw them as radically superseded in Christ – a very different position from that of many of the early Christians' contemporaries.

III

The eternal secrets of the heavenly world are as central a concern of the pseudonymous 'prophecy' written in New Testament times as they are of the way genuinely older Scripture was read. Rowland is fully justified in devoting a chapter to 'what is above', that is, the secrets of the heavens, in his survey of the contents of apocalypses, and pointing out that a number of them have virtually no concern with 'eschatology' but are devoted entirely to information about the heavenly world. The Enoch corpus, for example, contains much material of this sort, and the tales of 'heavenly journeys' that are characteristic of it became a common feature of later Jewish and Christian apocalypses, reaching their climax in Dante. 1 Enoch 14:8–24 is a classic example of the seer's ascent into heaven:

> Behold clouds called me in the vision, and mists called me, and the path of the stars and flashes of lightning hastened me and drove me, and in the vision winds caused me to fly and hastened me and lifted me up into heaven.

Enoch then proceeds through regions of fire and ice into the presence of God:

> I saw . . . a high throne, and its appearance was like ice and its surrounds like the shining sun and the sound of cherubim. And from underneath the high throne there flowed out rivers of burning fire so that it was impossible to look at it. And he who is great in glory sat on it, and his raiment was brighter than the sun, and whiter than any snow.[19]

In subsequent chapters Enoch is given a guided tour of the various regions of heaven (17–36) in which the only 'eschatological' interests are to be found in descriptions of the places in which those who are to sin or to act righteously in the days to come will be either punished or rewarded (for example, 19:1, 22:3). Rowland provides many more detailed examples of the sorts of secret that would be revealed to the seer on such a journey.

It should be noted – and by now this will not seem surprising – that revelation of heavenly mysteries is not confined to apocalypses, but occurs in other forms. Thus in the Testament of Levi 2–3 the patriarch describes for his descendants the geography of the seven heavens, which were revealed to him in a dream, and in chapter 5 we learn that it was while he was in heaven that God commissioned him to avenge the rape of Dinah.

A concomitant of the interest in the heavenly realm is the greatly increased importance attached to angels, and this of course is widely diffused in literature of the late post-exilic period, being found in narratives such as Tobit just as much as in apocalypses. One may state the relationship between apocalypses and an interest in the denizens of the other world as follows: many but not all apocalypses are interested in angels and in the events that take place in heaven; many but not all of the works with this interest are apocalypses. As soon as one tries to use the term 'apocalyptic' the fact that the two categories of literature overlap but are not conterminous becomes a problem[20] – the more so if one has a prior commitment to the idea that 'apocalyptic' is essentially about 'eschatology'. Thus Koch complains that 'apocalyptic' is used as a title 'not only (for) such writings as II Baruch and the Apocalypse of Abraham, which certainly derive from the Semitic linguistic area; it is also applied to originally Hellenistic works such as II Enoch, IV Baruch and the Apocalypse of Paul, which certainly treat of heavenly journeys and cosmic geography, like the Semitic books, but which are lacking in an account of the end-time'.[21] But in fact there is little basis for the distinctions which this implies. Heavenly journeys and cosmic geography appear as an interest both within and outside apocalypses, and may or may not be linked with eschatological questions. There is no reason to think that writers in our period would have felt there to be any oddity in any possible combinations of these features: 'prophecy' could include all or any of them.

Writers of pseudonymous works were equally concerned to

present the heroes of their books as capable of discerning the pattern and meaning in human history. Like Josephus, the great figures from the past who were supposed to be the authors of these books discoursed about human history in such a way as to bring out its inner purpose and to vindicate divine providence. The way in which history is treated is very far removed from 'eschatology' in any sense of that term that could apply to the genuine teaching of the pre- or early post-exilic prophets. Von Rad was entirely correct to argue that, despite the fact that many apocalypses are deeply concerned with 'history' if that means simply connected strings of narrated events, they had little interest in or understanding of history as a process within which a definite direction could be perceived.[22] What interests the sages who are the purported authors of so many pseudonymous books is not the movement of history but the *recurring* pattern of the divine purposes, seen in the moral ordering of human affairs. This may be seen, for instance, in several sections of 1 Enoch, and may be summed up in the words of 2:2, 'Consider the earth, and understand from the work that is done upon it, from the beginning to the end, that *no work of God changes as it becomes manifest*'. In each generation God's hand may be discerned from the way in which the wicked meet their fate and the righteous are delivered (compare 101:1–9). This is the thrust of the oracle attributed to Balaam in Josephus's *Antiquities* 4:128, where Balaam's words of blessing on Israel (Numbers 24:15–24) are reinterpreted to make them a prediction of a *repeated pattern* of suffering followed by exaltation:

> 'God is watching over them to preserve them from all ill and to suffer no such calamity to come upon them as would destroy them all. Yet misfortunes may well befall them of little moment and for a little while, whereby they will appear to be abased, though only thereafter to flourish once more to the terror of those who inflicted these injuries upon them.'

The classic case of this interpretation of history as manifesting the way God deals with the world and with his chosen people may be found in 4 Ezra 3–14. Formally this is an apocalypse; in content one would probably categorize it as 'wisdom', if it came from an earlier period. The umbrella term 'prophecy' covers both in our period, and there was nothing odd, for a contemporary reader, in an apocalypse whose concern was with general truths about divine

255

providence rather than with the prediction of coming events. 4 Ezra is also heir, of course, to the 'sceptical' wisdom of such books as Job and Ecclesiastes, stressing the difficulty of knowing how God's providence works in the world and the impossibility for man in general of plumbing the depths of the corrupt human heart (4:4). As Rowland points out, 4 Ezra shares with the Syriac Baruch and the Apocalypse of Abraham a concern with the lot of mankind in general, and although these works do contain substantial 'eschatological' hopes (in 4 Ezra, several different schemes are implied),[23] these seem to come in

> as a kind of final justification of God in the face of insoluble problems presented by existence. The burning question . . . is not "When will the end be?", but "How can one make sense of the present and the promises of the past when history seems to contradict all that was originally sacrosanct?" . . . Eschatological matters are usually the result of the divine reply to existential questions, whereas the thoughts which are on the mind of the apocalypticists are more concerned with the situation as it is.[24]

1 Enoch also contains passages that hint at this 'existential' question as central to the writer's interest. In 81:5 one of the truths revealed to Enoch, which he is to pass on to his descendants, is that 'no flesh is righteous before the Lord'; yet in the end God will discriminate between good and evil, and see to it that 'the righteous will rejoice with the righteous' and 'the sinner will die with the sinner'. The details of the events of the last days matter less because they provide accurate *predictions* of the future than because they vindicate the wisdom and justice of God, and looking forward to them one can set one's troubled heart at rest and continue to believe in the goodness of God in spite of everything. Thus we may say that *theodicy* is a central concern in these apocalypses as it had been in the wisdom literature of earlier times (and indeed as it continued to be in wisdom, both that which was written as the avowed instruction of contemporary teachers – for example, in Ecclesiasticus – and that which was dressed up as ancient prophecy – Wisdom of Solomon 1:16–3:19, say).

The same presentation of history, past or future, as important for the justice of God that it reveals, may be found in the testament literature, and in hymnody produced in our period. The Testament of Joseph, which is a specially clear example of this tendency, actually contains two hymnic passages in which God's loyalty to his faithful servants is affirmed, and illustrated from the history of Joseph:

> The Lord will not forsake those who fear him, whether it be darkness they are in, or distress, or need. . . . In all places he is near at hand, and gives comfort in different ways, though for a little while he may absent himself in order to test the disposition of the soul. By ten temptations he showed his approval of me, and in all of them I endured (2:4–7).

'Many are the afflictions of the righteous, but the LORD delivers him out of them all', as the Psalmist had put it (Psalm 34:19): 'If you live in accord with the Lord's commands, God will exalt you with good things for ever', says the Joseph of the Testament (18:1). The Testament of Joseph is indeed an example also of the first mode of prophecy, ethical instruction; but as H. C. Kee comments, 'Here ethical motivation is chiefly instrumentalist: obedience to the Law guarantees that God will exalt the obedient one.'[25] The author's concern is as much to convince his readers, from the way he tells Joseph's story, that God is just and faithful, as to encourage them to emulate Joseph's example.

Similar themes can be found in the Psalms of Solomon: 'When we are afflicted we will call upon thee for help, and thou wilt not turn back our prayer, because thou art our God' (5:5(7)); 'If thou sendest death, thou thyself givest it charge concerning us; for thou art merciful, and wilt not be angry and destroy us utterly' (7:4–5); 'Thy discipline is upon us as on a first-born, an only son, so as to turn the obedient soul away from ignorant stupidity' (18:4(5)). Finally, we may recall that Judith in her speech to the elders of Bethulia points to the history of the nation as revealing all that was needed of the purposes of God: 'The Lord our God is putting us to the test, as he did our forefathers' (8:25). God's plans cannot be wholly discovered; one must not 'try to bind the purposes of the Lord our God, for God is not like man, to be threatened, nor like a human being, to be won over by pleading' (8:16); yet his past record makes it reasonable to 'hope that he will not disdain us or any of our nation' (8:20).

257

IV

Thus in the pseudepigrapha just as in the 'exegetical' literature dealing with ancient prophecy we find both aspects of the fourth mode: history as an index to the character of God's ways of dealing with the world, and visionary experience revealing the secrets of the eternal world in which he dwells. It may have struck the reader, however, that in yoking these two aspects together under the fourth mode I have been guilty of some sleight of hand. The discernment of divine providence in historical events belongs, in modern categories, to systematic theology; knowledge of God 'in himself', or in the world of spirits, belongs more to mystical or speculative theology. Are these not in reality two separate modes of reading and writing prophecy?

I believe that in treating the religious literature of our period it makes perfectly good sense to see these two aspects, different as they seem to us, as two sides of the same coin; and I think that the lack of any firm distinction between them is in fact one of the most important points to be grasped. For us, certainly, the attempt to discern a pattern of providential guidance in historical events belongs to a quite different temper of mind than an interest in angels, demons, the geography of the heavens and the inhabitants of the divine realm. But for the writers we are studying I do not think that this was so. When Enoch saw 'all the secrets of heaven, and how the kingdom is divided, and how the deeds of men are weighed in the balance' (1 Enoch 41:1), he was acquiring knowledge of the heavenly realm *and* insight into the moral shape of human history at one and the same time. It is misleading to speak as though knowledge of angels, for example, was seen as a revealed secret, but understanding of the moral regularities of God's conduct of human affairs was thought of as a matter of rational reflection. For the authors of 1 Enoch or 4 Ezra *neither* was possible except through direct revelation. The kind of knowledge that in earlier times had been regarded as attainable through the right use of reason – knowledge of the cycles of nature, the fate of righteous and wicked, and the meaning of human life – was by the New Testament period very widely thought of as hidden from man. As the poem in Job 28 puts it – in this radically contradicting older wisdom – 'Man does not know the way to (wisdom), and it is not found in the land of the living. . . . It is hid from the eyes of all living, and concealed

258

from the birds of the air. (Only) God understands the way to it' (28:13, 21, 23).

Even those truths that can to our minds be worked out by reason were not so regarded in the world of the New Testament. They were truths for revelation to the wise alone, as 4 Ezra makes abundantly clear. In chapter 4, Ezra attempts to make just such a distinction as the one we are discussing. 'I did not wish to inquire about the ways above, but about those things which we daily experience: why Israel has been given over to the Gentiles as a reproach; why the people whom you love has been given over to godless tribes, and the law of our fathers has been made of no effect and the written covenants no longer exist; and why we pass from the world like locusts, and our life is like a mist, and we are not worthy to obtain mercy' (4:23–4). But Uriel makes it clear (as far as he makes anything clear) that such questions are every bit as hidden, reserved to God alone. They can be resolved for Ezra only if he fasts and prays, and accepts instruction from the angel. Only the knowledge of the nature of the end can make coherent sense of the present state of the world and show the divine purpose in all that happens, and such knowledge is not for the many, nor for any to discover through his own wit: 'I have not shown this to all men, but only to you and a few like you' (8:62). Thus the secrets of heaven and the meaning of human history are inextricably woven together. In this world of thought only a mystic has any chance of being a systematic theologian.

It is perhaps in Jubilees that this way of thinking is clearest. As we have already seen, little of the material in Jubilees is 'eschatological' in any sense to do with an imminent end; but much of it is about 'history', in that the work is in effect a midrash on Genesis and the first part of Exodus, retelling with embellishments the story of mankind from the creation. It is clear that this has a halakic purpose, that is, it functions in the first mode, since the story of the ancestors is shaped in such a way as to support the calendrical theories of the group that produced the book. But Jubilees also looks for patterns in the narrated history from which the character of God's activity in the world may be deduced. The punishment of the angels who sinned with the daughters of men, and of their descendants in the time of the Flood, illustrates the regular operation of God's retribution, much as it would, say, for the author of Chronicles or for Josephus: 'The judgement of every one is ordained

259

and written on the heavenly tablets, and there is no injustice in it: all who stray from the path marked out for them to follow, and do not follow it – judgement is written down for them, for every creature and for every kind of creature' (5:13).

Indeed, the whole history in the more accurate form which the angel of the presence delivers to Moses demonstrates the mercy and justice of God in all his dealings with Israel: 'Write it in a book, so that the generations to come may see how I have not forsaken them on account of all the evil they have done in transgressing the covenant that I am establishing between me and you on mount Sinai today for all their generations. And so, when all these things have happened to them, they will recognize that I am more righteous than they are in all they think and do, and they will recognize that I have kept faith with them' (1:5–6). The ensuing narrative is thus interpreted in advance, and we know that it will be told so as to bring out the moral of each incident – just as are the narratives in Chronicles, or in Josephus's *Antiquities*, or in Stephen's speech in Acts 7. But the details of the narrative which make it so edifying, and which in reality were of course concocted by the author, are presented as unknowable apart from revelation. Moses learns them because the angel of the presence reads them out from the 'tablets of the divisions of the years' (1:29). These stories are just as much secrets guarded in the divine realm as are the mysteries which are also revealed to Moses about the character of the angels and the organization of the heavenly world. Moses could not have known what was going on behind the scenes even during the events of his own life, if the angel had not revealed it to him (see, for instance, Jubilees 48 on the incident recorded in Exodus 4:24–6); equally, he could not have known what angels were like: no one would ever have guessed that the angels were created circumcised, for example, if the angel of the presence had not told him (15:27).

Similarly, the correct dates on which to celebrate all the festivals were revealed to Moses – Jubilees, as we have seen, represents an attempt to establish a ruling on this at variance with what became orthodox – but it is presupposed that these dates exist on the 'heavenly tablets': that is, the provisions of the calendar are also hidden secrets. We also learn a good deal about the role of the angels. They, like Israel, keep the sabbath (2:17–8); it was they who brought the animals to Adam for naming (3:1); and it is their duty to 'report all the sin that is committed in heaven and on earth, and in light and darkness, everywhere' (4:6). It was the angel of the presence himself who conveyed to Abraham God's command to leave his own country and go to Palestine, and taught him to speak and to read Hebrew, helping him to study 'his fathers' books' throughout the six rainy months of that year (12:22–7).

Thus knowledge of the providential character of God's dealing with his world and knowledge of the mysteries of the realm in which he dwells belong together for a book such as Jubilees; and I believe that most of the literature of our period makes good sense if read in the same way. The fourth mode thus generates pseudonymous works in which the reader is meant to learn from the ancient writer to whom they are attributed about what we should call *theology* or *doctrine*, and thus to acquire a better understanding both of this world and of the world to come, which already exists as the divine realm is which God is eternally king. As we have seen, in this mode history no longer has the central place in its own right that it is usually held to have had for a lot of earlier Israelite literature. It becomes merely the vehicle through which and in which God reveals aspects of his own nature or activity which in essence are eternally true or valid. This results in works which strike us as radically different from the books now in the Old Testament. But the difference will not have struck contemporary readers, for they read the genuinely old books in exactly the same way.

V

For the fourth and last time, we must now ask: Why? Why did people in New Testament times think that the prophets of old had been inspired to reveal either general truths about the recurring patterns of God's action, when in reality they had been utterly absorbed in, even obsessed by, one imminent divine act; or secrets of the heavenly realm, when the earthly society of Israel and its coming destruction had occupied all their attention? And once again we must have recourse to the general intellectual climate of the times to find an explanation. 'Prophets' were for them something between mystics and philosophers – indeed, both rolled into one. It is not hard to see how this should have been so, for example, for Philo, who makes Israelite prophets in the image of the Hellenistic mantic, and attributes to the ancient prophets of his people the same understanding of God and of the Scriptures that he had himself. For Philo, the highest form of ecstasy was a vision in which the true nature of things (in Platonic terms, their Ideas) became clear to the visionary. Thus in his own mystical states, 'I obtained language, ideas, an enjoyment of light, keenest vision, pellucid distinctness of objects, such as might be received through the eyes as the result of clearest showing.'[26] Once one translates this into Jewish terms, it is likely to become a vision of the nature of God and of the spiritual beings closest to God, such as the angels; and there is of course enough in the Old Testament references to prophetic visions to make it possible to think of the prophets as having been mystics in this sense, though without the encouragement of contemporary experience no one would have been likely to do so: see, for example, 1 Kings 22:19–22, 2 Kings 6:17, and – most important of all – Ezekiel 1–2.

But mention of Ezekiel's chariot-vision reminds us that many figures in what we think of as 'rabbinic' Judaism or its antecedents also practised a kind of mysticism, and there is every likelihood that they, too, would have thought of the prophets as very much like themselves, gaining special insight into the mysteries of God through ecstatic states. At the same time such people's tendency to meditate ceaselessly on the text of Scripture undoubtedly encouraged in them the sense that the Bible provided a complete interpretative framework within which to make sense of all experience. If one constantly thinks about the events narrated and the persons described in Scripture, it will become perfectly natural for one's own horizons to become those of the biblical world, as one perceives it. In particular the *patterns* of the history narrated in the Bible, which are already quite marked in the text itself, will become more and more the patterns one is likely to see in the rest of one's experience. For this to happen it is not necessary to have a high belief in the 'fulfilment' of prophecy in the sense assumed in the second, or even in the third mode. Rather, the whole of Scripture, including both historiographical and predictive prophecy, starts to function rather in the way that wisdom literature functioned in earlier times, providing ordered insights into the nature and course of human life. We might almost say that stories recorded in the Bible turn into parables of how human life unfolds under the hand of God, and predictions turn into assurances that it will continue to follow the same pattern in the future.[27] In the process, there is no doubt some loss of the sense of urgency that had really characterized biblical prophecy, and some tendency to turn the message of the prophets into a blandly reassuring one.

It seems likely that fourth-mode readings of prophecy could at times result more specifically from the 'failure' of prophecy, in R. P. Carroll's sense, or even from its 'success': at any rate, from the fact that it has slipped into the past. Instead of looking for the fulfilment of a prophetic prediction in one's own day, one may begin to see the prophet's message as really having been concerned with 'timeless' truths, for which the apparently strongly temporal form is merely a convenient vehicle. There would be strong similarities here with what happened to wisdom teaching, according to H. H. Schmid.[28] It seems inherently very improbable that this development should have taken place only within particular groups in Jewish society. Indeed, it may well be that the drive to interpret prophecy as teaching certain general truths, unrelated to specific circumstances, is a natural consequence of the fact that the prophetic books had come to be accepted as 'Scripture' by a much wider constituency than that which had either the ability or the inclination to read the signs of the times and look for 'fulfilments'.

The perception of prophets as mystagogues is only apparently at variance with this, for the same people who treat prophetic books as enshrining quite commonplace truths for the general reader generally have no difficulty in thinking that the less comprehensible passages in them may conceal special, secret information which only the learned, or the inspired, can interpret. Such an attitude towards 'holy books' is widely current today, and seems to have been common in New Testament times, too. Of course, anyone who claims to know what these hidden meanings are is immediately marked off from the generality of readers. Where we find authors who claim to know what the mysteries were to which the prophets had privileged access, we are dealing in all probability with 'sects', or at any rate with groups who had both the time and the inclination to give themselves to detailed study of the prophets in the hope of learning things concealed from the unlearned. But the belief that prophets had transmitted such mysterious information is not in itself a mark of any particular group: it evidently represented a very general perception.

Even to produce pseudo-prophecy that functions in the fourth mode does not necessarily demand any special or out-of-the-way vocation. I have suggested that history has more or less the character of parable in this mode, and to add fresh stories to the stock of those that can serve to illustrate God's ways with his world need not have been the prerogative of those who were themselves of a 'prophetic' temperament; in fact, it is more likely to have engaged those who were teachers of 'wisdom'. Stories which illustrate the same points about providence as do the primary historiographical documents of the Old Testament, without any 'eschatological' sense, belong to this category: Tobit, for example, and perhaps also Judith, Jonah, and even Esther (certainly the Greek version of that book) as well as many of the shorter tales that found their way into midrashic commentaries.

Some material in apocalypses may equally well be seen in this light. The discussions between Ezra and Uriel on the subject of theodicy in 4 Ezra 3–14 operate primarily in the fourth mode, and as we have seen the 'eschatological' sections, though they are seriously meant, seem secondary to this theme. The author need not have belonged to a sect which set all its hopes on the imminent arrival of 'the end'; he may have been a sage who used the apocalypse form, with its pseudonymous attribution, in order to give authority to a discussion of theodicy that would supplement those already in Scripture, such as Job.

Even the revelation of heavenly mysteries to the seer seems to indicate 'sectarian' origin only in cases where the mysteries have controversial implications – for example in Jubilees, where some of the astronomical and calendrical details written on the heavenly tablets have implications for halakah of a sort that many Jews would have contested. In other places the great secrets that the seer sees on his heavenly journey do not contradict popular belief, just as the moral instruction which is imparted to him for transmission to his eventual readers can be entirely traditional, even banal. A story in which a man is admitted to the presence of God himself need not imply that he learned very unexpected things about God before it can be accepted as important. Indeed, in some ways it will be more likely to prove acceptable if it sticks fairly closely to what its readers would expect to learn from it. What makes it important is the *fact* of the heavenly journey it relates.

All this is not to deny that some of the texts which represent the fourth mode of writing pseudo-prophecy may be the product of specialized sects, 'visionaries' who stood out from most of their contemporaries. The circle of Johanan ben Zakkai, as described by Rowland, would be an example of such people, and texts which speak of heavenly visions may well in some cases derive from groups like these. Again, however, there is no good reason to try to align them with one side or the other in the supposed 'theocracy and eschatology' conflict. For all I can see, the writing of books which imitated prophecy in the fourth mode had little to do with questions of 'eschatology' at all: in effect my own conclusions have the same effect, in their own terms, as Rowland's discussion of 'apocalyptic' – a link with eschatology is not of the essence of this literature. Furthermore, with some exceptions (such as Jubilees) it does not set itself against such tenets as we know to have been widely accepted by the leadership of the nation. What is said about divine providence is usually entirely 'safe', and the secrets that are revealed about the life of heaven rarely seem to have any revolutionary implications for political conduct on earth. So far as our interest in this alleged conflict reaches, then, we have seen once again in this chapter that it is a serious oversimplification.

Conclusion

I

Many societies are characterized by a tension between 'conservative' and 'radical' factions; and most scholars would agree that, in some periods at least, pre-exilic Israel was such a society, in which the 'opposition' was provided by the great prophets. Elijah, Amos, Hosea, and Jeremiah seem to epitomize the radical challenge to accepted patterns of political and social order which may arise when a burning conviction that God has purposes for humanity incompatible with a selfish desire to preserve the status quo comes into conflict with the vested interests of those in authority. As we saw at the beginning of this book, this has so strongly impressed itself on modern students of the Old Testament that 'prophecy' has come to carry with it overtones of such a radical challenge. To ask about the fortunes of 'prophecy' after the Exile, therefore, tends to be a matter of assessing how far the challenge continued, in the vastly changed circumstances of Persian domination and of life under the Ptolemies and Seleucids.

To the question of post-exilic prophecy, posed in these terms, this study gives an answer which is not far from the general modern consensus. Where scholars of an earlier generation spoke as if prophecy ceased altogether to exercise its role as the national conscience, it is now usual to say that the post-exilic reorganization of the life of Israel did not wholly quench an effective opposition. Prophets continued to function as they had in earlier times, and the pretensions of those in power did not go unchallenged. My quarrel has not been with this point in itself, for it is surely very reasonable, but only with the identification of the prophetic opposition with the 'apocalyptic movement'. This, I have argued, is the name of something that never existed. Certainly some of those who opposed

266

the existing state of affairs in God's name did so through the medium of apocalypses: either by making the seer whose name they assumed give or receive rulings on matters of halakah in contravention of common practice, or by practising 'charismatic exegesis' of older (or supposedly older) revelations and thereby supporting their own claim to represent the true Israel, by contrast with those currently in power. But this kind of prophetic challenge is only one of the uses of apocalyptic writing. There are many apocalypses which are not 'prophetic' at all, in this sense, but are either quite content with the way things are, or simply unconcerned with political matters in any form. And, equally, opposition did not by any means confine itself to the production of apocalypses. There are works in other genres altogether which present a challenge to influential groups in society. Yet, though these observations amount to a claim that (as I remarked at the end of the preceding chapter) some modern discussions of post-exilic Israelite society are oversimplified, they can be accommodated within the current frame of reference, and could be met by greater care in using such terms as 'apocalyptic'.

But so long as the discussion is conducted within this frame of reference an important shift in perspective, which in my judgement is crucial to the character of post-exilic Judaism, goes unnoticed; and it is with this that my real concern lies. Detailed disagreements about the extent to which prophetic protest continued after the Exile, though interesting and important in themselves, tend to occur against a background assumption which it is part of my purpose to question. This assumption is that those who protested against the post-exilic political and religious settlement must have seen themselves, just as we see them, as the heirs and successors of the great prophets. Whereas the 'establishment' view was that the time for prophecy – that is, for protest and challenge – was now past, these people carried forward *and were conscious of carrying forward* the torch lit by Elijah, Amos, and the rest. The question of how far prophecy survived is thus seen as a question about how many such people there were, and how far their influence was effective.

I believe that this assumption is false, and that our own terminology has here seriously misled us. 'Prophecy', of course, is an English word, not a Greek or Hebrew word, and we may use it how we choose. If we judge that the distinguishing marks of 'classical' prophecy – namely, challenge, protest, and moral seriousness – are

267

so important that we should regard them and them alone as truly 'prophecy', and so use the term only for movements that continue their special vocation, then we may do so without qualms. What we should not do is to assume that people in ancient times had formed the same judgement. There is, as we have seen, very little evidence to suggest that anyone in post-exilic Israel would have defined a *nabi'* or *prophêtês* in terms of these characteristics. 'Opposition' groups after the Exile may well have been the true heirs of the classical prophets, but the image of a 'prophet' which enables us to say this was not available to them. It may be protested that they had the books of the classical prophets, just as we have, and that one has only to read these books to see that true prophets were those who spoke out against authority in the name of the God of justice. But this protest miscarries. It is 'obvious' that the classical prophets were such people only in the same sense that many complex proofs in mathematics or logic are 'obvious' or self-evident. It can take many pages of demonstration to show that a mathematical proposition is self-evident; and in much the same way it has taken years of patient labour to show that the classical prophets were what most scholars now believe them to have been. It follows, indeed, from the 'plain sense' of books such as Amos or Isaiah. But who, in ancient times, read old prophetic books in their plain sense? Such reading was unusual to the point of eccentricity, and in most of the literature surveyed in this book it may be doubted whether it was even theoretically possible. Even those figures who were, to our mind, most like the classical prophets are unlikely to have seen themselves in that light, for 'prophecy' was scarcely thought of as the utterance of hard moral truths to one's contemporaries. What it was thought of as, the last four chapters have tried to make clear; and it should by now be apparent that there was little in the picture of a prophet in which Amos or Hosea would have recognized himself, if they were indeed the kinds of figure modern scholarship has reconstructed.

What is missing, in much modern discussion of the survival of prophecy in post-exilic times, is a sense of historical perspective, of cultural change. If this book has anything to contribute to broader issues within Old Testament study it is to illustrate and endorse the single insight with which Wellhausen changed the shape of our discipline: the insight that post-exilic Judaism is radically discontinuous with the religion and culture of pre-exilic Israel. For pre-exilic Israel, the classical prophets were eccentrics, strange and alarming figures who broke the mould of accepted beliefs and values but who, in the process, changed those values and altered the national religion into something scarcely parallelled in the ancient world. For post-exilic Judaism, especially in its development from the time of Ezra, the prophets were characters in a book written by the finger of God. Their utterances were not the words of mortal men, but divine oracles. This shift derived, to speak generally, from the widespread sense that an era had ended with the Exile and the Return, so that all that happened in 'former times' was qualitatively different from anything that could happen nowadays; more specifically, it is related to the treatment of writings from the older period as 'Scripture' (not the same, as I have tried to show, as their 'canonization'). The existence of prophetic Scripture, a two-dimensional ancient text set over against both the activities and the writings of later times, crucially changed the context within which the post-exilic community lived and thought. It makes no difference to this whether post-exilic writers thought that prophecy had survived or that it had come to an end; in either case the 'prophecy' of which they were thinking was a phenomenon distilled from the text of Scripture, rather than the continuation of a living tradition. What complicates the picture for us is that their very lack of a historical sense meant that they visualized scriptural prophecy in terms of the institutions they *did* know, even where these bore no resemblance to prophecy as it had actually been. Thus the *perceptions* of prophecy in Israel after the Exile are a kind of hybrid between the experiences of what was still called prophecy, even though it might bear little relation to what prophecy had originally been, and the institution to which the biblical text appeared to refer, when read with eyes wholly unaccustomed to the light in which it had been written.

Thus we arrive at a paradoxical conclusion. Many of those who seem to us, as a matter of the phenomenology of religious institutions, to have had a role close to that of the pre-exilic classical prophets, did not (indeed could not) realize that they stood in continuity with these illustrious predecessors. On the other hand, much that did pass as 'prophecy' in the post-exilic age corresponded not to prophecy as it had been in earlier times, but to prophecy as it was (falsely) imagined to have been. There is a crucial difference between post-exilic writers' self-understanding, and the reality of their role as reconstructed by a modern historian, and my suggestion is that this distinction has not been sufficiently allowed for in much discussion of the history of prophecy in Israel.

Once the question of people's perceptions of ancient prophecy is disentangled from the question of the survival or demise of prophecy as a living phenomenon, I have argued, these perceptions can be seen in a much sharper focus. The image of an 'ancient prophet', and the various modes in which prophetic writings were read, provide us with fascinating insights into the thought-world of Judaism in the post-exilic age. This – rather than classical prophecy as it actually was – is the background against which early Christian 'prophecy' has to be understood, and it is only by learning to read early Jewish and Christian writings with an imaginative grasp of the sorts of assumptions our inquiry has highlighted that we shall understand them properly.

II

Two issues remain on the agenda as a result of this study. First, we have discovered that a sharp dichotomy between pre- and post-exilic Israel is the only hypothesis that can make sense of the way old prophecy was read and understood in later times. There is not a smooth development from classical prophecy to its interpretation by such groups as the Qumran community or the early Church; rather, there is a sharp break, a dislocation, which seems to coincide with the point at which prophetic utterances cease to be the spring from which a living and continuous tradition flows and become instead a closed container in which the unalterable words of the prophet are preserved. All the indications seem to be that this point should be located some time early in the post-exilic age: in what we may call, with deliberate vagueness, 'the age of Ezra'.

But for all that the sense of a decisive break is real, the image of a point is an exaggeration. Cultural changes may occur rapidly, but the period over which they occur remains a period, a segment of the time-line of history, not a Euclidean point on it. The period out of which the post-exilic perception of prophecy arose must have begun when the actual prophetic activity of the classical prophets ceased; its end is marked by the coming into existence of a fixed corpus of prophetic scriptures. In other words, the period must coincide with the time in which the prophetic writings were being collected and edited to form the books we now possess. Of course the matter is far more complex than this. Redactional activity did not happen at the same time for all the books now in the canon, and some prophetic books still did not yet exist at a time when others were already approaching fixity in their present form. But broadly speaking we may say that there is a 'tunnel' period between the activity of named prophets and the emergence of finished books bearing their names, and that it is during that period that the shift in perception described in the present study must have begun to take place.

The process is infinitely complex. The very perceptions of prophecy I have described themselves generated additions to the prophetic books; on the other hand, some additional material seems to have existed in its own right as 'primary' prophecy before being incorporated into the book in which it now stands (one may think of Deutero-Isaiah). I have occasionally referred to stages in the redaction of prophetic books, where it seems clear that they can be correlated with one or other of our 'modes' of reading, or where they plainly reflect a post-exilic idea of what a 'prophet' was. But in general I have concentrated on the interpretation and imitation of the books we now have. A volume could be written on the perception of prophecy implied in the complex redactional history of the books, though it would need to be considerably more complex than the present study. But Fishbane's magisterial *Biblical Interpretation in Ancient Israel* already contains a great deal of the material that would be needed, and thanks to him the work of analysing and classifying redactional additions will not need to be done on this scale again. I hope at some future date to write something on the redaction of the prophets, which would be heavily dependent on his work but would attempt to correlate his findings with the scheme of 'modes of reading' developed in this book; but the primary, and vastly more laborious task of identifying and interpreting redactional material has been accomplished by him already.

Secondly, however, we are left with a very large question about the pre-exilic prophets. Throughout this book I have taken for granted that the picture of the pre-exilic prophets which we owe to Duhm and Wellhausen is approximately correct. The fact that people in post-exilic times did not read them in the way modern students of prophecy have learned to do does not at all mean

271

that the modern view is incorrect; for we have seen that there are innumerable reasons why a 'natural' reading was barred to ancient readers by their lack of historical sense and their preconceptions of the kind of information that 'ancient prophecies' could be expected to contain. Nevertheless, our study may give us pause. Ancient readers, we have found, consistently assumed that the prophets of whom the Old Testament told were visionaries, people whose message came by divine inspiration – understood to mean, not by any normal human channels. They also assumed that its content concerned questions which human insight could not in any case determine, since they were mysteries known to God alone. If we are to go on maintaining that the 'inspiration' of the classical prophets was as different from that of contemporary $n^ebi'im$ as was their message, then we must be clear that we are making claims for the originality of these figures which go considerably beyond the current general consensus, in which continuity between the different types of prophet in Israel is generally assumed.

It is not simply that, on the spectrum of paranormal experiences, the classical prophets are nearer to the 'rational' end than were, say, the ecstatics of Gibeah (1 Samuel 10); rather, they are not on this spectrum at all. They are different from what *any* ancient reader would have thought of as prophecy, they fit into no categories that were recognized even by very early readers of the prophetic scriptures. Rather than using 'prophecy' as the title proper to them, and then having to find other terms ('mantic', 'apocalyptist', 'ecstatic', etc.) for other figures in Israel who exhibited what later generations were to call 'prophetic' gifts, it would be less misleading to say that the classical 'prophets' were not prophets at all. We might do better, with E. W. Heaton, to speak of them as 'laymen', whose assumption of the prophet's mantle was just as much a ploy to command a hearing as was their use of forms of speech properly at home in the law-court, the diplomatic service, or the cult.[1] The designation of these figures as 'prophets', $n^ebi'im$, in a literal sense, would then appear simply as the earliest stage in their domestication within known 'traditions' of Israelite culture. In reality, we should have to say, they were not what the ancient world called prophets; they were individuals without a status, lone geniuses whom any generic title belittles.

For my part I think this probably a correct perception of what Amos, Hosea, and the other great prophets were: I think that Duhm and Wellhausen were essentially right. But my purpose here is chiefly to force this issue, which has been comfortably obscured in the more synthesizing aim adopted by studies of the prophets in the last fifty years or so, to the centre of attention once again. If 'prophet' is the proper title for Amos and his successors, then it is wildly inappropriate both for the $n^e bi'im$ who were his contemporaries and for the (really fictitious) heroes of the prophetic books in their present form, and still more for the people that readers in post-exilic times thought of as 'the old prophets'. If, on the other hand, it is a convenient designation for all these other religious figures, then it is misleading to perpetuate the post-exilic mistake of supposing that it can also serve to designate Amos and those like him. The compromise which treats all Israel's 'prophets' and, in addition, the interpretative tradition that grew up around them, as part of the history of a single phenomenon called 'prophecy', tends in practice to fudge an issue which for students of the Old Testament a hundred years ago was much more sharply and clearly focused: the question of just what was original and innovative in the work and teaching of men like Amos, Hosea, Isaiah, and Jeremiah. To a great extent the present study has shown that when post-exilic Judaism in its many varieties (including the Christian one) peered into the well of Israel's past and thought that it was looking at these great figures, it was seeing only its own reflection at the bottom. It remains to ask whether modern scholarship can do better in establishing what 'the old prophets' were really like. I believe that it can, but that it is first necessary to see clearly how great an obstacle to the task the ages that succeeded them have placed in our way.

Notes

INTRODUCTION

1 H. G. Gadamer, *Wahrheit und Methode*, p. 109: 'Im Hinblick auf Erkenntnis des Wahren ist das Sein der Darstellung mehr als das Sein des dargestellten Stoffes, der homerische Achilles mehr als sein Urbild'; compare *Truth and Method*, p. 103 where, however, a much more literal translation is to be found.

2 Cf. R. Smend, *Die Entstehung des Alten Testaments*, which similarly works from the finished books of the Old Testament back to hypothetical earlier stages. Smend argues (p. 11) that in this way 'vom relativ Sicheren wird schrittweise zum, in der Regel wenigstens, Unsicheren zurückgegangen'.

3 The general editors of this series are P. R. Ackroyd, A. R. C. Leaney, and J. W. Packer. At the time of writing, only volume 7 (Leaney's *The Jewish and Christian World 200 BC–AD 200*) had appeared. Cf. also the dates of the period covered by Schürer, *The History of the Jewish People in the Age of Jesus Christ*, ed. G. Vermes and F. Millar: 175 BC–AD 135.

CHAPTER 1: THE PROPHETS IN THE CANON

1 Duhm is generally regarded as the founder of the modern view of the prophets as concerned more with social criticism than with prognostications of the distant future: see B. Duhm, *Die Theologie der Propheten* (1875).

2 K. Thomas, *Religion and the Decline of Magic*, chapter 13.

3 See M. Buber, *The Prophetic Faith*.

4 See Maimonides, *Guide to the Perplexed* II, chapter 45, and the comments of A. J. Reines, *Maimonides and Abrabanel on Prophecy*, pp. 180–232. Cf. also the introduction to David Kimchi's *Psalms* commentary, where the Writings are said to have been uttered 'not in prophecy, but in the Holy Spirit': thus 'although Daniel saw visions and revelations, both sleeping and waking, still his power and knowledge in these visions did not approach the power of Isaiah and Ezekiel and the other prophets. For this reason

274

his book is not written in the collection of the books of the Prophets, but is written in that of the books which are called Writings, (which is as much as) to say that they were written in the Holy Spirit.'

5   Perrot, *La lecture de la Bible*, p. 15.

6   For the conception of the Prophets and the Writings as essentially commentary on the Torah see also A. C. Sundberg, *The Old Testament of the Early Church*, p. 73, and references there to older secondary literature. The matter is well treated in G. F. Moore, *Judaism* I, pp. 239–45; and for a recent discussion see J. Blenkinsopp, *Prophecy and Canon*, pp. 116–17 and notes, in which there are further useful bibliographical references.

7   Cf. D. Patte, *Early Jewish Hermeneutic in Palestine*, p. 22. For the Proverbs as Torah, see Baba Mezia 83a. The question is discussed in Montefiore and Loewe's *Rabbinic Anthology*, p. 158. See S. Z. Leiman, *The Canonization of Hebrew Scripture*, p. 170 for further examples, including some from the Qumran texts.

8   A similar application of a general principle which is said to be true of the Torah to texts from the other divisions as well can be found in the Mekhilta (Shirata 7). Commenting on Exod. 15:9–10 the text says, 'This really was the beginning of the section. Why then was it written here? Because no strict order as to earlier and later is observed in the Torah.' This principle, *'eyn môqedem ûmeaḥôr ba-tôrah* ('there is no before and after in the Torah'), is then illustrated by a number of passages which should logically have stood at the beginning of the book in which they occur. Only one of the passages is from the Pentateuch (Lev. 9:1); five are from the Prophets (Isa. 6:1; Jer. 2:2; Ezek. 2:1 and 17:2; and Hos. 10:1); the remaining one is from the Writings (Eccles. 1:12). Compare also the answers to the question 'Whence do we learn about the resurrection from the Torah?' (Sanhedrin 91b), which cite Ps. 84:5 and Isa. 52:8.

9   On traditional indifference to genre-distinctions, see below, pp. 141–9.

10   Schürer, *The History of the Jewish People in the Age of Jesus Christ* II, p. 321.

11   Pirqe Aboth 1:1.

12   Exodus Rabbah 42:8, cf. 47:7 and Taanith 9a. See the discussion in Sundberg, *The Old Testament of the Early Church*, p. 126, and Moore, *Judaism* I, p. 237. In Strack-Billerbeck IV/1, pp. 446–8 (Excursus 17, on the canon of the Old Testament), there is a discussion of the exact force of this theory: does it mean that Moses actually dictated the words of the prophets to them (as in a fourth century tradition in which he speaks on Sinai to the prophets' pre-existent souls: Tanhuma Yitro 11:124ab – see *Rabbinic Anthology*, p. 158 and cf. below, p. 155), or that he handed them down by a secret tradition like that which led to the oral Torah, or merely that there is nothing in the Prophets which is not implicit in the Pentateuch – a much tamer doctrine? Billerbeck favours the second of these explanations, I think probably rightly: compare the discussion in C. Rowland, *The Open Heaven*,

p. 67. Blenkinsopp (*Prophecy and Canon*, p. 182) points out that apparent halakic innovations by the prophets are sometimes explained as revelations to Moses which had subsequently been forgotten: see Pesahim 117a (on the recitation of the Hallel) and Sukkah 44a (on the 'four kinds' at Sukkoth). Note, however, Exodus Rabbah 28:6, where Isaiah is said to have been present at Sinai.

13 I am indebted to Selwyn Gross, OP, for drawing my attention to this example.

14 For other examples see Strack-Billerbeck IV/1, p. 422 (on Rom. 1:2).

15 Baba Bathra 14b–15a; translation from Leiman, *The Canonization of Hebrew Scripture*, p. 52.

16 The contrast between Isaiah and Jeremiah here is, however, fairly commonplace: cf. Berakoth 57b, where it is said that anyone who sees Ezekiel in a dream should expect to receive wisdom; Isaiah, consolation; Jeremiah, punishment: cf. C. Wolff, *Jeremia im Frühjudentum und Urchristentum*, p. 10. Jeremiah's reputation as a jeremiah is of long standing, as is the tendency to read the whole of Isaiah chiefly in the light of what we call 'Deutero-Isaiah'.

17 On this see my article, ' "The Law and the Prophets." Who are the Prophets?'.

18 For the way of reading the Prophets outlined here, see further chapter 7 below.

19 The Greek Bible reveals no trace of any awareness that there is any kind of break between Deuteronomy and Joshua. Writers of the patristic period freely use such terms as 'Heptateuch' and 'Octateuch' to refer to the historical books beginning with Genesis. See for example Pseudo-Chrysostom in *PG* 56, pp. 513ff. For other examples see H. B. Swete, *An Introduction to the Old Testament in Greek*, pp. 218ff.

20 This way of understanding the LXX arrangement of the Old Testament Scriptures is presented with great clarity in J. Goldingay, *Approaches to Old Testament Interpretation*, pp. 138–45. I have also been helped by an unpublished lecture by Selwyn Gross, OP.

21 See Swete, *An Introduction to the Old Testament in Greek*, pp. 197–230, for details of the various arrangements of the Greek canon.

22 On Levita see G. Weil, *Élie Lévita, humaniste et massorète (1469–1549)*. His classic work on the scriptural text is *Massoreth ha-massoreth*.

23 Thus in the work which marks the starting point for all modern discussion of the canon, H. E. Ryle, *The Canon of the Old Testament*, published in 1892: see especially pp. 182–3.

24 The general consensus summarized in this paragraph is essentially the position argued by G. W. Anderson in his excellent chapter 'Canonical and Non-canonical', in the *Cambridge History of the Bible* I. A briefer but very clear account can be found in J. Goldingay, *Approaches to Old Testament*

Interpretation, pp. 138–45. Full bibliographies for all aspects of the canon are in the new Schürer, vol. II, p. 314, and pp. 314–22 also give a good concise account of the consensus view, as does R. Smend, *Die Entstehung des Alten Testaments*, pp. 13–20. The idea that the three divisions of the canon correspond to a three-stage process of canonization is already found in Wellhausen: see *Prolegomena to the History of Israel*, p. 2.

25 Noth's theory is elaborated in his *A History of Pentateuchal Traditions*, von Rad's in 'The Form-Critical Problem of the Hexateuch'. If recent arguments for a much later dating for J are accepted, then of course the core of the Pentateuch is not earlier than the pre-exilic prophets, and the correspondence between theory and intuition becomes less neat. However, the works of Van Seters (*Abraham in History and Tradition*), Schmid (*Der sogenannte Jahwist*) and Rendtorff (*Das überlieferungsgeschichtliche Problem des Pentateuch*) have not yet established themselves sufficiently to dislodge the standard theories about the canon. As has often been observed, 'canon studies' tend to lag behind the study of the component parts of the Old Testament.

26 Thus classically L. Blau, 'Bible Canon: Traditional View' in the *Jewish Encyclopedia* of 1902: 'The fact that Daniel is not included in the Prophets is of importance, and demonstrates that the prophetical canon must have been closed before 165 BC; for the best of criticism is agreed that Daniel belongs to the Maccabean era; it would have been included in the Prophets had at that time the canon still been open.' This argument is especially important for Leiman – see *The Canonization of Hebrew Scripture*, p. 26.

27 Josephus, *Contra Apionem* 1:37–43.

28 Cf. J. Barr, *Holy Scripture: Canon, Authority, Criticism*, p. 58 (footnote).

29 In addition to these four points, and other arguments to be found in standard works, there is one document from Qumran that may conceivably refer to a tripartite canon. In a document from Cave IV (4QMess ar 1:5) we find the phrase *tlt' spry'* (the three books). But the interpretation of this is doubtful: for discussion and bibliography see the new Schürer, vol. II, p. 317.

30 D. N. Freedman, 'Canon of the OT', *IDB* Supplement.

31 G. Vermes, 'Bible and Midrash: Early Old Testament Exegesis', *Cambridge History of the Bible* I, p. 199.

32 Leiman, *The Canonization of Hebrew Scripture*, p. 28.

33 B. S. Childs, *Introduction to the Old Testament as Scripture*.

34 Leiman, *The Canonization of Hebrew Scripture*, p. 14.

35 A good summary of the consensus can be found in J. Blenkinsopp, *Prophecy and Canon*, a work which discusses the origin of the prophetic canon within the guidelines which acceptance of the consensus requires.

36 In J. E. Grabe and F. Lee, *Vetus Testamentum iuxta LXX interpretes* II, chapter 1, §§75–7. For full details of the 'Alexandrian canon' hypothesis

see P. Katz, 'The Old Testament Canon in Palestine and Alexandria', and Sundberg, *The Old Testament of the Early Church*. Uncontroversial statements of the hypothesis as it was learned by students before Sundberg can be found in R. H. Pfeiffer's article 'The Canon of the Old Testament', in the *IDB* I, pp. 510–11, or in O. Eissfeldt's *The Old Testament: An Introduction*, pp. 570–1.

37 Apart from his book *The Old Testament of the Early Church*, see also 'The "Old Testament": a Christian Canon?' and 'The Protestant Old Testament Canon: Should It be Re-examined?'

38 *The Old Testament of the Early Church*, p. 102, where Sundberg is building on the work of A. Jepsen, 'Kanon und Text'.

39 See Augustine, *de doctrina christiana* 2:8 (*PL* 34, pp. 40–1) and *de civitate dei* 17:20 and 18:26 (*PL* 41, pp. 554 and 582–3).

40 And is still defended as such by Barr, *Holy Scripture*, p. 55 (footnote), who points out that the distribution of books between the three sections into which Josephus's 'canon' appears to be divided correlates rather closely with the arrangement in the LXX.

41 See below, pp. 181–2.

CHAPTER 2: 'THE LAW AND THE PROPHETS'

1 My argument is in substantial agreement with that of Barr, *Holy Scripture*, especially pp. 49–74, but I am naturally concerned to spell out the implications for the canon of the Prophets in particular, and to provide more explicit documentation than is appropriate to a book which concentrates, as his does, on discussion of the theological implications of canonicity. I am indebted to him for help in clarifying many of the points with which this chapter deals.

2 Cf. Barr, *Holy Scripture*, p. 55.

3 See Anderson in 'Canonical and Non-canonical', p. 151, citing J. T. Milik, *Ten Years of Discovery in the Wilderness of Judaea*, p. 41. Material from Qumran sometimes introduces quotations with the words 'as it is written in the book of the prophet Daniel'.

4 *Ant.* 9:267–9; compare also 10:245–6; 249 ('Daniel the prophet').

5 Cf. *Ant.* 10:266.

6 Already in the Apostolic Fathers: see Barnabas 4:4, where 'The prophet says' is followed by a quotation from Daniel. See also the very interesting discussion by Origen in his letter to Africanus, cited below, p. 143.

7 L. Ginzberg, *The Legends of the Jews* VI, p. 413, note 76. (The note refers to vol. IV, p. 326, in the section on Daniel (pp. 326–50).) See also Leiman, *The Canonization of Hebrew Scripture*, p. 59, citing Megillah 15a, where Daniel is identified as one of a number of prophets who prophesied in the second year of Darius.

8   Ginzberg, ibid.

9   On the question of whether prophecy had ceased in Israel, see the careful discussion in R. Leivestad, 'Das Dogma von der prophetenlosen Zeit', considered in more detail below, p. 106.

10   Cf. Barr, *Holy Scripture*, p. 55.

11   See also Seder 'Olam 20, and cf. L. Blau, 'Bible Canon: Traditional View', p. 147.

12   See above, p. 18, and cf. N. M. Bronznick, 'Qabbalah as a Metonym for the Prophets and Hagiographa'.

13   j. Megillah 1.

14   Cf. Barr, *Holy Scripture*, p. 60.

15   This can be seen particularly in the way 'symbolic' meaning is given to liturgical customs which have lost their original *raison d'être*; there are good examples in A. Schmemann, *Introduction to Liturgical Theology*, especially pp. 130–1.

16   Leiman, *The Canonization of Hebrew Scripture*, p. 169 (note 293), with references to the medieval discussions.

17   Thus also Leiman, p. 64.

18   For a somewhat different interpretation of this passage see Rowland, *The Open Heaven*, pp. 307–8.

19   Cf. Barr, *Holy Scripture*, p. 60, from which this point is taken.

20   See below, pp. 75–9. There is a useful discussion of the antiquity of the system of lections in the liturgy of the synagogue (reaching somewhat sceptical conclusions) in P. F. Bradshaw, *Daily Prayer in the Early Church*.

21   Once again, cf. Barr, *Holy Scripture*, p. 61. This is the kind of 'canon' Philo has in mind when he says that 'the Jews alone opposed [Gaius] on principle, trained as they were we may say even from the cradle, by parents and tutors and instructors and by the far higher authority of *the sacred laws and also the unwritten customs [tôn hierôn nomôn kai eti tôn agraphôn ethôn]* to acknowledge one God who is the Father and Maker of the world' (*legatio ad Gaium* 115).

22   L. B. Wolfenson, 'Implications of the Place of the Book of Ruth in Editions, Manuscripts, and Canons of the Old Testament.'

23   See J. N. Lightstone, 'The Formation of the Biblical Canon in Judaism of Late Antiquity: Prolegomena to a General Reassessment.'

24   ' "The Law and the Prophets." Who are the Prophets?', p. 5.

25   'Implications of the Place of Ruth', p. 173. 'Proves conclusively' goes a bit too far for me. Wolfenson cites G. Wildeboer's *Het Ontstaen van den Kanon des Ouden Verbands* (2nd edition, German translation 1891) to the same effect: 'Wildeboer, "Entstehung des alttestamentlichen Kanons", 13, 17ff. has pointed out that originally the distinction between the last two divisions of the Jewish Bible was not strictly drawn. . . . This fact, however, has been lost sight of and Wildeboer's treatment of the subject not

sufficiently regarded ... the impression has gotten abroad that "the Hebrew canon is uniformly tripartite" (Swete, "Intro", p. 216). But this is an error; the tripartite division was not a rigid classification in its origin' (Wolfenson, ibid., note 54).

26   Indeed, the tendency to regard all of the Old Testament as 'prophecy' occasionally breaks down even this division: cf. Rom. 1:2, 'his prophets in the holy scriptures'.

27   Perrot thinks that 'the Law and the Prophets' represents a tendency to reduce the unique status of the Torah: 'Dans l'expression nouvelle *la Loi et les Prophètes*, on aligne en quelque sorte tous les écrits révélés au même niveau, cf. 4 Macc., XVIII, 10; Mt, v, 17; etc. Bref, on assiste à une sorte de nivellement de tous les écrits canoniques.' (*La lecture de la Bible*, p. 183.) I doubt whether this idea can be sustained, however.

28   Vol. II, pp. 316–17.

29   Cf. J. A. Goldstein, *II Maccabees*, ad loc. For Sundberg's discussion see *The Old Testament of the Early Church*, pp. 67–8, and compare Barr, *Holy Scripture*, pp. 54–5, and my ' "The Law and the Prophets." Who are the Prophets?', p. 17. Note that 1 Macc. 12:9 has the even simpler expression 'the holy books' for Scripture in general.

30   On Job as a prophet see also, of course, James 5:10–11, and compare my comments below, pp. 97–8.

31   On Ben Sira's canon see Koole, 'Die Bibel des Ben Sira', and Lebram, 'Aspekte der alttestamentlichen Kanonbildung'. It has occasionally been suggested that Ecclus. 39:1–2 reflects a tripartite canon divided into law, wisdom, and prophecy: see K. Frustorfer, 'Des Weisen Curriculum Vitae nach Sirach (39, 1–15)', p. 140, and the discussion in H. Stadelmann, *Ben Sira als Schriftgelehrter*, p. 224, where other suggestions of this kind are noted. Since the passage continues with further categories of literature with which the wise man is at home, without any clear sense that the three disciplines mentioned in the first two verses are in any special class of their own, the attempt to find hints of Ben Sira's 'canon' here seems to me unsuccessful. It remains interesting, though, that he should have seen it as characteristic of the Jewish wise man to be concerned with *prophecy* as well as 'wisdom', evidently seeing no opposition between the two.

32   Cf. Barr, *Holy Scripture*, pp. 55–6, and my ' "The Law and the Prophets." Who are the Prophets?', p. 6.

33   'Law, prophets, and psalms' (*de vita contemplativa* 3:25; see below, p. 58.

34   *de confusione linguarum* 39.

35   Ibid., 62.

36   *de congressu* 177, quoting Prov. 3:11–12 as written by Solomon.

37   Translation from Leiman, pp. 52–3, slightly amended.

38   Catechesis 4 (*de decem dogmatibus*) 33–6, *PG* 33, pp. 493–500.

39   *PG* 43, pp. 243 and 277–80. In *adversus haereses* 1:1:8 (*PG* 41, p. 213)

he produces a third list, this time more akin to the LXX arrangement with which we are familiar (though with the poetic books inserted between Ruth and Samuel), and describes all the books as 'prophets'.

40 Or *prologus galeatus*, *PL* 28, pp. 547–58. Cf. Leiman, *The Canonization of Hebrew Scripture*, p. 49. P. W. Skehan, 'St. Jerome and the Canon of the Holy Scriptures', is mistaken in asserting that Jerome here reckons Daniel a Prophetic book.

41 Cf. the *Preface to Daniel*: 'Admoneo non haberi Danielem apud Hebraeos inter prophetas, sed inter eos qui hagiographa conscripserunt.'

42 Augustine, *de doctrina christiana* 2:8:13.

43 See, for example, Hilary, *Tractatus in psalmos* on Psalm 127, *CSEL* 24, p. 630: 'Viae enim in lege, viae in prophetis, viae in evangeliis, viae in apostolis sunt . . . in quibus per timorem Dei ambulantes beati sunt.'

44 *The Canonization of Hebrew Scripture*, p. 168, note 287.

45 See above, p. 42. The same passage in 4 Macc. is cited by Perrot: see note 28 above.

46 See below, pp. 78–9.

47 *The Canonization of Hebrew Scripture*, p. 66.

48 'The "Old Testament": a Christian Canon?', p. 148.

49 *de agricultura* 50.

50 *de plantatione* 39.

51 L. Blau, 'Bible Canon: Traditional View', p. 147.

52 Cf. my ' "The Law and the Prophets." Who are the Prophets?', p. 6 for this point.

53 'The "Old Testament": a Christian Canon?', p. 147.

54 L. Blau, art. 'Bible Canon: Traditional View', p. 140. See also the discussion of this point in Barr, *Holy Scripture*, pp. 50–4.

55 'Canonical and Non-canonical', p. 130.

56 Cf. H. A. Wolfson, *Philo* I, p. 117.

57 See R. Meyer, 'Bemerkungen zum literargeschichtlichen Hintergrund der Kanontheorie des Josephus' (1974), building on his TWNT article 'Kanonisch und apokryph im Judentum' of 1938.

58 Ibid., pp. 289–90.

59 *BJ* 1:18.

60 See below, pp. 105–16.

61 Aune, *Prophecy in Early Christianity and the Ancient Mediterranean World*, p. 51.

62 Details of the debates about Ecclesiasticus may be found in Leiman, pp. 92–102. My argument that Ben Sira was not in the end admitted to the canon because he was known to have lived in the second century BC is in line with that of Smend, *Die Entstehung des Alten Testaments*, p. 18.

63 A possible reply to this might be that the book itself does not call

Daniel a prophet; but this proves too much, for the same is true of most of the books of the Twelve!

64 Lightstone well observes that the standard argument *presupposes* that there was such a thing as 'the Prophetic canon' in the second century BC; see 'The formation of the biblical canon in Judaism of late antiquity', p. 136.

65 The function of pseudonymity is discussed in more detail below, pp. 211–13. For a full bibliography on the pseudonymity of ancient works, see Rowland, *The Open Heaven*, pp. 61–70, and Aune, *Prophecy in Early Christianity*, p. 376, note 47.

66 This is noticeably the case in Jerome, who from 390, the year of the *prologus galeatus*, espoused a rigorous line on deuterocanonical books: his later works still quote them freely; cf. A. Penna, *S. Gerolamo*, pp. 387–9. See P. W. Skehan, 'St. Jerome and the Canon of the Holy Scriptures', which tries to show (I think unsuccessfully) that Jerome did not therefore really believe in his own theory but adopted it only for apologetic purposes, in order to give himself a stronger hand when arguing with Jewish thinkers; contrast J. N. D. Kelly, *Jerome*, p. 161. My own impression is that he fully believed in his own theory about the canon, but that his practice continued to reflect the earlier and less self-conscious attitude found in all the Fathers: that ancient books bearing the names of figures from the hallowed past were naturally to be venerated and could be expected to contain divine truth.

67 See W. G. Lambert, 'Ancestors, Authors, and Canonicity', p. 9.

68 Cf. C. S. Lewis's comment on medieval writers: 'They are bookish. They are indeed very credulous of books. They find it hard to believe that anything an old *auctor* has said is simply untrue' (*The Discarded Image*, p. 11). As Sir Thomas Browne put it, 'most men of ages present so superstitiously do look on Ages past, that the authorities of the one exceed the reasons of the other' (*Pseudodoxia Epidemica*, chapter 6).

69 Lightstone points out that some evidence that even the division between Law and Prophets may be artificial may be found in the contents of the Samaritan Pentateuch. While it is often said that the Samaritan schism (whenever that was) gives us a *terminus ante quem* for the closing of the canon of the Pentateuch, since that alone is shared between Samaritans and Jews, it should be noted that parts of the book of Joshua in fact find a place within the Samaritan Pentateuch. Lightstone argued that this might suggest that there was a stage at which there existed a Hexateuch (or even a Heptateuch or Octateuch) in Judaism; and that in that case such terms would not represent a purely Christian reading of the Old Testament. Compare perhaps the tradition in the Talmud that if Israel had not sinned there would have been no need for God to have given the Prophets and the Writings, since the Torah, together with the book of Joshua (a Hexa-

teuch?) would have sufficed. In the age to come, when there is no more sin, the *qabbalah* may cease, while the Law endures (Nedarim 22b). There can be no doubt here that the status of scriptural books diminishes as one moves further from the Pentateuch. On these points see Barr, *Holy Scripture*, pp. 53–4.

70   Cf. Leiman, *The Canonization of Hebrew Scripture*, p. 30.

71   Of course the passage entirely confirms, as Leiman argues, that the twenty-four books were already accepted by everyone as 'Scripture' by the time of 4 Ezra. And there is no difficulty, from our point of view, in understanding why the 'seventy books' were not similarly accepted by all: assuming that they existed at all, they were a good deal newer than the books that were accepted. The reason why no one had used most of the Enoch or Ezra literature was simply that it had not existed. The theory that Ezra had been told to conceal it was part of the fiction by which it could be promoted as hidden lore from the remote past. The fiction enables the author to claim the most superlative authority for works which had not been known to past generations, by invoking a divine decision which had led to their being hidden.

72   G. W. Anderson, 'Canonical and Non-canonical', p. 115.

73   The esoteric character of 1 Enoch is strikingly confirmed in chapter 42, a midrash on Prov. 8 (perhaps also on Ecclus. 24, itself a midrash on the same passage), where it is said (contrary to those earlier texts) that Wisdom did *not* settle anywhere on earth, not even in Israel, but dwells still with the angels. This is very good publicity for books such as 1 Enoch itself, whose author had of course been among the angels, but hardly reflects flatteringly on the Torah, which Ben Sira had said *was* the Wisdom of God dwelling on the earth and choosing Israel as its dwelling. In other places 1 Enoch may even imply that the ordinary Scriptures have been falsified by sinners (cf. 104:10–13; 108:6). If one accepts the claims that 1 Enoch makes for itself, one is almost inevitably committed to regarding the Torah as less than perfect.

74   *The Canonization of Hebrew Scripture*, pp. 72–8.

75   For a bibliography on this point see Leiman, ibid., pp. 173–4.

76   See above, p. 42.

77   Moore, *Judaism* I, p. 247. Cf. also Anderson, 'Canonical and Non-canonical', p. 134.

78   Leiman, p. 190, note 502, reports a Palestinian tradition which reads 'all the *songs* are holy, but . . .'.

79   *Holy Scripture*, pp. 50–1.

80   The modern reader's sense that it is odd to speak of holy books as conveying *un*cleanness does not rest wholly on a misunderstanding of purity laws, since rabbinic literature also has to explain the expression: see M. Yadaim 4:6; Tosefta Yadaim 2:19; j. Sotah 5 (18a). Purification is needed

after handling a scroll of the Torah or certain other books *as if* it were unclean, in order to avoid its being accidentally contaminated. This is however a very good illustration of the fact that to incur uncleanness is not to sin: the two categories exist in a different universe of discourse – see the excellent discussion of this point in E. P. Sanders, *Jesus and Judaism*, pp. 182–7.

81 See Leiman, pp. 106–7, for a full discussion with bibliographical notes.

82 Rowland, *The Open Heaven*, p. 272. Rowland's discussion of 'The Esoteric Tradition in Early Rabbinic Judaism' (pp. 271–348) is extremely illuminating, and my ideas on this subject largely derive from him, though I am trying to draw rather different conclusions about the status of canonical and non-canonical books in the New Testament period than his treatment generally presupposes.

83 D. Patte, *Early Jewish Hermeneutic in Palestine*, p. 152.

84 See *Jewish Encyclopedia* s.v. *haftarah* (pp. 135–7, by Adolf Büchler), for a complete list.

85 See Perrot, *La lecture de la Bible*, pp. 45–7.

86 H. Danby, *The Mishnah*, p. 114.

87 See Perrot, *La lecture de la Bible*, pp. 175–93.

88 See above, pp. 71–2.

89 This is also argued by Büchler in the *Jewish Encyclopedia* article on *haftarah*.

90 Perrot, p. 138.

91 Leiman, *The Canonization of Hebrew Scripture*, p. 168, note 287.

92 'The Formation of the Biblical Canon in Judaism of Late Antiquity' lists five false assumptions, of which this is one.

93 Ibid., p. 141.

94 See Blenkinsopp, *Prophecy and Canon*, pp. 120–3. Cf. my own reference to the passage on p. 16 above.

95 P. 121.

96 This is the title of section IV of Blenkinsopp's chapter 'The Making of the Prophetic Canon', *Prophecy and Canon*, pp. 96–123.

97 Pp. 122–3.

98 Wolfenson, 'Implications of the Place of the Book of Ruth', p. 171 (note 49); cf. Barr, *Holy Scripture*, p. 57. The same point is already made in Swete, *An Introduction to the Old Testament in Greek*, p. 225, and picked up by Anderson, 'Canonical and Non-canonical', p. 131 (footnote); but scholars rarely seem to allow this (actually rather obvious and literal-minded) observation to affect their discussion of the ordering of Scripture.

99 See E. Würthwein, *The Text of the Old Testament*, especially p. 10.

100 Cf. Smend, *Die Entstehung des Alten Testaments*, p. 15. The Leningrad codex is not unique in arranging these three books in their 'correct' chrono-

284

logical order: some Spanish mss. do the same. See Anderson, 'Canonical and Non-canonical', p. 141.

101   Wolfenson, pp. 154–5, note 13, referring to 'the *editio princeps* of the entire Old Test., Soncino, 1488; 2nd edition of the entire O.T., Naples, 1491–3; 3rd edition of the O.T., Brescia, 1494; 4th edition of the O.T., Pesaro, 1511–17.'

102   Ibid.

103   N. M. Sarna, 'The Order of the Books'.

104   See R. E. Wolfe, 'The Editing of the Book of the Twelve', for one of the few attempts to present a complete history of the redaction of the Minor Prophets. Few since 1935 have been so ambitious, or so confident about their conjectures in this difficult area.

105   Thus Blenkinsopp, *Prophecy and Canon*, pp. 120–1.

106   Numbers I, II, and III of the *Apocryphal Psalms*, ed. W. Baars.

107   See J. A. Sanders, *The Psalms Scroll of Qumran Cave 11 (11QPs^a)* (1965).

108   Sanders, *'Variorum* in the Psalms Scroll', p. 89.

109   Cf. R. Meyer, 'Bemerkungen zum literargeschichtlichen Hintergrund der Kanontheorie des Josephus'. So far as I know, the only clear reference to a psalm-number in our period is Acts 13:33, citing Psalm 2:7 with the words 'as it is written in the second psalm'. It is a wry twist of fate that makes this verse also a witness to the very variety of usage we are discussing here; for, as is well known, the verse is textually uncertain, Codex Bezae reading instead 'in the first psalm'.

110   M. H. Goshen-Gottstein, 'The Psalms Scroll (11QPs^a): a Problem of Canon and Text', p. 26. Further discussions of the scroll may be found in J. A. Sanders, 'Pre-Masoretic Psalter Texts'; P. W. Skehan, 'A Psalm Manuscript from Qumran (4QPs^b)' and 'The Qumran Manuscripts and Textual Criticism'; J. P. M. van der Ploeg, 'Le psaume xci dans une recension de Qumran'.

111   Cf. Acts 1:20.

112   This point is made by Katz, 'The Old Testament Canon in Palestine and Alexandria'.

113   *The Canonization of Hebrew Scripture*, p. 56.

114   Ibid., p. 166 (note 271).

115   'Implications of the Place of the Book of Ruth', pp. 167–8.

116   Contrast Schmidt, 'Bible Canon: Untraditional View', who thinks the arrangement is thematic. I am inclined to think that this takes too much at face value the 'explanations' of the order, such as that ascribed to Johanan b. Zakkai.

117   'Implications of the Place of the Book of Ruth', p. 175.

118   Katz, 'The Old Testament Canon in Palestine and Alexandria', p. 198, says that Augustine sometimes mentions Ruth as if it were appended to *Kings* rather than to Judges. I think, however, that this may rest on a

misreading of *de doctrina christiana* 2:8:13, where Augustine notes that the book of Ruth, which he names after Judges in his list, 'magis ad Regnorum principium videtur pertinere' – that is, though it is a separate book, it seems rather to belong to the beginning of 'Kingdoms', in other words, to the beginning of 1 Samuel. It is sometimes argued that the assignment of both Ruth and Lamentations to the Writings must be older than their position in the LXX after Judges and Jeremiah respectively, since the LXX arrangement is so natural that no one would ever have changed it if it had been the original order: see, for example, Anderson, 'Canonical and Non-canonical', p. 139. The thesis being argued here undercuts this perfectly reasonable but in my view anachronistic argument by denying that *either* order is 'original'.

119   The text of all three is quoted in Leiman, *The Canonization of Hebrew Scripture*, pp. 41–3, where there are full bibliographical references.

120   See above, p. 50.

CHAPTER 3: PROPHETS AND THEIR MESSAGE

1   Cf. Ignatius, *Philadelphians* 9: 'Abraham, and Isaac, and Jacob, and the prophets, and the apostles, and the whole church'.

2   Cf. 1 Clement 17: 'those who went about in sheepskins and goatskins, preceding the coming of Christ. We mean Elijah and Elisha and likewise Ezekiel the prophet, and besides them those also who obtained a good report.'

3   It is also possible that the existence of 'prophets' in the early churches coloured Christians' understanding of what the ancient prophets had been like, though this is more likely to have encouraged them to use the term with a rather narrowly-defined content, not in this more general sense. Nevertheless the persecuted prophets of Revelation could be Christian prophets rather than those of old.

4   Cf. J. Lindblom, *Gesichte und Offenbarungen*, p. 165.

5   Tertullian, *de oratione* 23 (*PL* 1, p. 1303).

6   See R. P. Carroll, *From Chaos to Covenant*, for one possible theory about the elaboration of the stories about Jeremiah.

7   See Sanhedrin 93a–94a, and compare Ginzberg, *The Legends of the Jews* VI, p. 413, and chapter 2, note 7 above.

8   Cf. P. W. Barnett, 'The Jewish Sign-Prophets – AD 40–70 – Their Intentions and Origin'; see also the discussion in E. P. Sanders, *Jesus and Judaism*, pp. 157–73, especially pp. 170–2. What term *we* should use to describe such wonder-workers is a question that need not concern us here: contemporaries evidently saw them as prophets, though Josephus refuses them this title.

9   In the Mekhilta Moses, already a miracle-worker in Exodus itself, is

attributed with a miracle which derives directly from one of Elisha's. According to 2 Kings 6:1–7, Elisha recovered an axe-head which had fallen into the Jordan by throwing a stick in after it, thereby (?) causing the iron to float. Applying the principle of *qal wa-ḥomer* (*a minore ad maius*, as it is known in English), the Mekhilta argues: how much more was Moses able to cause the coffin of Joseph to rise from the waters of the Nile, in which it was submerged! On its own terms there is no way of refuting this argument.

10 Cf. Josephus, *Ant.* 4:165: 'Moses . . . appointed Joshua to succeed him both in his prophetical functions (*epi te tais prophêteiais*) and as commander-in-chief.'

11 M. Hengel, *Judaism and Hellenism* I, p. 136; cf. Stadelmann, *Ben Sira als Schriftgelehrter*, p. 207, quoting the original German from *Judaismus und Hellenismus*, p. 248.

12 See Stadelmann, *Ben Sira als Schriftgelehrter*, pp. 204–7, with reference both to the passage from Hengel just quoted, and also to G. von Rad, *Wisdom in Israel*, p. 258 ('Sirach's idea of prophets is astonishingly inadequate, for he regards the prophets almost solely as wonder-workers').

13 Cf. Syriac Baruch 85:12: 'When the Most High brings all these things to pass, there will be there no further opportunity for repentance . . . no intercession by the fathers nor prayer by the prophets nor help from the righteous.'

14 For this understanding of the 'pseudepigrapha' see above, p. 8.

15 This passage occurs in the vision of the sheep, bulls, asses, wolves, etc. in chapter 89, a chapter which induces in the reader a trance of a kind quite different from that which apparently enabled Enoch to write it. It is possible that the sheep to whom is given the task of recording the sins of the seventy shepherds against the sheep should be understood as an angel.

16 *Ant.* 6:66; cf. the discussion in G. I. Davies, 'Apocalyptic and Historiography'. The extent of Samuel's knowledge of things to come is equally well illustrated by a story told of him by Pseudo-Philo. After retelling the incident narrated in 1 Sam. 9:15–21, where Samuel tells Saul that he is to be king, the author continues: 'And Saul said to Samuel, Who am I, and what is my father's house, that my lord should speak thus unto me? For I understand not what thou sayest, because I am a youth. And Samuel said to Saul: Who will grant that thy word should come unto accomplishment of itself, that thou shouldest live many days? but consider this, that thy words shall be likened to the words of a prophet, who shall be called Jeremiah': *Biblical Antiquities* 56:6 – cf. Jer. 1:6.

17 For a full discussion with bibliography see D. L. Petersen, *Late Israelite Prophecy*, pp. 19–45.

18 Thus R. Leivestad, 'Das Dogma von der prophetenlosen Zeit'.

19 Cf. Sanders, *Jesus and Judaism*, p. 271: 'Scholars sometimes say that

prophecy was regarded as having ceased in Israel, but quite evidently that was not the case. John the Baptist preceded Jesus, and other spokesmen followed him. They were all prophets, or claimed to be, and they all had followings.' See also A. E. Harvey, *Jesus and the Constraints of History*, pp. 58–65.

20   Cf. Syriac Baruch 85:3, where we read 'the prophets have fallen asleep' – but the reference is similarly to the situation of the community in exile.

21   See Goldstein, *I Maccabees*, p. 285 and J. R. Bartlett, *The First and Second Books of the Maccabees*, p. 65; and cf. Leiman, *The Canonization of Hebrew Scripture*, p. 198.

22   My reason for putting the term 'eschatological' in inverted commas will emerge later: see below, pp. 214–23.

23   For recent work in this area, see Aune, *Prophecy in Early Christianity*.

24   Cf. Leivestad, 'Das Dogma von der prophetenlosen Zeit', p. 290 (on the saying in Tosefta Sotah 13:2): 'Der Spruch zeigt, daβ der heilige Geist nicht nur an die Prophetie, sondern an die heilige Schrift geknüpft wird. Haggai, Sacharja und Maleachi kommen in Betracht als die letzten Propheten der kanonischen Schriftsammlung.'

25   See O. Plöger, *Theocracy and Eschatology*.

26   See P. D. Hanson, *The Dawn of Apocalyptic*.

27   Seder ʿOlam Rabbah 30 – see above, p. 110.

28   Cf. Yoma 21b: 'Rab Samuel bar Inia said in the name of Rab Aha, The second Temple lacked five things which the first Temple possessed, namely, the fire, the ark, the Urim and Thummim, the oil of anointing, and the holy spirit.' Prophecy ('the holy spirit') is by no means unique in being absent from 'modern' Judaism here; it is simply one of the features that made the pre-exilic period so special. (Haggai, Zechariah, and Malachi seem here to be ignored.)

29   See J. Lindblom, *Prophecy in Ancient Israel*, pp. 105–219, for the most thorough discussion of the possibilities, which are also explored in his article 'Die Vorstellung vom Sprechen Jahwes zu den Menschen im Alten Testament'.

30   Gen. 37:5–11.

31   1 Kings 22:20–2.

32   1 Sam. 28:13.

33   Zechariah 1:9.

34   It used to be said that E differed from J in according a greater role to intermediaries in God's communication with man. But though this may reflect differences of assumption between the two sources, it is not clear that either regarded the difference as theologically important.

35   See the footnote in Thackeray's translation, ad loc.

36   *de somniis* 1:1–2; 2:1–4.

37   *de somniis* 1:190: 'the Divine word proclaims as dreams sent from God

288

not only those which appear before the mind under the direct action of the Highest of Causes, but those also which are revealed through the agency of His interpreters and attendant messengers who have been held meet to receive from the Father to Whom they owe their being a divine and happy portion.'

38 See *de vita Mosis* 2:188–91.

39 See Aune, *Prophecy in Early Christianity*, pp. 147–8.

40 See especially D. S. Russell, *The Method and Message of Jewish Apocalyptic*, p. 161.

41 *de somniis* 1:190 (in accordance with Gen. 31:11 itself).

42 Gal. 3:19; cf. Acts 7:30 and 38, where Stephen refers to 'the angel' who spoke to Moses in the burning bush.

43 See the excellent discussion in W. Eichrodt, *Theology of the Old Testament* I, pp. 23–9. I am not sure that the distinction is so clear as the consensus would have it. For example, Gen. 19:1 implies that of the three 'men' who visit Abraham, one is Yahweh and the other two are 'angels'. Israel was certainly aware of a plurality of divine or semi-divine beings from its earliest days in Palestine, and the multiplicity of angelic beings in the post-exilic period does not seem particularly novel. However, it would take us too far afield to examine this widely-accepted part of the consensus picture of the difference between pre- and post-exilic thought. At least it can be said that the rise of 'apocalyptic' is hardly the *explanation* for so far-reaching a change; rather, if apocalyptists adopted an advanced angelology they did so because it was part of their religious environment.

44 Rowland, *The Open Heaven*, pp. 52–7.

45 See Lindblom, *Gesichte und Offenbarungen*, and the extremely interesting attempt by Rowland to apply a similar approach to rabbinic visionary traditions, in *The Open Heaven*, pp. 282–348. Contrast Koch, *The Rediscovery of Apocalyptic*, p. 25: 'It is hardly possible to ascertain how far descriptions of this kind [sc. trances, etc.] are representations of actual experience and how far they are a literary fashion.'

46 See Aune, *Prophecy in Early Christianity*, pp. 25–6. Very much the same may be said about the assumption that prophetic inspiration is a matter of ecstasy, in which the mind of the prophet is taken over by God: see pp. 32–4. I do not know what evidence there is for the view of J. J. Collins, 'The Court-Tales in Daniel and the Development of Apocalyptic', p. 230, that the use of dreams for prognostication was felt to be a Gentile phenomenon which Jews would avoid: it is certainly not favoured in the Old Testament, as we have seen, but it is difficult to find any indication that this was widely noticed. Collins writes: 'A good Israelite like Joseph might interpret the dreams of a Gentile, but the Hebrew prophets had visions rather than dreams.' The dividing-line, however, is hard to draw (though Lindblom, *Gesichte und Offenbarungen*, shows that it may not be impossible)

and in any case does not seem to be drawn in the book of Daniel. There is a good study of the role of dreams in Talmudic and post-Talmudic times in J. Trachtenberg, *Jewish Magic and Superstition*, pp. 230–48 – who also offers evidence of bibliomancy (divination by opening the Bible at random), the vulgarized descendant of the rabbis' meditations on particular texts such as the *merkabah*. For interesting parallels from a much later time and a different culture cf. Thomas, *Religion and the Decline of Magic*, pp. 139–53.

47   F. F. Bruce, 'Josephus and Daniel', p. 159, who notes, 'This was the form of prophetic inspiration which Josephus claimed for himself, and which impelled him to proclaim Vespasian as emperor-to-be.'

48   Lindblom, *Gesichte und Offenbarungen*, pp. 175ff.

49   I agree with Stadelmann, *Ben Sira als Schriftgelehrter*, pp. 216–52, that Ben Sira's occasional references to his own teaching as being 'like prophecy' (see Ecclus. 24:33; 39:12; 50:27) do not indicate that he shared such a conception of the wise man's task. Ben Sira represents the old wisdom tradition in its non-mystical, non-mantic form, and he does not think that the revelation of mysteries is to be desired (cf. 3:21ff.).

50   See H.-P. Müller, 'Mantische Weisheit und Apokalyptik'.

51   Lindblom, *Gesichte und Offenbarungen*, p. 175. Note that Paul is specifically called a prophet in Acts 13:1, and in v. 2 'the Holy Spirit said' surely refers to a prophetic utterance.

52   Thomas in *Religion and the Decline of Magic*, p. 466, shows how in sixteenth- and seventeenth-century England historical figures who had originally been moralists and religious leaders, warning of disasters that would overtake their audience unless they repented, were turned in the popular mind into 'prophets', that is, prognosticators of coming events who had supernatural knowledge of the future. 'A good example of this process was provided by the poet George Wither, whose reiterated predictions of the woes in store for unregenerate England seemed, after the coming of the Civil War, to have been based on real foreknowledge, an illusion their author was happy to encourage.'

53   See Stadelmann, *Ben Sira als Schriftgelehrter*, p. 180, quoting Hengel, *Judaism and Hellenism*, pp. 135–6 (= *Judaismus und Hellenismus*, pp. 248–9).

54.   Cf. above, p. 100.

55   See Stadelmann, p. 204.

56   See J. F. Stenning, *The Targum of Isaiah*, ad loc.

57   *PG* 22, p. 343; quoted by R. P. C. Hanson in 'Biblical Exegesis in the Early Church', p. 422.

58   Cf. Barr, *Holy Scripture*, pp. 44–5: '. . . reading Genesis or Isaiah, the western Christian may probably ask himself "what is this saying to me today?", but on reading Enoch or Jubilees he is not likely even to ask the question. But this is not because of the intrinsic merits or demerits of the books: it is because the books are canonical and uncanonical respectively

. . . If Ecclesiastes had not in fact been canonical, no one would ever have dreamt of the salutary contributions to Christian doctrine that its presence is supposed to furnish.'

CHAPTER 4: MODES OF READING THE PROPHETS

1 For a discussion of the importance of genre in reading the Bible see my *Reading the Old Testament*, especially pp. 8–19.

2 The correspondence is in *PG* 11, pp. 42–86. See the discussion in Sundberg, *The Old Testament of the Early Church*, p. 137.

3 Cf. Barnabas 13:4: 'Jacob says, in another prophecy . . .' (referring to Gen. 48:8–22); Josephus, *Ant.* 2:194; Philo, *quis rerum divinarum heres* 261, where Isaac and Jacob are both shown as prophets by foretelling the future on their death-beds; Jubilees 32:21; and Testament of Levi 9:2–3.

4 The distinction between 'prophecy' and 'apocalyptic' was certainly unknown to Josephus, if it is true that the second book of Ezekiel to which he refers was in fact the apocalyptic Ezekiel Apocryphon: see *Ant.* 10:78 '. . . the prophet Ezekiel, who left behind two books which he was the first to write about these matters [sc, the Roman capture of Jerusalem]'.

5 Cf. my *Reading the Old Testament*, pp. 40–3.

6 Cf. Wellhausen, *Prolegomena to the History of Israel*, p. 345, where it is noted that the same mixture of law and historical narrative already characterizes both JE and, following its example, the book of Deuteronomy: 'This manner of setting forth the Torah in the form of a history-book is not in the least involved in the nature of the case; on the contrary, it introduces the greatest amount of awkwardness.'

7 See B. S. Childs, *Introduction to the Old Testament as Scripture*, and compare the discussion in Barr, *Holy Scripture*, and in my own *Reading the Old Testament*. The point about the Torah is made in my article ' "The Law and the Prophets." Who are the Prophets?', p. 8, with reference to unpublished lectures by Paul Ricoeur.

8 Volume 1 is called *Apocalyptic Literature and Testaments*, and consists of two parts: 'Apocalyptic Literature and Related Works' and 'Testaments (Often with Apocalyptic Sections)'. Volume 2 is called *Expansions of the 'Old Testament' and Other Legends, Wisdom and Philosophical Literature, Prayers, Psalms, and Odes, Fragments of Lost Judeo-Hellenistic Works*.

9 Compare my discussion of Childs in *Reading the Old Testament*, pp. 77–103 and 140–57; also in my article 'Classifying Biblical Criticism'.

CHAPTER 5: PROPHECY AS ETHICAL INSTRUCTION

1 Cf. my comments in *Reading the Old Testament*, pp. 129–33.

2 See above, p. 43.

3 Tanhuma Yitro 124ab: quoted from Montefiore and Loewe, *A Rabbinic Anthology*, p. 158. See also above, pp. 18 and 275–6.

4 Cf. D. Daube, *Studies in Biblical Law*, pp. 3–15, where it is argued that various legal principles find expression in the stories of the patriarchs. For example, Jacob's 'recognition' of the bloodstained coat (Gen. 37:33) as proof that Joseph has been killed by wild animals is said to reflect a legal custom. It does not imply that Jacob believes the brothers' story (the narrative later shows that he did not: see Gen. 42:36), but simply that he followed the legal forms prescribed within a system of 'objective' justice. In Daube's work there is a hint that the Pentateuchal system of law is therefore older than the Graf–Wellhausen hypothesis implies, since already in the patriarchal stories there are cases where rabbinic methods of legal exposition can be found in operation; cf. J. Weingreen, *From Bible to Mishna*, for a similar argument about Deuteronomy. Whether or not one accepts this corollary of Daube's suggestions, they are an excellent example of the way the Pentateuch is treated once it is supposed that its primary function is halakic.

5 M. Noth, 'The Laws in the Pentateuch', p. 87.

6 See Noth, *The Deuteronomistic History*, pp. 89–99; E. Janssen, *Juda in der Exilszeit*, pp. 12–18; and P. R. Ackroyd, *Exile and Restoration*, pp. 72–8.

7 Cf. E. W. Nicholson, *Preaching to the Exiles*, and R. P. Carroll, *From Chaos to Covenant*, especially pp. 84–106. Further discussion of the deuteronomistic redaction of Jeremiah can be found in H. Weippert, *Die Prosareden des Jeremiabuches*.

8 Cf. G. von Rad, 'The Levitical Sermon in I and II Chronicles'. The prophet as one who *instructs* people in right conduct appears in a number of places in Chronicles: see, for example, 1 Chron. 21, where Gad gives David directions concerning the altar; 2 Chron. 11:2 and 12:5, where Shemaiah gives directions to Rehoboam; 16:7, 19:2–3, 20:14 and 20, and 25:15 for other cases where prophets tell kings how to behave; and 29:25 for prophetic guidance in establishing the correct forms of worship.

9 R. A. Mason, 'Some Echoes of the Preaching in the Second Temple? Tradition Elements in Zechariah 1–8'.

10 Ibid., p. 234.

11 On this see also H. W. Hertzberg, 'Die Nachgeschichte alttestamentlicher Texte innerhalb des Alten Testaments', who stresses that glossing and redaction in the interests of ethical instruction is the commonest case of 'inner-biblical' exegesis; cf. J. Koenig, 'L'activité herméneutique des scribes dans la transmission du texte de l'Ancien Testament', who concentrates on the same process during the later stages of textual transmission. There is an attractive account of the way in which one passage has influenced another in the Prophets in J. Day, 'A Case of Inner Scriptural Interpretation'. The major study of inner-biblical exegesis is now M. Fish-

bane, *Biblical Interpretation in Ancient Israel*. Fishbane classifies the editorial additions to biblical books under three types: legal, aggadic, and mantological. It will be found that his 'legal' category corresponds to the first mode in which the scriptural books were read once their redaction was complete, and with which we are concerned in the present chapter; 'aggadic' exegesis covers much of what I have assigned to the fourth mode (speculative theology); and 'mantological exegesis' concerns the matters that appear in my second and third modes. Fishbane's book is a monumental, exhaustive, and fascinating treatment of the redactional development of Scripture, on a scale never attempted before. It appeared too late for me to include references to it in the many places where it is relevant to my own concerns, much to my regret.

12 *Ant.* 10:260–2; cf. Bruce, 'Josephus and Daniel', p. 150.

13 *Ant.* 6:340–2.

14 N. Walter, *Der Thoraausleger Aristobulos*, p. 31, note 1; cited in H. von Campenhausen, *The Formation of the Christian Bible*, p. 4.

15 Philo's other references to Hannah are in *de cherubim* 2; *de somniis* 1:254; *de mutatione nominum* 144; and *quod deus immutabilis sit* 2.

16 For a similar spiritualization see *de somniis* 2:250–4.

17 A good statement of the principle of exemplification from a later, Christian writer may be found in Ambrose *de sacramentis* 1 (*Sources chrétiennes* 25 bis, p. 156): 'De moralibus cotidianum sermonem habuimus, cum vel patriarcharum gesta vel proverbiorum legerentur praecepta, ut his informati atque instituti assuesceretis maiorum ingredi vias eorumque iter carpere ac divinis oboedire oraculis.'

18 On Philo's use of Scripture see W. L. Knox, 'A Note on Philo's Use of the Old Testament'.

19 On this see E. P. Sanders, *Jesus and Judaism*, pp. 256–60.

20 See above, pp. 111–13.

21 See Mason, 'Some Echoes of the Preaching in the Second Temple', p. 234, with reference to R. P. Carroll's important study *When Prophecy Failed*. The present argument is not meant to counter Carroll's general presentation of the way in which the adherents of 'prophetic' groups adjust their expectations to changing circumstances, which is very acute, but merely to question it as it relates to the transformation of prophetic oracles into *moral advice* in redaction and interpretation. See also Mason's 'The Prophets of the Restoration'.

22 Schmid, *Wesen und Geschichte der Weisheit*, p. 74: 'Was ursprünglich – im Rahmen des damaligen Weltgefühls – erfahrbare, „empirische" Beschreibung der Wirklichkeit war, wurde zum Postulat, zum Wirklichkeitsbild, das ungeschichtlich über jede begegnende Situation gelegt wird und bestrebt ist, die Wirklichkeit mit allen Mitteln sich anzupassen.'

23 Ibid., p. 77: 'Was einst für die spezifische Beamtenausbildung und

damit – wie die gesamte damalige Erziehung – nur für Fürstenkinder bestimmt war, wurde später als Schulbuch für den Lese- und Schreibunterricht verwendet.'

24 Ibid., p. 79: 'Die sprachliche Fixierung und Tradierung solcher Maximen, die Allgemeingültigkeit beansprucht, entkleidet diese der Bindung an ihrem geschichtlichen Ort und ihrer Einmaligkeit. Die unmittelbar erlebten und verstandenen Zusammenhänge werden objektiviert und damit ungeschichtlich. Sie verlieren den direkten Bezug zur begegnenden Wirklichkeit und stehen in der Vorratskammer der Sprache bereit, in einer neuen geschichtlichen Situation Verwendung zu finden and dort Hilfe zu sein. In diesem Sinne ist alle Weisheitsliteratur – als Literatur, als auswendig gelerntes, geschriebenes oder sonstwie konserviertes Wort – ungeschichtlich.'

25 On this see Sanders, *Jesus and Judaism*, p. 67.

26 Cf. Wellhausen's comments on *midrash*: 'It is a high estimate of tradition that leads to its being thus modernized; but in the process it is twisted and perverted, and set off with foreign accretions in the most arbitrary way' (*Prolegomena to the History of Israel*, p. 227). The adaptation of older works to new situations is very neatly summed up by I. L. Seeligmann, 'Voraussetzungen der Midrasch-Exegese', p. 181: 'In der Tat wohnt ihr die Spannung eines gewissen Paradoxes inne. Auch nachdem der Midrasch zur richtigen Auslegung eines festen und fertigen Textgebildes geworden ist, bleiben ihm Elemente der Beweglichkeit, des Spiels und der Aktualisierung anhaften: einerseits will er einen abgeschlossenen Text erklären, andererseits ist er bestrebt denselben ... offenzuhalten, vor Versteinerung zu behüten und mit immer neuem Leben zu erfüllen – für jede Situation und für jeden neuen Tag!'

27 Noth, 'The Laws in the Pentateuch', p. 87, note 202.

28 Cf. Isa. 2:8, Jer. 2:9–13.

CHAPTER 6: PROPHETIC FOREKNOWLEDGE OF THE PRESENT DAY

1 Aune, *Prophecy in Early Christianity*, p. 133. (The word 'eschatological' will be qualified a little in our discussion.)

2 Cf. the discussion of meditation on Scripture as a preparation for receiving prophetic inspiration on p. 126 above.

3 See above, pp. 105 and 130.

4 On which see K. Stendahl, *The School of St Matthew*.

5 Cf. B. Lindars, *New Testament Apologetic*, especially pp. 89–93. Lindars' discussion is a fascinating study of the mutual influence of event and prophecy in the evolution of the gospel narratives.

6 Much typological interpretation in modern English-speaking scholarship derives from the work of A. M. Farrer: see, for example, *A Study in St*

Mark or *A Rebirth of Images*, and the theoretical discussion of the typological approach in *The Glass of Vision*. Farrer toyed with lectionary theories (e.g. in his essay 'On Dispensing with Q'), but the credit for making the connection in a consistent way is due to his pupils Aileen Guilding (see *The Fourth Gospel and Jewish Worship*) and Michael Goulder (already in his book on Acts, *Type and History in Acts*, but more clearly in *Midrash and Lection in Matthew* and *The Evangelists' Calendar*). Why lectionary theories should be regarded as peculiarly disreputable, rather than merely mistaken, I do not understand (but then I was myself taught by Farrer), but there is no denying that they are highly speculative. The study of the state of the canon in New Testament times with which the early chapters of the present book is concerned may have added more difficulties to them, by showing how fluid was the notion of 'Scripture'. But it would be a pity if in rejecting them one were also to shut one's eyes to the presence of typology in early Christian literature. To acknowledge its presence is not necessarily to regard it as a good thing (as Farrer undoubtedly did), and it is merely confused thinking to deny that it exists because one disapproves of it. Obviously some passages in the New Testament are richer in typological allusion than others: the birth-narratives in Matthew and Luke, in particular, show the desire to present Jesus' birth and all the circumstances surrounding it as combining all the best features of similar narratives in the Old Testament.

7   Many examples can be found in Barnabas (see especially 5; 6; and 11–14) and 1 Clement (e.g. 12:7, on the scarlet cord which Rahab hung in her window, to be a type of the blood of Christ bringing salvation to those who rely on it); and see also Justin's *Dialogue with Trypho* (on which I commented briefly in my article 'Judaism and Christianity: Prophecy and Fulfilment'. J. Daniélou, *The Theology of Jewish Christianity*, is a rich source of information and examples.

8   *Essays on Biblical Interpretation*, p. 50; cf. the critical comments in Barr, *Holy Scripture*, p. 70.

9   Further examples of the fulfilment of prophecy in Acts are to be found in the following passages: 3:18–26; 4:24–30; 7:52; 8:28–34; 10:43; 13:27–41; 15:15; 26:22–7; 28:23; 28:25.

10   And also in Justin's Dialogue with Trypho, where for example we find a 'proof' that the prophecy of Isaiah 7:14 cannot be explained as a reference to Hezekiah, as Trypho maintains.

11   See Sanders, *Jesus and Judaism*, p. 217.

12   In Jude 14 Enoch is perhaps presented as prophesying events which the author of the Epistle was experiencing: in this case, the heretical activities of 'ungodly persons who pervert the grace of our God into licentiousness, and deny our only Master and Lord, Jesus Christ' (v. 4). If

this interpretation is correct, the extremely vague prediction of 1 Enoch 1:9 is taken as 'fulfilled' in the present generation; but see below, p. 223.

13   I made this point in my article 'Judaism and Christianity: Prophecy and Fulfilment', p. 261: 'the argument [in Christian claims that Jesus had 'fulfilled' prophecy] is at least as much about the claim of Jesus to be a definitive revelation from God and hence the key to the Scriptures, as it is about the reference of the Scriptures, considered as infallible oracles, to Christ. The process is a two-way one, but on the whole Christ, rather than the Scriptures, is the given – even in arguments ostensibly relying on Scriptural proof texts.' Cf. also Barr, *Escaping from Fundamentalism*, pp. 9–10.

14   R. Longenecker, *Biblical Exegesis in the Apostolic Period*, p. 41.

15   F. F. Bruce, *Biblical Exegesis in the Qumran Texts*, p. 8; quoted by Longenecker on p. 42.

16   This difference of usage in the term 'messianic', for which see B. Wilson, *Magic and the Millennium*, can be confusing. In sociological writing a sect can be 'messianic' without expecting a 'messiah', still less *the* Messiah often supposed to have been awaited in Second Temple Judaism (but see A. E. Harvey, *Jesus and the Constraints of History*, pp. 120–53).

17   See, for example, Russell, *The Method and Message of Jewish Apocalyptic*, pp. 224–9.

18   *The Open Heaven*, pp. 9–48.

19   Ibid., especially pp. 70–2.

20   One of the four types of inquiry proscribed in M. Hagigah 2:1: 'Whosoever gives his mind to four things, it were better for him if he had not come into the world – what is above, what is beneath, what was beforetime, and what will be hereafter.' This provides Rowland with a fourfold classification of the types of secret with which apocalyptic texts are concerned. As will be seen, my own view is that similar concerns underlie the four 'modes' of reading (and writing) prophecy in our period, though they do not correspond to the 'four things' of this text. The first mode, revelation about halakah, does not appear among them – and it is interesting that Rowland does not deal with the ethical teaching in the apocalypses, which remains as puzzling on his view as it has appeared to be to most of those who have regarded the eschatological interest as primary. The second mode and the third are both concerned with 'what will be hereafter' and with 'what was beforetime'. 'What is above' and 'what is beneath' – that is, secrets of the heavenly and earthly realms – all fall under my fourth mode.

21   See, for example, Russell, *The Method and Message of Jewish Apocalyptic*, pp. 297–303.

22   Cf. G. B. Caird, *The Language and Imagery of the Bible*, pp. 243–71, for a detailed argument in favour of a generally 'metaphorical' interpretation of such language.

23   *The Open Heaven*, pp. 160–76.

24 Ibid., p. 167.

25 See, for example, R. Loewe, ' "Salvation" is not of the Jews'.

26 In the Testaments of the Twelve Patriarchs, for instance, and the Ascension of Isaiah.

27 *The Open Heaven*, pp. 162–3.

28 'Schweitzer's Influence – Blessing or Bane?'. See the discussion in Sanders, *Jesus and Judaism*, pp. 124–5, which accepts Glasson's contention that there is little evidence for an otherworldly hope in Judaism, while noting that Glasson's criticism of Schweitzer for being mistaken about this tries to prove too much.

29 Bultmann, 'History and Eschatology in the New Testament', p. 6; quoted by Glasson on p. 297.

30 H. H. Rowley, *The Relevance of Apocalyptic*, p. 38; cf. Rowland, *The Open Heaven*, p. 25.

31 See the interesting discussion in Lindblom, *Prophecy in Ancient Israel*, pp. 137–48.

32 See *The Open Heaven*, p. 427.

33 Cf. Russell, *The Method and Message of Jewish Apocalyptic*, pp. 92–6.

34 For the classical prophets' exploitation of forms likely to appeal to their hearers cf. C. Westermann, *Basic Forms of Prophetic Speech* and H. W. Wolff, 'Das Zitat im Prophetenspruch'.

35 See above, pp. 61–2, and compare the discussion of pseudonymity, with full bibliography, in Rowland, *The Open Heaven*, pp. 61–70.

36 See Rowland, *The Open Heaven*, pp. 240–5, which travels some way down the road towards this conclusion but stops short of suggesting, as I am doing, virtually a theory of automatic writing to account for those pseudepigrapha which speak of imminent divine intervention. Rowland writes: 'Though we may expect that the bulk of the material in the apocalypses may have been inserted within a fictitious framework deliberately, in order to gain authority for the visions, it seems that a case can be made for some visions at least being linked with a pseudonymous author precisely because the character of the experience itself drove the visionary to the conclusion that narrating in the name of some other person was the only way in which he could do justice to the nature of his experience' (p. 245). Rowland draws on much of the material in Lindblom's *Gesichte und Offenbarungen* related to the experience of *Objektivierung des Ichs*, a phenomenon related to 'out-of-the-body' experiences and some forms of depersonalization or derealization. His suggestion is that in describing such experiences the subject feels a need to talk about himself in the third person, as Paul does in 2 Cor. 12:1–10, and that the figures of well-known sages and mystics may have offered themselves as a way of naming the *alter ego*. As Rowland observes, however, there is a logical gap here, in that no reason can be suggested why the 'apocalyptists', unlike Paul, did not simply leave the

alter ego anonymous. My suggestion (and that is all it is) is that we need to move still one more stage away from the mentality of most people who have undergone no strange psychic experiences, and contemplate the possibility that these visionaries had a sense of becoming one with, or a vehicle for, Enoch or Moses or whichever was their preferred predecessor.

37 See, *inter alia*, N. Cohn, *The Pursuit of the Millennium*; R. Bauckham, *Tudor Apocalypse*; and K. R. Firth, *The Apocalyptic Tradition in Reformation Britain*.

38 *Religion and the Decline of Magic*, pp. 502–3. This reason probably accounts also for some Mesopotamian pseudo-prophecy. I am indebted to Dr Stephanie Dalley for pointing this out to me.

CHAPTER 7: PROPHECY AND THE DIVINE PLAN FOR HISTORY

1 Origen, *Homilies on Joshua* 6:4, *PG* 12, pp. 885–6.

2 Eusebius, *praeparatio evangelica* 7:5:1, quoted in Hanson, 'Biblical Exegesis in the Early Church', p. 422.

3 S. Schechter, *Some Aspects of Rabbinic Theology* (1909), p. 102. Cf. Moore, *Judaism* II, pp. 279–395, where it is taken for granted that there is no essential conflict between the eschatological expectations of rabbis and apocalyptists.

4 See above, pp. 197 and 190.

5 Cf. also Mekhilta on Exod. 20:15–19, where God is said to have shown Abraham the following: Gehenna, the giving of the Law, the division of the Red Sea, the Temple, the order of the sacrifices, and the four kingdoms that would oppress his descendants. Of course this means that Abraham is presented as a prophet, but there is no sense that his visions concerned matters with an immediate contemporary relevance for the reader of Genesis: it simply implies that God has accurate knowledge of all that is to be throughout his people's history, from first to last, and reveals it to his prophets. What else would anyone expect?

6 E. W. Heaton, *The Hebrew Kingdoms*, p. 59.

7 Cf. above, p. 130.

8 See *Ant.* 1:240, where Alexander Polyhistor is said to have made use of a history by 'Cleodomus the prophet'.

9 See above, p. 20.

10 Barr, 'Historical Reading and the Theological Interpretation of Scripture', p. 36. Compare Cornill's description of Israelite historiography as *rückwärts gekehrte Prophetie* (cited in L. H. K. Bleeker, 'De geschiedenis van het Oude Testament (Hoseah 11, 1–3)', pp. 32 and 39).

11 The two foregoing sentences are a slightly adapted version of my comments on the same quotation from Barr in ' "The Law and the Prophets." Who are the Prophets?', p. 9.

12   Mekhilta, on Exod. 15:1.

13   *The Open Heaven*, p. 137. Compare Philo on Moses: 'He prophesied to each tribe in particular the things which were to be and hereafter must come to pass. Some of these have already taken place, others are still looked for, since confidence in the future is assured by fulfilment in the past' (*de vita Mosis* 2:288).

14   Ibid., p. 142.

15   Ibid., p. 143.

16   Compare the discussion in R. E. Clements, *Isaiah and the Deliverance of Jerusalem*, pp. 52–71, where a full bibliography may be found.

17   See the discussion in Aune, *Prophecy in Early Christianity*, p. 37, and p. 357 note 166.

18   Cf. Vermes, 'Bible and Midrash: Early Old Testament Exegesis', p. 207.

19   See the study of periodization in Noth, *The Deuteronomistic History*, pp. 18–78.

20   Cf. J. Van Seters, *In Search of History*, pp. 38 and 358.

21   For these points about 'P' I am indebted to an unpublished paper, read to a seminar in Oxford, by my colleague Mr Jeremy Hughes, who has made a detailed study of the chronological systems of the Hebrew Bible.

22   See, again, Van Seters, *In Search of History*, pp. 68–76. Information about the background of the four world-empires and their association with metals can be found in Hengel, *Judaism and Hellenism*, p. 182, and cf. H. H. Rowley, *Darius the Mede and the Four World Empires*, p. 69. See also Barr, 'The Question of Religious Influence: the Case of Zoroastrianism, Judaism, and Christianity', pp. 224–5, and the bibliography there; and A. Momigliano, 'The Origins of Universal History'.

23   See the discussion of periodization and *vaticinia ex eventu* in Sibylline oracles by J. J. Collins in *The Old Testament Pseudepigrapha* I, p. 319, referring to K. Kerenyi, 'Das persische Millennium im Mahabharta, bei der Sibylle und Vergil' and D. Flusser, 'The Four Empires in the Fourth Sibyl and in the book of Daniel'.

24   This is an objection, for example, to the explanations offered by von Rad in *Old Testament Theology* II, pp. 301–8.

CHAPTER 8: THE PROPHET AS THEOLOGIAN AND MYSTIC

1   Cf. H. W. Wolff, 'The Kerygma of the Deuteronomic Historical Work'.

2   Cf. also *BJ* 5:375–419 (Josephus's own lengthy exhortation, which takes the form of a retelling of Israel's history to bring out the 'moral'), and the Slavonic Addition after *BJ* 1:644, where Abraham is used as an example of the operation of divine providence in making rewards fit deserts.

3   J. Mann, *The Bible as Read and Preached in the Old Synagogue* I, p. 134; cited in Patte, *Early Jewish Hermeneutic in Palestine*, p. 40.

4   The possibility is discussed (though rejected) in Clements, 'Patterns in the Prophetic Canon', p. 47.

5   'Auguries of Innocence', *circa* 1803.

6   Chronicles is full of prophecy in the fourth mode: prophets regularly appear to preach sermons on the general truths about God's attitude to his people evinced by Israel's history. See especially 2 Chron. 12:5; 13:4–12; 15:2–7; 16:7–9; 24:20; and 28:9–13. See on this Wellhausen, *Prolegomena to the History of Israel*, p. 203.

7   The contrast is made more explicit in those manuscripts (ADWΘ*f*1*f*13) which insert 'as Elijah did' after the disciples' question, and make Jesus reply: 'You do not know what manner of spirit you are of; for the Son of man came not to destroy men's lives but to save them.'

8   See the full discussion of this passage in Hanson, *The New Testament Interpretation of Scripture*, pp. 21–96, which discusses in particular the problem of identifying the quotations.

9   An enormous literature could no doubt be cited on both sides of the dispute referred to here, but see at any rate J. Munck, *Paul and the Salvation of Mankind* for the 'eschatological' interpretation.

10   Subject to the same qualification as in the preceding note, see R. Bultmann, *Theology of the New Testament* I, pp. 301–2.

11   Cf. J. A. Emerton, 'The Origin of the Son of Man Imagery'.

12   'Biblical Theology' was somewhat equivocal on this point; as well as producing works that stressed 'actions' rather than 'concepts' as the nub of Old Testament theology, it also found expression in such books as N. H. Snaith's *The Distinctive Ideas of the Old Testament*. Perhaps the best and most nuanced approach is still that of Eichrodt in his great *Theology of the Old Testament*, a work which has stood the test of time better than some of the biblical 'Theologies' produced after the Second World War.

13   Cf. above, p. 72.

14   *The Open Heaven*, pp. 282–305: 'The Meditation of Rabban Johanan Ben Zakkai and His Circle on the Chariot-Chapter'.

15   The relevant texts, all fully discussed by Rowland, are Hagigah 14b, j. Hagigah 77a (= 2:1), Tosefta Hagigah 2:1, and Mekilta de R. Simeon b. Yohai (*Mishpatim* 21:1).

16   Cf. Ignatius, *Smyrneans* 7:2; Barnabas 5:6–7.

17   See the illuminating discussion in F. Kermode, *The Genesis of Secrecy*, pp. 23–47, where the possibility that Jesus is being presented as a teacher of arcane knowledge is seriously grappled with.

18   Cf. C. K. Barrett, 'The Eschatology of the Epistle to the Hebrews'.

19   The very late 3 Enoch is a particularly clear example of an apocalypse concerned with the details of the divine realm; see the exceptionally useful

introduction by P. S. Alexander in *The Old Testament Pseudepigrapha* I, pp. 223–54.

20 Cf. M. E. Stone, 'Apocalyptic Literature' in *Jewish Writings of the Second Temple Period*, p. 393: 'Many works which belong to the genre "apocalypse" contain much that is not covered or rendered comprehensible by [standard definitions of "apocalypticism"], while many works not formally apocalypses are imbued with this apocalypticism.'

21 *The Rediscovery of Apocalyptic*, p. 22. In the light of our discussion, and the arguments of Rowland, Koch's definition of 'apocalyptic' stands in need of revision: he says that apocalypses 'reveal something about the destiny of mankind which has hitherto been a secret (*raz, mysterion*) guarded in heaven but which will soon come to pass on earth'. In fact the most we can say is that they 'reveal something which has hitherto been a secret guarded in heaven', full stop; and we then need to add that it is not only apocalypses which are concerned with such revelations, for it is a general interest of much of the literature of our period, including 'wisdom' and psalmody.

22 Cf. von Rad, *Old Testament Theology* II, pp. 304–6.

23 Compare B. M. Metzger's comments in *The Old Testament Pseudepigrapha* I, p. 521.

24 *The Open Heaven*, p. 134.

25 See *The Old Testament Pseudepigrapha* I, p. 823, footnote.

26 *de migratione Abrahami* 35, cf. *de cherubim* 27; cited in Aune, *Prophecy in Early Christianity*, p. 147.

27 See H. Frei, *The Eclipse of Biblical Narrative*, pp. 17–50, for an account of how the biblical narrative framework functioned in this way in much Christian thought until the Enlightenment. Of course it still does function in this way in many contexts, such as the liturgical and the devotional reading of Scripture, and for many mainstream Jews and Christians this is in practice one of the most important roles the Bible has to play.

28 See above, pp. 170–2.

CONCLUSION

1 See E. W. Heaton, *The Old Testament Prophets*, p. 36.

Bibliography

Ackroyd, P. R., *Exile and Restoration*. London 1968.

Anderson, G. W., 'Canonical and Non-canonical', in *Cambridge History of the Bible* I, q.v., pp. 113–59.

Aune, D. E., *Prophecy in Early Christianity and the Ancient Mediterranean World*. Grand Rapids, Michigan 1983.

Barnett, P. W., 'The Jewish Sign Prophets – AD 40–70 – Their Intentions and Origin', *NTS* 27 (1981), pp. 679–97.

Barr, J., *Escaping from Fundamentalism*. London 1984.

—, 'Historical Reading and the Theological Interpretation of Scripture', *Explorations in Theology 7: The Scope and Authority of the Bible* (London 1980), pp. 30–51.

—, *Holy Scripture. Canon, Authority, Criticism*. Oxford and Philadelphia 1983.

—, 'The Question of Religious Influence: the Case of Zoroastrianism, Judaism, and Christianity', *JAAR* 53 (1985), pp. 201–35.

Barrett, C. K., 'The Eschatology of the Epistle to the Hebrews', in *The Background of the New Testament and its Eschatology* (Cambridge 1956), pp. 363–93.

Bartlett, J. R., *The First and Second Books of the Maccabees* (Cambridge Bible Commentary). Cambridge 1973.

Barton, J., 'Classifying Biblical Criticism', *JSOT* 29 (1984), pp. 19–35.

—, 'Judaism and Christianity: Prophecy and Fulfilment', *Theology* 79 (1976), pp. 260–6.

—, ' "The Law and the Prophets." Who are the Prophets?', *OS* 23 (1984), pp. 1–18.

—, *Reading the Old Testament. Method in Biblical Study*. London and Philadelphia 1984.

Bauckham, R., *Tudor Apocalypse. Sixteenth Century Apocalypticism, Millenarianism and the English Reformation* (Courtenay Library of Reformation Classics 8). Appleford, Abingdon 1975.

Blau, L., 'Bible Canon: Traditional View', *JE* III, pp. 140–50.

Bleeker, L. H. K., 'De geschiedenis van het Oude Testament (Hoseah 11,

Bibliography

1–3)', in *Geschiedenis, een bundel studiën over de zin der geschiedenis*. Assen 1944.

Blenkinsopp, J., *A History of Prophecy in Israel. From the Settlement in the Land to the Hellenistic Period*. London 1984.

—, *Prophecy and Canon. A Contribution to the Study of Jewish Origins*. Notre Dame, Indiana 1977.

Bradshaw, P. F., *Daily Prayer in the Early Church. A Study of the Origin and Early Development of the Divine Office* (Alcuin Club Collections 63). London 1981.

Bronznick, N. M., 'Qabbalah as a Metonym for the Prophets and Hagiographa', HUCA 38 (1967), pp. 285–95.

Browne, Sir Thomas, *Pseudodoxia Epidemica* or *Enquiries into Vulgar and Common Errors*. London 1646 (ed. R. Robbins, Oxford 1981).

Bruce, F. F., *Biblical Exegesis in the Qumran Texts*. London 1960.

—, 'Josephus and Daniel', ASTI 4 (1965), pp. 148–62.

Buber, M., *The Prophetic Faith*. New York 1960.

Büchler, A., 'Haftarah', *JE* VI, pp. 135–7.

Bultmann, R., 'History and Eschatology in the New Testament', *NTS* 1 (1954–5), pp. 5–16.

—, *Theologie des Neuen Testaments*. Tübingen, I 1948, II 1953 = *Theology of the New Testament*, 2 vols. London 1958.

Caird, G. B., *The Language and Imagery of the Bible*. London 1980.

The Cambridge History of the Bible, I, edd. P. R. Ackroyd and C. F. Evans. Cambridge 1970.

von Campenhausen, H., *Die Entstehung der christlichen Bibel*. Tübingen 1968 = *The Formation of the Christian Bible*. London 1972.

Carroll, R. P., *From Chaos to Covenant. Uses of Prophecy in the Book of Jeremiah*. London 1981.

—, *When Prophecy Failed. Reactions and Responses to Failure in the Old Testament Prophetic Tradition*. London 1979.

Charles, R. H., *The Apocrypha and Pseudepigrapha of the Old Testament in English, with Introductions and Critical and Explanatory Notes to the Several Books*, 2 vols. Oxford 1913.

Charlesworth, J. H., *The Old Testament Pseudepigrapha*, 2 vols. London 1983 and 1985.

Childs, B. S., *Introduction to the Old Testament as Scripture*. Philadelphia and London 1979.

Clements, R. E., *Isaiah and the Deliverance of Jerusalem. A Study of the Interpretation of Prophecy in the Old Testament* (JSOTS 13). Sheffield 1980.

—, 'Patterns in the Prophetic Canon', in *Canon and Authority*, ed. G. W. Coats and B. O. Long (Philadelphia 1977), pp. 42–55.

Cohn, N., *The Pursuit of the Millennium. Revolutionary Millenarians and Mystical Anarchists of the Middle Ages*. London 1957.

Bibliography

Collins, J. J., 'The Court-Tales in Daniel and the Development of Apocalyptic', *JBL* 94 (1975), pp. 218–34.

Danby, H., *The Mishnah*. London 1933.

Daniélou, J., *The Theology of Jewish Christianity* (volume I of *A History of Early Christian Doctrine before the Council of Nicea*). London 1964.

Daube, D., *Studies in Biblical Law*. Cambridge 1947.

Davies, G. I., 'Apocalyptic and Historiography', *JSOT* 5 (1978), pp. 15–28.

Day, J., 'A Case of Inner Scriptural Interpretation', *JTS* 31 (1980), pp. 309–19.

Duhm, B., *Die Theologie der Propheten*. Bonn 1875.

Eichrodt, W., *Theologie des Alten Testaments*. Stuttgart, I 1933, II 1935, III 1939 = *Theology of the Old Testament*. London, I 1960 (from sixth edn of the German, 1959), II 1967 (from fifth edn of the German of vols. II and III in one vol., 1964).

Eissfeldt, O., *The Old Testament – an Introduction*. Oxford 1965.

Emerton, J. A., 'The Origin of the Son of Man Imagery', *JTS* 9 (1958), pp. 225–42.

Farrer, A. M., *The Glass of Vision*. London 1948.

—, *A Rebirth of Images*. London 1950.

—, *A Study in St Mark*. London 1951.

Firth, K. R., *The Apocalyptic Tradition in Reformation Britain 1530–1645*. Oxford 1979.

Fishbane, M., *Biblical Interpretation in Ancient Israel*. Oxford 1985.

Flusser, D., 'The Four Empires in the Fourth Sybil and in the Book of Daniel', *Israel Oriental Studies* 2 (1972), pp. 148–75.

Freedman, D. N., 'Canon of the OT', *IDB* Supplement.

Frei, H. W., *The Eclipse of Biblical Narrative: A Study in Eighteenth and Nineteenth Century Hermeneutics*. New Haven and London 1974.

Frustorfer, K., 'Des Weisen Curriculum Vitae nach Sirach (39, 1–15)', *ThPQ* 94 (1941).

Frye, Northrop, *The Great Code. The Bible and Literature*. London, Melbourne and Henley 1982.

Gadamer, H. G., *Wahrheit und Methode*. Tübingen 1960 = *Truth and Method*. New York 1975.

Ginzberg, L., *Legends of the Jews*. 7 vols. Philadelphia 1909–38.

Glasson, T. F., 'Schweitzer's Influence – Blessing or Bane?', *JTS* 28 (1977), pp. 289–302.

Goldingay, J., *Approaches to Old Testament Interpretation*. Leicester 1981.

Goldstein, J. A., I *and* II *Maccabees*. 2 vols., New York 1976 and 1983.

Goshen-Gottstein, M. H., 'The Psalms Scroll (11QPs^a): A Problem of Canon and Text', *Textus* 5 (1966), pp. 22–33.

Goulder, M. D., *The Evangelists' Calendar*. London 1978.

—, *Midrash and Lection in Matthew*. London 1974.

304

Bibliography

—, *Type and History in Acts*. London 1964.

Grabe, J. E. and Lee, F., *Vetus Testamentum iuxta LXX interpretes*. Oxford 1707–20.

Guilding, A., *The Fourth Gospel and Jewish Worship. A Study of the Relation of St John's Gospel to the Ancient Jewish Lectionary System*. Oxford 1960.

Hanson, A. T., *The New Testament Interpretation of Scripture*. London 1980.

Hanson, P. D., *The Dawn of Apocalyptic*. Philadelphia 1975.

Hanson, R. P. C., 'Biblical Exegesis in the Early Church', in *Cambridge History of the Bible* I, q.v., pp. 412–53.

Harvey, A. E., *Jesus and the Constraints of History*. London and Philadelphia 1982.

Heaton, E. W., *The Hebrew Kingdoms*. Oxford 1968.

—, *The Old Testament Prophets*. London 1958, revised edn 1977.

Hengel, M., *Judentum und Hellenismus: Wissenschaftliche Untersuchungen zum Neuen Testament*, second edn Tübingen 1973 = *Judaism and Hellenism*. London 1974.

Hertzberg, H. W., 'Die Nachgeschichte alttestamentlicher Texte innerhalb des Alten Testaments', *Werden und Wesen des Alten Testaments* (Berlin 1936), pp. 110–21.

Janssen, E., *Juda in der Exilszeit*. Göttingen 1956.

Jepsen, A., 'Kanon und Text des Alten Testaments', *TLZ* 74 (1949), cols. 65–74.

Josephus, translated and ed. by H. StJ. Thackeray (vols. 1–5), R. Marcus (vols. 5–8), and L. Feldman (vols. 9 and 10), 10 vols. London and Cambridge, Mass. 1926–65.

Katz, P., 'The Old Testament Canon in Palestine and Alexandria', *ZNW* 47 (1956), pp. 191–217.

Kelly, J. N. D., *Jerome: His Life, Writings, and Controversies*. London 1975.

Kerenyi, K., 'Das persische Millennium im Mahabharta, bei der Sybille und Vergil', *Klio* 29 (1936), pp. 1–35.

Kermode, F., *The Genesis of Secrecy*. Cambridge, Mass., and London 1979.

Knox, W. L., 'A Note on Philo's Use of the Old Testament', *JTS* 41 (1940), pp. 30–4.

Koch, K., *Ratlos vor der Apokalyptik*. Gütersloh 1970 = *The Rediscovery of Apocalyptic* (SBTh II:22). London 1972.

Koenig, J., 'L'activité herméneutique des scribes dans la transmission du texte de l'Ancien Testament', *RHR* 1961, pp. 141–74 and 1962, pp. 1–43.

Koole, J. L., 'Die Bibel des Ben Sira', *OS* 14 (1965), pp. 374–96.

Lambert, W. G., 'Ancestors, Authors, and Canonicity', *JCS* 11 (1957), pp. 1–14.

Leaney, A. R. C., *The Jewish and Christian World 200 BC–AD 200*. Cambridge 1984.

305

Bibliography

Lebram, J. C. H., 'Aspekte der alttestamentlichen Kanonbildung', *VT* 18 (1968), pp. 173–89.

Leiman, S. Z., *The Canonization of Hebrew Scripture: The Talmudic and Midrashic Evidence*. Hamden, Conn. 1976.

Leivestad, R., 'Das Dogma von der prophetenlosen Zeit', *NTS* 19 (1972–3), pp. 288–99.

Lewis, C. S., *The Discarded Image*. Cambridge 1964.

Lightstone, J. N., 'The Formation of the Biblical Canon in Judaism of Late Antiquity: Prolegomena to a General Reassessment', *SR* 8 (1979), pp. 135–42.

Lindars, B., *New Testament Apologetic. The Doctrinal Significance of the Old Testament Quotations*. London 1961.

Lindblom, J., *Gesichte und Offenbarungen (Vorstellungen von göttlichen Weisungen und übernatürlichen Erscheinungen im ältesten Christentum)*, Skrifter utgivna av Kungl. Humanistika Vetenskapssamfundet i Lund LXV. Lund 1968.

—, *Prophecy in Ancient Israel*. Oxford 1962.

Loewe, R., ' "Salvation" is not of the Jews', *JTS* 32 (1981), pp. 341–68.

Longenecker, R., *Biblical Exegesis in the Apostolic Period*. Grand Rapids, Mich. 1975.

Mann, J. and Sonne, I., *The Bible as Read and Preached in the Old Synagogue: A Study in the Cycles of the Readings from Torah and Prophets, as well as from Psalms, and in the Structure of the Midrashic Homilies*. Cincinnati 1940.

Mason, R. A., 'The Prophets of the Restoration', in *Israel's Prophetic Tradition. Essays in Honour of Peter R. Ackroyd*, edd. R. Coggins, A. Phillips and M. Knibb (Cambridge 1982), pp. 137–54.

—, 'Some Echoes of the Preaching in the Second Temple? Tradition Elements in Zechariah 1–8', *ZAW* 96 (1984), pp. 221–35.

Meyer, R., 'Bemerkungen zum literargeschichtlichen Hintergrund der Kanontheorie des Josephus', in *Josephus-Studien: Untersuchungen zu Josephus, dem antiken Judentum und dem Neuen Testament, Otto Michel zum 70. Geburtstag gewidmet*, edd. O. Betz, K. Hacker and M. Hengel (Göttingen 1974), pp. 285–99.

—, 'Kanonisch und apokryph im Judentum', appendix to art. *kruptô* in *TWNT* III, pp. 979–87.

Milik, J. T., *Dix ans de découvertes dans le désert de Juda*. Paris 1957 = *Ten Years of Discovery in the Wilderness of Judaea* (SBTh I:26). London 1959.

Momigliano, A., 'The Origins of Universal History', in *The Poet and the Historian. Essays in Literary and Historical Biblical Criticism*, ed. R. E. Friedman (Chico, California 1983), pp. 133–48.

Montefiore, C. G., and Loewe, H., *A Rabbinic Anthology*. Cleveland, N. Y., and Philadelphia 1938 (reprinted 1960).

Moore, G. F., *Judaism in the First Centuries of the Christian Era*. Cambridge, Mass. 1927.

Müller, H.-P., 'Mantische Weisheit und Apokalyptik', VTS 22 (1972), pp. 268–93.

Munck, J., *Paulus und die Heilsgeschichte*. Aarhus and Copenhagen 1954 = *Paul and the Salvation of Mankind*. London 1959.

Nicholson, E. W., *Preaching to the Exiles. A Study of the Prose Tradition in the Book of Jeremiah*. Oxford 1970.

Noth, M., *Die Gesetze im Pentateuch (ihre Voraussetzungen und ihr Sinn)*. Schriften der Königsberger Gelehrten Gesellschaft, geisteswissenschaftliche Klasse 17. Halle 1940 = 'The Laws in the Pentateuch: their Assumptions and Meaning', *The Laws in the Pentateuch and Other Essays* (Edinburgh and London 1966), pp. 1–107.

—, *Überlieferungsgeschichte des Pentateuch*. Stuttgart 1948 = *A History of Pentateuchal Traditions*. Englewood Cliffs, N. J. 1972.

—, *Überlieferungsgeschichtliche Studien I*, Schriften der Königsberger Gelehrten Gesellschaft 18 (1943), pp. 43–266; second edn (Tübingen 1957), pp. 1–110 = *The Deuteronomistic History* (JSOTS 15). Sheffield 1981.

Patte, D., *Early Jewish Hermeneutic in Palestine* (SBL Dissertation Series 22). Missoula, Montana 1975.

Penna, A., *S. Gerolamo*. Turin and Rome 1949.

Perrot, C., *La lecture de la Bible. Les anciennes lectures palestiniennes du Shabbat et des fêtes*. Hildesheim 1973.

Petersen, D. L., *Late Israelite Prophecy: Studies in Deutero-Prophetic Literature and in Chronicles* (SBL Monograph Series 23). Ann Arbor, Michigan 1977.

Pfeiffer, R. H., 'The Canon of the Old Testament', *IDB* I, pp. 510–11.

Philo, translated and ed. F. H. Colson (vols. 1–10) and G. H. Whitaker (vols. 1–5), 10 vols. London and Cambridge, Mass. 1929–43.

van der Ploeg, J. P. M., 'Le psaume xci dans une recension de Qumran', *RB* 72 (1965), pp. 210–17.

Plöger, O., *Theokratie und Eschatologie* (WMANT 2). Neukirchen 1959 = *Theocracy and Eschatology*. Oxford 1968.

von Rad, G., *Das formgeschichtliche Problem des Hexateuch* (BWANT 4.26). Stuttgart 1938 = *Gesammelte Studien zum Alten Testament* (Munich 1958), pp. 9–86 = 'The Form-Critical Problem of the Hexateuch', *The Problem of the Hexateuch and Other Essays* (Edinburgh and London 1966), pp. 1–78.

—, 'The Levitical Sermon in I and II Chronicles', *The Problem of the Hexateuch and Other Essays* (Edinburgh and London 1966), pp. 267–80 (from *Festschrift für Otto Procksch* (Leipzig 1934), pp. 113–24 = *Gesammelte Studien zum Alten Testament* (Munich 1958), pp. 248–61).

—, *Theologie des Alten Testaments*. Munich I 1957, II 1960 = *Old Testament*

Bibliography

Theology. Edinburgh and London I 1962 (from second German edn, 1957), II 1965 (from third German edn, 1960).

—, *Weisheit in Israel*. Neukirchen-Vluyn 1970 = *Wisdom in Israel*. London 1972.

Reines, A. J., *Maimonides and Abrabanel on Prophecy*. Cincinnati 1970.

Rendtorff, R., *Das Überlieferungsgeschichtliche Problem des Pentateuch*, (BZAW 147). Berlin 1977.

Ricoeur, P., *Essays on Biblical Interpretation*. Philadelphia 1980, London 1981.

Rowland, C., *The Open Heaven. A Study of Apocalyptic in Judaism and Early Christianity*. London 1982.

Rowley, H. H., *Darius the Mede and the Four World Empires in the Book of Daniel*. Cardiff 1935.

—, *The Relevance of Apocalyptic*. London 1947.

Russell, D. S., *The Method and Message of Jewish Apocalyptic*. London 1964.

Ryle, H. E., *The Canon of the Old Testament*. London 1892.

Sanders, E. P., *Jesus and Judaism*. London 1985.

Sanders, J. A., 'Pre-Masoretic Psalter Texts', *CBQ* 27 (1965), pp. 114–23.

—, *The Psalms Scroll of Qumran Cave 11 (11QPs^a)* (Discoveries in the Judaean Desert 4). Oxford 1965.

—, '*Variorum* in the Psalms Scroll', *HTR* 59 (1966), pp. 83ff.

Sarna, N. M., 'The Order of the Books', in *Studies in Jewish Bibliography, History and Literature in honor of I. Edward Kiev*, ed. C. Berlin (New York 1971), pp. 407–13.

Schechter, S., *Some Aspects of Rabbinic Theology*. London 1909.

Schmemann, A., *Introduction to Liturgical Theology*. Leighton Buzzard and New York 1975.

Schmid, H. H., *Der sogenannte Jahwist: Beobachtungen und Fragen zur Pentateuch-forschung*. Zürich 1976.

—, *Wesen und Geschichte der Weisheit. Eine Untersuchung zur altorientalischen und israelitischen Weisheitsliteratur* (BZAW 101). Berlin 1966.

Schmidt, N., 'Bible Canon: Untraditional View', *JE* III, pp. 150–4.

Schürer, E., *The History of the Jewish People in the Age of Jesus Christ (175 BC–AD 135): a New English Edition revised and edited by G. Vermes and F. Millar*. Edinburgh I 1973, II 1979.

Seeligmann, I. L., 'Voraussetzungen der Midrasch-Exegese', VTS 1 (1953), pp. 150–81.

Skehan, P. W., 'A Psalm Manuscript from Qumran (4QPs^b)', *CBQ* 26 (1964), pp. 313–22.

—, 'The Qumran Manuscripts and Textual Criticism', VTS 4 (1956), pp. 148–60.

—, 'St Jerome and the Canon of the Holy Scriptures', in *A Monument to Saint Jerome: Essays on Some Aspects of his Life, Works and Influence*, ed. F. X. Murphy (New York 1952), pp. 257–87.

Smend, R., *Die Entstehung des Alten Testaments*, second edn Stuttgart 1981.

Snaith, N. H., *The Distinctive Ideas of the Old Testament*. London 1944.

Stadelmann, H., *Ben Sira als Schriftgelehrter* (WUNT, second series, 6). Tübingen 1980.

Stendahl, K., *The School of St. Matthew and its Use of the Old Testament*. Philadelphia 1954.

Stenning, J. F., *The Targum of Isaiah*. Oxford 1949.

Stone, M. E., 'Apocalyptic Literature', in *Jewish Writings of the Second Temple Period: Apocrypha, Pseudepigrapha, Qumran Sectarian Writings, Philo, Josephus (Compendium Iudaicarum ad Novum Testamentum)*. Assen 1984.

Strack, H. L. and Billerbeck, P., *Kommentar zum Neuen Testament aus Talmud und Midrasch*. 4 vols., Munich 1922–8.

Sundberg, A. C., 'The "Old Testament": a Christian Canon', *CBQ* 30 (1968), pp. 143–55.

—, *The Old Testament of the Early Church*. Cambridge, Mass., and London 1964.

—, 'The Protestant Old Testament Canon: Should it be Re-examined?', *CBQ* 28 (1966), pp. 194–203.

Swete, H. B., *An Introduction to the Old Testament in Greek*. Cambridge 1900.

Thomas, K., *Religion and the Decline of Magic. Studies of Popular Beliefs in Sixteenth- and Seventeenth-Century England*. London 1971; paperback edn, London 1973.

Trachtenberg, J., *Jewish Magic and Superstition. A Study in Folk Religion*. New York 1939.

Van Seters, J., *Abraham in History and Tradition*. New Haven and London 1975.

—, *In Search of History. Historiography in the Ancient World and the Origin of Biblical History*. New Haven 1983.

Vermes, G., 'Bible and Midrash: Early Old Testament Exegesis', in *Cambridge History of the Bible* I, q.v., pp. 199–231.

Walter, N., *Der Thoraausleger Aristobulos. Untersuchungen zu seinen Fragmenten und zu pseudepigrafischen Resten der judäisch-hellenistischen Literatur*. Berlin 1964.

Weil, G., *Élie Lévita, humaniste et massorète* (1469–1549) (Studia Post-Biblica 7). Leiden 1963.

Weingreen, J., *From Bible to Mishna. The Continuity of Tradition*. Manchester 1976.

Weippert, H., *Die Prosareden des Jeremiabuches* (BZAW 132). Berlin 1973.

Wellhausen, J., *Geschichte Israels I*. Marburg 1878; second edn 1883 as *Prolegomena zur Geschichte Israels = Prolegomena to the History of Israel*. Edinburgh 1885 (reprinted as *Prolegomena to the History of Ancient Israel*. New York 1957).

Bibliography

Westermann, C., *Grundformen prophetischer Rede*, (EvThBeih 31). Munich 1964 = *Basic Forms of Prophetic Speech*. London 1967.

Wildeboer, G., *Het Ontstaen van den Kanon des Ouden Verbands*, second edn. Assen 1891 = *Die Entstehung des alttestamentlichen Kanons*. 1891 = *The Origin of the Canon of the Old Testament*. London 1895.

Wilson, B., *Magic and the Millennium. A Sociological Study of Religious Movements of Protest among Tribal Third World Peoples*. London 1973.

Wolfe, R. E., 'The Editing of the Book of the Twelve', *ZAW* 53 (1935), pp. 90–129.

Wolfenson, L. B., 'Implications of the Place of the Book of Ruth in Editions, Manuscripts, and Canon of the Old Testament', *HUCA* 1 (1924), pp. 151–78.

Wolff, C., *Jeremia im Frühjudentum und Urchristentum* (TU 118). Berlin 1976.

Wolff, H. W., 'Das Kerygma des deuteronomischen Geschichtswerks', *ZAW* 73 (1961), pp. 171–86 = 'The Kerygma of the Deuteronomic Historical Work', in *The Vitality of Old Testament Traditions*, edd. W. Brueggemann and H. W. Wolff (Atlanta 1975).

—, 'Das Zitat im Prophetenspruch', EvThBeih 4 (1937), pp. 3–112 = *Gesammelte Studien* (Munich 1964), pp. 36–129.

Wolfson, H. A., *Philo*. Cambridge, Mass. 1947.

Würthwein, E., *Der Text des Alten Testaments*. Stuttgart 1952 = *The Text of the Old Testament. An Introduction to Kittel-Kahle's Biblia Hebraica*. Oxford 1957.

Index of Modern Authors

Index of Modern Authors

312

Index of Subjects

Index of Scriptural and other Primary Sources

Bible
(Books are listed in the order usual in English Bibles; English verse-numbering is followed)

315

Index of Scriptural and other Primary Sources

316

Index of Scriptural and other Primary Sources

321